THE ROSES OF
NO MAN'S LAND

THE ROSES OF NO MAN'S LAND

Lyn Macdonald

ATHENEUM   NEW YORK   1989

Atheneum
Macmillan Publishing Company
866 Third Avenue, New York, N.Y. 10022

Library of Congress Cataloging-in-Publication Data
Macdonald, Lyn.
 The roses of no man's land / Lyn Macdonald.
  p.   cm.
 Reprint. Originally published: London : Joseph, 1980.
 Bibliography: p.
 Includes index.
 ISBN 0-689-70810-6
 1. World War, 1914–1918—Medical care—Great Britain.   2. Nursing
—Great Britain—History—20th century.   3. World War, 1914–1918—
Personal narratives, British.   I. Title.
 D629.G7M18   1989
 940.4'7541—dc19   88-39134   CIP

Macmillan books are available at special discounts for bulk
purchases for sales promotions, premiums, fund-raising, or
educational use. For details, contact:

Special Sales Director
Macmillan Publishing Company
866 Third Avenue
New York, N.Y. 10022

10 9 8 7 6 5 4 3 2 1

Printed in the United States of America

Contents

List of Illustrations

The Rose Of "No Man's Land".

Written by J. CADDIGAN.

Composed by JAMES A. BRENNAN.

I've seen some beau_ti_ful flow_ers
Out in the Heav_en_ly splen_dour,

Grow in life's gar_den fair,_____
Down to the trail of woe,_____

I've spent some won_der_ful
God in His mer_cy has

hours,_____
sent her,

Lost in their frag_rance rare,_____
Cheer_ing the world be_low._____

This book is dedicated to the nurses, the doctors and the soldiers whose stories it tells, to the tens of thousands whose stories will never be told and, in salute, to the generation to which they all belonged.

Author's Foreword and Acknowledgements

This is not a 'woman's book' – even though it is based to a large extent on women's recollections of their experiences. It is the story of a remarkable generation of people which shows another facet of the Great War that changed the world, although not entirely in the way that those who went off to fight in it and serve in it intended.

If the ghost that haunts the towns of Ypres and Arras and Albert is the statutory British Tommy, slogging with rifle and pack through its ruined streets to his well-documented destiny 'up the line', then the ghost of Boulogne and Etaples and Rouen ought to be a girl. She's called Elsie or Gladys or Dorothy, her ankles are swollen, her feet are aching, her hands reddened and rough. She has little money, no vote, and has almost forgotten what it feels like to be really warm. She sleeps in a tent. Unless she has told a diplomatic lie about her age, she is twenty-three. She is the daughter of a clergyman, a lawyer or a prosperous businessman, and has been privately educated and groomed to be a 'lady'. She wears the unbecoming outdoor uniform of a VAD or an army nurse. She is on active service, and as much a part of the war as Tommy Atkins.

On the face of it, no one could have been less equipped for the job than these gently nurtured girls who walked straight out of Edwardian drawingrooms into the manifold horrors of the First World War. It was all a far cry from the old myth of the 'ministering angel'. These girls had to be tough. They worked in flooded operating theatres in Flanders where, in a big 'push', there might be four operations going on at one time, and as many as ten amputations an hour. They nursed men with terrible wounds and saw them off to convalescent camp, or laid them out when they died. They nursed in wards where the stench of gas-gangrenous wounds was almost overpowering. They nursed men choking to death as the fluid rose in their gassed lungs, men whose faces were mutilated beyond recognition, whose bodies were mangled beyond repair, whose nerves were shattered beyond redemption.

They turned into a generation of redoubtable grandmothers or, more precisely, maiden aunts – because most of the men of their age-group whom they might have married never came back from that war to end wars, and they themselves came back to a changed world.

Of course, some did marry, but the others were not content to return to the old life of busy idleness, even if circumstances had made it possible – nor were they content to sit around mourning their lot as the 'surplus women' which society unflatteringly called them in the Twenties and Thirties. They shortened their skirts, bobbed their hair, flattened their chests and, having proved beyond argument during the war that women could do anything, set out to carve themselves a place in what was still a man's world. They moved wholesale into commerce. They became teachers, doctors, social workers, pharmacists, journalists, ran dairies and chicken farms. They won the vote and the right to work in the face of formidable opposition and the obdurate philosophy that a woman's place was in the home, even though such hopes as most marriageable girls had had of husband and children lay buried with their men on some far-off battlefield. They earned liberation long before Liberation earned itself a capital L.

In the course of more than two years' research and preparation of this book (the writing is always the least of it!) I have spent hundreds of hours talking to octogenarians who were nurses, soldiers, orderlies and doctors. What comes through most strongly is their remarkable resilience, the casualness with which they refer to work in circumstances and situations which would appall most other people, the matter-of-fact way in which they refer to their 'war wounds'. 'Oh dear, I'm sorry to be so clumsy. It's these stupid stiff fingers of mine.' It was an apology I heard literally scores of times as a photograph slipped to the floor, or two drops of tea slopped into a saucer. The 'stupid stiff fingers' are mostly scarred where they were lanced to release the pus from a septic hand. The soldiers' wounds were pouring with sepsis and inevitably, through a cut or a graze or a broken chilblain, the nurses who dressed them caught the infection.

The nurses and doctors were fighting death and disease without the benefit of the modern weapons of antibiotics, sulphonamide drugs or penicillin. It is not an overstatement to say that drugs like these – together with modern methods of plastic surgery, blood transfusion, skingrafting and the treatment of burns – had their beginnings in research which was born of necessity during the war. If nothing much came out of the battles at the Front, the same cannot be said of the mirror-image battles in the hospitals and laboratories behind it.

It is always difficult to know where to begin thanking people, but first and foremost I have to record my deep gratitude to the many people who took the time and trouble to talk to me or to write at length to 'tell it like it was', to generously lend me letters, diaries and photographs, and to ply me with hospitality. I've had more good teas in the last two years than normally fall to my lot! In Leeds, one ninety-six year old (it was Sister Mary Stollard) walked a mile to the shops and back again so that she could offer me the local delicacy, Eccles cakes. In America I was not only magnificently fed and watered but frequently invited to spend the night – generous hospitality which enabled me to cover long distances and keep to a necessarily tight schedule.

The names of all those who contributed in one way or another to this book are at the back, listed in a more impersonal way than I would wish to thank each person individually if time and space allowed, but certain people deserve particular thanks.

In the USA Janice and Eric Anthony not only allowed me to turn their home into an office cum travel agency cum telephone exchange during my stay, but drove me many miles to meet American doctors and nurses and, even after I had left, uncomplainingly took on the job of photocopying papers and documents, procuring photographs and following up information which I had not had time to pursue myself.

Elizabeth Ogilvie wrote out of the blue from New Zealand after she had read my book *They Called it Passchendaele* and volunteered to contact and to interview New Zealand nurses who had served in the war, and my much-missed colleague and assistant Vivien Bilbow (now Vivien Riches and living in Melbourne) undertook to do the same job in Australia. If this book reflects a picture that is not one-sided, it is largely due to their efforts and to the efforts of the many people in other countries who so enthusiastically co-operated.

On the Home Front I have been dependent, as always, on a squad of volunteers 'acting unpaid' (to continue the army metaphor) who have given up many hours of leisure-time to helping with the accumulation and organization of such a mass of information and material. John Woodroff, a veteran of the Passchendaele team, was as indefatigable as ever in checking often-obscure facts buried in regimental histories, tracking down information, helping with the interviewing, checking a long manuscript page by page, and always being patiently available for hours of discussion on points arising. Martin Pegler, another new recruit, earned his stripes by his enthusiastic and valuable help with the paperwork and by doing some useful interviews, and Don Dean, another reader who has become a helper and friend, scoured his part of the country for 'Roses' and spent most of his holidays interviewing old soldiers. Tony Spagnoly, a greatly valued member of the 'team', for personal and business reasons was unfortunately unable to devote much time to this particular project, but he was nevertheless always ready to answer queries and put his knowledge at my disposal.

My thanks are also due to Frank Ellis, MS, FRCS, who helped me to 'translate' Dr Reardon's case-notes (and explained them!) and to Dr E. J. Raftery, who kindly read the completed manuscript with an eye to the medical details.

Various members of the British Red Cross Society have been kind and helpful, even to the extent of allowing me to keep for nearly two years some of their valuable and irreplaceable records so that I could constantly refer to them. In Washington, the American Red Cross, in the person of Rudolf A. Clemen Jnr, was most co-operative and helped me to make the most of my limited time there, as did the staff of the Nathan Pusey Library at Harvard University.

The Commonwealth War Graves Commission has an august-sounding title which I always feel tends to obscure the almost passionate human interest its officials take in their work and the enthusiastic help they give to requests for background information about long-dead soldiers. I am particularly grateful to Gordon Cheater, who has willingly embarked on the trail of some mysterious stories and, on the basis of such scant information as I was able to supply, has unfailingly come up with an answer about casualties or circumstances, and has channelled much interesting information and contacts in my direction.

Although this book is based almost entirely on new information and I have not drawn on the archives of the Imperial War Museum, Rod Suddaby, Head of the Documents Department, has taken a lively and helpful interest in it, and has willingly answered queries as well as pointing me in the direction of some useful information.

I am most grateful to Leo Feist, Inc., for allowing me to use the words and music of 'The Rose of No Man's Land', to Messrs Francis, Day and Hunter for permission to quote the words of 'My Girl's a Yorkshire Girl', and to the following publishers for permission to quote from their books: William Blackwood & Sons Ltd, for *Diary of a Nursing Sister on the Western Front; The Times*, for *Six Weeks at the War* by Millicent, Duchess of Sutherland and for permission to use several extracts from the newspaper; William Heinemann Ltd, for *Medicine and Duty* by Harold Dearden; and Messrs Constable, for *From a Surgeon's Journal* by Harvey Cushing.

It is customary to conclude by thanking the person responsible for typing the manuscript, but no simple thanks or acknowledgement could possibly reflect my gratitude to Alma Woodroff. Producing a final typescript to her customary standard of meticulous perfection was the least of her contribution. She also typed every transcript of every interview over the last two and a half years, remembered things that I had forgotten, sustained me by her interest and encouragement throughout the long process of writing what was technically a complicated book to construct, and acted as quartermaster to up to a dozen hungry footsloggers on research trips to the battlefields. Above all, she has been the never-failing prop that every writer would like to have to lean on – and all too seldom has.

LYN MACDONALD
LONDON, FEBRUARY 1980

Part One
1914 – 1915

Chapter One

The coast of France was the frontier between two worlds. For the unseasoned soldiers packed into the cross-Channel ferries, the pleasure steamers and the cattleboats pressed into service as troopships it was the gateway to the war, the real start of the journey towards that unknown 'front' where the guns rumbled and flashed in the east. For the battle-weary troops pouring joyfully out of ramshackle trains at the *Gare Maritime,* kicking the sticky trench-mud from their boots as they bounded up the gangway of the leave-boat, it was the first stop on the journey home. For many of the badly wounded whose journey ended at one of the camp-hospitals on the edge of the sea, it was the last stop before eternity.

From the packed deck of a troopship on a dull day, even before the denser grey of the coastline itself began to peer through the Channel mist, the marquees of the clifftop encampments were the first sign of landfall. They stretched along the cliffs snaking south from Calais round Cap Gris Nez to Wimereux. They straggled up the slopes of the hills around Boulogne. They stood ranked behind the line of sand-dunes along the road to Etaples, ran on to Merlimont and Berck Plage beyond Le Touquet and swept into Normandy by way of Le Tréport, Deauville and Trouville.

Yet even that long line of hospitals, whose canvas tents flapped in the sea winds on the French side of the English Channel, was a mere drop in an ocean of sickness and suffering that beggared description.

A European war had long been thought to be inevitable, but before 1914 no lunatic imagination could have envisaged that half the youth of half the world could be sucked into a conflict that would rage across the sodden wastelands of France and Belgium; among the sandstorms of Egypt and Mesopotamia; on the high peaks of Alsace; among the mountain passes of the Tyrol; on the barren rocks of Gallipoli; in the hinterland of Africa; and across half the oceans of the world. It would likewise have been dismissed as the half-crazed ravings of an idiot had it been suggested that the invincible British army – which had beaten Napoleon at Waterloo, tamed the Russian Bear in the Crimea, sorted out the Boers on the South African veldt and garrisoned an Empire which stretched around the globe – would be ordered to retire as it fired the first shots in its first engagement, and that the name of Mons would go down in history not as a famous battle but as a famous retreat.

On the heels of its burnished cavalry the first infantry contingents of the British Expeditionary Force made their way towards Mons in the manner of a rambling club setting out on an enjoyable holiday hike. It was true that the hobnails of their army boots slipped on the deceptively round and smooth-looking cobbles of the French roads, and that there were twisted ankles and mammoth blisters to be doctored and cursed at the end of the day, but even that was not sufficient to dampen the festive spirit of the troops. There had been a holiday atmosphere ever since they had disembarked a few days before at Boulogne. It seemed as if the entire population had turned out to welcome the BEF with flags and flowers, kisses and cheers of welcome. They swept in a babbling, enthusiastic throng alongside the soldiers marching to the transit camps, occasionally sweeping a rank or two of stragglers into a convenient roadside café to toast the *entente cordiale,* and bearing them back to their units many convivial hours later. It was fortunate that their officers, only too relieved to find themselves with a full complement at morning roll-call, and perhaps too concerned with grappling with the problems of transporting their forces from Point A to Point B in a foreign country, discreetly turned a blind eye to the excesses of the previous evening.

Point B, in the case of the 4th Battalion, The Middlesex Regiment, turned out to be the village of Taisenières, twenty-five kilometres east of Valenciennes. They travelled in comfort by passenger train, and the sensation caused by their arrival in the midst of the peasants harvesting in the fields only added to the hilarity of the soldiers, already agog with the excitement of the strange sights and sounds of France. At the appearance of a thousand men, in unfamiliar but unmistakably foreign uniforms, pouring out of the train at the country station, the peasants ran for their lives, shrieking in panic, apparently under the impression that the dreaded German invaders had adopted the simple expedient of purchasing rail tickets to French destinations.

When they realized their mistake, the villagers rose heroically to the occasion, which was more than the troops could say of their officers. The colonel had been given a lead as to what was expected, in the form of a smacking, hairy embrace administered by the mayor, but, to the ill-concealed derision of the battalion drawn up behind them on the village square, the officers received the bouquets presented to them by a bevy of expectant village girls with salutes which were uncompromisingly military. Fortunately for the honour of the regiment, the disappointed welcome committee, which was only too anxious to be compromised, proceeded to present single blossoms to all the rest of the battalion, which was only too happy to oblige. The manifestation of mutual esteem was only temporarily interrupted by the troops being marched off to billets in the barns and outhouses of local farms.

The fact that the local estaminet was put out of bounds was of small consequence, because in the haste of mobilization and departure there had been no time to hold pay-parades, and aggrieved reminders to the officers failed to elicit any response in the way of hard cash. 'They seem to think we carry their pay around with us in our pockets,' complained Lieutenant Rory Macleod of the 80th Battery, Royal Field Artillery, in his first letter home from France. But the men of the 4th Middlesex succeeded in striking a chord of sympathy with their officers, who sportingly clubbed together one evening and had barrels of free beer set up in the village square to ensure that the men and the villagers would have at least one merry evening.

It was in the nature of a farewell party. On the scorching morning of 20 August the troops marched off, festooned with flowers – in their hands, round their necks, wreathed hoop-la style round the barrels of their rifles – accompanied by a cheering escort of villagers who kept up with the column for more than a kilometre along the cobbled highroad and stood waving it out of sight for another. When the civilians had been left behind, the soldiers started to sing. *'Who were you with last night, out in the pale moonlight?'* It was a pertinent question.

As time went on and feet began to swell in the August heat, the singing became desultory. Accustomed though they were to long route marches on British highways, every passing kilometre reinforced the soldiers in their opinion that the French pavé was an invention of the devil and increased the sensation that they were marching on swords all the way to Mons. They were not alone in this impression. There was not a man in any one of the three British Divisions plodding painfully northwards in the same direction who would have denied it. Long before they reached their destination, every ounce of excess weight had been jettisoned, and the march of the BEF could be traced by a trail of trampled bouquets tossed aside on the roadside verges.

Not that either the soldiers, their officers or their commanders realized Mons was their destination. The British army was on its way to take up its position on the left of the French and, with them, push up into Belgium to trap the Kaiser's army in a pincer movement, administer a sound thrashing and send it packing, in much the same manner as it had been accustomed to dealing with marauding tribesmen and upstart natives for the best part of a century. If the area had any significance at all, it was merely in the mild interest of the fact that it was near here that the Duke of Marlborough, at the head of another army, had beaten the French at Malplaquet. Mons had been in the thick of those earlier wars, and people had lost count of the number of times it had been besieged. But who cared about Mons nowadays? There was a coalfield or two among the spreading fields which surround it, a fifteenth-century town hall to stand testimony to past grandeur, a straggle of cobbled streets, some simple houses and small industrial concerns based on the modest prosperity of an agricultural market-town.

On the afternoon of the 21st, parched and sunburnt, weary and footsore, and only slightly cheered by the enthusiasm of their welcome, the first of the troops entered Mons and passed through it to the suburb of Nimy. The seventeen-year-old daughter of a local schoolmaster, together with her friends Germaine Ochier and Georgine Bott, found their arrival a little less than triumphal.

Germaine
Lauryssen

I saw fifty or more soldiers turning the corner of the street and they were completely exhausted. Every fifty yards or so the officer gave an order and they simply collapsed on the ground. They just let go and fell backwards, landing on their packs as if they were pillows. There was an old gutter overgrown with grass, and one of the soldiers put his hand in the gutter right on to a piece of glass and made a really nasty gash all round the inside of his hand. I dashed back to my house where we had some brown powder which was a strong disinfectant. I took some, and some scissors and bandage, and dashed back again and bandaged his hand. My friend, Georgine Bott, had been a governess in America and spoke English very well, so I asked her to ask the officer where they were going, and he replied, 'Over the railway line to dig some trenches'. I felt really indignant. 'These men aren't fit to dig trenches', I said. 'They're worn out!' There were crowds in the street, so we called to some of the local boys and asked them if they would dig for them. They said, 'Yes, of course we will'. But when Georgine told the officer this he only replied, 'No, thank you'.

Georgine and Germaine were incensed. But the officers and soldiers who heard the exchange realized, as the girls did not, that if the Germans arrived and got wind of civilians assisting the army they might have been shot as *francs-tireurs*. Still, there was nothing in the rules of war to prevent the soldiers accepting food. No field kitchens had arrived, but eggs were sustaining even when they had to be consumed raw. There were greengages at their juicy prime – Germaine's mother had bought a tree full of them, and they lay in the yard of her house in vast linen-baskets ready for jamming and bottling. The girls carried them, bushels at a time, to the soldiers digging across the field behind the house. In the thick mist of early morning they staggered across with milk churns brimming with hot coffee; in the heat of the day with baskets of bottled beer and wine brazenly pilfered from their fathers' cellars. Although the trenches were taking shape in front of their eyes, although the soldiers kept warning them to keep away, although there were rumours that patrols of Germans were already in a wood just across the fields, the picnic atmosphere was hard to dispel. The soldiers adopted by the Nimy girls were the Royal Fusiliers. Half a mile down the road, the 4th Middlesex were experiencing some difficulty in preventing other local girls from leaping up beside the lookouts on their hastily erected barricades to join them in the jolly game of spotting non-existent Germans.

Lance-Corporal Alf Vivian had been relieved to find that if the Germans were not precisely non-existent, they were at least not yet in the immediate vicinity, for the 4th Middlesex had entered its sector of the war in the time-honoured manner in which British troops had sortied in the Crimea. Intended to protect the main body from surprise attack, one man designated as 'Point' proceeded in conspicuous and solitary splendour well ahead of his comrades, followed by groups in single file at intervals of fifty yards. So far as the unfortunate 'Point' was concerned it might as well have been fifty miles, for his function (and well he knew it) was to draw enemy fire. Although there happened to be no fire to draw, it was not an experience that the lance-corporal would have cared to repeat. It so happened that it was the last time in history that such a manoeuvre would ever be carried out. The cavalry away to his right, the enemy Uhlans in the wood across the way and Sir John French in his headquarters at Le Cateau would all have been equally incredulous had they realized that the battle of Mons in which they were about to engage would be the last of the old-style European battles which their armies had been fighting out on the soil of Europe since time immemorial.

It started on Sunday morning as the sun began to filter through the mist with the promise of yet another hot day.

> At nine o'clock, Père, Mère and I went to Mass at Nimy church. It was very hot in church and the priest had left both the main doors open so that you could hear the street noises. Suddenly, in the middle of Mass, we heard rifle-fire quite near. Every head in the church turned round. I looked at the priest to see how he was going to react, but he continued without any pause. But when he went into the pulpit he said that there would be no sermon today. He just gave out the notices and advised us to go straight home. But Père and I walked towards the canal to see what was happening. There were three rows of sandbags, the height of a man, one near the canal bridge and the others further back. The soldiers had taken up paving stones and put them in the sandbag walls to make little windows to fire through. They told us to go away, because the Germans were on the other side of the canal. So we finally turned towards home. Later, when the firing got bad, we went down to the cellar.
>
> *Germaine Lauryssen*

To the soldiers waiting to engage the enemy in front of Mons, and doubtless to the German forces in the woods, the sound of the church bells chiming across the Sunday morning landscape struck a strange dreamlike note, a reminder of the ordered world they had so recently left behind. The first patrol of German cavalry to appear on the front of the 4th Middlesex burst out of a wood under the horrified eyes of Lance-Corporal Vivian and a section of six men who had set up a forward outpost in an abandoned cottage. Nonplussed though they were, they had been trained to instant reaction and the pay of every man among them had depended on his skill and proficiency with a rifle. The first tentative sorties of the German Uhlans were met all along the line by such vicious and rapid fire, brought to crack perfection on the peacetime rifle-ranges of the British army, that those who survived it were convinced that the British troops were equipped with machine-guns. The soldiers of Vivian's section, which had easily annihilated its target, were overcome by a strange feeling of guilt. From a village across the fields the church bells were still ringing, and there in front of them, eighty yards away, were the still bodies of eight Uhlans and their horses, whom they had undoubtedly killed.

L/Cpl.
Alfred Vivian,
4th Battalion,
The Middlesex
Regiment

We stood trembling. I felt, unaccountably, physically sick. I had a distinct fear of the consequences of breaking one of the most solemn laws of civilization.

By the end of that day of fierce action they had all quite forgotten that they had ever had any such qualms, and the bulk of the army was retiring slowly through the silent, shuttered villages, which three days earlier had been so loud in their welcome. Of the 1,050 officers and men of the 4th Middlesex who had gone into action, there were just 380 left to answer their names at a scratch roll-call.

At the end of that day, Germaine Lauryssen was still sheltering with her family in the cellar when there was a sudden clattering in the street outside. A moment later, the low shaft of evening sunlight streaming through the grating at street-level was broken by a jagged line of shadows that bobbed across the cellar floor. They tried to tell each other that they were cast by the barrels of British rifles carried at the slope, but they knew very well, for the outlines of the spiked helmets were unmistakable, that the Germans were marching down the street on their way into Mons.

The explicit instructions which had been given to Sir John French in command of the BEF boiled down to two vital points. Firstly, he was to do everything in his power to assist and co-operate with the French army. Secondly, bearing in mind the limited numbers of men at his disposal in the BEF, he must do his best to conserve his troops and avoid wastage. Outnumbered by vastly superior forces, the French line on the right of the British at Mons had been broken and the French were forced to withdraw. Under those circumstances, and in accordance with his orders, the British Commander had no choice but to withdraw his own troops and to plan to make a new and firmer stand alongside the French army at a more advantageous position further to the south and west. Given the fluctuating situation and the hasty last-minute decisions, given that the troops, though skilled in professional soldiering, were unschooled in large-scale warfare, the retreat was masterly.

Inevitably there were stragglers. The artillery fire had been devastating. There were bitter rearguard actions and small groups of men were cut off from the main force and had to make their escape as best they could. Many of the wounded lay unconscious and in the haste of withdrawal were left for dead. Either they were captured by the Germans or, like Lance-Corporal Vivian, whose scalp was sliced open by a shell splinter on the third day, they managed to scramble back alone in the confusion. Wandering the forests and by-ways of Northern France, without rations or equipment, with swollen, bleeding feet, with little sense of direction and no compass other than the sun to guide them, it was as much as ten days before the last exhausted groups of stragglers caught up with the army. The Germans, on the other hand, caught up with it on 27 August at Le Cateau, where, in a fierce artillery battle in support of the cavalry, Lieutenant Rory Macleod was wounded by shrapnel in the head and shoulder. On the same day, Lance-Corporal Vivian, who had sufficiently recovered from his first wound to be able to take part in another skirmish, was wounded for a second time, in the arm and in the lungs.

Ever since the Crimean War, when Florence Nightingale had cudgelled the authorities into the realization that they must make better provision for the care of the wounded than the rough ministrations of one army surgeon to 350 men, the army had prided itself on its medical services. There was a corps of army nurses which, after sterling service in South Africa a dozen years before, justifiably considered itself to be an élite. There were well-equipped military hospitals in each command area of Great Britain capable between them of caring for 7,000 wounded. There were three hospital ships. There were cadres of trained personnel, ready to set up field ambulance units, casualty clearing stations and base hospitals. There was provision for a back-up organization of volunteers, for the army had realized that in the event of a European war its own resources would have to be supplemented by outside help. Everything had been thought of – except the unimaginable difficulties involved in rescuing and tending thousands of badly wounded men in the midst of a wholesale retreat.

Stretcher-bearers and orderlies did magnificent work. Doctors toiled to the last minute in temporary dressing-stations which all too soon had to be evacuated, leaving the worst of the wounded to the mercy of the fast-approaching enemy. Hospital units had arrived with the BEF, but they had hardly had time to unpack, still less to organize the reception of several thousand wounded. Nor were the transport arrangements all that they might have been. Lieutenant Macleod, after a lurching, painful ride on a supply lorry, was astonished to find himself being carried away from the battle-zone in a hastily commandeered London bus, emblazoned with an advertisement extolling the virtues of 'Grapenuts for Breakfast'. It struck him with some irony that he had indulged in neither breakfast, lunch nor dinner for the past forty-eight hours. His spirits were not improved by a long, hungry rail journey, packed with other walking wounded into a cattle truck, nor by finding that on reaching Rouen they were expected to proceed to hospital by tram-car.

Lieutenant Rory Macleod, 80th Battery, Royal Field Artillery

The hospital had not properly unpacked and had little food available, but they gave us some soup and bread. I was thankful to get to bed as my head was bothering me, and I felt very hungry, weak and dizzy. We stayed in the hospital for two days and the most solid food we had was bottled chicken (which was mostly jelly, skin and bone!). Then, as the Germans were advancing, the hospital packed up. We were put on a hospital ship for Southampton on Sunday, 30 August.

It was exactly one week since the ringing of church bells had mingled with the first shots in the battle of Mons, and seventeen days since the first contingents of the BEF had been happily basking in a heroes' welcome. Of the 90,000 men who had landed in France, one in every six had become a casualty. The ranks of the BEF were horribly depleted and before many more days had passed, its remnants would be fighting shoulder to shoulder with its French allies in the battle of the Marne.

The Germans were almost at the gates of Paris, but in the hospital which had been hastily set up in the Grand Trianon Hotel at Versailles, the doctors and nurses had little time to brood on the progress of the war. What worried them a great deal more was the unprecedented character of the wounds they were trying to treat – almost all of them infected with gas gangrene.

Captain Geoffrey Keynes, RAMC

We knew nothing about it at all. Nothing like it had ever been experienced in South Africa on the clean, sandy battleground of the veldt, which had been the army's last experience. Here, on the heavily manured soil of France, it was a different matter. You got this appalling infection with anaerobic bacteria and the men just died like flies. We got the casualties straight from Mons and the infection had usually set in by the time they got to us. If they had compound fractures, full of mud, it was the ideal site for the bacteria to flourish, and, if the men had been several days on the the way, as most of them had, the wound was simply a mass of putrid muscle rotting with gas gangrene. Nothing to do with gas as we knew it later in the war. It was called that because the bacillus that grows in the wound creates gas. The whole thing balloons up. You can tap it under your fingers and it sounds hollow. Even with quite a slight wound, when soil and shreds of uniform are carried in by the missile, it starts up. They soon died. We simply didn't know how to treat it. We'd never come across it before. Of course, there were no antibiotics. No effective disinfectants. We would cut away as much of the diseased tissue as we could. On a leg or an arm we would remove the limb, but that didn't stop it. It just went on up, and still the men would die from the toxic effects of the products of the bacteria. That was the worst thing in the first few months of the war.

Already, the doctors had an inkling that this was to be a different kind of war, and it was a suspicion that the army commanders were beginning to share. Like Le Cateau and the actions on the Marne and the Aisne, the action at Mons clearly demonstrated to British, French and Germans alike that the technical development of modern weaponry had rendered completely useless the old methods of attack, and with them all the military ideas which had governed warfare and training for half a millenium.

It was a lesson they were slow to learn. After four years of bitter contemplation, Field-Marshal Lord French wrote with admirable candour:

> It is easy to be 'wise after the event'; but I cannot help wondering why none of us realized what the modern rifle, the machine-gun, motor traction, the aeroplane and wireless telegraphy would bring about. It seems so simple when judged by actual results. . . . All my thoughts, all my prospective plans, all my possible alternatives of action were concentrated upon a war of movement and manoeuvre.*

By November 1914, their strategy defeated by the deadliness of their own weapons, the opposing armies had ground to a halt, each entrenched in a fixed position which, give or take a mile or so, would hardly alter for the next three years and a half. Already, two-thirds of Europe was alight, and the flames were licking outwards to engulf half the world. Years later, when they struck the medals, they called it The Great War for Civilization. The truth was that Civilization would never be quite the same again.

* *1914*, Field-Marshal Viscount French of Ypres (Constable, 1919).

Chapter Two

There was hardly a hint, in that golden summer of 1914, that the world was about to come to an end.

The great British lion, basking at the heart of its Empire, gave the slightest twitch of its ears at the echo of a double pistol shot far away in the Balkans. But on that summer Sunday when the Austrian Archduke Ferdinand was assinated at Sarajevo, the anxieties of politically conscious people were concentrated on Ireland, where there was a real risk of civil war.

The weather was beautiful. Garden parties, tennis parties, village fêtes could all be looked forward to in the happy certainty that the sun would co-operate. No 'best hats' would wilt in the damp. Picnics would not be rained off. No sudden showers would interrupt the delicate flirtations of couples strolling discreetly in shrubberies within earshot of lawns and tennis courts where middle-aged ladies, heads bobbing under silk sunshades, cluck-clucked together over the free and easy behaviour of the modern generation.

In its own eyes it was a startlingly modern generation. Born in the last decade of the nineteenth century, in their brief lifetime twenty-year-olds had seen the horse make way for the motor car, gaslight ousted by electricity, the telephone become an almost everyday convenience, and, if aeroplanes were not exactly commonplace, they no longer caused neck-craning crowds to gather as they had done a decade earlier. Every drawing-room and all but the poorest front parlours still boasted a piano, but the old parlour songs had long ago been relegated to the recesses of piano stools. It was ragtime that stood on the music stands, and ragtime that caused parents to cover their ears as it jangled from the horns of the newfangled gramophones, beloved by the young.

'Hitchy koo, hitchy koo, hitchy koo,' they sang, as they two-stepped to the tinkling of the latest hit. 'Oh, you *beautiful* doll,' warbled young men, gazing meaningfully into the eyes of pretty partners. 'Hello, hello, who's your lady friend?' enquired more robustly melodious crowds, free and easy on day trips to the sea.

But in spite of their up-to-date ideas, in spite of their easy acceptance of mechanical toys and scientific advances, and in spite of an awakening social conscience far removed from the soup-kitchen philosophy of their Victorian parents, the roots of the young generation were still firmly embedded in the Victorian age into which they had been born. It was to that high noon of power and Empire, of prosperity and expansion, of national pride and security, that they owed their unshakeable confidence, their patriotism and the unquestioning sense of duty that went with it.

It was pleasant to be newly grown up. Girls of the élite were presented at Court and admitted to the butterfly social round. Girls of the working class merely exchanged the discipline of the classroom for the factory bench, the sewing machine or the drudgery of domestic service. For the daughters of the industrious professional and business men who made up the middle classes, 'growing up' meant putting down their skirts, putting up their hair and 'coming out' at whatever local dance happened to take place nearest to their eighteenth birthdays. Kit Dodsworth, daughter of a Yorkshire lawyer, was typical of her generation.

We were terribly strictly brought up. Until I was eighteen, I lived up in the schoolroom. If the grown-ups had a tennis party we were allowed to come down and field the balls for them, but we had to go back to the schoolroom for tea and then go down again. We never met anyone, and I was petrified with shyness.   **Kit Dodsworth**

I came out at a big dance. It was the Yorkshire Hussars Ball, and I had a marvellous dress. It was white satin, all beaded. It cost twelve pounds – and that was a frightful price! After that one evening you were grown up; until then you were a child.

We lived very comfortably with lots of servants, so there was no real work to do. We tidied our rooms. We paid calls; we had tea-parties; we sewed; we taught at Sunday School; we organized bazaars and fêtes, made sweets and cakes for them. We always seemed to be busy.

Even with an abundance of servants, there was plenty to do in the home. Some girls, more adventurous or more persistent, bored with the small-change of domestic life, succeeded in cajoling parents into allowing them to take up a career. Nursing and teaching were acceptable, and social work was not frowned on so long as it was unpaid. But the universal attitude was that girls who didn't need to work should not take jobs away from those who did.

Hilda and Gladys Pole, the youngest of the five daughters of a clergyman in Kent, just back from six absorbing months at finishing school at Stuttgart, settled down to enjoy the social life of Chislehurst, and to help their mother and elder sisters. They joined the Red Cross because it was regarded as the sensible thing to do.

Girls who were unlikely ever to have to light a fire, cook a meal or sweep a floor would nevertheless, in their future married state, have to cope with illness, to deal with household accidents and eventually to nurse children ailing with the unavoidable fevers and infectious diseases which no amount of comfortable prosperity could prevent and only careful nursing could cure. So they joined the Red Cross or St John Ambulance Brigade, met their friends at the sociable weekly classes, did a little studying and sat the exams. The First Aid Certificate qualified them to dress cuts and grazes and bandage broken limbs. The Home Nursing Certificate demanded proficiency in the elementary skills of smoothing pillows, making beds and concocting beef tea. It was laudable as well as useful. Best of all, it was a sociable afternoon out. Kit Dodsworth was motivated less by the cause of suffering humanity than by the fact that she had a crush on a local doctor who gave occasional lectures. Millicent Norton found it a heaven-sent excuse to spend two afternoons a week out of the house, away from the baleful gaze of a repressive father who had failed to notice the ending of the prudish Victorian era thirteen years earlier.

Millicent Norton, later Commandant of Sussex 66 VAD Convalescent Hospital

My father was old. He was nearly seventy when I was twenty, and very, very old-fashioned. My sister and I were both terrified of my father. You never dared go against your parents. After I left school, a friend asked me to go and stay with her family in Ireland, and by some miracle my mother managed to persuade Father to let me go. When I got to the station I discovered that he had brought his own luggage with him. I simply couldn't believe it. He said, 'You don't think I'd be letting you go alone, do you? I am coming over too. I have booked into a hotel opposite their house'. I shall never forget how embarrassed I was, having to explain that my father had come too. Of course, they were very polite and said, 'Well, do ask him to call'. But he wouldn't. He just stood at the window of this hotel. We could see him watching us every time we went out.

Setting sail from New York on 1 July 1914, Mary Ludlum had a more sympathetic chaperone in the form of a kindly aunt, Mrs Higbie. The party was completed by her brother, Spink, and her cousin, Robert, who took pride in staying upright while Mary was prostrated by sea-sickness, almost before they reached the open sea. She managed to totter up on deck half-way through the voyage. 'Which way did the seasick pills taste best?' jeered Spink. 'Going down or coming up?'

They were due to land in Sweden on 11 July at the start of a whirlwind tour that would take in eight countries and a dozen or more cities. Sweden, Finland and Denmark were routine tourist fare, but when they reached Berlin a fortnight later they would find a city steaming with war fever as the European crisis bubbled up to the boil.

In 1914, Britain was not entirely unprepared for war. Every public school and many grammar schools had Officers' Training Corps and thousands of less privileged young people were in the ranks of the Territorial Force. They called themselves the Saturday Afternoon Soldiers. At weekends they trained and drilled and through the long winter months looked forward to the annual summer camp. They slept under canvas, drilled and marched in the sunshine, relished the good and copious food dished out by the field kitchens and enjoyed the friendly competition of rifle-range and sports field. In the summer of 1914 there was an added attraction. For the first time Voluntary Aid Detachments went with the local troops to camp. The VADs, as they were popularly known, had been formed four years earlier in 1909.

Britannia prided herself on ruling the waves, but was shrewd enough to realize that no matter how strong her navy a group of islands was always vulnerable to invasion. It was not so long ago that her shores had been threatened by Napoleon and, with the disturbing resurgence of militarism in Europe, it was not impossible that they would be threatened again. The job of the Territorials was to protect the homeland in case of invasion, or take over the home duties of the regular army if an emergency sent it abroad. Local branches of the Red Cross and the St John Ambulance Association could provide assistance to the Territorial medical services in case of need, but what was badly needed was a central organization to co-ordinate their individual efforts, raise new detachments, and gather them all under one national umbrella in case of a rainy day.

People flocked to join, not only for motives of patriotism, but because the activities of the new detachments were to go a good deal beyond the provision of bandages and beef tea. They were to be prepared to organize transport, provide food and dressings for improvised ambulance trains, set up emergency field kitchens and even auxiliary hospitals if the need arose. Above all, they were to be trained in the art of improvisation. It promised, at least in peacetime, to add up to quite a lot of fun. By the summer of 1914 there were two and a half thousand Voluntary Aid Detachments spread across the country manned by 74,000 enthusiastic volunteers, two-thirds of them women and girls. As a member of Voluntary Aid Detachment, Dorset 52, Gladys Stanford went off joyfully with the local Territorial battalion of the Dorsetshire Regiment to their annual camp.

We went for a whole fortnight in the month of May, living in tents just like the men, but, of course, in a separate field, and we were given strict instructions by our VAD officers that we must have nothing to do with the men. But they overlooked the fact that there was no water in our camp, so we had to get all our water from the men's camp. They carried it for us and handed the buckets over the hedge, so naturally a lot of chaffing went on, but we behaved very nicely on the whole.

The soldiers had exercises and mock battles and we set up a field hospital to take care of the 'wounded'. It was very interesting and great fun after practising putting splints and bandages on unwilling children or Boy Scouts. And towards the end of the fortnight we were

Gladys Stanford, VAD, Dorset 52

absolutely thrilled to have a real casualty. One of the men was kicked
by a horse and had his leg broken. We practically fought over him –
but of course in the end he was taken off to hospital! Still, we did
have a few tummy upsets and minor cuts and grazes to deal with. We
took it all very seriously, but we hardly thought we'd be nursing the
wounded in earnest before the winter set in.

Winter and war alike were far from the minds of most people as July
trailed towards August through a succession of hot, cloudless days. But
on the 23rd, news reached Whitehall that Austria had delivered an
outrageous ultimatum to Serbia, and Foreign Office officials, raising an
eyebrow as they contemplated the interlinked treaties and alliances
which supported a precarious peace in Europe, could envisage without
much difficulty a chain reaction that might just conceivably force Great
Britain to mobilize. But it seemed a remote possibility. Even if the
mighty Austrian-Hungarian Empire was determined to kick little Serbia
into submission, deplorable though such an event would be, it was
unlikely that the ring of its iron heel on the ancient cobbles of an
insignificant Balkan state would strike a spark that would ignite
Europe.
    But two days later, at nine o'clock in the evening of 25 July, despite
the placatory nature of Serbia's reply to her ultimatum, Austria
announced that her troops were to mobilize on the Serbian border.
    The news was flashed from Vienna to Berlin, where tension had been
rising for the past two days. An hour later a special single-sheet edition
of the evening newspaper was on sale in the streets, and excited crowds
began to gather. The taxi taking Mrs Higbie and her young American
party from the Stettiner station to their hotel had some difficulty in
getting through them.

Mary Ludlum   By the time we settled into the hotel it was too late to do much, but
                the boys went out to see what was going on. They found the streets
                full of people and handbills being thrown about, something to do
                with some government decision between Austria and Serbia. We
                couldn't find out any more, except that people seemed to think there
                might be a war. But the boys said, 'It's nothing. There's always some
                tin-pot little war brewing over here!' So we didn't bother about it.

But next day, despite the fact that it was Sunday, they could not help
but notice the news-hungry crowds gathered at government buildings in
the Wilhelmstrasse, waiting outside the Kaiser's palace in the Schloss-
platz, besieging news-stands in the Potsdamer Platz, and arguing noisily
in cafés along Unter den Linden. The knife-edge atmosphere only served
to heighten their impression that Berlin was the most exciting place
they'd ever seen.
    Potsdam, where royal palaces and military barracks stood side by

side in monumental Prussian splendour, was the Kaiser's weekend retreat. Under normal circumstances, he would already have left for a cruising holiday on the royal yacht *Hohenzollern*. As things were, at a moment's notice the royal train could whisk him back to Berlin, a mere twenty minutes away. The Kaiser was a worried man, for at the start of the crisis he had pledged Germany's support to Austria. Now, the fact of Austria's mobilization was forcing his hand, and he was beginning to have second thoughts. Monday was another scorching day. Potsdam was crowded with visitors, among them Mary and Spink, Robert and Mrs Higbie. They had toured *Sans Souci,* the summer palace of Frederick the Great, strolled in its grounds, glimpsed the Neue Palais from a distance, visited the Friedenskirche and were back in the town when outriders of the Royal Guard appeared and the crowd surged to the edge of the pavement. A moment later, the royal carriage passed en route to Berlin.

> The carriage passed just a few feet from where we were standing. The Kaiser was in full uniform, with an aide-de-camp sitting opposite. He looked absolutely splendid and I thought he was *very* handsome.
>
> Mary Ludlum

It was the climax of their two-day visit. Next day they left for Cologne. And next day, exactly a month after the assassination at Sarajevo, Austria declared war on Serbia.

In London it was Speech Day at St Paul's Girls' School, and something of a special occasion, for the concert given by the girls took the form of a musical première – the first performance of the fourth movement of Gustav Holst's *St Paul's Suite*. It was played by the school orchestra, and the seventeen-year-old twin sisters of Lieutenant Rory Macleod were in the choir that sang the Dargason theme:

> *It was a maid of my countrie,*
> *As she came by a hawthorn tree,*
> *As full of flowers as might be seen,*
> *She marvelled to see the tree so green.*

It was the twins' last day at school. There were six weeks of summer holiday to look forward to before they left home again, this time for Germany, where they were to spend the winter at Marburg studying German.

Their elder brother, Rory, serving with a regular brigade of the Royal Field Artillery at the Curragh in Ireland, was looking forward to a fortnight under canvas at the annual 'practice camp', and the advance party had already gone ahead in charge of the adjutant. Late that evening, as acting-adjutant, it was Lieutenant Macleod who received the message that went out to all units from the War Office. It instructed the Army to regard itself as being in a Precautionary Period and to prepare for mobilization. The colonel was dining out and could not be found, so, on his own initiative, Macleod recalled the advance party and issued the order.

Reassured by the announcement that the Foreign Secretary proposed a meeting of the four major powers – Germany, France, Russia and Great Britain – to try to pull Austria and Serbia apart before it was too late, people went on making plans for the August Bank Holiday weekend. But it was already too late. Russia, too close for comfort to remain aloof, mobilized her troops along her border with Austria. Germany, in support of her ally, promptly declared war on Russia, demanded an assurance from France that she would remain neutral and threatened dire consequences if she refused. France mobilized and sent her army streaming to the north and east to stand along her border with Germany. One by one the cards were dealt out for the first hand of a macabre game in which war was trumps and the winner would take all.

Still the British government hesitated to issue the order for general mobilization, but faced with the worsening situation and fearful of the threat to her vital sea-lanes, the Home Fleet was ordered to sail north to take up a strategic position at Scapa Flow. Admiralty staff worked all through Saturday night preparing the telegrams that would be sent off in the morning to call up the naval reservists.

On the following day, Bank Holiday Monday, Germany declared war on France.

Gladys Stanford, VAD, Dorset 52

On that Monday my family had planned a very big and special picnic at a lovely spot nearby called Larner Tree on an estate owned by General Pitt-Rivers. It was my young brother's twenty-first birthday, and a double celebration because a cousin was twenty-one, too. We had asked masses of people and spent days planning it and preparing the food and hoping that the fine weather wouldn't break. We were going to have cricket in the afternoon and dancing in the evening, by the light of lanterns among the trees.

Overnight we got messages from some of the guests to say that they would be unable to come, because all the railway trains were taken over by the government to transport reservists called up to report to their depots. During the party several young men had to leave to report. They did return that night, but they were called up again two days later. They were all in the Dorset Yeomanry.

It was still the Precautionary Period, but when, early next morning, German troops marched into Belgium hoping for a clear passage through it to strike a blow at north-western France, Britain – as guarantor of Belgian neutrality – could stand aside no longer. An ultimatum was handed to the German Ambassador in London and, by eleven o'clock that evening, Russia, France and Great Britain were at war with Germany and Austria.

From the safety of Lucerne in neutral Switzerland, Mary Ludlum wrote excitedly in her diary:

WAR! It's thrilling! Everything is in turmoil. All the countries are mobilizing their armies. Saw the Lion of Lucerne, went shopping and spent some good money we now wish we had, as we find the coin of the realm tied up and we can't cash Express checks.

We were safe and comfortable in Lucerne and everyone urged us to stay, but finding that there was no way to communicate with the USA, and knowing that our families would be worrying, we decided against it, despite all warnings. We had become friendly with a Dr Lee and his little boy, so we decided to make our way to Paris together. This new-made friend almost literally saved our lives. He carried gold, the only acceptable currency after we crossed the border into France. I've often wondered who or what could have warned him.

Mary Ludlum

It was difficult enough to get to the French border; once across it their troubles began in earnest, for all the trains had been requisitioned by the French army. Suddenly the tourists had become refugees. It took them two days to reach Pontarlier in a succession of friendly haycarts and farm wagons. Sitting on the pile of baggage at the railway station through the long, hot day while the men looked for accommodation, Mary and Mrs Higbie watched the trains come and go. They could see for themselves that there was no chance of getting a train to Paris, for it was perfectly evident that they were all bound for the front.

It was pitiful to see the soldiers saying goodbye to wives and sweethearts, and daughters and mothers and sisters. Really heart-rending. It made us feel that we weren't by any means the worst-off females in town. Dr Lee and the boys spent the whole day scouring the town from the mayor down, but they couldn't get a room for love or money. Finally, they went back the the mayor and told him that one of the women was desperately ill. Somewhat to their consternation, the mayor said he would come see for himself. By a stroke of luck, when they arrived at the station I had fallen sound asleep, sitting on my biggest bag, with my head hanging down. (Rob said later, 'And you never did see a sicker-looking woman in your life'!) *'Oh, la pauvre fille'*, said the mayor. He took us to a small hostelry and ordered them to give us a room. It wasn't much, and all six of us had to share, but we were glad of it. The mayor gave us passports to stay a few days and permission to eat and sleep here and pay later. Three days later we did manage to travel on to Paris – on a cattle-truck train. It took us twenty-four hours to get there. We kept the doors open for ventilation and the train travelled so slowly that the

Mary Ludlum

boys and I were able to sit on the floor with our feet dangling over-side.

Hot and dirty, travel-stained and exhausted, the refugees reached Paris to discover that their hotel reservations had been cancelled. Despite another wearisome trek in search of lodgings, this irksome event (which would have loomed large in normal times) seemed a pinprick of such little importance that Mary did not trouble to record it in her diary. She noted, however, that Mrs Higbie, doubtless now past caring, had relaxed the rules and changed her views on the amount of freedom that might be permitted to young Americans travelling abroad.

Mary Ludlum (her diary)

Still in Paris. Our new abode is a pension. Spink and I are allowed to do more now. Spink is a fellow, and my French, though a small thing, is a big factor. We first of all decided to live here for a while, then changed our minds and later decided we'd only stay until Monday and then go on. It looks as though the Aquitania will sail on schedule. Everyone tells you differently. . . . Go to this or that man and get this or that permit or pass. Should like to stay here a while, but Rob has a strong hunch the Aquitania will sail.

But first they had to get to Boulogne and across the Channel to England. It was a hot, dusty, gruelling journey to the coast in a passenger train that clanked along at a snail's pace, sometimes being shunted on to a siding to make way for a military train, often standing for hours at a station seething with troops.

Mary Ludlum (her diary)

The French soldiers are so messy. Their gaudy uniforms remind me of Wallace Irwin's pun on French trousers, 'Toulon, Toulouse, and too baggy'. But you can't help being impressed by their ardent esprit de corps. Their eyes fairly brim when they cry out, 'Vive La France!', and they grip our hands and beat their breasts. The English soldiers look so different. We saw a lot of them when we got to Boulogne and they look like regular men, trimly dressed in khaki. Nice, clean-looking fellows.

Mary Ludlum could justifiably claim to have had a grandstand view of the so-called 'tin-pot little war'. Two weeks ago she had stood in the crowd that cheered the Kaiser on his way to a council of war. Now she had arrived in Boulogne on the same day as the first of the British soldiers who would confront his armies.

Already the giant *Aquitania* had been requisitioned for war service, so on 15 August, the day after Mary's twentieth birthday, Mrs Higbie's party sailed from Liverpool in the *Campania*. She was a condemned ship, hastily reprieved from the breaker's yard, and they had only been able to get steerage passages, but they were glad to get any at all.

With the exception of the unfortunate Mrs Higbie, who never wanted to see Europe again, in three years time the whole party would be back – Spink and Rob as soldiers of the United States Army and Mary as an army nurse. But for the moment, as the ship steamed out of the River Mersey and headed west into the Atlantic, although it had been the adventure of their lives they were thankful to turn their backs on Europe's war. The only war that could be reasonably supposed to affect the interests of America was on her own back doorstep, where the small regular army was engaged in an intermittent squabble with Pancho Villa on the Mexican border. Citizens of the United States could hardly be expected to feel personally threatened by a dispute that had started up on the back doorstep of tiny neutral Belgium, several thousand miles away on the other side of the Atlantic Ocean.

Chapter Three

At the beginning all eyes were on Belgium. GALLANT LITTLE BEL-GIUM shrieked the newspaper headlines and no cause was more calcu-lated to appeal to the British sense of fair play. Had neutral Belgium allowed the German army to march through unimpeded on its way to invade France, no one could have blamed her. But the Belgians exhi-bited pluck, and pluck in the circumstances was something to be admired. Faced with overwhelming odds, Belgium squared up to the invader and appealed to her allies for help. The public imagination was caught by the justness of the cause. Germany had been sabre-rattling for too long, and, if she were allowed to get away with this outrage, might soon be rattling her sabre over Britain itself.

Indignation was fanned by atrocity stories (the Germans were auto-matically supposed to rape women and bayonet children as a matter of course) and refugees, flying from the path of the invaders with their salvaged possessions piled high on rickety carts, and their imaginations inflamed by hardship, added rumour to rumour and horror to horror. It was no wonder that it was a popular war.

Everyone wanted to do their bit. The trouble at the beginning was that there weren't quite enough bits to go round. Young men besieged recruiting offices in answer to Lord Kitchener's call to arms. Reservists had been recalled to bring battalions of the regular army up to active service strength and the Territorial Force had been mobilized, soldiers and nurses alike. The peacetime strength of army nurses, serving with Queen Alexandra's Imperial Military Nursing Service, was only 300, but there were almost 2,000 trained nurses attached to the Territorial Force and the QAIMNS Reserve, and many thousands more who were working in civilian hospitals and could be recruited later. At the moment they had their hands full. Hardly had the war begun than there was an outbreak of infectious diseases. It was hardly surprising, for the whole country was on the move.

The Territorial Highland Division was taken *en masse* from the pure mountain air of its native Scotland, where communities were small and infection did not travel far, and deposited in highly populated Bedford. The town was the home of a famous public school with an enthusiastic juvenile population of its own, all eager to mix with the soldiers. Within weeks the Highlanders succumbed to a virulent epidemic of measles. Everywhere it was the same story. There were men from the hills and valleys of Wales, from farms and villages in the north country, from the moors of Devon and from rural areas all over the country who were not only living in close proximity to each other, but were often for the first time mixing with townspeople in large numbers. Epidemics of childish ailments spread like a powder trail through the uprooted recruits, and many a village lad who had swaggered into the ranks with heroic ideas of fighting the Germans spent his first weeks as a soldier fighting a fever, scratching his spots or nursing a painful case of mumps. The isolation hospitals were soon full of sick soldiers, so there was no alternative but to send them to be nursed in civilian hospitals, which were hastily forced to convert part of their accommodation into fever wards. The nurses were rushed off their feet, because these were serious cases.

In the Highland Division alone, eighty-five soldiers died between the beginning of the school term and the end of November. With hundreds of others out of action for weeks at a time the effect of the epidemic on the carefully planned training programme was chaotic. But it did give the VADs of Bedford an opportunity to 'do their bit' for sick soldiers a good deal earlier than many other frustrated detachments, whose members had little to do but knit socks, roll bandages and wonder when more important services would be needed.

They acted as unpaid orderlies in the 'measles hospital', dishing out tea, scrubbing floors and lockers and willingly performing any other menial task that would relieve the overworked nurses. They organized recreation rooms and took it in turns to prepare gargantuan supplies of porridge which the soldiers consumed as fast as it could be doled out. They organized concerts and entertainments, put chairs and tables in their gardens and stuck hospitable notices on their gates inviting the soldiers to come in. In circumstances that were not always easy they took the Highlanders to their hearts.

These rough and simple men from the remoter parts of Scotland had some trying habits which people who lived along the leafy avenues of Bedford found it hard to come to terms with, and it was along these avenues that most of the soldiers were billeted. Their landladies looked after them like mothers, washing and mending their clothes, making sure that they wrote home, nursing their lodgers when they were sick and taking such a personal interest in the Jocks that Colonel Nicholson became quite accustomed to finding half a dozen ladies waiting on the doorstep of his headquarters office every morning. Each had come to explain that Hamish or Duncan or Sandy had a cold coming on, that she had packed him off to bed with a hot-water bottle and that, in her opinion, he was not fit to do any soldiering today.

Nevertheless, there were occasions on which their patience was sorely tried. When the soldiers were actually under their own roofs, the women of Bedford could exercise a certain amount of control; when they were merely 'neighbours' it was less easy. Houses that were 'To let' had been requisitioned by the Army and used as billets for anything up to twenty young soldiers, whose limited experiences had not included that of living in 'a desirable villa-residence with modern conveniences'. They were not barbarians. But boys from Scottish farms who were accustomed to seeing household refuse thrown into a pit or on to a midden-heap in the farmyard were naturally unfamiliar with the use of the dustbins supplied by the army. Acting on the principle of some crofters' wives who made a week's supply of porridge at a time, the soldiers brewed a week's supply of tea in the shiny new dustbins and continued to throw their rubbish into the garden. They could have filled and trimmed oil lamps without a second thought, but gaslight was a disconcerting mystery. Once they had solved it the Jocks simply left it on all the time, an expensive habit which was only noticed at the end of the quarter when the army received the bills. Lacking a handy supply of peat, they were not above pulling up a few loose floorboards to light a fire of an evening or even, in extreme cases, demolishing the railing of a staircase. And when a man had been used to washing under a pump in a yard in spartan Scotland and attending to his more personal require-ments in an earth closet outside the back door, what was he to make of those 'mod cons' which were taken for granted in the select purlieus of Bedford? The answer, in many cases, was, 'very little'.

One soldier returning to his new billet after a long day's route march was washing his muddy kilt-hose in what house agents euphemistically referred to as the downstairs convenience. 'Hey, Willie,' he shouted to a fellow soldier, 'what do I do when I want more water?' 'Pull the plug,' answered Willie. This helpful advice was followed by a pause – a clank – a rush of water – and a startled cry of 'Jesus Christ!' as the socks made a rapid watery exit. At the next kit inspection their owner's long-suffering officer had no difficulty in understanding his aggrieved expla-nation. By that time he would have believed anything.

The Territorial Highland Division was not popular with solicitors and house agents and the civilians would not have been human had they not complained. With remarkable indulgence they went on pampering the unruly Jocks and looked on it as 'doing their bit'.

Members of the Voluntary Aid Detachments in Southampton also managed to find useful work, for although their nursing skills were not yet needed Southampton had become one vast transit camp. More than two-thirds of the common was covered with tents and marquees where soldiers spent the hours before embarkation. The rest had been turned into a vast remount camp where horses requisitioned from all over the country were concentrated before being shipped to France, and the overpowering proximity of thousands of horses caused acute attacks of asthma and hay fever among men who had never before realized that they were allergic to them. This was a temporary condition that could be dealt with by Battalion Medical Officers, but in transit there was little that the individual units could do in the way of providing their men with creature comforts. So the VADs commandeered a marquee and set up a canteen in which the men could while away a few reasonably pleasant hours before going to sleep as best they could under canvas, or marching to the docks en route to France. Night after night the streets of Southampton rang with the sound of marching feet.

Where the army went their nurses went too. They had landed in France with the first contingents of the BEF, looking very much as they had looked at the beginning of the century when they had landed in South Africa to nurse the soldiers of the Boer War. They wore close-fitting grey bonnets, tied with a bow under the chin, and, under their travelling cloaks, ankle-length dresses covered with the short scarlet cape which had been designed by Florence Nightingale to conceal curvaceous bosoms from the eyes of the licentious soldiery. Many of the capes bore the red, yellow and blue ribbon of the South African Campaign medal; all of them bore the stiff, pink Alexandra rose at the back, between the shoulder-blades. The legend went that they were placed in that position in order to prevent the Sisters from falling asleep on night duty. The first of the nurses reached France on 12 August.

Good works had always been based on the concept of *noblesse oblige*, and, when their country called, *noblesse* automatically obliged, undeterred by the fact that the country had not yet called in particularly stentorious tones. Overnight, it seemed, stately homes and country houses were transformed into convalescent homes for officers, and the London houses of the rich became private hospitals financed by their owners and by contributions from wealthy friends. Suddenly, the one autumn fashion everyone wanted to be seen wearing was a nurse's uniform, preferably moulded to voluptuous perfection by Monsieur Worth. Soon the streets of Mayfair were fluttering with veils of the finest organdie flowing from aristocratic heads. Lucky the soldier who was evacuated from the nightmare of Mons to a haven presided over by a 'Lady'. At Mrs Freddie Guest's in Park Lane it was blue silk pyjamas for junior officers on the ground floor and pink silk for senior officers on the floor above.

At the Duchess of Leinster's in Bryanston Square, Second Lieutenant Peter Mason (still under the weather from the operation he had undergone two days earlier before being transferred to the ducal residence) woke from a drugged sleep to find the ducal butler standing at the foot of his bed. 'What', enquired the butler, 'would you care to have for dinner this evening, sir?' Disinclined to eat at all, Mason was unable to express any positive preference, but the butler was insistent. 'Then, may I suggest, sir, Lamb Cutlets Reform, and perhaps half a bottle of Bollinger?' In his befuddled state, Second Lieutenant Mason came to the conclusion that he must be delirious and went back to sleep.

With the unexpected rush of wounded arriving before the war was a month old, the authorities were only too glad to make use of the private hospitals and looked approvingly on the angels of mercy who ran them. The 'Flying Angels', on the other hand, although they were equally rich and powerful, equally anxious to do good, the authorities were privately inclined to consign to the Devil. No one could doubt the 'Flying Angels'' patriotism or the purity of their motives, but while the situation was so fluid at the front, while no one knew precisely where the front was, the last thing that was needed was the worry of knowing that there were a dozen or so flying columns of nurses and would-be nurses chasing hither and thither on the heels of the armies in France and Belgium.*

In the vanguard of them all was the Dowager Duchess of Sutherland. Attired in the uniform of a Red Cross nurse, she marched down the gangway of a cross-Channel steamer and set her feet firmly on the soil of France before the war was a hundred hours old. Her intention was to attach herself to the *Secours aux Blessés*, a branch of the French Red Cross whose president, the Comtesse d'Haussonville, was her personal friend. It was a strict rule that no foreigners were allowed to nurse in French hospitals, but in the Duchess's philosophy rules did not apply to her. Escorted by the British Ambassador, she called on the French Minister of War, who 'broke every regulation in my favour, gave me a permit and expressed devoted gratitude for my services!' Armed with her permit, the Duchess was able to join a group of nurses (countesses every one!) travelling to Belgium.

Brussels was a disappointment. It still had the air of a peacetime city and was packed with Red Cross workers, and was already well-supplied with hospitals and detachments of trained nurses, which included a group from Guy's Hospital in London. Fate intervened in the person of Dr Depage of the Brussels Red Cross. 'How splendid it would be,' he remarked, 'if groups of English nurses could be formed into ambulance units and sent to the provinces of Belgium.' The Duchess was enchanted with the idea. She promptly resigned from the French Red Cross, joined the Belgian *Service de Santé de l'Armée* and wired her instructions to England. A surgeon and eight trained nurses must be engaged at once and sent to join her in Belgium. They would be known as the 'Millicent Sutherland Ambulance' and the Duchess would be their commandant. Two days later, on 16 August, the doctor and nurses arrived, bringing with them drugs, disinfectant, dressings and, in accordance with Her Grace's special instructions, a plentiful supply of glycerine for the hands.

Their destination was Namur, a border town surrounded by nine forts. It had seemed reasonable to assume that the Germans would

* In the event, most of these unofficial, private ambulance groups did invaluable work. The story of the two women of Pervyse (who nursed virtually in the trenches) is well known. Others nursed under bombardment at Antwerp, Furnes and Ypres as the armies retreated. Some groups set up centres to care for refugees. But despite their good work and goodwill, their impetuous and premature departures for the front were a distinct embarrassment to the Government.

by-pass Namur in their anxiety to push on into France. But within a few hours of the arrival of the 'Millicent Sutherland Ambulance', communications with the outside world were completely cut and the town was rapidly emptying as people fled from the advancing Germans. The Duchess was made of sterner stuff. Under her supervision the ambulance set up in a local convent, unpacked its equipment and prepared for action. There were no wounded to nurse as yet but the 'Commandant' let it be known that henceforth she wished to be addressed as 'Sister Millicent'.

On 21 August, gunfire was heard outside the town, refugees began to pour in from the surrounding countryside and Namur itself was bombed.

Namur . . . Never shall I forget the afternoon of 22 August. The shelling of the past hours having suddenly ceased I went to my dormitory. I was falling asleep when Sister Kirby rushed into my room calling out, 'Sister Millicent! The wounded!'

I rushed down the stone stairs. Six motor cars and as many wagons were at the door. In less than twenty minutes we had forty-five wounded on our hands. They were all Belgian – Flemish and Walloon – or French. Our young surgeon, Mr Morgan, was perfectly cool and so were our nurses. What I thought would be for me an impossible task became absolutely natural; to wash wounds, to drag off rags and clothing soaked in blood, to hold basins equally full of blood, to soothe a soldier's groans, and to raise a wounded man while he was receiving extreme unction. These actions seemed suddenly to become an insistent duty, perfectly easy to carry out. Hundreds of wounded, we believed, were still waiting to be brought in and, owing to the German cannonading, it was impossible to get near them. The guns never cease.

The Belgian gendarmerie have just been in and collected all arms and ammunition. Quite late in the afternoon we heard a tremendous explosion. The Belgians had blown up the new railway bridge, but unfortunately there are others by which the Germans can cross, and presently we hear that they are in the town. There is some rapid fusillading through the streets and two frightened old Belgian officers run into the convent and ask for Red Cross bands, throwing down their arms and maps.

Millicent, Duchess of Sutherland (her diary, 23 August 1914)

In the light of the fact that all further resistance would obviously be useless, the idea of posing as Red Cross workers must have seemed eminently practical to two elderly reservists anxious to return with all possible speed to the homes and families they had left unprotected. They reckoned without 'Sister Millicent'. She never did admit that she had threatened them with a loaded revolver, but merely recorded laconically that 'in a few minutes, however, they regained self-control and went out into the streets – without the Red Cross bands. Heaven knows what happened to them. . .'

But she had not been one of those who had meekly handed over her firearm to the Belgian authorities, and a suspiciously few moments after the cowed departure of the Belgian officers who had been so quick to regain self-control, the Duchess was to be found 'burying my revolver under an apple tree when the bombardment began once more'.

When the flames and the smoke died down an uneasy peace descended on Namur and the Germans were in full possession of the town.

Millicent, Duchess of Sutherland

What a change in three days! German sentries stood outside the military hospital, Germans filled every café, and up and down the streets there was a perpetual march of German soldiers. There was a look of terror on each face amongst the inhabitants.

But not on the face of Sister Millicent. As soon as it was safe to leave the shelter of the convent she marched off to German headquarters and sent in her card to the commandant, General von Bulow, whose acquaintance she had made at Homburg before the war. She was also acquainted with his aide-de-camp, Baron Kessler, with whom she had frequently discussed 'Art and opera' at social gatherings during the past London season. She demanded and obtained a written order that the sacks of flour which the nuns had stored in their cellar should not be commandeered by the Germans, who had already started requisitioning food. The following day she was back complaining about the treatment of British prisoners whom she had heard were passing through the town on their way to Germany. Every day the Duchess appeared at the Kommandantur with a fresh demand or complaint, quoting the Geneva Convention at the Germans until they were sick of the sight of her. It was extraordinary, in the face of this onslaught, that they remained so consistently civil and courteous but then, as the Duchess remarked, 'the Germans like well-known people.'

They had rather more than enough of them, for there were an extraordinary number of intrepid English ladies on errands of mercy in occupied Belgium, calmly ignoring the annoying presence of the Germans unless they required them to perform some service. The Duchess heard that Miss Angela Manners and Miss Nellie Hozier had gone down with an ambulance of London Hospital nurses to Mons. They had obtained a permit to do so from the German authorities by freely using the name of Miss Hozier's brother-in-law, Mr Winston Churchill.

This news sent the Duchess hot-foot back to the Kommandantur. She too wished to go to Mons. It was imperative that she should visit the captured British wounded. They would kindly issue a permit immediately and in addition (going one better than the Misses Manners and Hozier) they would also supply a motor car and a driver to take her.

The Germans meekly complied, but it was all getting too much, even for them. Their liking for well-known people was rapidly waning in the formidable presence of this blue-blooded tormentor.

On returning to the convent after her sponsored visit to the German lines, the Duchess was infuriated to discover that the Germans, taking advantage of her absence, had closed down all private ambulances and ordered the wounded to be removed to German military hospitals. The unkindest cut was that she was unable to storm down to make her protest in person at the Kommandantur, 'as the fatal hour of nine was past when all who ventured into the streets were shot'. For once the Germans had won a round, and there was nothing the Duchess could do about it but stand by, loudly quoting the Geneva Convention at the officer in charge of the party which carried the wounded out.

It was a Sunday and, as a consequence, the Kommandantur was manned only by a skeleton staff. Undeterred, the Duchess pursued the German commandant to early morning service at the cathedral, and when she failed to intercept him there, followed him to the Hotel St Aubain, where he was at lunch. Meek as a lamb he came out of the dining-room in response to Her Grace's summons. He would be delighted, he said, to help them in any way to leave Namur. Where did they wish to go? Perhaps, he suggested, Maubeuge. If so, he would arrange for a special carriage in a military train to transport them there.

It is difficult to understand the motive behind this proposal, for Maubeuge was still being shelled by the German artillery; the French were still in possession and did not finally surrender until six o'clock that evening, several hours after the German Commandant suggested to the Duchess that she and her ambulance should go there. Maubeuge or perdition; it was doubtless all one to him, and he perhaps also took into consideration the fact that this troublesome lady might bully her way through the German lines and take her valuable services back where they belonged – with the Allies. This possibility had not escaped the Duchess herself.

It was a gruelling journey to Maubeuge. The train took them as far as Erquelinnes, ten kilometres from their destination, and they were informed that it would go no further. Very well, then, they would walk. 'After all,' the Duchess airily remarked to her nurses, 'one very nearly does that in a day's golfing.' But on a newly conquered battlefield there were rather more obstacles than are normally found on a golf course.

It was utterly deserted, save for the German troops marching up the rough, dusty roads and the French prisoners marching down them. After a time we cut across country to shorten our walk, but we were perpetually tripped up by barbed wire or hindered by the deserted trenches and the huge pit-like holes which had been made by the shells. Presently we came to a village. Every house was either ruined or deserted. All around the village we saw dead cattle and horses

Millicent, Duchess of Sutherland (her diary, 10 September 1914)

swollen and stiff, killed by shellfire. There was a dreadful smell. I saw
no human dead bodies but numbers and numbers of long mounds,
which were graves marked by empty shells and German helmets
stuck on top. It was all heart-breaking, but still we walked.

It was late in the evening when the footsore party limped into
Maubeuge, where, with confidence unimpaired, the Duchess of Sutherland presented herself at the German headquarters and sent in her card
to its astounded commander, Major Abercron. He was appalled to see
'a high-born lady in an invidious position'. He regretted that he was not
in a position to avail himself of the services of the 'Millicent Sutherland
Ambulance' and suggested that they would be well-advised to leave
Maubeuge as soon as possible. What under these circumstances, he
enquired, did they wish to do? 'Get through the lines,' replied the
Duchess firmly, looking him straight in the eye, 'to our own troops.' It
was a good try! But no German officer – not even one so obviously
admiring as the commandant of Maubeuge – could possibly have
connived at such a blatantly madcap scheme. But such was the commandant's liking for 'well-known people' that he wrote out a pass for
the Duchess, giving her permission to make her way to England, and put
a charabanc at her disposal so that the party might travel north again
and perhaps reach Ostend. Two members of the French Red Cross were
to accompany the party to drive the motor car and bring it back.

Of course, it was impossible to get through the German lines to
Ostend. They got as far as Renaix, where the brigadier in charge of
German headquarters was reduced to tears of laughter at the very idea.
The party was ordered to proceed to Brussels to report to Feld-
Marschal von der Goltz, and this time a military escort went with them
to make sure that they did.

Furious and, for once, exhausted, the Duchess of Sutherland arrived
with her ambulance in German-occupied Brussels. The nine trained
sisters were sent off to lodge in hospital. 'Sister Millicent' repaired to a
suite at the Hotel Astoria, and the following morning was thrown into a
towering rage by the discovery that two German soldiers were on guard
outside her door and that she was in effect a prisoner. It was a state of
affairs which did not last long. There was no longer a British Ambassador in Brussels but there was an American Ambassador, Mr Brand
Whitlock, who was only too ready to champion the cause of the
Duchess of Sutherland. But unknown to them both, another of Her
Grace's extensive acquaintances, an aristocratic count working with
the German Red Cross, was in a position to help her. He arrived shortly
after the ambassador, kissed the Duchess's hand, had the guard
removed from the door and informed her that she and her ambulance
were free to leave by the next train for neutral Holland. It was a
tongue-in-cheek *laissez-passer*, in view of the fact that there were now
no trains to Holland. But the Duchess was still in possession of the

Maubeuge motor. The military governor of Brussels, General von Lüttwitz, was summoned to wait on her at her hotel. He would allow the 'Millicent Sutherland Ambulance' to go to Holland. He would provide two German drivers for the motor car. But they must travel via Aachen. He furnished a passport accordingly. 'Sister Millicent' was a trifle uneasy. Aachen was in Germany and she did not trust the Germans, but Mr Brand Whitlock came to the rescue. He too was not immune to a liking for important people and the Duchess had been grateful for his many attentions, from bouquets of red roses to copies of *The Times* smuggled into her hotel buttoned under his waistcoat. Now he came up with a brilliant idea.

'What about Jim Barnes going with you?' Jim Barnes was an American journalist working in Brussels and as a neutral could travel freely to Holland.

'He seemed the very man for us,' exulted the Duchess. 'He readily agreed to come with us, and by this means he prevented a German officer from occupying the front seat. He sat between the two German soldiers, a fine, burly protector, and the German officer was left behind. The Stars and Stripes seemed to flap in Brussels a little uncomfortably in the eyes of the Prussian dictators.' Within a few hours they had crossed the border at Canne. A procession of horse-drawn carriages was driven from Maastricht to meet the travellers, a courtesy which had been arranged in advance by the splendid Mr Barnes. The German charabanc, having carried the party on a tortuous journey of some hundreds of miles from the front at Maubeuge, turned around and drove back into occupied Belgium, and the Duchess of Sutherland watched it go with the greatest satisfaction, not merely because the journey had been safely accomplished but because she had the pleasure of knowing 'that Germany had paid for all the petrol we used from Maubeuge to Maastricht!'

After a rousing welcome at The Hague (where the British Ambassador, Sir Alan Johnston, naturally put himself at the disposal of the Duchess of Sutherland) the 'Millicent Sutherland Ambulance' sailed from Flushing on 18 September. Blatantly capitalizing on the publicity she received the Duchess, with hardly a pause for breath, set about raising funds and preparing to go back again.*

But there were those who felt that the impetuous 'Flying Angels' had had more than their fair share of the war. Hardly anyone else had had a chance to do anything at all. Unless, perhaps, it was Lieutenant-General Sir Douglas Haig, commanding the First Army Corps. On the day on which the Duchess and her entourage left Flushing for England, he

---

* This time she had to act through the official channels of the Red Cross. The Duchess of Sutherland's Red Cross Hospital was soon set up just outside Calais, where it remained for the duration of the war. It was an uncommonly efficient hospital and the Duchess, as commandant, was superb.

pulled off something of a coup by trading 10,000 tins of bully beef with the French zouaves in reserve on his right, in return for the loan of two heavy guns. He needed them badly, for although the Germans had been pushed back to the River Aisne it was plain that they could be pushed back no further. It was equally plain that the French and British armies massed in front of them could not advance.

Chapter Four

The German artillery had now been able to bring up heavy guns from the captured Belgian forts and to augment them with British field guns captured at Mons and Le Cateau. It was true that the Germans had had to send two divisions of infantry to the Russian front and they were not, for the moment, in a position to advance. What they could do was dig in and fortify their position with an arsenal of weapons of such power and effectiveness as to render impotent any attempt at conventional attack. It was now that the British and French were introduced to the terrors of the 'Jack Johnsons' — huge shells fired from eight-inch siege howitzers which burst in black, death-dealing clouds. Machine-gun fire and short-range shells fired from trench mortar guns, deadly accurate in front-line positions, could easily put an infantry attack to rout and the soldiers, armed with rifles and bayonets, who survived to reach the enemy trenches were blown to pieces by bombs and hand-grenades hurled at point-blank range by the practised German infantry.

It was impasse, and every move ended, as Field-Marshal Sir John French bitterly remarked, 'in the same trench! trench! trench!'

The casualties were frightful. In the first weeks of the war the medical services were uncertain whether they should advance or retire with the armies over the fluctuating front, and in trying to establish base hospitals in the rear they were equally uncertain as to where the rear would finally be. Scores of the army nurses who had originally disembarked with the BEF were shunted from place to place without being given any definite work to do. Among them was Sister Luard, who killed time, marked linen and waited for orders at Le Mans. The big battles were over, but on 20 September three train-loads of wounded arrived. They were the casualties of the impasse, the first harvest of the new and deadly weapons that had sliced through the ranks of the French and British armies standing opposite the Germans on the Aisne. There were no facilities to take care of any but the very worst of the wounded, and nothing for it but for the nurses and doctors to go to the station and tend the others there.

> You boarded a cattle truck, armed with a tray of dressings and a pail; the men were lying on straw, had been in trains for several days. Most had only been dressed once, and many were gangrenous. If you found one urgently needed amputation or operation, or was likely to

Sister K. Luard, Queen Alexandra's

die, you called an MO, to have him taken off the train for hospital.
The platform was soon packed with stretchers with all the bad cases
waiting patiently to be taken to hospital. The staple dressing is
tincture of iodine; you don't attempt anything but swabbing with
lysol, and then gauze dipped in iodine. They were nearly all
shrapnel-shell wounds – more ghastly than anything I have ever seen
or smelt; the Mauser wounds of the Boer War were pinpricks compared with them. When I think of the Red Cross practices on Boy
Scouts and the grim reality, it makes one wonder.

The wounded soldiers of the BEF arrived home to a warm welcome.
Everyone wanted to do something for them. They cheered them in the
streets and threw them packets of cigarettes; volunteers at railway
stations dished out hot tea by the gallon; children lined the streets
waving flags as the ambulances passed; work parties redoubled their
efforts in bandage rolling and knitting; and, learning that soldiers who
had sustained bad wounds in the back or in the chest could not be
dressed in conventional pyjamas, old ladies all over the country assiduously combed a regiment of reluctant Pekinese dogs once, twice, even
three times a day. It was their contribution to the war effort, for the
collected combings of dog hair could be woven into the lightest of
garments to cover the shoulders of wounded soldiers who could bear no
other weight on their bandaged bodies. They had to be kept warm,
because already it was beginning to turn cold. The days were shorten-
ing, summer had drifted imperceptibly into autumn and still a legion of
volunteers waited to be mobilized. The most impatient of all were the
Voluntary Aid Detachments.

Premises had been earmarked for auxiliary hospitals. Empty houses,
village schools, church halls were ready to be occupied at a moment's
notice. Lists had been drawn up of the equipment and furnishings that
would be required, and it was many months since local residents had
been canvassed for contributions. Most households had a brass bed-
stead which could be spared, and few could not part with a pair of sheets,
a couple of blankets, a few towels, knives and forks, cutlery, chairs and
tables, pillows and cushions – even saucepans, china, kettles, scrubbing
brushes and buckets. All were ready to be collected at a moment's
notice. But nothing happened, and it began to seem as if nothing ever
would.

There was still fighting along the comparatively narrow strip of land
where the Belgian army stood between Germany and the sea, but like a
school bully who with a single hand can hold a struggling small boy at
arm's length behind him while inflicting a bloody nose on a second with
the other, the Germans were having no trouble in dealing with the
demoralized remnants of Belgium's field army. One swift blow would
finish it altogether. And with a single stride the Germans would be in
possession not only of the Belgian ports of Zeebrugge and Ostend but of

the vital French ports of Dunkirk, Calais and Boulogne. In the absence of the British forces still fighting with the French further south, they lay open and vulnerable within the German grasp, and once in possession of these ports the Germans would not only have deprived the British army of its most vital supply lines at the narrowest point of the channel which divided Britain from France, but, with such a springboard to leap from, might in a few short weeks be astride the Channel itself. In France, in Germany, in London, in the headquarters on either side of the front where General von Kluck and Field-Marshal Sir John French conferred with their commanders, pored over maps and tried to read each other's mind, the situation was quickly appreciated, and the Race to the Sea began.

Now that the enemy advance had been thwarted and the Germans driven back to the Aisne, Sir John French was anxious to withdraw his forces from the French and take up his 'natural position' on the left of the French, where he would be nearer his own lines of communication and supply and in a favourable position to try to manoeuvre round the right flank of the Germans while they were occupied on the Aisne. But it takes time to move an army, and leaving aside the question of transport, they could hardly decamp wholesale leaving the French to patch the holes in their line as best they could. Meanwhile, Antwerp was wavering, was in danger and then – devastatingly – was on the point of collapse. This news reached London on 2 October, the day before the British army was to begin its move to the north. Something had to be done, if not to save Antwerp, then at least to hold the Germans there until the British could arrive in force.

The million men who had enlisted in Kitchener's Army during the first months of the war had hardly begun their training. Some Territorials or reservists had already been sent to stiffen the ranks of the sorely tried BEF, which had fought three major battles in as many weeks, and the rest were either on the high seas on their way to India, where they would release seasoned fighting troops to join the war on the Western Front, or were protecting the shores of Britain from an invasion that was now a grim possibility. The only body of trained and efficient troops which could possibly be spared to help at Antwerp were 3,000 men of the Royal Marines – and they had already been sent there at the end of September when the first misgivings had been felt. Now they would have to be reinforced, but by whom? It was a case of Hobson's Choice.

'Hobson's Choice' was at present disporting itself on the Downs behind Walmer and Deal and having a thoroughly enjoyable time. They were the men of the two Royal Naval Brigades newly formed from the ranks of the Royal Fleet Reserve, the Royal Naval Reserve and the Royal Naval Volunteer Reserve who had been called up at the beginning of August when the Navy was mobilized. Now they were to be turned into soldiers. It was unfortunate that very few of their officers, to whom this task was entrusted, had more than a glimmering of an idea as to how this was to be accomplished.

Able Seaman
(later
Sub-Lieutenant)
Jeremy
Bentham,
Benbow
Battalion, 1st
Royal Naval
Brigade

We had some Royal Marine Sergeants attached to us and they knew all about how to drill, but there weren't nearly enough of them to train us directly. All they could do was brief our own officers how to go about it. The routine was that every morning after breakfast we were marched out on to the Downs and then we'd immediately be told to fall out while the Royal Marine sergeant tried to give the officers a bit of instruction. After he'd gone they went through the motions, reading out of the Army Training Manual, but our platoon officers were just young midshipmen – seventeen or eighteen – and they didn't have the first idea. As soon as the Marine sergeants were out of the way they'd just tell us to fall out again and have a smoke, or we'd have the odd game of football, maybe some physical jerks, and in the evening we'd march back to camp. Day after day it was the same thing. Eventually we were issued with rifles and tried to do a bit of rifle drill, but they were very old ones and there was no ammunition. When we were told we were going to France I'd never even fired out of my rifle!

We got the order on 4 October at about five o'clock in the morning, when the bugles summoned us to assemble at the double and Commodore Henderson announced that we were going to France. Pandemonium wasn't the word! Even the Commodore had to go to Deal and wake up the shopkeepers to buy up all the school satchels and linen bags he could find to serve as ammunition pouches.

When we eventually reached Antwerp early in the morning of 6 October, we were marched through the town and out into the country, told to dig a light trench and stand by for a Uhlan charge. We said, 'What's that? Never heard of it.' For none of us had ever fired a gun and hardly knew one end of a rifle from the other. During the night, lying there in the open, I kept hearing this roaring sound over my head. It was exactly like the sound of the District Line Underground train I used to travel in to the bank every day, and it was a long time before I realized that it was heavy shells going over our heads on their way to Antwerp. There were explosions going on all over the place, but somehow I didn't connect them with this noise, just like the sound of a Tube train rushing past.

Miss Sarah Macnaughton, who was a well-known novelist of the day, had arrived in Antwerp on 22 September as a helper with a private ambulance unit run by Mrs St Clair Stobart with the blessing of the Red Cross. She was asleep when the shelling began.

Miss
Sarah
Macnaughton

At midnight the first shell came over us with a shriek, and I went down and woke the orderlies and nurses and doctors. We dressed and went over to help move the wounded at the hospital. The shells began to scream overhead. It was a bright moonlit night, and we walked without haste – a small body of women – across the road to the hospital. Here we found the wounded all yelling like mad things, thinking they were going to be left behind.

Nearly all the moving to the cellars had already been done – only three stretchers remained to be moved. One wounded English sergeant helped us. We sat in the cellars with one night-light burning in each, and with seventy wounded men to take care of. Two of them were dying. There was only one line of bricks between us and the shells. One shell fell into the garden, making a hole six feet deep; the next crashed through a house on the opposite side of the road and set it on fire.

We stayed there all night. The worst cases among the wounded lay on the floor, and these wanted constant attention. The others were in their greatcoats and stood about the cellar leaning on crutches and sticks. In the morning Miss Benjamin went and stood at the gate, while the shells still flew, and picked up an ambulance. In this we got away six men, including the two dying ones. Mrs Stobart was walking about for three hours trying to find anything on wheels to remove us and the wounded. At last we got a motor ambulance and packed in twenty men. We told them to go as far as the bridge and send it back for us. It never came. Nothing seemed to come.

We were told that we were supporting the Marines, but we didn't see any until we moved on again, and then we met a bunch of them coming away from the trenches. They were in a filthy state, some of them wounded and bandaged, and they looked absolutely exhausted. They shouted out to us, 'Where are you going?' and we called out, 'Fort 4'. We didn't feel too easy in our minds when they called back, 'Poor little buggers!'

When we eventually did arrive at Fort 4 we were even more unhappy. It was chaos. As we arrived the Belgian soldiers were putting the guns out of action, and after they'd done that they disappeared altogether. After a while the young midshipman who was our platoon commander thought he'd better send a messenger back to HQ, to ask for orders. But when the chap got back to us he told us that there was no one left at HQ, except for one man who'd volunteered to stay behind to pass on the message to any stragglers that we were retiring, so it was unanimously decided that we'd better get out of it. We didn't seem to have done much, but nobody was prepared to argue.

Able Seaman (later Sub-Lieutenant) Jeremy Bentham, Benbow Battalion, 1st Royal Naval Brigade

They hadn't done much but they had done something. Even if the efforts of the Royal Marines and the two Royal Naval Brigades between them had not been able to save Antwerp, they had enabled it to hold out against the Germans while the British army turned north and barred the way to the Channel ports, and also allowed the Belgian field army –

whose collapse would have possibly led to the collapse of Belgium itself
– to be relieved a few days earlier and escape to safety further south.

Now everyone was trying to escape. The rearguard of the Belgian army;
the wounded from hastily evacuated hospitals; and every inhabitant
who could cycle or walk, crawl, be carried or push a handcart jostled
out of the city through one single bottleneck to the road to Ghent. There
was no other way to go because the German army was closing in to the
north and east of the city, and behind it to the west the Dutch border
looped across the estuary of the River Scheldt, cutting off all means of
esacpe by the sea. *

Behind them shells pounded into the city until it seemed that hardly
one brick could be left standing. When dusk fell, the sky over Antwerp
was lit with a lurid incandescence that sent its light flickering for many
miles across the streaming crowds of refugees. The great petroleum
plant at Hoboken had been set on fire. The flames were shooting 200
feet into the sky, and the sound of the massive petrol tanks exploding
could be heard as far away as Ghent. Some said it could be heard all over
unoccupied Belgium; it was quite possible, for Belgium was shrinking
fast. All that was left was a strip of land some eighty miles from north to
south and a mere forty miles from the German lines to the sea. Soon
even this would be reduced to a tiny foothold above the extreme
north-western frontier of France. That at least would be secured, for as
the great evacuation proceeded southward King Albert of the Belgians ordered the dykes to be opened and the land to be flooded to bar
the passage from the north, and in the south the main force of the British
army, having completed its complicated move north, was in position
and had already thrust out an arm to encircle the city of Ypres. It had
not been in time to save Antwerp but the siege of Antwerp had saved
Ypres. Ypres, in its turn, was to save the Channel ports, for Dunkirk lay
not far behind it, and a little to the south, through Calais and Boulogne,
lay the lifeline to England.

Every ship that could be spared went to the rescue. The sailors and
Marines had to be brought home and thousands of destitute refugees
brought to asylum. And there were huge numbers of wounded Belgian
soldiers evacuated from hospitals as the Germans advanced.

The hospital ships waited at the quayside, and on that dark night of
15 October they were the first of the rescuing armada to be loaded up
and set sail for England. On the other side of the Channel, hospital
trains, hurriedly assembled, steamed towards the ports to meet them as
frantic messages buzzed over the wires and across the Home Counties.

Military hospitals agreed to take as many wounded as they could, but

* In the confusion some fifteen hundred sailors, including Jeremy Bentham,
were forced to cross the river into Holland, where they were interned at
Groeningen. Bentham and a few others eventually escaped and made their way
back to England, but the majority remained in Holland for the duration of the
war.

warned that it would be precious few, and only the most serious cases must be sent. The next line of reserve was the big civilian hospitals. In The London Hospital, Staff Nurse Lucilla Bailey had just gone on night duty in Harrison Ward.

The first we knew of it was a telephone message to prepare room in the ward for ten extra beds each side of the ward. This was at 10.30. My ward was quite quiet, everyone sleeping soundly. Sister was still on duty, thank goodness, so we all set to work and pushed beds up against a wall, and by and by the extra beds arrived. All the patients were awakened, there was such a clatter and banging all over the hospital. The three huge lifts were clanging up and down, carrying beds and patients from one floor to another, bales of bedding, piles of food, everybody working as hard as they could go. There were sisters at one end of the beds and lift boys and porters at the other. In Harrison a regular army of sisters, doctors, surgeons, porters, etc., invaded the ward. Before you could say Jack Robinson, all my patients, the little rheumatism children, the bank clerk, theatre attendant, the whole go, were switched out and into another men's medical ward. You see, they turned Harrison into a proper soldier's ward with twenty beds each side, which meant forty altogether.

> *Staff Nurse Lucilla Mary Bailey, Harrison Ward, The London Hospital*

By midnight that ward looked beautiful. Each bed was quite close to the next and was already made up with clean things and half-opened ready to lay the soldiers in. Each locker was provided with a clean flannel, towel and soap, clean suit of pyjamas, pretty ones, blue, pink, mauve, etc. A clothes bag to put the patients' clothes in and labels to tie on. I can tell you, we felt proud of ourselves. There was a big cheerful fire on each side and the electric lights full on. Then we went and sat on the balcony looking over the garden. There was another scene of bustle because it had been decided that the soldiers should be brought in the garden way, and electricians were busy arranging a temporary set of electric lights and another army of porters was bringing out rows and rows of stretchers, wheelchairs, etc. Then, as we watched and it got along to three o'clock and then four, all the hospital staff, first and foremost Matron and Mr Morris the Secretary, and then Matron's assistants and all the doctors and surgeons, students, every member of the hospital staff who was up, and nurses on the balconies were collected on the steps in the garden waiting to receive them. It was weird. The big lighted wards behind us, and in front just the stillest hour of the night, with only a faint blur of sound over London. Then a telephone bell rang in one of the wards and they had arrived at Charing Cross. Probationers were sent flying to call up the sleeping Day Sisters. Of course, all this time the Day Nurses were in bed quite oblivious.

By and by we heard the sound of many cars whirring along, then a hooting of horns sounded at the gates and business began. The first hundred who arrived were all able to walk into hospital, because they were just wounded in their arms or the upper part of their body. The last lot were worse and had to be laid on stretchers. We rushed back to the wards to receive our soldiers. Then arose the difficulty. They were Belgians and Flemish, every one of them, who had had to be turned out of the Antwerp hospital when the Germans bombarded it. Not one of them could speak a word of English. Many of them died on the journey and food was scarce too, and their wounds had not been dressed for ever so long. It was so difficult to get them undressed. Sisters, doctors and porters came in to help until there were nearly as many as soldiers.

When we had got them into bed we washed their faces and hands and then we fed them. My word, didn't they eat! It was a sight for sore eyes. Eggs, bacon, soup – anything! All our bread and butter vanished as if by magic. I never saw men eat so much, but they were surgical patients and their wounds did not interfere with their appetites. About ten of the forty men were suffering from acute rheumatism, owing to cold and wet and insufficient food. They slept and slept all that day and the next night, and well one can understand why. Many of them were natives of Mons, Louvain and Malines and had fought at each place. I felt as if I were in a big glorious library but unable to read one of the books. What these men could have told if only we could have spoken their lingo properly. They were very good and docile and so funny.

They got up to some tricks. Some of them, about ten, were only slightly wounded and were allowed to get up in dressing-gown and slippers. The next night, at 2 am, I went round the ward to each bed to see if everyone was sleeping all right and in bed. When I got to the end of the ward I smelt smoke and saw a hand quickly bundle a *lighted* cigarette under his pillow. I switched on the electric light over his bed and looked at him and then, oh Lor! Didn't I wish I could grip his lingo. I made do with English, though, and he understood anyway. I could tell by his face.

By dint of doubling up they had managed to pack 300 wounded Belgians into The London Hospital, and about the same number went to St Thomas's and Guy's; but with upwards of 15,000 arriving, there was nothing for it but to mobilize the auxiliary hospitals and also the VADs.

They had waited so long, gone over the preparations so many times and their eager services had been by-passed so often that when the call eventually came it seemed like practical joke. Certainly Gladys Pole thought so when she answered the telephone in the vicarage at Bromley at half-past nine in the evening of 15 October. She laughed and hung up, and returned to the drawing-room where the Pole girls and their mother sat knitting as their father dozed over *The Times*. It seemed that they had knitted up miles of khaki wool and rolled leagues of bandages since the war had begun nine weeks ago. 'That was some idiot trying to pull our legs, saying we've got to mobilize the hospital!' Lily, who, as quartermaster, was a VAD officer, flew to the telephone. She knew the number of Headquarters off by heart. There was a hasty conversation and Lily hung up. 'It's true!' she said. 'They're sending a batch of wounded soldiers first thing in the morning. *Come on!*'

As the floodlit hospital ships sailed through the night to England, lights sprang up in windows all over the Home Counties and burned until daylight. VADs on bicycles, policemen and Boy Scouts who had been roped in to help, rapped on doors and windows with the news that the wounded were on their way. It was inconvenient that the call had come at night, that the notice was so short, because most of the vans earmarked for use in this long-foreseen emergency belonged to local firms and were garaged in business premises shuttered for the night. The drivers had to be roused, the owners knocked up to produce keys and it was past one o'clock before some of the vehicles were ready to start on the collecting run to bring in the equipment. Bedsteads had to be manhandled down several flights of stairs from attic bedrooms, and mattresses, boxes of china and kitchen equipment to be heaved into vans and carts. Private cars, whose owners a scant two hours ago had been nodding over their bedtime cocoa, drove from house to house collecting smaller items until the springs protested under the weight of mountainous bundles of towels and sheets, blankets and pillows. Whole villages were now awake, because people who had been knocked up to hand over the things they had promised to give in an emergency had no intention of going back to bed now that the emergency was here. They dressed and flocked to the houses, the village schools and the parish halls which were all supposed to be turned into hospitals by the morning.

We were very glad to see them, not just because we needed as much help as we could possibly get but because a lot of them were people who'd pooh-poohed us before and said things like, 'Oh, you'll never be used, you know. The Red Cross will never be used. You're wasting your time.' They were always saying things like that until we began to believe it ourselves – which is why I thought it was a hoax when the telephone rang that night.

Gladys Pole,
VAD, Kent 60

Our first hospital was at Christchurch Hall and a church hall was ideal in a way, because we already had a kitchen there and plenty of china and cutlery that we used for parish functions – cups and saucers and teaspoons, mainly – and of course we had plenty of chairs and tables, so we didn't have to get as much ready as some of the other detachments, which were starting from scratch. And we had all our medical supplies ready in a locked cupboard. Disinfectant and iodine and piles and piles of dressings and bandages. My sister

Hilda Pole,
VAD, Kent 60

Lily had arranged all that. She was the quartermaster, and the commandant of our detachment was Trixie Batten.

They were both magnificent that night, dashing back and forwards in the church hall as people carried in these beds and piles of mattresses and blankets – everything you could think of! Of course, once they got there the bedsteads had to be put up and arranged in the big parish room. We had heaps of volunteers and Trixie and Lily organized everything. Then people started putting on the big tea-urns and making soup and getting hot water ready so that the soldiers could have tea or Bovril. Of course, we had no food in, and there were naturally no shops open, so later, when we'd got things more or less square, the volunteers went home and came back with whatever bread they had in the house, a few eggs and a bit of butter, so that we'd be able to give the wounded some breakfast.

It was all very exciting. We were sorry when Lily sent us home to bed in the middle of the night. It seemed awful to go to bed when everyone was still working and there was so much to do, but Lily wasn't only an officer, she was very much the elder sister, and we weren't in the habit of arguing with her.

We were too excited to sleep much, so we were back by half-past eight the following morning – all spick and span in our uniforms and very proud to feel that we were actually going on duty as nurses. And when we walked in, we could hardly believe it. There were the soldiers all tucked up in bed and everything arranged, looking just like a real hospital with not a thing out of place. There were even flowers on the tables in the middle of the ward. We were dying to speak to the soldiers, but they were all Belgians, and Flemish Belgians at that. They couldn't speak a word of English and our schoolgirl French was no good either!

Muriel Pole, VAD, Kent 60

It didn't really matter that we couldn't communicate with the soldiers, because we weren't really allowed to have anything to do with them. The trained nurses and the officers saw to that! All we saw of them was when we were taking trays round with their meals or when we were sweeping the floors or cleaning the windows in the ward, because we had to do all that. But that first day all they wanted to do was sleep. After they'd been cleaned up and put to bed and had their wounds seen to – and mostly they were lightly wounded – all they wanted to do was sleep and sleep and sleep. I remember that first day very well. It was my twenty-first birthday. Normally, of course, there would have been a party or some sort of celebration. As it was, I sat in the church hall kitchen and had my tea all by myself. You could hear a pin drop, all the men were sleeping so deeply.

It was a brief interlude of peace. The thirty-three wounded Belgians asleep in Christchurch Hall were the first of many. As the wounded kept arriving by the boat-load there was another emergency call and Kent 60 Detachment performed the mammoth feat of mobilizing a second hospital in a large empty villa, just forty-eight hours after they had set up the first.

The same thing was happening all over the country. If the VADs had been trained to improvise they were now using their training to good effect, for improvisation was the order of the day. The British wounded soldiers who arrived in the early morning joked about having come in on the milk train and it was literally true, for the shelves on which the milk churns were stacked on their journey from the country to the towns were ideal for stretchers, and twenty 'lying' cases could be accommodated in every wagon. The ambulances that met them at country stations were improvised from farmcarts with white tarpaulins – which the volunteers had not omitted to decorate with a red cross – thrown over a light framework manufactured from flexible garden canes. A mobile canteen, which could be wheeled up and down the length of a hospital train or a troop train stopping at a wayside station, could be improvised from an ice-cream barrow, which kept the tea as hot as, in its peacetime role, it had kept the ice-cream cool.

Heating the makeshift hospitals was a problem. Oil stoves had to be brought in to warm draughty halls, and their fumes, the smell of antiseptics and the less pleasant odours that were unavoidable in even a small hospital ward created an unpleasant fug. There was a constant running battle between Sisters going briskly about their business and patients lying immobile in bed on the thorny question of open windows. The Sister in charge of Kent 2 Auxiliary Hospital at Ramsgate ordered a large notice to be put up, 'Night air is NOT poisonous!' It meant as little to the seventy-two wounded Belgians, lying there in the erstwhile Mission Hall of the Royal Sailors' Rest, as the plaque which decorated the wall above the harmonium on the stage. 'Oh hear us when we cry to Thee,' it read, 'for those in peril on the sea.' They went on shivering under the multicoloured counterpanes donated by local ladies, and if they were the slightest bit mobile, continued to hop out of bed to close the window whenever Sister's back was turned.

The trained nurses attached to each auxiliary hospital were generally paid by the Red Cross. The VAD officers, who ran the administrative side of the hospitals, and the VAD members, who did everything else, worked entirely voluntarily. It never occurred to them to expect payment. They belonged to the vast army of leisured women and girls which extended from the upper echelons of the wealthy to the limits of genteel sufficiency. Not many had led completely idle lives, but none of them had ever had to work like this before.

Oh, the washing up we had to do! That was the worst thing. There were mountains and mountains of it and as soon as you finished one lot it was time to set the trays for another meal, and in half an hour

Hilda Pole, VAD, Kent 60

you had to start all over again. The wards were all bare wooden floors and every morning, after breakfast, we had to take all the tea-leaves from the kitchen and scatter them over the floors to lay the dust and then sweep them up again. We had to clean and polish and scrub. We didn't mind doing it because it was what we were there for, to take all the everyday chores off the shoulders of the trained nurses so that they could concentrate on looking after the wounded, and they kept us very much in our place because they'd been used to the discipline of big hospitals, which was very strict in those days. Our Sister Treasure was a very good nurse and very efficient but she was a real tartar. We had a VAD called Elsie Doran. She was a much older person than we were and quite an important one because her husband was a general in the army, so we thought she was quite somebody.*

One day, when we had moved to the hospital in the big house, Abbey Lodge, Sister Treasure met her in the hall one day and said, 'Nurse Doran, I want you to take these sheets upstairs.' And Sister handed her an armful of sheets and proceeded to walk up the main staircase. Naturally, Elsie Doran obediently followed her carrying the sheets, and Sister put her head over her shoulder and said in the most chilling voice, 'Nurse Doran, nurses use the *back* stairs!' We did have a laugh over that and no one enjoyed the joke more than Nurse Doran.

We were supposed to be very humble and we had to be very polite to our officers, who were Trixie Batten and my own sister. When we went in and out of the office we had to be like parlourmaids, bringing the tea in perfectly set out on the tray and taking it out again later. Always on our very best behaviour. In those days we had parlour-maids at home so we knew just how it was done. We thought it was rather good fun. It was amusing when we came off duty and went home tired and the maid brought in *our* tea, just as we had been doing a little while before!

Gladys Stanford, VAD, Dorset 52

Our little hospital was in a house at Stirminster Marshall. We *did* have a time at first! There were coal fires in little wards that only held four or five patients and we had to do it in turns to do the housework. Every morning we had to light these dreadful fires. They had old-fashioned grates and it was so difficult. I never mastered it because I'd never had to light a fire in my life. But I did learn one trick that used to work. I'd do my best to get it going – which wasn't very good – and when I saw that it was going to go out any minute, if there was a man who could get out of bed, I used to say, 'Oh, I must go. Will you keep an eye on the fire for me?' I knew perfectly well that it was

* Brigadier-General Beauchamp J. C. Doran, CB, Commander of the 8th Infantry Brigade, Third Division.

going to go out any moment and that the poor man would have to light it all over again. But the men never minded and they were much better at making them burn than we were.

They had to put up with rather a lot from us, I'm afraid. When the first wounded came in they were in a terrible state. They were light cases, as they sent the most severely wounded, the ones that needed really expert care, to the big hospitals, but they were covered in dust and dirt because they'd been on the road for so long and perhaps lying out in the fields before that. As a matter of fact our first wounded weren't soldiers at all, they were Belgians of the Civil Guard who'd had to go out and fight before Antwerp fell, and there were so many wounded going through at the time that there was no chance of cleaning them up in France. They were put on boats just as they were and arrived in these filthy uniforms. We'd put them to bed in pyjamas, of course, but we hadn't the first idea how to clean these uniforms for when they got up.

There was an old-fashioned wash-house attached to this place with an old copper in it, so another VAD and I got a fire going under the copper and boiled these uniforms up with plenty of soap. Then we scrubbed them on a washing board, and when they came out they were absolutely ruined. They looked dreadful, with all the colour run out of them, all shrunk and shapeless, nothing but rags really. Later in the war they had blue suits, like cardigan suits, that were soft and comfortable for the wounded soldiers to wear when they were convalescing, but in those days there were none, or if there were, certainly not enough to go round. We had to beg from all our friends for cast-off clothing, odd trousers and jackets, so that the boys would have something to wear when they got up. We started to call it the Ragtime Hospital, and it was no wonder.

There was little of the 'ragtime' atmosphere in the military hospitals where the severely wounded soldiers were being nursed. The war had suddenly arrived on the doorstep, and it was not just the sight of convalescent soldiers in the streets that began to bring it home. There were also the casualty lists. Day after day, column after column, they filled whole pages of the newspapers. The fact was that the Army which had first crossed the Channel in August was by now practically wiped out. The war, they had said, would be 'over by Christmas' but the slogan was beginning to ring hollow. It would only be over by Christmas for 90,000 of the 100,000 men who had first crossed to France in August. By Christmas 1914, the original British Expeditionary Force had suffered 90 per cent casualties, and although many who were wounded would recover to fight again, as a composite force the BEF would have ceased to exist.

Although the full and horrifying extent of the losses had not been fully realized, it was becoming painfully obvious that there was no

question of cutting and thrusting to speedy glory. It was equally obvious
that the Army would need more men. After the first enthusiastic weeks
when young men had tumbled by the thousand into the welcoming
arms of recruiting sergeants, and men with physical defects had lied
their way past harassed Medical Officers, recruiting had fallen off. In
the countryside where the numbers had been initially disappointing, the
war had come at a bad time, but after the harvest was brought in at the
end of September there was a sudden upsurge as farm lads and coun-
trymen turned up in their own good time at the recruiting offices in
county towns. But it was not enough. The Army, or at least that part of
it which was facing the problem of equipping 100,000 newly enlisted
civilians and turning them into soldiers, might have been glad of a
moratorium but the country was only too anxious to hustle every
available man into khaki. Join Up, Join Up, Join Up was the cry.
Recruiting posters bellowed it from billboards. It was urged from a
thousand platforms at recruiting meetings, where wounded soldiers
were invited to reinforce the call. Lieutenant Rory Macleod, on convalescent leave at home in Cambridge, was forced by his insistent twin
sisters to submit to his now-healed wounds being rebandaged when he
went to recount his adventures at Le Cateau, and so add a bit of local
colour at recruiting meetings presided over by his father.

Join Up, Join Up, Join Up. They even started to sing about it, and held
special recruiting nights at theatres and music halls. Ivy Donegan, who
was working at a private nursing home in Duke's Avenue, Chiswick,
where one ward had been set aside for wounded soldiers, was invited to
escort a party of her walking-wounded Belgian patients to the Chiswick
Empire. They were given seats of honour in the first row, and when the
show reached its climax she and the other nurse in the party were
surprised to find themselves being ushered firmly on to the stage. It took
a little longer to get the wounded up the steps, for some were still on
crutches, but the audience was happy to wait. Abashed, but not dis-
pleased with the applause, they were ranged across the stage. A curtain
rose behind them to reveal a spectacular representation of the burning
of Rheims Cathedral, with realistic flames that spurted dangerously
through an open trapdoor on the stage. In front of them strutted Hetty
King, and as the orchestra played the opening bars she started to sing
the hit song of the year:

> We don't want to lose you but we think you ought to go,
> For your King and your country both need you so.
> We shall want you and miss you,
> But with all our might and main,
> We shall cheer you, thank you, kiss you,
> When you come back again.

It brought the house down.

Chapter Five

The Gothic splendour of 'Rheims Cathedral Set Alight by the Barbarous Hun' was an image which caught the imagination of people on the other side of the Atlantic. Every newspaper carried the story, and *The Sun* blazoned a cartoon across its pages in which Joan of Arc, sword in hand, gazed up for divine inspiration as she galloped off to avenge the blazing ruins in the background.

America was well informed about the war. As a neutral country the correspondents of her newspapers were able to move freely in all the belligerent countries, and their reports were read with distinctly mixed feelings. Politically, Europe's war had nothing to do with America. There was no threat to American lives, American territory or American property. It was 134 years since George Washington had bidden Europe a long goodbye in his farewell speech, and in the intervening years America had augmented her sparse population with immigrants who had been driven by wars and pogroms to escape from Mother Europe into the arms of Uncle Sam. And Uncle Sam had domestic problems of his own on the Mexican border.

There was no reason to suppose that the United States would enter the lists or ally herself to either side, but America could prove to be a rich and influential friend and whichever side succeeded in enlisting American sympathy would have a powerful advantage. The propaganda began at the very start of the war with the publication of an elaborate pro-German journal entitled *The Fatherland*. It contained signed articles virulently hostile to the Allies written by Hermann Schoenfeld, Professor of History at George Washington University, and, among others, Hugo Muensterberg and Kuno Francke of Harvard University. There was page after page of abuse and tortuous argument justifying 'peace-loving' Germany's entry into the war. *The Fatherland* also contained a poem which, in nine ringing stanzas, presented the Kaiser in the unlikely guise of 'Wilhelm II, Prince of Peace'. It was a masterpiece of bellicose piety:

> May thy victorious armies rout
> The savage tribes against thee hurled,
> The Czar whose sceptre is the Knout,
> And France, the harlot of the world!

But thy great task will not be done
Until thou vanquish utterly
The Norman brother of the Hun,
England, the serpent of the sea.

The flame of war her tradesmen fanned
Shall yet consume her, fleet and field;
The star of Frederick guide they hand,
The god of Bismarck for thy shield!

When it appeared on 10 August the Americans were quick to observe that such a publication could not possibly have been composed, edited and published in the six days which had elapsed since the declaration of war. Public opinion, at least as reflected in the American press, was more inclined to favour the Allies and showed all the sympathy that Americans traditionally felt for the 'little guy' on the receiving end. The cartoons summed it up.

The Kaiser was shown standing by a savage gun, pouter-breasted and mouthing, *'Deutschland Uber Alles!' 'The Kaiser's terms of peace'*, read the caption. Another showed post-war tourists inspecting the shattered remains of a noble building as the guide remarks, *'These are the ruins of William II'*. In the *New York World*, a baby duckling representing England paddles in a rough sea, brightly enquiring of an American eagle glowering from the shore, *'Dare you to come in?'*. In the *New York Evening World*, Uncle Sam, in the guise of fireman, stands above the extinguished fire of Mexico looking thoughtfully across the Atlantic to the conflagration raging on the other side. The caption punches home the point, *'My fire is out.'* Some thousands of young Americans, captivated by reports of derring-do on the battlefield, were not inclined to wait for Uncle Sam to make up his mind, and poured across the border into British Canada and enlisted there. As they had done in Britain, women and girls flocked to join the Red Cross. But the American Red Cross, while anxious to make use of their services as fund raisers, knitters and bandage rollers, felt obliged to make it plain that graduation from first-aid classes did not 'qualify women for the actual nursing care of the sick under the Red Cross, nor for enrolment as Red Cross nurses'.

With professional nurses it was quite a different matter. As soon as war broke out in Europe the Red Cross started appealing for volunteers, and units drawn from most of the eastern states arrived in New York on Wednesday evening, 3 September 1914. A few days later they sailed for Europe on a chartered steamer whose name had been hastily changed from the *Hamburg* to the *Red Cross*.

Departing from a neutral country as part of an international organization, the American Red Cross could afford to show no favours. There was no question of their serving one side or the other. Units were sent to Britain, France, Russia and Serbia, but they were also sent to care for the wounded in Germany and Austria.*

But Americans resident in Europe, particularly in France, had no such reservations. In Paris there was a ready-made base at the American hospital at Neuilly, and within hours of Germany going to war with France it became the rallying point for the American residents, travellers and students who happened to be in Paris at the time – a disparate bunch of people with only one thing in common. They wanted to help. Before the German army had reached the Marne they had opened a hospital for French wounded in the Lycée Pasteur near the American hospital in Neuilly and were in the process of setting up another near Meaux. Rich Americans donated their automobiles, mostly open tourers and limousines, and they were quickly converted into makeshift ambulances to carry the wounded. Money poured in from America to buy supplies and equipment and even ten Ford ambulances, with bodies made out of packing cases, to form the nucleus of the American Field Ambulance. There was no shortage of volunteers to drive them.

Under United States law any man who enlisted in a foreign army automatically relinquished his US citizenship.** The boys who had gone to enlist with the Canadian Forces had taken that risk, but many more who were equally eager to join in the war were more cautious. Besides, the Canadian government, having recruited a thousand Americans (enough to form a separate American Legion), was having difficulty in training and equipping her own flood of volunteers. Reluctantly she slammed the door on United States citizens. The American Ambulance was a heaven-sent answer to the would-be volunteers.

Graham Carey was one of the first to arrive. He was twenty-two and had just graduated from Harvard. He arrived in Paris on 14 December.

I went to France with the idea of being a hospital orderly, but when I got to the American hospital in Neuilly in Paris I found they were organizing ambulances, so I immediately signed up. I already knew how to drive because my father had one of the first private cars. Of course, in those days you had to have a chauffeur, not only to drive it but to attend to it and be responsible for it, and there were great difficulties in driving those early cars. Unbeknown to my father I went out on various occasions with the chauffeur and took over the wheel and got some knowledge of how to drive. I don't know about the other boys. Some of them probably had never driven at all and I certainly wasn't very good, but somehow we managed and soon I was an old hand.

Graham
Carey,
American Field
Service,
Ambulance
Section No. 3

* After the sinking of the *Lusitania* in May 1915, prompted by cries of outrage in the United States, the American Red Cross felt justified in withdrawing its medical units from Germany and her allies.
** A provision which was quietly waived when the United States entered the war in 1917, and citizens of the United States serving in the British and French armies were given the opportunity of transferring to the US Forces.

Fresh from high school and college, fresh from stirring tales of Lafayette's army of young Frenchmen, much like themselves, who had fought alongside George Washington's army in the War of Independence, the allegiance of patriotic young Americans lay naturally with the French. They were Francophiles to a man, but it was a strange time to be in Paris. The bustling boulevards were strangely quiet; the restaurants and cafés were ordered to turn out their last customers by nine o'clock in the evening; the lights were dimmed in the cité lumière.

In the vast Place de la Concorde, where the windows of the Red Cross headquarters looked out on the massive stone statues representing the major cities of France, that of Strasbourg was still swathed in the black mourning drapery in which it had been draped for the forty years that had elapsed since France had lost Alsace and Lorraine to Germany in the Franco-Prussian War. The loss of these eastern provinces still rankled bitterly with the French, and it was this which had been to some extent responsible for the ease with which the German invaders had broken through in the north. The German strategy (known as the Schlieffen Plan) had been planned some years before as part of Germany's general military precautions, and if it was not precisely common knowledge, its broad outlines, through intelligence channels, were reasonably widely known. But Marshal Joffre, myopically enthralled by the idea of snatching back the lost territories in a swift war of manoeuvre that would once and for all drive the German army back over the other side of the Rhine, had rushed the bulk of his army to the eastern frontier and the border forts in the north-east. This left a token force to meet the Germans when they eventually broke through from Belgium. The French army had been in the wrong place at the wrong time, and now it was fighting for its life. The hospital trains, packed with casualties from the heavy German shells, clanked interminably into Paris and within a fortnight of his arrival Graham Carey had become a veteran.

Ambulance de l' Hôpital Americain de Paris
Lycée Pasteur,
Boulevard d'Inkermann.
10 January 1915.

Dear Mother,
I'm afraid that my last two or three letters have been pretty stupid, so to liven things up a little I propose to write you out just what I have done for one day, by way of a sample. I shall choose yesterday as a little more interesting than some and easier to remember, being nearer to the present.

When I got up at eight-thirty, I only had to dash down into the dining-room basement here for my breakfast. After this I called my orderly, and we cleaned and tinkered with my ambulance, number

78, which I have named Suzanne. Suzanne is at present the handsomest and best car in our squad. Only much toil and study have made her so, and I and Richardson – my orderly – strain every nerve to keep her in the lead.

After lunch, Charley Lovering appeared with our first really definite orders as to our destination and time of departure, and to my lot fell the pleasant task of greasing and oiling all the cars. This took till after dusk, and then I was informed that I was to go on the Aubervilliers service at seven, with my car and orderly. So I had to get them both ready for that – full tanks and lamps, blankets, pillows, *brancards** ready, etc., etc.

At seven we left for the Aubervilliers station (where the *blessés*** are taken out of the southbound train), which is about seven or eight miles from Neuilly. I reported to the major in charge, who eventually gave me two lying cases. Blessés that can walk are known as sitting cases or 'hoppers'. Both my men were shot through the head, one very badly indeed. I had to drive very slowly, as the roads outside of Paris are very rough, but eventually we got to Saint Antoine and saw my patients into bed. When I got back to Aubervilliers there were two more 'lyers' for me, but these were both very cheerful, and talked and laughed together all the way to the Hôpital de la Pitié. One had a broken leg and I don't know what was wrong with the other, but they were both very cheerful nevertheless. At Aubervilliers they were waiting for another train, and had no more blessés for us.

At four I was so sleepy that I got into a railway carriage that we have on a siding there and immediately went sound asleep. At six-thirty, however, Richardson and I were waked up and given two sitting cases, officers this time, for the improvised hospital at the Hôtel Ritz. Almost all the big hotels in Paris have been converted in whole or in part into hospitals for the military, and this is one of them. Our officers were not badly hurt, and it did not take long to get them to their destination, where an English Red Cross fellow set us up to a whisky apiece to start the new day on. By the time we got back to Aubervilliers it was light, and all we had to do was to wait for our relief at eight o'clock. This brings me to the end of my brief sample twenty-four hours.

So after this rather long day, you can imagine that I was rather weary when I finished the first three pages of this letter last night. My next one shall be from Jouilly, and as the life there will probably be different from this, I am glad that I have been able to give you a sample, however hasty, of what our day here in Neuilly is like.

Good night, Mother. Pray for
your loving son, Graham

* Stretchers.
** Wounded.

In the first five months of the war the American Red Cross had sent abroad 150 nurses and forty-five surgeons. But hundreds of other volunteers who did not come under its sponsorship were working to help the French wounded. Two hospitals were completely staffed by American personnel. There were young men like Graham Carey acting as mechanics and ambulance drivers, and ladies of the American community acting as nurses, orderlies and general helpers; there were American doctors working there permanently, and others who came from America for short periods to give badly needed help. One of them was Harvey Cushing, whose wide experience of surgery in the United States had not prepared him for anything he met in France.

Dr Harvey
Cushing
It is difficult to say just what are one's most vivid impressions: the amazing patience of the seriously wounded, some of them hanging on for months; the dreadful deformities (not so much in the way of amputations but broken jaws and twisted, scarred faces); the tedious healing of infected wounds, with discharging sinuses, tubes, irrigations and repeated dressings – so much so that grating and painful fractures are simply abandoned to wait for wounds to heal, which they don't seem to do.

In the American hospitals, in the British hospitals, in the French hospitals, men were dying like flies from terrible suppurating wounds. Something had do be done, for the gas gangrene was killing more men than the bullets themselves. In laboratories set up at Boulogne, where Sir Almroth Wright was working on the development of a bactericide, and in the French hospital in the forest of Compiègne, where the American Dr Henry Dakin and the French Dr Alexis Carrel were engaged on the same task, it became top priority to find a cure. Dr Cushing visited his colleague Henry Dakin in his laboratory.

Dr Harvey
Cushing
The lines along which they have started to work include the suction treatment of suppurating wounds without dressings; the employment of irrigation with bactericidal fluids; methods of increasing resistance to pathogenic organisms by turpentine injections, etc., etc.

There were other problems of almost equal magnitude – strange diseases brought to Europe by troops from the French colonies in Africa and from the British Dominion of India, and all the illnesses and ailments which were the inevitable result of exposure.

Dr Harvey
Cushing
There are erythromelalgia-like feet – painful, blue, cold, macerated-looking extremities; and indeed the whole circulatory condition of many of the blessés is very bad. Some of these poor devils must have stood for days in hastily dug trenches without a chance of getting off their boots.

Almost from the start the majority of the men have been admitted with bronchitis, and many with influenza-like colds.

It was winter and it was deadlock. From the North Sea to the mountains of Switzerland, in a line that straggled and twisted on a circuitous route that covered a thousand miles, the armies shivered in a labyrinth of miserable ditches. Swept by the biting north-east winds, and wading in icy water that no amount of baling or pumping could clear from the trenches, they succumbed in droves to bronchitis and pneumonia. The regulation puttees, which every soldier wore tightly bound from ankle to knee, shrank in the wet, cut off the circulation and turned feet black and rotting with frostbite. Lacking drinking water but desperate for a drink of even lukewarm tea, the soldiers skimmed the cleanest-seeming liquid from the top of waterlogged ditches and trenches without investigating what horrors of ordure or decay might lie in the murk beneath. The result was an outbreak of enteric and dysentery. For Europeans, hardened to cold if not to exposure, the conditions were appalling. For the Indian troops they were insupportable. No amount of drilling on the torrid plains of the subcontinent, no amount of hard fighting in the cold, jagged uplands of the Himalayas or on the North-West Frontier had prepared them for the dank, bitter chill of Europe in winter. Coughing in an infernal chorus, painfully racked with rheumatism, and bleeding from their wounds, they were brought to the hospital trains that travelled slowly up and down behind the front, from Ypres to Rouen and Le Havre. 'Indian men too cold,' moaned a bearded Sikh, shivering on a stretcher. 'Kill more Germans if not too cold.'

Sister Luard on hospital train No. 5, aching with pity for all the men, was sorrier for the Indians than for any of them.

They are such pathetic babes, just as inarticulate to us and crying as if it was a crèche. I've done a great trade in Hindustani, picked up at a desperate pace from a Hindu officer today! If you write it down you can soon learn it, and I've got all the necessary medical jargon now; you read it off, and then spout it without looking at your notebook. The awkward part is when they answer something you haven't got! They are nearly all 47th Sikhs, perfect lambs; they hold up their wounded hands and arms like babies for you to see. They behave like gentlemen, and *salaam* after you've dressed them. They have masses of long, fine, dark hair under their turbans done up with yellow combs, glorious teeth and melting dark eyes. One died.

Those of a different caste had to sleep on the floor of the corridors, as the others wouldn't have them in. One compartment of four lying-down ones got restless with the pain of their arms, and I found them all sitting up rocking their arms and wailing, 'Aie, Aie, Aie.' Poor pets. They all had morphia, and subsided.

This long journey from Belgium down to Havre has been a strange

Sister K. Luard, QAIMNS (her diary, 25 November 1914)

mixture. Glorious country, towns and valleys. Glorious British Army lying broken in the train – sleep (or the chance of it) three hours one night and four the next, with all the hours between hard working putting the British Army together again.

There were six hospital trains trundling up and down behind the front carrying 400 sick and wounded at a time, manned by two or three medical officers, four nursing sisters and forty RAMC orderlies. It was a strange and primitive life. On 8 January, Sister Luard recorded, 'It is nearly three months since I sat in a chair, except at meals, and that is only a flap-down seat, or saw a fire, except the pails of coke the Tommies have on the lines. I expect we shall be off again tonight somewhere.'

It was always 'somewhere', no one ever knew precisely where – slow hours of clanking north or inland, punctuated by long waits on sidings while the troop trains or supply trains went through. Then more rumbling through the night, and at last loading up at a shattered station or a wayside halt somewhere in the back of beyond, where long rows of stretchers and huddled groups of walking wounded waited in the wintry weather to board the train. If they were lucky they would unload at Boulogne. If Boulogne was full the train had to go on, to Le Touquet, to Rouen or, furthest of all, to Le Havre, a journey of 200 miles. When conditions were at their worst it could take up to three days.

Theoretically, the care of casualties on the field was well organized. A man who was wounded would make his way, or be carried, to the regimental aid-post, virtually in the line. From there, after his wound had been dressed, he would be taken further back to a field dressing-station, where he was given an anti-tetanus injection and where, with luck, there would be an ambulance to take him back still further to the casualty clearing station eight or ten miles behind the line. There he would be kept until he was fit to be sent by hospital train to a base hospital, where he would either be treated until he was well enough to return to his unit or to be shipped directly home across the Channel. It was an admirable scheme and it was no one's fault that it went wrong. It was no one's fault that the casualty clearing stations in commandeered breweries, convents and colleges at a 'safe' distance from the line were well within reach of heavy shells, that they were swamped with more wounded and sick than they could possibly have anticipated or could cope with. It was no one's fault that, although hospitals had been set up in the casinos at Boulogne and Le Touquet, in commandeered buildings in Rouen, in the old first-class waiting rooms of the ocean terminal at Le Havre, there were not nearly enough of them for the mass of casualties that had to be cared for.

Sister K. Luard, QAIMNS (her diary Friday,

We did a record loading up in fifty minutes last night, chiefly medical cases, and took eight hours to crawl to Boulogne. Now we are on the way to Havre but shall not get there till about 10 pm tonight, so they will have a long day in the train.

. . . This is an interminable journey – have not yet reached Rouen and shan't get to Havre till perhaps 2 am. The patients are getting very weary, especially the sitting-ups.

. . . Still on the way to Havre! And we loaded up on Thursday. This journey is another revelation of what the British soldier will stick without grumbling. The sitting-ups are eight in a carriage, some with painful feet, some with wounded arms, and some with coughs and rheumatism, etc., but you don't hear a word of grousing.

It is a mercy we got our bad cases off at Boulogne – pneumonia, enterics, and some badly wounded with only rifles for splints, including an officer dressed in bandages all over. He was such a nice boy. When he was put in clean pyjamas and had a clean hankie with eau-de-Cologne, he said, 'By Jove, it's worth getting hit for this, after the smells of dead horses, dead men and dead everything.'

The 'home' of the hospital train nurse was a first-class compartment. Here she slept, dressed, stowed all her kit, and mended rips in the long cotton dresses that were so irritatingly prone to catch on protruding corners as she negotiated the swaying length of the train a hundred times a day. Here she brushed thick layers of dirt from the hems of garments that trailed in the mud when she scrambled down the high steps on to the track. Here she spent long hours fine-combing her long hair and searching her clothing for the lice which the troops straight from the trenches unavoidably brought with them. Here, in lukewarm water in a folding canvas basin, she washed collars, cuffs, caps and as much of herself as she could, and dreamt almost with passion of the hot bath she would have a week or ten days hence at the base at Rouen or, if the train stopped long enough, on board a friendly hospital ship at Boulogne.

With space at a premium on board the train, and with every available inch that was not set aside for the wounded occupied by medical stores, kitchen, laboratory and, even on some, a tiny theatre for emergency operations, the Sisters' 'bunks' – which were not quite six feet square – also had to accommodate boxes and bales of 'comforts'. In the first disorganized winter, they were the obvious people to distribute them, not just to the wounded but to the troops they met as they travelled up and down the lines of communication. The soldiers soon got to know. 'Any soap, Sister?' they would cry as the train drew into a station where they were waiting to go up the line, or where a party of Tommies was unloading ammunition or at work on maintaining the track. 'Any cigarettes? Socks? Gloves? Mufflers? Chocolate? Magazines?'' The Sisters were usually able to oblige.

Comforts arrived in France by the boat-load. The Red Cross was inundated with gifts that ranged from valuables which could be sold for cash to the homely, useful items that almost every woman in the country was busy sewing or knitting.

Mabel Bone,
VAD,
Staffordshire 2

The Stoke-on-Trent War Hospital Supplies Depot was started by Mrs Eric Young, the wife of a local surgeon. It was in a large villa in Shelton, Stoke-on-Trent. Mrs Young was assisted by a number of local ladies, and I, at the tender age of fifteen, was allowed to join.

We bought our own uniform, white drill full-length coats and white squares folded into triangles and worn flowing for caps. We paid ninepence each time we went, and at half-time were given a cup of tea and a biscuit. The profits were used to buy more materials. We padded splints, rolled bandages on little hand-worked machines called 'donkeys', and sewed many-tailed bandages (used for abdominal wounds). In another room splints were made of papier mâché, which had been made from the strong paper bags that sugar came in. And of course we made shirts, knitted helmets, scarves, mittens, socks and woollen gloves by the ton.

I had just started work in the bookshop, and spent my Sunday afternoons working at the War Supplies Depot. On Saturday evenings we used to go to the Hippodrome to collect money from the audience, and sometimes we took our collecting boxes to local dances and collected there.

Not all the supplies of comforts were sent directly to the Red Cross. Where a local battalion was on active service the people of their home town showered them with treats. The 1st Battalion, The Hertfordshire Regiment, marched off from St Albans and an endless flow of parcels from home followed it wherever it went. Schoolchildren were particularly enthusiastic in their efforts, and one enlightened teacher realized that writing lessons could be given added interest by allowing her pupils to write letters to the troops. At Christmas time the 1st Herts, in billets in France, received a consignment of parcels from a local primary school accompanied by letters from all the children. Corporal Gordon Fisher's letter was laboriously penned in copperplate by ten-year-old Gerty:

> 10, Lower Marlboro Road,
> St Albans,
> Herts,
> 7 December 1914

My Dear Soldier Friend,
We are always thinking of you here in old England, and my classmates and I are knitting and sewing as fast as we can to make you

warm clothes for the cold weather that is approaching so soon. We are sending a great many parcels, which contain mittens, scarves or socks and some peppermints and some chocolate or toffee to help you when you are in the trenches.

The week before last we had a party and each gave a small contribution, and afterwards we sent the amount taken to make shelters for the soldiers in Hertfordshire.

Yesterday the soldiers here had a sham fight. The enemy had white bands round their hats and they used blank bullets. Every time one was hit he had to call out 'Dead' and fall out. Ah! Yours is more deadly work, is it not?

If your parcel contains any clothes that do not fit you, you can easily change with somebody else. We have knitted many loving thoughts and wishes among the stitches. I wonder if you have any of the chocolate we sent from St Albans. All of we schoolgirls took a small quantity, and in the local paper afterwards we found the whole of St Albans had collected a ton and a quarter of chocolate.

Do try to shoot the Kaiser in the legs – not fatally, because he must have time to repent before he dies.

I must close now because my time is getting short, with lots of love,
I remain, my dear soldier friend,
Your unknown friend,
Gerty

PS I hope you will answer my letter if you have a moment to spare.

In York, Kit and Eve Dodsworth were still waiting for their auxiliary hospital to be mobilized. Everything was ready, and now that the first excitement had worn off and no wounded had yet arrived, it was becoming tedious hanging around waiting for phone calls and constantly changing the hot-water bottles to air beds that were never occupied. Nevertheless, they managed to keep busy.

Lovely fine day. Went into town and bought more wool. I shall be ruined! Then collected for Belgian Fund. We were awfully amused after lunch. There was a wedding at Clifton Church, one of the 6th West Yorks officers. Great excitement. Guard of Honour with crossed bayonets, officers with crossed swords. Such a scrubby bride! We watched from a window and saw all the wedding party coming out. So funny! Went to YMCA as usual. Place very crowded and amusing. A Tommy sang and played most beautifully. Kit very tired and feeble tonight.

Eve Dodsworth (her diary, Saturday, 30 January 1915)

Kit was 'tired and feeble' because she was recovering from measles, caught almost certainly from the soldiers the girls met when helping at the YMCA canteen. The soldiers (apart from being a source of infection!) were a constant source of amusement – particularly the boys of 'H' Company of the 4th Battalion, West Yorks, who trained on the open space in front of the Dodsworth house and vastly improved the outlook from the big bay window on the ground floor, where the girls often sat knitting. Now, with the first part of their training completed, the West Yorks were moving south.

Eve
Dodsworth
(her diary,
Thursday, 25
February
1915)

Sat in window all the afternoon, very sad. Had window open and talked to lots of Tommies. We called out 'Goodbye' again when they went. Put Do to bed after dinner with temperature of 101, so suppose *she* has measles now. Simply *too* boring. When we were in her room about ten o'clock this evening, Reg and someone else serenaded us outside and made such a noise that we opened the window and talked to them. Disgraceful! They promised to 'Coo-ee' for us when they march out in the morning and to come and see us when the war is over. Dear boys, I do wish they weren't going.

Friday, 26
February 1915

. . . We got our 'Coo-ee' all right this morning. I slept in Kit's bed until they had gone. Hardly slept a wink! Said they were off at 3.30 but didn't go until nearly five. We lay awake listening. At last heard their whistling in the distance, then 'Now then!' – and they shouted 'Coo-ee'. We put on the light to show we had heard and they all yelled 'Goodbye'. Too sad for words! I went to my bed after that. It was rotten all day. Town lost and empty now the Brigade has gone. New ones came in and they are a nasty dirty-looking lot. KOYLIs at this end of town.

Now that there was so much war work to do many more people were working part-time, particularly in London and the south where most of the wounded were still concentrated. A shopgirl or a factory worker who could not afford to work full-time as an unpaid nursing orderly could nevertheless give up her Sundays and one or two evenings a week to scrub floors at a local hospital, or to help in the kitchen at a rest centre or canteen, where her services were frequently found to be a good deal more efficient than those of the well-meaning but inexperienced helpers of the more prosperous classes.

Claire Elise
Tisdall, VAD
Ambulance
Column, The
Ambulance
Service,
London
District

I got very friendly with a couple of VADs who always came together. One was much older than the other and I only knew that they were two friends living together. One night the older woman asked me back to their flat. I accepted with pleasure, and it was only when Miss Robinson turned to the other and ordered cocoa, which was duly served, that it dawned on me that they were mistress and maid.

'*Nah then, Lady Halexandra*', chortled *Punch* in the caption to a cartoon portraying a competent skivvy berating a harassed aristocrat who staggered under the weight of a loaded tray, ' *'urry up with them tea things or it'll be time to feed 'em agine afore you've done'*. And *The Sketch* joined in the joke with a much-bandaged Tommy muttering to an orderly as a beaming ministering angel prepared to descend on him. '*Lummy, 'er Ladyship again? Look 'ere George! Be a sport. Go and tell 'er I'm too bloomin' ill to be nussed today'*.

The press never tired of satirizing the efforts of the rich and the fashionable who adorned the wards, and frequently the commandant's office, of private and auxiliary hospitals both at home and abroad. Mostly, their criticism was unfounded. After a few false starts, the ladies had been quick to learn and were doing valuable jobs organizing and financing badly needed hospitals, now run on Red Cross lines under military authority. But sometimes Tommies returning home on convalescent leave had surprising tales to tell.

At first I was sent to a casualty clearing station, which was simply an engine shed at the railhead nearest the front made into a hospital. The men were brought in on stretchers and we nursed them on stretchers.

Lynette Powell, QAIMNS (R)

Then I was sent to the Duchess of Westminster's hospital at Le Touquet. The Duchess was a splendid lady, quite young and really beautiful. She had the most lovely uniform and always wore a very dainty cap, and wherever she went her great wolfhound followed her – into the wards, everywhere. She had a villa at Le Touquet, and very soon after war broke out she went there with some other ladies who were all friends of hers to start a hospital.

But, of course, they couldn't manage on their own. Having seen the wounded coming from Mons myself I always thought it was rather splendid of them not to give up, and as they realized that a hospital was badly needed, they sent to the Red Cross asking for trained nurses to go there and nurse the wounded. They stayed on themselves, of course, and they were very useful because we didn't have time to do things for the men, like write letters for them and read to them and do other things to keep them happy and entertained. So the ladies did that, and they also did all the administration and clerical work and saw to the medical supplies and the food. The Duchess thought that one of the best things they could do was to raise the morale of the soldiers. When the convoys came in we all rushed to attend to them, and as they arrived they had to have their particulars taken down on slips of paper. The Duchess and the other ladies used to do that and they always dressed themselves up in full evening dress! 'It's the least we can do to cheer up the men', the Duchess always used to say. Whenever we got word that a convoy was coming in, even if it was nine o'clock in the morning, that's what they always used to do – went upstairs and changed into full evening dress, with diamond tiaras and everything. Then they would parade themselves and stand at the entrance to take the names of the men. They used to set the gramophone going too, so that they would have a welcome. They meant very well, but it did look funny, these ladies all dressed up and the men, all muddy on the stretchers, looking at them as if they couldn't believe their eyes. I remember one man saying, 'We thought we were going to Hell and now it seems we are in Heaven!' These lovely ladies taking their names down. . . .

Later in the war there would be no time for such refinements. But the hospital was badly needed, and soon it was transferred to larger premises in the big casino in the forest. In the gaming rooms the elaborate chandeliers were swathed in linen covers, the tables were moved out to make room for hospital beds, and the *salles privées* were transformed into operating theatres.

But it was not enough, not nearly enough, for the scarcity of hospitals in France meant that men who were seriously wounded and should have been nursed on the spot were frequently shipped off on gruelling journeys to England because there was nowhere else to send them. Trained nurses who had volunteered to serve and were sent to military hospitals at home grumbled that they had wished to serve at the front. It had to be pointed out to them that, so far as nursing was concerned, Britain *was* 'the front'. In the sense that a man might easily be admitted to a hospital in Blighty within forty-eight hours of being wounded, it was quite true.

There was a desperate need for more hospitals in France, but they had to be in exactly the right place, near the lines of communication that ran along the 'back of the front', and near the supply depots and the ports from which the wounded could be shipped back home. In those areas the most suitable of the large buildings had already been requisitioned; now there was no alternative but to build.

In the middle of March, Sister Luard, glancing from the window of No. 5 hospital train as it steamed slowly along the track a few miles south of Boulogne, saw an army of workmen busy erecting an encampment of huts and tents for a new hospital complex planned to take 12,000 wounded. A similar camp was being prepared on the racecourse at Rouen. On the other side of the Channel tent stores were being rifled, and marquees long-unused being overhauled and repaired, before they were shipped off to France in time for the battles which would certainly take place in the spring. Up to the end of March 180,000 casualties had passed through the hospitals in France.

Noting the end of her first six months' service, Sister Luard remarked to her diary, 'This time last year the last thing one intended to do was to go and travel about France for six months, with occasional excursions into Belgium.'

'This time last year' was a whole world away from the present.

When I wanted to take up nursing before the war my mother exclaimed, 'But darling, it would ruin your hands!' She was right. Within a few months of the start of the war my hands were ruined for ever.

Kathleen Rhodes, VAD No. 11 Stationary Hospital, Rouen

Now the VADs, whose hands 'this time last year' had seldom touched anything so down to earth as a dishcloth or a sweeping brush, were scrubbing and polishing until their arms ached; running at the beck and call of harassed nurses and sisters until their feet swelled through the laces of their sensible shoes; emptying bedpans with hardly a wrinkle of their dainty noses; sterilizing instruments in operating theatres; holding kidney trays of instruments, and looking on as nurses and doctors probed and dressed wounds so terrible that only the most hardened of stomachs could look on them with equinamity. Now they were accepted in war hospitals that were desperately short of staff – though not always with a good grace.

Grace Bignold, working as a VAD in No. 1 London General Hospital, which was run on strict military lines, was kept firmly in her place and often on her day off went home to Dulwich exhausted and discouraged. Her mother wrote a poem to cheer her up:

'Valueless, A Duffer!' says the Sister's face,
When I try to do her orders with my bestest grace.
'Vain And Disappointing!' says Staff Nurse's eye,
If I dare to put my cap straight while she's walking by.

'Very Active Danger', looks the angry pro.,
If I sometimes score a wee bit over her, you know.
'Virtuous And Dumpy!' that's the way I feel,
When I'm uniformed from cap strings to each wardroom heel.
'Vague And Disillusioned' that's my mood each night,
When I've tried all day to please 'em and done nothing right.

'Valiant And Determined', I arise next day,
As I tell myself it's *duty* and I must obey.
'Very Anxious Daily' I await my leave,
Which I spend with my *own* soldier, as you may believe.
'Verily A Darling' That's his name for me,
When I meet him in my uniform of VAD.*

The soldiers coined their own epithets. 'Very Artful Darlings' was a favourite, with 'Very Active Dusters', and – less kindly – 'Victim Always Dies'. But by the time the war was six months old, the VADs had proved their usefulness, and the trained nurses and Army alike

* Grace Bignold married her 'own soldier' and became Mrs Francke.

realized that they could not do without them. It was decided that when the new camp hospitals opened in the spring, a selected few might be allowed to go to work in them as an experiment, and VADs with some hospital experience were invited to volunteer for service abroad.

They volunteered in droves, for now everyone was on the move. The first batch of the civilians who had stampeded to join up in the heady early days of the war had been trained and licked into shape as soldiers of the New Army. The leave-rota had been completed, foreign service equipment issued and the troops were ready to go to France. In Yorkshire the KOYLIs, like other battalions all over the country, were standing by for orders. In the eyes of the Dodsworth girls it was many weeks since they had been transformed from 'a nasty, dirty-looking lot' to 'such nice, cheery boys!'

Eve Dodsworth (her diary, Sunday, 11 April 1915)

Sat in the window and watched the Tommies all afternoon. We really thought they were off. They came on to the green with packs and rifles; were there for ages, were inspected and went back again. I expect they'll be off tonight.

Monday, 12 April

KOYLIs not gone yet. Don't go till tomorrow. Crowds in at the canteen in the parish hall. We heard them singing 'God Save the King'. I wept. Had a letter from Edward which worried me awfully. He says he goes into Ypres every day and it's being heavily shelled. Do hope he's all right.*

Tuesday, 13 April

. . . Most pathetic morning. Sat in window and watched KOYLIs. All yelled 'Goodbye'. They assembled on the green first and went off waving to us. Wept! We rushed out and followed them to the station. All the reserves lined the road as they marched through. Some friends recognized us again, and we were glad they knew we went to see them off. We went up on the station bridge and saw the train go out with all of them waving and the band playing 'Auld Lang Syne'. Simply *horrid!* Such patriotic scenes. Saw the Yorks and Lancs go too. They go straight to Folkestone and then across to France. So depressed. I can't bear it. Kit's arm very bad tonight and I feel a bit sickly myself.

Kit and Eve had both been innoculated. Soon, they too would be following the KOYLIs to France. It was the end of the beginning and for the girls and the soldiers alike, the war was about to start in earnest.

* Edward Dodsworth, Eve's brother.

Chapter Six

The trench was six feet deep with a high sandbagged parapet. At intervals there were trench periscopes – a long wooden box with an arrangement of mirrors which enabled an observer to look out over No Man's Land without getting a sniper's bullet in the head. There was a fire step which could be manned in an emergency or used as a seat at other times. On the right was a roomy dugout furnished with table and chairs, a couple of wire bunks and a few carefully selected photographs pinned to the close-boarded walls. In the dugout and along the bottom of the trench itself was a neat line of wooden duckboards which constituted a token attempt to provide a dry pathway above the squelching mud and seeping water that, even in the dryest weather, permeated the trenches. The Tommies cursed it, slipped on it, waded in it and often, struck down by the force of a bullet or an explosion, died in it.

But in this particular trench the duckboards were merely an attractive amenity, for there was no mud and the trench was not 'Somewhere in France'. It was in the grounds of the Moss Bridge Red Cross and St John's Hospital in Manchester, and the soldiers who had built and manned it were not dressed in mudstained khaki but in the now familiar 'convalescent blue'. The trench was the star attraction of a fund-raising garden party held in the hospital grounds.

The ladies in particular loved it, and queued up to pick their way along the realistically rough path that led through the shrubbery to the trench where the wounded proudly showed off all its amenities; demonstrated the use of a rifle; helped them over the rough patches; and let them have a go with the periscope, so that they could look through the wire entanglement in front of the parapet to the smartly dressed crowd strolling on the smooth lawn of the hospital beyond. But the crowning glory, when the visitors left the trench, was to find a 'camp-life scene' where groups of wounded soldiers brewed tea in a dixie over a real campfire and sold it to the delighted civilians at threepence a cup. No one complained about the inflated price. 'GIVE, GIVE, GIVE', the public was constantly exhorted. 'SAVE, SAVE, SAVE'. And when a million young men had given up their own civilian freedom and comfort to go soldiering, it seemed only right that these civilians who remained at home should dig deep into their pockets and purses to provide them with comforts and with all the care that money could provide when they came back wounded. When soldiers were prepared to risk their lives, it was surely not too much to ask that people at home should sacrifice the luxury of meat on just one day a week; should save fuel by giving up their motor cars; economize light by retiring to bed an hour earlier; and that women should assist in saving raw materials, badly needed for uniforms and blankets, by adopting the new short skirt.

The last item was not much of a sacrifice, for it had to be admitted that the new short skirt was undoubtedly chic. No one approved of it more than the soldiers home on leave, whose hearts were rejoiced by the sight of so many pretty ankles which last year had been modestly concealed by long skirts. But the soldiers in France had no such delightful spectacles to distract them. The few Frenchwomen they saw in villages behind the lines were cocooned in peasant black, and at the base the nursing authorities still frowned on any modification of the uniform designed in Victoria's reign. Queen Victoria herself would not have raised an eyebrow at the picture presented by Kit and Eve Dodsworth as they left for service in France.

Kit
Dodsworth,
VAD, No. 12
General
Hospital,
Rouen

We were arrayed in the most unbecoming uniform it was ever the misfortune of any poor woman to wear. It consisted of long black cloaks with little braid-edged shoulder capes; and small black bonnets made of straw and trimmed with black velvet bows which were secured to our heads by narrow white strings. The cloaks came to within an inch or two of the ground and thus hid most of our thick black woollen stockings.

When we arrived in London we hurried to headquarters, where we were interviewed by various officials. There was one rather unnerving moment when I was asked my age. The minimum age for overseas service was twenty-three, and of course I was nothing like that. However, I put a brave face on it and replied that I *was* twenty-three. My inquisitor looked a bit incredulous and I could feel myself blushing. Then to my great relief he grinned, and all was well. It would have been terrible to have been turned back at the last moment.

Then there was a rather disturbing episode. While we were waiting in a corridor a very wild young man appeared and asked if we were going to France. When we said that we were he said, 'God help you.' We both stared at him. 'It's Hell out there,' he went on. 'Don't let them send you to the casino, whatever you do. They're cutting legs and arms off so fast that there's no time to clear them away, and you can see amputated limbs piled on trays lying about the corridors.' We decided that he must be a bit off his head (and he probably was!), but we felt a bit uneasy just the same. However, we forgot all about that next morning when we got to Victoria Station. It was the most thrilling moment of my life, and perhaps the saddest as well. I shall always remember the sorrow of that station platform. You could just feel the sorrow and fear everywhere, cloaked by smiles and jokes that were heartbreaking to see.

Victoria Station was the hub of wartime London. In the early morning, just before the leave-train steamed out at half-past eight, it was a seething mass of khaki. Lines of Woodbine-puffing Tommies, weighed down by packs and rifles, jostled and joked as they waited to report to the Railway Transport Officer. A sprinkling of officers and an occasional ranker stood near Platform 7, where an old bookstall did a new kind of business under a large noticeboard: FRENCH MONEY EXCHANGED HERE FOR TROOPS IN UNIFORM ONLY. (But it was apt to do brisker business later in the day when the leave-train arrived from France, for it was a point of honour with the men to have spent every penny in their pockets before going back to the front.)

In the canteens that had taken over the peacetime waiting rooms, soldiers crowded round the counters for a last mug of strong Blighty tea, which was dished out by weary volunteers at the end of their night's shift. Outside by the platform gates soldiers, weighed down though they were with equipment and accoutrements, swung small children high in their arms for a last look and a last hug. Mothers and wives were pressed against the rough khaki tunics they had spent much of the last seven days scrubbing and sponging into a semblance of cleanliness, and sisters and sweethearts, wearing best hats and small strained smiles, cared not a jot about the propriety of kissing in public as the engine of the long leave-train whistled ominously at their backs.

Solitary soldiers, unable to face station farewells, plodded up the platform to secure an early seat on the train, before the final order to board and the last-minute rush through the barrier. Then the clatter of running boots, shouts, a banging of doors, the crashing down of windows as the best part of a thousand troops tried to hang out for a last look and a last wave. A final hiss of steam, a slow rumbling that slowly gathered momentum behind the bravado of cheers and yells, and the train pulled out of the station, leaving in its wake an emptiness that wiped the brave smiles from faces now buried in the pocket handkerchiefs that half a minute before had been fluttering a courageous farewell.

Then the women turned and walked dejectedly out of the station through the carved stone archway, once known as the Gateway to the Continent. Now they called it 'The Gate of Goodbye'. The happy crowds of relatives who came later in the afternoon to meet the homecoming leave-trains, and tried to pick out one particular warrior from the mass of soldiers streaming joyously through the barrier, superstitiously avoided it and used the entrance to the Brighton line instead.

But long before the first leave-train reached London in the afternoon, Kit and Eve Dodsworth had arrived in Boulogne.

Kit
Dodsworth,
VAD, No. 12
General
Hospital,
Rouen

My sister and I were to go to Rouen with about eight others, and as the train didn't go until the evening we had the rest of the day to ourselves. We were sent to an hotel where we were able to get lunch, and after that we went out to explore the town. Almost the first place we found was the casino. We were agreeably surprised that we were not led to it by the anguished cries of the patients, nor did we see any unattached limbs lying around! However, we were duly impressed. After a while it started to rain, and as dresses only three inches off the ground are not very suitable for paddling about in wet streets we went back to the hotel to get out of it.

There was a boat to England that night, and one by one officers arrived to wait there till they went on board. To us, straight from home, who had seen none of our people until they had had time to get clean and more or less de-loused, these men thrilled us to the marrow; so muddy and so tired. They dragged their chairs up to the stoves and almost all of them went straight to sleep. Once in England the excitement of being home lights up their faces and brightens their eyes. There, they were just resting after such tiredness as we at home could never even imagine. Their faces seemed almost expressionless with exhaustion.

Can you picture that big room? It was furnished with just a few wicker chairs, a large assortment of wooden ones and several large palms by way of decoration. A seedy-looking waiter and several buxom waitresses came in and out from time to time, but what struck us most was the silence. The atmosphere seemed to be impregnated with this feeling of utter weariness. We were hardly able to speak ourselves, we were so overawed, like new girls at school. They seemed such veterans to us.

The New Army was arriving and there had never been an army like it for strength and youth and fitness, every man a volunteer. The 'Old Army', or what was left of it, and that included any man who had been at the Front for more than a month or so, certainly considered itself to consist of seasoned campaigners. Graham Carey undoubtedly did so, for he was serving with his ambulance section 800 miles away where the battle was raging among the summits of the Vosges mountains on the edge of what was proudly known as 'Alsace Reconquise'. There, the French army struggled to maintain its grip on the few miles of territory it had managed to wrest back from the Germans in its first patriotic foray at the start of the war.

It was no easy job manoeuvring the erratic and temperamental motor ambulances up under bombardment to aid-posts in the high peaks, and it was a long, comfortless journey back for the wounded as the ambulances careered down the tortuous rock-strewn roads on their two-hour journey to safety in the valley below. But it was an improvement. Before the arrival of the Americans the wounded had been carried tied to the backs of mules, or, if conditions permitted, on two-wheeled springless mule-carts. By either method it had taken five hours to reach the field hospital, and alarming numbers of the wounded were found to be dead on arrival. Now that there were fewer fatalities among these less severely wounded, the French authorities were touching in their gratitude and were happy to regard the *Section Sanitaire Américaine* as a recognized unit of the French army. Bit by bit, the boys had discarded the official uniform for attire which identified them even more closely with the poilus.

Graham Carey – although omitting to mention that he now sported a fine, bushy beard – described it in a letter to his mother.

I have completely discarded the regular ambulance uniform bit by bit, until not a single original garment is left, and I am accordingly quite happy. As you know the French go in for all sorts of fancy cuts and colours in their clothes, and you can get all sorts of gorgeous clothes in any little country store. I have got our officer so subdued at last that he doesn't object to *bleu azure* velour breeches and *mouflières* – and he was even moved to admire them this morning! These plus a red *ceinture*, leather coat with brass buttons and *beret* is about the best combination I have yet struck, and has the added advantage of preventing excitable *chasseurs* from shooting one for a Boche, which I've narrowly escaped once or twice when up near the lines. Our khaki is very close in colour to the green-grey of some of the *Jaegers* and Bavarian regiments.

How I do wish I could be in Portsmouth with you this summer! I freeze so solid every night that I find it hard to realize thay we are well on in July. We celebrated the 4th by having champagne with our supper in the evening and drinking to America's joining the Allies as soon as possible. We have just had a new squad sent out from Paris to reinforce us, but they seem to be a pretty sick lot on the whole, a regular Neuilly outfit. However, they may work into shape later.

Graham Carey, American Field Service, Ambulance Section No. 3

Spurred equally by their admiration of their swashbuckling predecessors and their resentment at being so blatantly patronized, the newcomers were quick to shed their rookie ways and uniforms, and after their first spell in the lines they were ready in their own turn to sneer at the next lot of new recruits. Since its tatterdemalion beginnings the Field Ambulance, with the blessing of the French authorities, had been put on a regular and official basis. There was nothing in the neutrality laws which forbade the recruitment of non-combatants in the United States, and in April an advertisement had gone into East Coast newspapers:

VOLUNTEER AMBULANCE DRIVERS ARE WANTED

New men are also needed from time to time to fill up the places of those who return to America on leave or who are unable to re-enlist at the expiration of their six months in the field.

REQUISITE QUALIFICATIONS

American Citizenship – Good Health – Clean Record – Ability to Drive Automobiles (Superficial Knowledge of Repair Work an Advantage) – No Salary, but Living Expenses Paid.

For Further Details and Terms of Service
Apply to:

WILLIAM R. HEREFORD,   HENRY D. SLEEPER,
Headquarters American Ambulance,   c/o Lee, Higginson & Co.,
14 Wall Street,   State Street,
New York   Boston

There was no shortage of would-be recruits, and a large and growing appeal fund meant that more and better ambulances could be bought and that the volunteer drivers would no longer have to pay their own fares across the Atlantic. America was giving generously to a variety of war charities, and opinion was hardening in favour of the Allied cause. The Germans had seen to that when they sank the *Lusitania*. The loss of life among the citizens of the neutral United States on board a neutral ship had outraged public feelings, particularly on the East Coast, and it was remarked at the time that 'New England has become positively bellicose'.

While the drivers of the American Field Ambulance celebrated 4 July by drinking champagne in a leaky billet at the foot of the Vosges mountains, another celebration was taking place in mid-Atlantic on the steamer *Noordam*. On board were 110 American surgeons and nurses who had signed on for varying periods to help staff the new camp hospitals that were now nearing completion on the coast of France. These were no youthful enthusiasts impelled by a sense of adventure to get as near as they could to the war. They were skilled and experienced men and women, well established in their professions, who were travelling as a unit organized by Harvard University. On 4 July the day started with a flag-raising ceremony on deck and a lusty rendering of 'The Star Spangled Banner'. It was followed by an even louder rendering of 'Fair Harvard'. The Harvard contingent were still smarting at what they had considered an insult to their Alma Mater as well as to themselves. 'Fair Harvard' was their anthem. It had resounded through a thousand graduation ceremonies. It was sung at reunion dinners wherever Harvard men met. It was bellowed on Saturday afternoons at Harvard football matches. It was unthinkable that it should not be sung on the quayside as the first Harvard Unit set sail for Europe. But the unthinkable had happened.

The grand farewell had been at Boston's South Station on the eve of the unit's departure, but a fair number of friends and relatives had gone with the unit to New Jersey, so there was quite a crowd assembled at No. 5 Pier at Hoboken when they boarded the *Noordam* on 26 June. There was also a band, and Dr Frank Lund had even gone to the trouble of arranging for a supply of sheet music to be on hand, so that there should be no mistake. He reckoned without the band, for the song was sung to the old Irish air, 'Believe me if all those Endearing Young Charms' – and the band was anti-Irish. They refused to play 'Fair Harvard'. As the gangway was lowered and the mooring ropes loosened, the band obstinately struck up a Sousa march. But the unit lining the deck of the *Noordam* were cheered up by one final excitement, later reported in *The Boston Globe*.

There was no last-minute passenger, but there was one last-minute fareweller. He had come from Poughkeepsie, had run himself out of breath and could only gasp, when he reached the rail as the ship was already moving, 'Goodbye, Bessie!'.

And on the face of the prettiest of the nurses the sorrow at parting was illuminated by the triumph of this proof of affection. 'Goodbye, Harold,' she called out, a world of sentiment in the tone.

'Whoo,' hooted the *Noordam*, and backed out into the hot haze of a June noon.

Now, a week out at sea on 4 July, standing on the deck of the *Noordam* beneath the fluttering Stars and Stripes of the United States of America, the Harvard Unit bellowed out *'Fair Harvard'* for all they were worth.

Fair Harvard! thy sons to thy Jubilee throng,
And with blessings surrender thee o'er,
By these festival rites, from the age that is past
To the age that is waiting before . . .

. . . Thou then wert our parent,
The nurse of our soul;
We were moulded to manhood by thee,
Till freighted with treasure, thoughts, friendships and hopes,
Thou didst launch us on Destiny's sea.

The verses did not constitute the world's greatest poetry, but now, well and truly launched on 'Destiny's sea', the men and girls of the Harvard Unit sang the words as loud as they could. Far out on the grey Atlantic there was nothing but the waves and the sea winds to hear them. But it made them feel good.

Two days later they arrived in London.

Dr Daniel Reardon of Quincy, Massachusetts, was thirty-seven years old, a married man and father of two, a neutral and a non-combatant. He was not surprised that the doctors of the party had to be kitted out in British military uniform, but it did astonish him that a considerable portion of the briefing time in London was devoted to teaching the American doctors how to deliver a full military salute. But while they awaited delivery of their kit and, in spite of the enjoyable distractions of London, chafed to get to France, there was one medical diversion.

Dr Daniel
Reardon,
1st Harvard
Medical Unit
(his diary,
Thursday, 8
July 1915)

Hotel Cecil London. At 5 pm went to King George's Military Hospital and was shown through by the colonel-surgeon in charge. This was formerly a stationery factory which had been transformed into a military hospital. We saw many wounded soldiers, who related very sad and sorrowful experiences. Saw sixty-five cases of paraplegia from wounds of spine in one ward, hopeless cases. Several at Ypres.

The 2nd Battle of Ypres, just a few weeks before, had hit the headlines in America and shocked the civilized world. In another bid to reach the Channel ports the Germans had used poison gas, and it was only by a miracle and the staunchness of a weak force of Canadian and British troops that they had not broken through the huge gap in the Allied line. The line had held, but the casualties were appalling. It is likely that, prior to April 1915, both sides had developed and held supplies of chemical gases which could be used in warfare, although as signatories to the document drawn up at The Hague Conference in 1907 – which renounced the use of asphyxiating or harmful gases in time of war – neither wished to be the first to use them. In retrospect it was regarded as a 'warning' when Germany leaked a protest to the world's press that the British were using asphyxiating gases on the Western Front a week before Germany herself attacked with gas. The gas attack at Ypres unleashed a whole new area of warfare, which in the next four years reached ever new heights of diabolical refinement. The early gases, chlorine (Cl_2) and phosgene ($COCL_2$) were acute lung irritants. A two-minute exposure to chlorine, breathed in a concentration of as little as one part gas to 10,000 parts air, was sufficient to cause pulmonary lesions. The more powerful phosgene could be distributed in an even lower concentration (one to 50,000) and needed to be inhaled in for only one minute in order to reduce a man to helplessness.

Four days after the gas attack, Dr J. S. Haldane and Professor H. B. Baker were sent to France by the British government to investigate this new horror. Dr Haldane found the casualties still lying in the casualty clearing stations at Bailleul.

Dr J. S.
Haldane

These men were lying struggling for breath and blue in the face. On examining the blood with the spectroscope and by other means, I ascertained that the blueness was not owing to the presence of any abnormal pigment. There was nothing to account for the blueness (cyanosis) and struggle for air but the fact that they were suffering from acute bronchitis, such as is caused by inhalation of an irritant gas. One of them died shortly after arrival. A postmortem examination was conducted in our presence by Lieutenant McNee. The examination showed that death was due to acute bronchitis and its secondary effects. Lieutenant McNee also examined yesterday the body of a Canadian sergeant who had died in the casualty clearing station from the effects of gas. In this case also, very acute bronchitis and oedema of the lungs caused death by asphyxiation. . . . The symptoms and the other facts so ascertained point to the use by the German troops of chlorine or bromine for purposes of asphyxiation. There are also facts pointing to the use in German shells of other irritant substances, though in some cases at least these agents are not of the same brutally barbarous character as the gas used in the attack on the Canadians. The effects are not those of any of the ordinary products of the combustion of explosives.

Dr Haldane's report was given wide coverage in the newspapers and aroused both horror and indignation. The nurses were appalled. Nothing in their experience, nor in the experience of the doctors, had equipped them to deal with wards full of men gasping for breath; with the terrible rasping sound of their struggle; with their blue faces and livid skins; and, worst of all, with their terror as the fluid rose higher and higher in their lungs until eventually they drowned in it. The terror was made worse by the fact that most of the men were blinded and trapped in darkness in their suffocating bodies.

It was the responsibility of the RAMC laboratories to try to analyse the gas, to try to produce some some alleviating treatment, and devise masks to protect the troops in the trenches. On 25 April, only three days after the first gas attack at Ypres, Sister Luard – now relieved from the hospital train and working in a casualty clearing station a few miles south of Ypres – had an unexpected casualty. It was the Assistant Director of Medical Services of the 5th Division.

This afternoon the medical staffs of both divisions have been trying experiments in a barn with chlorine gas, with and without different kinds of masks soaked with some antidote, such as lime. All were busy coughing and choking when they found the ADMS of the 5th Division getting blue and suffocated. He'd had too much chlorine and was brought here looking very bad, and for an hour we had to give him fumes of ammonia till he could breathe properly. He will probably have bronchitis. But they found out what they wanted to know – that if you put on this mask, you can go to the assistance of men overpowered by the gas, with less chance of finding yourself dead too when you get there.

Sister
K. Luard,
QAIMNS (her
diary, 25 April
1915)

The masks were primitive affairs but they were better than nothing, and work parties and hospital supply depots at home in Blighty set to work to turn them out as fast as they could. They were simple to make — cotton wool pads enclosed in butter muslin, large enough to cover the mouth and nose, and with tapes at each corner to tie at the back of the head. Within a week, 300,000 had been sent to France. As the medical authorities struggled to evolve more efficient protection, the army authorities put in hand the business of manufacturing quantities of asphyxiating gas on their own account to use against the Germans.

The new soldiers of Kitchener's Army, massing at the ports to board the troopships that would take them to France, were travelling towards a new kind of war, governed by new rules, filled with new horrors, and of a deadliness that was unsurpassed in human experience.

Chapter Seven

The weather was changeable all that summer, and remembering the heatwave and the cloudless skies of the year before, people began to mutter darkly that the fearsome bombardments on the Western Front were causing vibration in the atmosphere and affecting the climate.

But although there were showers and occasional chilly winds, the soldiers of the New Army were able to settle down and become used to the primitive conditions with less hardship than the unfortunates who had been rushed to the Western Front during the hard winter weather. The new arrivals were almost a million strong. For every battalion of front-line infantry there was a battery of artillery; for every brigade a transport column; for every division a motor lorry unit for the distribution of ammunition, stores and rations, and a battalion of pioneers to construct new trench lines, lay military roads and build bridges. Despatch riders and messengers burned up the roads, and in the skies young airmen flying in flimsy planes were the eyes of the army. Signallers of the Royal Engineers, several thousand strong, festooned the great hinterland with telephone wires and cables to connect the army at the Front to the base depots, where another army of ordnance men, instructors, printers and mapmakers, quartermasters and storemen, clerks, cooks and bottlewashers, laboured to keep it there. It took seven men working behind the lines to put one soldier into battle, and now there was a whole host of doctors and nurses to care for him if he was wounded and got out.

The Harvard Unit, having mastered the intricacies of the military salute and donned their newly delivered uniforms, crossed to France on the hospital ship *St Patrick* and arrived at their destination on 18 July at seven o'clock in the evening.

No. 22 General Camp Hospital was one of half a dozen newly erected around the twin villages of Dannes and Camiers. They lay behind the sand dunes of the coast, just under the slopes of a line of low hills near the railway line that served the hospitals, the Machine Gun School, the training camps and base camps strung out along its length as it ran from Etaples and the south to Boulogne and the north. Dr Daniel Reardon, who at the age of thirty-seven considered himself to be a little past the age of enjoying Boy Scouting, passed an uncomfortable night in a bell-tent shared with Dr Nat Hunting. He slept on a collapsible bed-chair covered with the three thin 'biscuits' which made up an army mattress, and was kept awake by the cold and by the trains which rumbled past at intervals through the night. Next morning the doctors climbed the hills behind the camp. There was time to take a stroll, for there was 'not much doing' and no convoy was expected, but everywhere they looked there was bustle and activity.

The extent of the hospitals alone was impressive, for five camps had been set up, and the tents, which between them could hold almost 7,000 wounded, stretched far to the south, where No. 18 and No. 25 General Hospitals lay in the direction of Etaples, and to the north, where No. 26 General and No. 20 Canadian Hospital (run by a unit from McGill University) reached towards Boulogne. Beyond the camps where the dunes ran towards the sea was the vast area the troops called the Bull Ring, and from the hill the doctors could see them swarming across it, drilling and marching. Between the chattering bursts of fire from the ranges of the Machine Gun School, they could faintly hear bloodthirsty yells whipped up by NCO instructors as squads of soldiers – antlike in the distance – leapt out of 'practice' trenches to rush with fixed bayonets at a line of limply dangling straw-filled sacks that represented the enemy. Lorries, ambulances and staff cars raced up and down the roads, and in their own camp below, inspired by the maple leaf emblem picked out in stones at the entrance to the Canadian hospital next door, RAMC orderlies were engaged in constructing the Stars and Stripes in limestone and crushed brick. Later, when time permitted, they would add the Harvard shield, but for the moment they only had time to complete their handiwork with the word 'Welcome'. It was 30 July before the Harvard Unit received its first convoy.

Dr D. B. Reardon, 1st Harvard Medical Unit, (his diary, 31 July 1915)

Our first convoy of 108 soldiers came into the hospital during the night between 2 and 5 am. About half and half, medical and surgical. After breakfast, went to my ward (C.6) and found new patients. Most were injured at Ypres and Hill 60. They say that Ypres is entirely wiped out. There's a man with wounds of fingers and shrapnel wounds of the head, arms and thigh. One boy had a bullet wound through the left humerus (at Hill 60), breaking humerus (septic). A soldier had shrapnel in the back. He is an artillery man and had been at the front since the beginning of the war. A shell burst five feet from him. He was knocked out temporarily but not injured badly. Says that the nearer a man is to the shell the less liable to great danger, unless struck.

Another man was an old veteran who had been twenty years in service. He says that his battalion had 1,160 men at the start and now contained sixty. All had been killed or wounded. Another boy had bullet wound through the right cheek, and many showed how near a man can come to death without being killed. Another man was sighting a gun when a bullet went through a finger of his left hand and struck the breech, otherwise he would have been killed.

It had been a long and busy day. It was ten o'clock before Dan Reardon closed his diary, opened his writing case and started a letter to his wife in Quincy, Massachusetts:

> 22 General Hospital,
> British Expeditionary Force,
> Harvard American Unit,
> France

My Darling Minnie,

It is now 10 am, and after a strenuous day's work I thought I would give you a few experiences since my last note. First of all, imagine me in my tent sitting in my solitary chair beside a canvas table with a tent lantern with candles in it, cot over in one corner, a few boxes in the tent with clothes and shoes in them, and you have a picture of yours truly. I have taken off my leggings and the only companions I have are a few earwigs (insects half an inch long) running about the tent. In the adjoining tents some of the boys are having a coffee party with cake and coffee, but I have had a fairly hard day and have decided to retire as I hear another convoy of wounded soldiers is due tonight and tomorrow it will mean more work. However, it is very interesting and we are so glad to help these poor lads.

You may have read with passing glance of an engagement about Ypres at Hooge two days ago and taken no notice of it. We drew about 150 of the wounded boys who were able to drag themselves out.

They were put to bed and washed and some were so tired that they fell to sleep sitting up in bed while talking to you. Some had not washed their faces for eleven days, and water was a 'Godsend' to them. Our doctors passed cigarettes to them and the way those poor chaps would take one and smoke it with a smile was a sight that will never be forgotten. We got those boys within twenty-four hours after being wounded. They lost their colonel and all the officers of their regiment. Today we have been operating most of the day, fixing broken bones and extracting shrapnel and bullets from their bodies. They also told of the Germans playing hot pitch from a hose on to them, which shows the methods that the Germans are adopting in this terrible war.

Time is flying and it will not be long before we will all be joined together and happy again. 'War is Hell' – and more, and I am having a glimpse of it close at hand.

I hope that you and kiddies are enjoying yourselves and had a pleasant time at the beach.

The soldier boy is a happy individual and seems contented, and those we see are anxious to get to the Front. The boys who came in last night were a fine lot and appeared to be very respectable young fellows, but shot and shell has no regard for respectability!

Well, my dear, Nat Hunting is snoring and I guess it is time for me to retire, so I will close with a goodnight to you and may God bless you all. Love to you and my darlings,

from Daddy

xxxx Mary
xxxx Paul
xxxx Mama

In spite of repeated promptings from London, where they were already thinking of the information that would be required for a future Medical History of the war, medical officers in base hospitals were too busy caring for the wounded to make more than the cursory scribbled notes that were absolutely essential to guide their colleagues or to accompany the wounded back to England. But newly arrived from the United States, absorbed by the challenge of surgical work which was entirely new in his fourteen years' experience as a surgeon, Dan Reardon made time to record details of the cases which came under his care:

1. General gunshot wound, pelvis. First serious case observed was case of through and through gunshot wound of pelvis. Bullet entered posterior to left trochanter, went through and out behind right trochanter. Discharged pus and faeces with considerable blood from left-side wound. Wound evidently of lower bowel with haemorrhage.
2. Shrapnel wound, head. Boy, nineteen, piece of shrapnel entered right side of head above ear two inches. Probe entered brain four inches. Had left hemiplegia, delirium and was unconcious six days before we arrived. X-ray showed piece of shrapnel on spheroid bone which was left alone. Kept in hospital four weeks. Hemiplegia cleared up. Wound healed and patient was discharged. Returned to England.
3. Gas Bacillus Cases.
   (a) First one we saw here had been here for shrapnel wound, left thigh. Had mid-thigh amputation and secondary operation for haemorrhage. Recovered and was sent home to England. Treated by Dr Hunting. By English MO first.
   (b) Mr Bragg. Entered hospital thirty-six hours after receiving shrapnel wound left mid-thigh. Temperature 102 to 104. Pulse 120 to 140. Gas bacillus in wound. Operation with large incisions. Piece of shrapnel extracted. Temp. came down to normal. Wound treated by granulations and he returned retired to England in four weeks. The patient was E. Bragg, 6th Somerset Light Infantry, Company 'D'.
   (c) Dr Allan had case of wound from shrapnel. Right arm.

Patient doing well. At 1 pm was good. 3 pm went bad and died at 8 pm.

(d) Dr Hartwell had three cases of gas infection of arms from shrapnel with recovery.

(e) Dr Starkey had case of a gas-infected wound of the arm that necessitated amputation above the elbow. Severe prostration for two days, then eventual recovery.

4. Septic Knee Cases. Sir Charles Makins, consulting surgeon to our various hospitals about here, made a statement that 80 per cent of septic knees in this ward have led to amputations.

5. Gas Bacillus Cases. Irrigate with Hypochlorous Acid ¼% Solution. Also dress wounds with same solution.

The figure of 80 per cent amputations that resulted from sepsis and gas gangrene was about to reduce slightly, because 'Hypochlorous Acid ¼% Solution' was the result of the experiments conducted by Doctors Carrel and Dakin which Harvey Cushing had remarked on earlier in the year. It was not the complete answer, but it was undeniably a help. But it only worked when the gangrene was not too far gone and if the patients could be treated before it spread.

We used to have to make this stuff up by the gallon and we kept it in big demi-johns. There were drainage tubes in the bad wounds, and another long tube came up from the wound with about five other small tubes at intervals along the way. We had a big syringe filled with this solution, and we used to have to inject it into the tubes every three hours so that it would wash round the wound. Of course, it was very painful for the men. They hated it, it was so cold – it didn't seem to soothe the wound at all but very often the infection started to diminish if the wound was well irrigated. We used to have to do it every three hours – even at night we had to wake the men up. Of course, even so, the limb often still had to be amputated if it was too far gone; or, if it were on the body, the man died. But we did manage to save a great many with no other treatment but the Carrel and Dakin solution.

Gwynedd Lloyd, VAD, No. 6 General Hospital, Rouen

I could never get the smell of that stuff out of my nose. I can still smell it even now, a sort of chlorate of lime smell, and of course the smell of the wounds themselves was terrible. If there was a case of gas gangrene in a ward you could smell it as you opened the door. We used to put on enormous dressings of lint soaked in this stuff – Eusol, we called it, but it was just Carrel and Dakin's under another name.

You couldn't clean a wound up properly, it was absolutely suppurating. All you could do was slap on this quite large dressing soaked in the solution and then dress it again every four hours. So there was a tremendous amount of dressings to be done and a lot of

Hester Cotton, VAD, Rusthall Grange Auxiliary Hospital, Tunbridge Wells

pain for the men, because there weren't all the pain killers there are now. I don't know how they survived what they did.

Irrigation wasn't done much in this country, because they couldn't be shipped back home until that was finished with, but we still went on using the solution on the wounds. We had to make it up every morning, so much powder to every pint of water – boiled water, of course – and the jars were taken on a trolley round the wards and used on the worst ones. We soaked the lint in it, put it straight on to the open wounds and then wrapped them in Jackinette, which was sort of mackintoshy stuff that helped to keep the bed dry. It also kept the dressing moist, which was essential.

It was very hard to do the dressings sometimes, because we weren't trained nurses and were only helping to hold things and pass them to Sister, but it was dreadful to have to look at them nevertheless. I only had to leave the ward once, and that was for the very first wound I saw. It was a man who'd had half his buttocks shot off, all the fleshy part, and never having seen a real wound before I was a bit taken aback. If the wound had been clean it would have been red, because it was absolutely raw flesh. As it was, it was full of pus, absolutely suppurating with pus. You simply couldn't clean it up; you just had to keep on putting these wet things on until gradually it got cleaner and cleaner. He did get better, that man, but he had a terrible time. He had to be kept lying on his stomach and I remember when he was first able to inch round on to one side for the first time. That was a great day.

Drusilla (Maisie) Bowcott, Nursing Probationer

At first I only hovered around the edges and didn't see much, but the third morning after I started, the senior probationer upset Sister in some way, so she was banished and I was called to replace her. I was absolutely shaking at the knees as I approached the team at the bed where the dressing trolley stood. 'Hold that stump', said Sister, and the poor chap must have felt dreadful because I gripped his leg well above the knee, and as the solution of Eusol and Peroxide was poured on to the stump the pus was pouring over my hands. Then I saw *two* stumps, *two* Sisters, and I must have started to sway because I was carted out very ignominiously to the fire escape. Someone said, 'Put your head between your knees and you'll be all right'. It was the only time I ever disgraced myself like that.

It's amazing what you get hardened to. But the pain the men suffered was frightful and we had nothing to give them. Aspirin was not much good but there was nothing, no pain killer, between that and a morphine injection at the other end of the scale, which they got if they were very bad. But that made them unconcious, so it was only given in very extreme cases. Most of the time they just had to bear it – and they were very stoical.

We had a very heavy ward and one man was very badly wounded. He was a Scots sergeant–major, an elderly man. He'd lost one eye and he was wounded in his arm and leg. The orderly had to lift him up to have his dressing done, and the Sister and the MO did the dressing together with the orderly and myself lending a hand. It was such a difficult dressing to do. The poor man used to scream. He was the only man I ever knew who did. They were most extraordinarily brave, most of them, absolutely marvellous.

I used to hate it if they died when I was on night duty, because then you had to lay them out yourself. But if they died during the day, the orderlies always did that. My first night duty was on this very heavy ward. There was one man, he'd been a fisherman in civil life and he had dreadful wounds, internal wounds, all fastened up with tubes that ran into a bucket underneath his bed. His bed was up against the door of the marquee, because anyone who was likely to die was always put there so that they could be taken out without fuss and depressing the rest of the wounded. I was terrified that he would die when I was on night duty, and the first thing I used to ask the day nurse when I went on was, 'Is the fisherman still alive?' She said he was, but he was very near death. But as soon as I went in and got into the marquee he called me and said, 'Sister, can you give me the drink you gave me last night?' I'd given him some port warmed with a bit of water and sugar and he wanted it again. I gave him the drink and I sat with him.

A little while before he died he opened his eyes and said, 'You've been an angel to me.' It made me feel absolutely dreadful. I thought, 'Thank goodness he doesn't know what I've been thinking, just hoping all the time that he wouldn't die when I was on duty.' But he died that night. The night superintendent came in. She was an elderly Scotswoman, and very kind. She said, 'I'll do the laying out and you hold the lantern for me.' So we put the screens round and started to lay out this poor man, ready for the orderlies to take him away. Of course, the rest of the ward was in darkness and the men were sleeping, and there was only a dim light and us behind the screens in this shadowy corner with the poor, dead soldier. Half-way through, as we turned the body over, Sister looked at me and shook her head. 'We do have to do some things, don't we!' she said.

Kitty Kenyon, VAD, No. 4 General Hospital, Camiers

There was a very young lad who was badly wounded. He had all his genital parts blown off. Bad as he was, he was always cheerful about it. I used to wonder how he stood it. It was a terrible dressing to do, and very, very hard on him. We used to see him watching us as the dressing trolley came down the ward, and you could see that he was dreading the moment we would get to him. The wound – it was just a hole – was packed with gauze with just a silver tube coming out of it; that was the catheter that led into his bladder. Every morning all the

Sister Christina Hastings, QUAIMNS Reserve

packing had to be pulled out bit by bit, the hole cleaned, and the gauze packed back in again. It was agony. We all used to dread it because it was so very hard on him. He used to cry. He couldn't help it but he felt very badly about crying, and we used to cover his face with a handkerchief so that he wouldn't be embarrassed about it. He was no good for about an hour after the dressing was done. He just lay there and we would give him a drop of brandy or a glass of champagne. He was about twenty-five. He recovered. Eventually, we were able to send him back to England and I expect he was discharged from the Army, but he'd never be any good as a man after that.

Kitty Kenyon
VAD, No. 4
General
Hospital,
Camiers

The other man I remember very distinctly, because he was my first real patient. We had been told there was a convoy coming in. I went off for my tea, and when I came back again the whole tent was full of huge men in their overcoats. They were all muddy, some with bandages, and moving about in the dimness. Sister told me to attend to a man who was sitting on a bed. He was a huge Scots sergeant with a very mud-stained, blood-stained tunic. So I made him lie down on the bed and cut off his uniform. We had these great, huge scissors and you simply sliced through the clothing with them. I gave him a blanket bath and made him tidy and comfortable. You could tell that he was in terrible pain, and he should really have been a stretcher case.

The first few days he just lay quiet, seldom speaking, gritting his teeth when his dressing was done. But it was a very bad dressing and one day he nearly fainted with the pain of it. Sister, as a joke, said to him that she knew perfectly well he was playing up for a drink of brandy. She turned away from the bed when the dressing was finished and said to me, 'Give him some brandy, Nurse, he really needs it.' I brought the brandy, but he was so furious with Sister that he wouldn't touch it. It stood on his locker all day. He'd been a regular soldier in the Black Watch and had deserted before the war. But on the day war broke out, on 4 August, he'd joined up again with another battalion, and so many were joining at the time that they'd never caught up with him. He'd twice been promoted, and twice been reduced to the ranks.

When he was getting better I remember making his bed one day. There had been something in the papers about the Germans killing prisoners, which had shocked me and I was laying off about how terrible I thought it was. He fell absolutely silent, made no answer at all. It was as if a shutter had come down over his face, and I realized in a flash that he must have done the same thing.

He had a beautiful baritone voice and he used to sing Scottish songs, 'Ye Banks and Braes' and 'Loch Lomond' and 'Bonnie Mary of Argyll'. So I asked him if he would sing 'Annie Laurie', which was a favourite of mine. But he just shook his head. Then I asked him a second time, and after he'd refused twice I knew I mustn't ask again – that it was obviously a song that meant something to him. Then one morning we were doing the dressings. A number of bad cases had come in, and there was one in particular which he must have been able to see that I dreaded doing. It was a very difficult, painful dressing on an arm, and I was helping Sister and the MO, handing them things, when suddenly, further down the ward, I heard him singing, very softly. He was singing 'Annie Laurie', and I knew he sang it for me because he saw that I was doing something difficult – so he sang the song I'd asked him to sing. And he never sang it again.

Besides the extra and willing hands that provided badly needed help, the Americans brought with them a priceless asset – the technique of successful blood transfusion. Until their arrival the method had been primitive and there were a large number of failures, when the donor's blood formed into clots in the patient's veins so that he died of thrombosis. Early in 1915 the Americans had developed a method which prevented the donor's blood from coagulating. The Harvard Unit brought the new technique with them to the camp hospital at Dannes-Camiers. Lieutenant Geoffrey Keynes was one of the British doctors who spent two weeks there in order to learn it.

The first thing to do was to get the group of the donor and the patient matching, and we had the serum for doing that. It had just been discovered as well as the method by which we could prevent the blood from clotting. It turned out to be very simple. You simply put sodium citrate solution in the flask, a certain amount, then ran in the pint of blood, shook it around, and gave it to the patient through a pipe. You took it from the donor into a flask and then from the flask to the patient. I spent two weeks with the Harvard Unit and during that time I contributed something by devising an improved apparatus, which in fact continued to be used until the 1930s. After a fortnight studying this technique I went back to the casualty clearing station where I was working, and introduced the method there. It saved countless lives of men who would otherwise have died from shock and loss of blood.

    Captain Geoffrey Keynes, RAMC

It provided an incomparable extension to the possibilities of life-saving surgery. Trained anaesthetists were scarce and often I dispensed with their services. A preliminary transfusion, followed by a spinal analgesic, enabled me to do a major amputation single-handed. A second transfusion then established the patient so firmly on the road to recovery that he could be dismissed to the ward without any further anxiety. When the convoys came in, the wounded whom the responsible officer thought had no chance of recovery were put all together in one tent – because the thing that mattered was to do the best one could as quickly as one could for the men whose lives you could possibly save. So the others were all put into this 'moribund' ward and made as comfortable as possible, and were looked after until they died. The possibility of blood transfusion now gave hope to a lot of these people, and I made it my business during any lull in the work to go into the 'moribund' ward, choose a patient who was still breathing and had a perceptible pulse, transfuse him and then carry out the necessary operation. Most of them were suffering primarily from shock and loss of blood, and in this way I had the satisfaction of pulling many men back from death.

One young man came in practically dead – he'd got twelve holes in his intestine. He'd got his brachial artery severed in one of his arms and several other wounds. I spent a long time on him and gave him a transfusion. Believe it or not, next morning he was alive and perky. He was a Newcastle boy. He would certainly have died without a blood transfusion. It saved countless lives.

Rifleman Charlie Shepherd, 13th Service Battalion, The Rifle Brigade

I was in this camp hospital and they was all Americans in there. The man who used to look after me, the orderly, was a man called Packard. He was one of the Packard Car Company. Well, suddenly out of the blue they called for a volunteer for a blood transfusion. All the chaps on the other side of the ward was legless, both legs off, so I said, 'Here you are.' And this Major Hopkins, I always remember him, an American surgeon, said, 'Are you willing to give blood?' I said, 'Yes, you can try me,' so they pricked my finger and I was the same group as the chap who was wanting blood. So they said, 'Right.'

They wheeled me into this operating place and this chap was lying there, his head at one end and my head at the other – heads and tails. I've still got the scar where they opened me up to get the tube into the vein, and it came up to a thing like a pint bottle. I had a piece of board under my arm and a rolled-up bandage in my hand, and I had to keep on opening and closing my fist. The blood was running up into the bottle and from there it was running into the other chap's left arm. He'd lost a leg – been down in No Man's Land. Gangrene had set in and they'd had to amputate it. Oh, he was like death! As white as a sheet! There was a nice American nurse stroking my forehead, because I was only a boy and so was he. I was lying watching the other bloke and, believe me, you could see the colour coming into that man's face. The American staff sewed me up – five stitches. Then they put us both back to bed and the nurse came along and brought me some champagne. They *did* make a fuss of me. Oh, I was the unsung hero!

In those days if somebody was thought to be dying – and this bloke certainly was! – they brought their relatives out to see them, and this boy's mother had come. She was a devout Christian woman, a Welsh woman, and she knelt at my bedside and prayed. Oh, I was embarrassed! She said, 'My dear boy, anything I've got in this world you can have' – because they'd told her I'd saved his life, you see. I said, 'Look, Ma, you've got your son, and that's *all* I want. I don't want no earthly possessions, I've done my duty, and he'd have done the same for me.'

But, of course, the best bit was that I only had a slight wound and I'd have been back up the line in no time, just a day or two later at the most. But next morning this Major Hopkins came over to me and the Sister was there, and they were both beaming and Major Hopkins said, 'Sonny boy' – you know how the Americans speak – 'you're going to be sent to England.' I said, 'Am I really?' – I could hardly believe it, you see. He said, 'Yes, you're being sent back to England on the next boat.' So I came home on a boat called the *Grantully Castle* and I came home 'boat sitting' – I wasn't a stretcher case. You had a label on you, 'BS'. I wouldn't have got home if it hadn't been for that blood transfusion. Oh no! I'd have been sent to convalescent camp for a fortnight's rest and back up the Bumper again.

To get to Blighty was the dream of every wounded soldier. Before the morning ward round the tension mounted until you could almost feel it hanging in the air. Who would be 'marked for Blighty'? Sister met the Medical Officer at the entrance to the ward, or as he ducked through the flap of the marquee; there was a low voiced consultation; then the round started – Sister, the MO, the Staff Nurse and often a VAD, trailing behind. It was a slow progress from bed to bed. Wounds had to be looked at, treatment discussed, decisions made. The seriously wounded were often too ill to care, but the others hoped against hope, at best for a 'ticket to Blighty' or at least for a few more days in hospital before being marked out for convalescent camp and the inevitable posting back up the line. The MO gave the verdict. Sister carried the labels and they were written out there and then. One tied to the end of the bed; the other round a pyjama button. BL – 'Boat lying', for the serious cases. BS – Boat sitting, for the fitter men, who nevertheless would require long convalescence; and red labels for the cases which required careful watching on the journey and which should have immediate attention on arrival.

There were two majors among the MOs, one in command of the medical side and the other surgical. One of them was very good-looking and I was always very thrilled when it was my duty to take him round the wards. It was his unenviable job to decide which of the patients were to be sent home, and often the major would ask me which I thought were the most deserving cases. They were usually obvious, so I generally took him to the right ones. Because of this the men used to think that I had some influence, and they started to say

Kit Dodsworth, VAD, No. 12 General Hospital, Rouen

that I had 'The Blighty Touch'. They were really superstitious about it. When we got to the side of the bed they would reach out and touch my apron. They seemed to think that if only they could touch my apron as I walked round, they would get home. It used to make me miserable the way they believed so firmly that I could work it for them – and, of course, I couldn't. They used to call a synovitis knee a 'Sign o'Blighty knee', and it certainly was serious enough to get them a trip home.

There was one boy I always remember. His wound was really on the mend, and on this one particular day the MO looked at him and wrote on his sheet that he was marked for convalescent camp. He was very young and I'd never seen such a stricken look on any face before or since. It haunted me all the way round the ward. Eventually I plucked up my courage, and in between patients I spoke to the MO about him and asked him to let him go home. He didn't say anything, just walked back across the ward, scored out what he'd written and said, 'Give him a ticket, Nurse. BS'. I'll never forget the look on his face.

The convalescent camp was not far away, and between the hospital and the camp was the road. All the drafts going up the line had to pass along it.

In the evening after supper we often went down to see the drafts going up. Often there would be one of our patients, either Eve's or mine, in the draft, and quite frequently an old patient would come to say goodbye before leaving and would ask us to go to the gate to wave him off. There was always someone at the gate, every time we went. There was a long straight road, lit by the light of the camp opposite and a little cluster of white-capped nurses standing by the gate. Then, in the distance, came the faint sound of men's voices singing and it got louder and louder until you could hear the sound of their marching feet. There was something terrible and heart-breaking about it. They used to sing 'Tipperary' as they passed, and now and again someone would shout, 'Are we downhearted?' and there was a huge, almost hysterical shout of 'No!'

They weren't new, excited troops. They were men who had been up before and they had all had any excitement knocked out of them by cruel experience. One evening I saw a man fall down and refuse to get up. The officer in charge of the draft came back and spoke to him. I couldn't hear what he said, but I heard the man moaning that he couldn't face it again. The Company halted for a moment, then the man got up slowly and went back into the ranks. The officer walked beside him as they moved off.

But that was only one occasion. Usually, as they passed the gate, they would shout, 'Goodbye, Sister, wish me luck!' or, 'Wish me a Blighty one next time. I'll be back again soon.'

One day a little Jock came back to me in the ward to say goodbye.

He had a small gunshot wound in his arm which had healed very quickly, to his great sorrow, and he was now warned for a draft going back to the line that night. Poor little fellow! He was only seventeen and had thought himself exceedingly clever when he had succeeded in fooling the recruiting people about his age. Now he was regretting it sadly. He sat down on an empty bed and cried like a baby. He simply could not face going over the top again. I did my best to comfort him and eventually all I could do was promise to be at the gate to say goodbye that night. When they went past he was singing with the rest. I couldn't bear to look at them. As soon as the draft had gone by I rushed back to my tent to cry in private. It all seemed so futile. We were doing our best to get them well and then they had to go back and get another wound, or worse. We used to call that boy 'Baby Jock' in the ward. After he went back to the line I heard from him, and it was a great relief to know that he had been sent to the ammunition column. I felt much happier when I knew that he was in no great danger.

I hated it this afternoon. There was one boy who couldn't have been more than twenty. His seven brothers were all killed and his mother had died – he said it was from grief. He wasn't ill enough to be marked for Blighty. His quartermaster-sergeant is in the next bed to his and told me it was all true. Fenny was up, and I shall never forget seeing him sitting reading by the stove. The sun was shining through the little tail window above the stove pipe, making a brilliant patch of sunshine in the dark marquee, and there was Fenny in his blue suit and red tie. Behind him was a blue bowl full of red and purple anemones, and then later his anxious ugly face waiting for his fate to be sealed by the MO. He isn't fit, but he isn't ill and it had to be convalescent camp and 'Up the Line' once more.

Kitty Kenyon, VAD, No. 4 General Hospital, Camiers (her diary)

'Is it a Blighty?' 'Is it a Blighty?' It was all a matter of luck. When the MO looked particularly harassed, when there was a big 'push' in the offing, when as many beds as possible had to be cleared to make way for the convoys of fresh casualties that would inevitably pour in, there was a very good chance that a man who was on the road to recovery but not yet fit enough to discharge to convalescent camp would make it to Blighty.

Blighty. Home. Respite. The blessed relief after months of fighting made it almost worth the pain and discomfort of a wound. Eventually, of course, you would recover. Eventually, they would send you back. But that would be another day. In the meantime, as you hobbled on to the hospital ship it didn't do to think about that. There was time enough to think of tomorrow when it came.

Chapter Eight

The course of the camp hospital day was punctuated by bugle calls that rang out over the camp and bounced back from the hills behind. They sounded for reveille, for breakfast, for lunch and for supper; they sounded for 'Lights out' at the end of the day and, whatever the hour, the summons to 'Fall in' when a convoy arrived. At No. 22 General Hospital the five buglers took up their position in a field deafeningly close to the doctors' quarters on the southern edge of the camp. But Dan Reardon, caught up in the fascination of his new life, and absorbed in the interest of the surgical work, was willing to put up with discomfort, and even with the eternal bugle calls blasting directly into his ears. He wrote magnanimously to his 'Darling Minnie', 'It is interesting to hear the trumpet calls, especially Tattoo at 9.30 and Taps at 10'.

It was the sound of the Last Post that drove into the heart. Just down the coast, on the open slopes by the sea, was the fast-growing cemetery where they buried the men who died in the hospitals.

Captain
Harold
Deardon,
RAMC

After lunch today I went for a walk for some fresh air, and coming past the cemetery I saw there was an officer's funeral on. It was a very simple affair and yet awfully impressive. The coffin was wheeled up on a little hand-bier covered with the Union Jack, and behind it was marching a firing squad of about twenty men. When they got near the grave the coffin was carried down and the soldiers formed up by the graveside while the service was read. There were two of the boy's people there, an elderly lady and a younger girl, and they stood almost alone in a little space on the other side of the grave from the soldiers' ranks.

So far as the relatives of the wounded were concerned the Army had a heart, and if they could not afford to pay for the journey their expenses were met by the public purse. There was a standard formula for the telegrams which were automatically sent out if a man was on the Dangerously Ill List:

REGRET INFORM YOU PRIVATE SMITH 19 MANCHESTER REGIMENT DANGEROUSLY ILL AT THIS HOSPITAL. IF YOU WISH TO VISIT HIM AND ARE UNABLE TO BEAR EXPENSE TAKE THIS TELEGRAM TO THE NEAREST POLICE STATION.

Every day small groups of anxious relatives arrived on the Channel ferries at Boulogne, often to face a long train journey to Rouen or to a hospital on the Normandy coast. Sometimes there was a happy ending. At No. 4 General Hospital, Kitty Kenyon spent many nights by the bedside of Private Linton before he took a joyously unexpected turn for the better.

I'm able to sit in the bunk again now that Linton is so much better. Captain Walker said to the Night Super some nights ago that he didn't think he'd pull through. So we're awfully bucked over him! His wife is out and arrived just when he was first beginning to be better. She came at 9 pm when I was on duty, and Night Super went and told him and then I took her in. His face! And when she'd gone back to the relatives' hostel he simply couldn't stop smiling, and at last turned on his side and fell asleep like a child. 'Some wimmen do get excited,' he said to me next day when I was giving him his breakfast. 'She must 'a bin excited to come rushing across the water like that!' The darling!

Kitty Kenyon, VAD, No. 4 General Hospital, Camiers (her diary)

But all too often the relatives reached a soldier's bedside only to watch him breathe his last or, sadder still, too late to see him at all. If a wife or a parent was known to be on the way the funeral would be delayed, so that at least there would be some comfort in being able to follow a boy to his grave, to see him buried with honour, to hear the last staccato salute of the firing party and the notes of the Last Post.

For weeks after every 'big push', wherever you went in the base hospitals you could hear faintly in the distance the sound of the bugles drifting inland on the sea wind. Sometimes they sounded twenty times or more in a single day.

Our chaplain told me he attended thirteen funerals yesterday and sixteen the day before. This is the side that those who are not here do not see. They are buried in a military cemetery a mile or so away. It is a beautiful but tragic place with its rows and rows of white crosses. There are fresh flowers on some of the graves which have been sent by the relatives.

Dr D. B. Reardon, 1st Harvard Medical Unit (his diary, 8 August 1915)

That week there were many funerals of men brought down from the bitter fighting in the salient around Ypres where, hard on the heels of the terrible poison gas, a new horror had erupted. At the tip of the salient was the most miserable, the most desolate, the most violent and dangerous spot on the Western Front. When the British and Germans had started fighting for it a few short months before, they had called it Hooge Château; now they called it Hooge Crater. So bitter was the fighting at this point where the line had crystallized, so intense the bombing and shelling, so pulverizing the mining and counter-mining, that nothing remained but a vast pit in which a whole battalion of soldiers might have been drawn up with room to spare. Here the tenacity of the British troops was tested to the limit, for Hooge, little more than a mile from what remained of the gates of Ypres, was the last outpost that protected it. If the line broke here, or even gave way, the city would fall into the hands of the Germans.

In trenches which were battered every day almost out of existence by incessant shellfire, and patched up every night with sandbags into some semblance of protection, the Tommies held on, even attacked and captured the first line of German trenches in an effort to inch the enemy back. The attacking German troops brought up their new 'wonder weapon' to burn them out. The petrol ran from back packs through rubber hoses ending in long, steel nozzles. Out of the nozzles spurted a vicious stream of liquid fire.

It was The Rifle Brigade, in tenacious possession of the newly captured German trenches, which bore the appalling brunt of the first liquid fire attack, but the 8th Battalion of the King's Royal Rifle Corps on the fringe of the attack came off nearly as badly. Few of them survived it, but those who were dragged burnt, blackened or bleeding and yet still breathing from the inferno, together with the wounded who survived the savage fighting to the right and left of them, made up the second convoy to arrive at No. 22 General Hospital at Camiers. The badly burned who were still alive at the end of the journey were treated in a special ward, but the soldiers with 'straightforward' wounds who were brought to C6 Surgical Ward and into the care of Dr Reardon had nightmare tales to tell of the fighting. They told them again and again.

The American doctors listened incredulously, and Dan Reardon, concerned but not astonished that his patients woke screaming with nightmares, suggested that they should write about their experiences. It was a shrewd therapeutic move, and it kept the men busy through the weary days of painful convalescence – scribbling, with pencils on paper supplied by the YMCA hut, drafting, scoring out and eventually proudly handing over fair copies in 'best writing'. Dr Reardon collected the accounts, read them aloud to the other doctors in the Mess, studied them again by the light of the candle-lantern in his tent, shook his head over them in disbelief, packed them carefully in his valise to take back to America and kept the accounts for the rest of his life.*

---

* He kept them without fully realizing the unique historical value of first-hand eyewitness descriptions written while small details were still fresh in the mind. Now, at the author's suggestion, his son Judge P. C. Reardon (the 'Paul' of Dr Reardon's affectionate letters) has most generously placed the accounts, together with other letters and the diary relating to his father's service with the British army, in the care of the Department of Documents in the Imperial War Museum.

I arrived in France with a draft of fifty men from the 7th Battalion, King's Royal Rifle Corps, on 30 June and was wounded on 30 July.

We had only been in occupation of the trench for two hours, and had scarcely had time to get our bearings when the enemy commenced a most terrific artillery bombardment in which they used every conceivable variety of projectile and which lasted for several hours. There was also heavy rifle fire, and liquid fire was used for the first time. Its appearance added to the disconcerting effect produced by the terrible gunfire to which we were being subjected. . . .

After the enemy took the trench on our left and burnt it out and all the men in it, they were able to get round behind us and were preparing to attack us in the rear, which would have meant complete annihilation. But the danger was seen in the nick of time by a Second Lieutenant who was a mere lad of nineteen. Without the slightest hesitation he leapt over the back of the trench and called on the men near him to follow. About a dozen did so, and although the enemy's fire was withering and they kept falling as they went they charged the Germans and the danger was averted. . . .

One of our bombers, when passing us on his way down the trench for a further supply of bombs, shouted that he had got hold of the helmet of a German who'd come too near, but he had had to leave it for the time being where the battle was raging between the German bombers and ours. Another man came past on his way to the bomb dump and was complaining that the other chap had taken the helmet from him. But neither of these poor fellows got away with their precious souvenirs, as the whole party was wiped out after standing their ground to the last man and the last bomb. I was hit in the morning, but I understand that the few remaining men in the battalion, after their terrible experiences and exertions of the morning, joined another battalion in an attack on the enemy in the afternoon to regain some lost ground. The attempt was unsuccessful, but it was a fine example of dogged pluck and dauntless courage.

The incidents I have quoted are just a few of those I witnessed that day.

Signed, T. J. Harrington

25 September 1915

From the account of Rifleman T. J. Harrington, 7th Battalion King's Royal Rifle Corps

I am a rifleman in the 8th Battalion, King's Royal Rifles, and I just write my little experience in the trenches at Hooge and the attack we made on 30 July. We had been in the trenches for seven days and on the eighth day, about 1.30 am, we were relieved by another battalion of our regiment. We were all glad to get out of the trenches. Every man was dead beat and tired, but the same tired look was on the officers' faces. We trudged along at a slow pace. Just as we arrived at

From the account of Rifleman Arthur Dickings, 8th Battalion, King's Royal Rifle Corps the camp we were shelled very heavy, and our own guns commenced talking, and very loudly too. I caught a glance at our officer's face and I saw something had happened. I overheard him say, 'I believe these Germans have made an attack'. It wasn't many minutes afterwards his words came true, for the order was given, 'Stand to. These Germans have made an attack on our trenches as soon as we left. It is up to every man to do his best.' 'I know you're all very tired,' the officer said, 'and had seven weary days, but something must be done, and *will* be done.'

We lined up and the order was given to load magazines with five rounds. We then marched off until we came to the field we had to cross leading to the trenches. And I tell you, it was broad daylight by this time, which made it more difficult for us and better for the German aeroplanes that were overhead. We crossed the field in extended order and the shells were dropping everywhere. It was while crossing the field that we lost our doctor. A shell exploded very close to him, carrying away his head and shoulders. We had to push on, under orders even after such a sight as this. We lay in the woods very near the trenches for some time awaiting further orders. By this time the Germans had been counter-attacked by another regiment (I believe them to be the Irish Rifles), who drove them back. As we lay in the woods the bombardment was terrible on both sides. Shells were pouring into the woods, breaking down large trees and splintering branches.

By this time we were getting very hungry, as we had not had a decent meal for many days. We only had biscuits which we had got at the last minute. The next order given was 'We make an attack on these Germans at 2.45 pm.' Well! It was simply agony waiting for the final minute, but it came. Our officer called out, 'Sixteen, fifteen, fourteen, thirteen sections advance'. Then it was just one wild yell, several chaps losing their heads and I thought I should lose mine, for then a lyddite shell burst some yards away and the fumes that ascended were terrible. I thought I should choke for the minute. It was Hell, nothing more. . . .

As I pushed on I came in contact with our officer. There he was, directing orders under fire, as cool as you please. Then the barriers of sandbags were taken down. They called out for swordsmen. A chum and I fixed bayonets, and went over into the German trench, but there were no Germans to be seen. Just then the order came, 'Advance as far as you can and barricade the trench.' We had to stay in the trenches. They had to be held at all costs. We stayed until dark. I lost sight of many of the officers, but the news came that our adjutant was killed. Our captain was shot through both legs and my officer was shot through one of his legs. First Lieutenant Watson killed, First Lieutenant Bourdillon wounded (I don't know what part of his body) and a number of sergeants killed. All my own mates

went. One sergeant came to me in the trench and remarked, 'Dickings − you're a section on your own now'.

As we went out of the line I happened to be in front, and Assistant
Captain Rothschild asked me on returning how I felt. I said, 'I don't
feel well at all, sir.' He was an awful colour himself. He said, 'I'm sure
you don't feel well. You all did splendid for the first attack the 8th
had ever made.' He had to leave us owing to a nervous breakdown.
Two days later I was wounded myself.

God, bring this War to a Speedy End.

I stay in hospital at present and I am comfortable and doing very
well.

Signed: Arthur Dickings,
8th Battalion, King's Royal Rifles

16 August 1915

In all my experience I have never seen anything like Hooge. We went
into the line on 9 August and there were still British and Germans
dead, lying all over the place, and no chance of burying them, for the
enemy keeps a continuous artillery fire both day and night. I often
wonder if this position is really worth the price paid for it in casualties.

     *From the
account of
Sergeant
J. Beaumont,
The Leinster
Regiment*

Now at present I'm in the American hospital at Camiers, France,
where I soon expect to leave to join my regiment again. This is the
second time I have been wounded. I must mention that the doctors
and nurses of this hospital are extremely nice people and don't seem
to carry the same amount of importance about them as our Military
Medical Staff. In a hospital like this, one seems to be more at home,
and I believe patients recover much more quickly than when treated
in a stiff military manner.

But as the pace quickened on the Western Front and the flow of
casualties increased, and everyone was thrown willy-nilly into the
never-ending work of tending ever-increasing numbers of wounded,
even in the British hospitals the 'stiff military manner' was on the wane.
The army nursing sisters who just a few months ago had been so doubtful about the usefulness of untrained VADs were now working alongside
them, treating them as colleagues, and of necessity giving them more
responsibility than the sisters or the VADs themselves would ever have
believed to be possible only a short time ago.

There was only the briefest of respites before the order came, 'Clear
the hospitals.' It was the eve of the battle of Loos. In yet another attempt
to break the German line before the winter set in, the troops were
moving into position a little way to the north-east where the black slag
heaps jutted from the flat northern plains. They were working overtime
in the hospitals, sending out convoys of recovering wounded, scrubbing
out the wards, making up the empty beds, snatching a few hours' rest

when they could. The only certain outcome of the battle was that in every hospital from Calais to Le Havre, every bed that was available would be needed.

But at least the wounded who arrived at a base hospital would have had some rudimentary attention, and would be to some extent cleaned up. It was in the casualty clearing stations a few miles behind the line that the worst of the pressure would be felt, as the wounded were brought in straight from the battlefield. It was there that help would be most badly needed, and it had to be skilled help. Ten days before the battle, many VADs learned with not a little anxiety that the Ward Sister had been ordered up the line, and that they would have to cope as best they could with such help as the Sister of other wards could spare. VADs were not alone in dreading the Sister's departure.

Sister Grace Buffard, Territorial Force Nursing Service

While I was waiting to go up to a clearing station I had five young-sters together in one hut whom I'd been looking after for quite some time. They were just young boys, but officers. Baby officers! I don't suppose there was one over twenty-one. One boy was wounded on the abdomen. It was getting better and there was strapping on it, sticky strapping like Elastoplast, which we'd only just begun to use. And one morning he knew that he had to have the strapping removed and he was a bit nervous about it. He said, 'Sister, does it hurt?' And I got hold of the end of it and pulled and said, 'No. You just pull it off like that.' 'Oh,' he said, 'is that what you do?' I said, 'Yes. That's what you do!' And of course it had been done while he was still wondering about it.

When I got my movement orders, they knew about it, of course, and they had given the orderly some money to buy me a present at the shops in Le Touquet. It was a little white curly-haired toy dog. They said it was to guard my tent when I went up the line. Round the dog's neck was an envelope with a poem in it which they'd made up between them. The real joke was in the title, because I'm very tall. I was probably the tallest of all the girls.

TO *LITTLE* SISTER
From No. 16

Have you seen our Little Sister?
Officers can ne'er resist her.
She will flay and burn and blister
Someone every day.
Does she tend poor wounded wretches?
No! Their wounds she probes and stretches
Till the brandy flask she fetches
When they faint away.

Not for them the gentle touches
Of a Matron or a Duchess –
Little Sister simply BUTCHERS
Everyone she gets.
Rubber gloves her hands adorning
Give to us a daily warning
That the bone she cleans each morning
Never, never sets.

Though our misery's unending,
Though with pain our wounds she's tending,
Yet with courage still unbending
We can bear the strain.
But if once we woke and missed her
We should cry with tears that blister,
'Have you seen our Little Sister?
Send her back again!'

The Sisters moved up the line to the casualty clearing stations. The bombardment started. The troops went over the top and the battle of Loos began.

When the convoys started to come in, they were very different from any we had seen before. The casualty stations simply couldn't cope and many of the wounded arrived with their first field dressings on. Stretchers were scarce, and it was no uncommon sight to see one wounded man almost carrying another. Many of them who were walking were in no condition to do so. There was one man who came to my tents who had a large piece of shrapnel in his side and at least one fractured rib. One of the other men told me that he'd seen that man put on a stretcher three times, and each time he had given it up to someone he thought worse than himself. Of course it was madness – he might so easily have shifted that bit of shrapnel into his heart or some equally vital part. As it was he was terribly ill, and at one time we were very doubtful if he would live. He was a splendid man. His name was Robertson and he was in the Cameron Highlanders, and his main topic of conversation when he began to get better was his Commanding Officer, Cameron of Lochiel. No one ever had, or according to him ever could have, such a wonderful man to command them. Robertson simply worshipped him.

Most of the new patients were Kitchener's Army men and they'd never been in hospital before. They were horrified when I told them that I was going to bath them. One man with a smashed leg assured me that he could easily get to the bath-house if one of the others helped him. Another badly wounded man actually succeeded in getting to the bath-house while my back was turned, but he had to be

Kit Dodsworth, VAD, No. 12 General Hospital, Rouen

carried back in a state of collapse. After I had bathed him he was very penitent and promised that he would never funk it again. They didn't funk the battle but they were desperately embarrassed about having a girl to wash them.

We were terribly overworked. One Sister and I had six tents to cope with alone. The orderly was fully occupied with the men's kits when he wasn't carrying the stretchers of the new arrivals. Normally, when a new patient was admitted, the orderly undressed him and took his clothes to be de-loused; but in this rush I very often had to see to the undressing of the men myself. Their things, as can be imagined, were in a pretty foul condition, and as all the pockets had to be emptied before they were taken to be de-loused, it was almost impossible to avoid the creatures swarming all over them.

For over a fortnight we worked unceasingly, just as hard as we could go. The Sister of my ward handed over to me three of the tents, and told me to carry on with them and appeal to her only if something unusual occurred or if I were in any difficulty. She came round and inspected them twice a day, otherwise I had complete charge. There was no off-duty time for over a fortnight and we slept with one ear open in case the 'Fall In' went, which meant the arrival of a fresh convoy of patients. We had no time to feel tired. It was just a case of rushing through the work and, when a spare moment arrived, flying up to the Mess to get a meal. Often we didn't get supper until we came off duty at about eleven o'clock at night. By then we were too tired to eat.

One night, very late when I was going to bed, I discovered that I had collected some of the notorious 'grey backs', as the lice were called. I found them when I was brushing my hair, and I was so exhausted that I just collapsed in tears. It seemed the last straw. I sat up nearly all night crying and washing my long hair again and again in disinfectant. I felt as if I'd never be clean again.

After the rush, rather belatedly, in about the middle of October, a new lot of trained nurses were sent to us straight from the Cambridge Hospital in Aldershot, They were very smart and grand, and very critical of our rough and ready ways. One of these new people was sent to my ward. Sister told me to show her round myself, as she would be taking over my tents and (as Sister pointed out) I really knew more about the patients and their treatment than she did. The poor lady was horror-stricken to think that she would have to keep the linen in packing cases stood on end. 'In the Cambridge Hospital,' she said, 'we had wonderful linen cupboards. I never imagined we should have to put up with this sort of thing.' I'm afraid that I was a bit irritated and couldn't resist pointing out that we were, after all, on Active Service.

Dorothy Nicol,   It was quite different from a military hospital in England. There was no running water, every drop had to be brought in a bucket from a boiler outside. There was no Sisters' Room, just a small table at the centre of the ward with a camp stool. Behind it were several sugar boxes which had been converted into medicine chests, and standing at right-angles to the side of the marquee was a large wooden table for the sterilizer and for larger containers to stand on after they had been burned out with the methylated spirit that had sterilized them, with a biscuit tin as a windshield. We had a wooden trolley, but that was about all.

VAD, No 11
General
Hospital,
Camiers

The so-called kitchen was at the far end of the ward, and there was a large table where the men who were up had their meals. There were several wire cages at this end of the marquee which I discovered to my horror were rat traps. Outside the marquee was a bell tent, where the orderly left all the articles which would normally be kept in the sick-bay of an ordinary hospital. At night the marquee was lit by electric light, but in the daytime, however dark it was, we only used hurricane lamps. The gloom was added to by the fact that the beds were covered with brown or red blankets. White counterpanes would have been out of the question here.

How I longed for the bright wards I'd left behind in the Military Hospital in Bramshot. It now seemed to be the acme of comfort. I pictured the light, dazzling light it seemed in retrospect, with heaps of windows, shining taps, the floors dry and draught-proof and, the greatest luxury of all, unlimited quantities of hot water. A proper kitchen. A bathroom . . .

It was all very different from what the newly arrived Sisters had been used to. I had become rather spoilt, as most of us had, because during the rush there was no time for differences between trained staff and mere VADs. We each did what we could, and it was no uncommon sight to see a Sister scrubbing a locker top in one ward while a couple of tents away a VAD would be doing a dressing. The new Sister would stand none of that sort of thing, and I was quickly told that in future I was to give no more medicines, nor was I to presume to take a temperature. There was doubtless plenty of scrubbing and cleaning that I could do, declared Sister. In the end she had to give in a bit, with rather bad grace, because the men were furious about it. There was one boy I had had all through the rush, who had been very seriously ill with pneumonia and pericarditis. He had needed really careful nursing and was still on the Dangerously Ill List. He got terribly upset when I was forbidden to do anything for him. He refused to let the new Sister near him. She just had to give in, but she hated me for it.

But the thing that upset them most was that we were always called 'Sister'. Soon after the arrival of the new batch of trained nurses, it was posted up in orders that in future VADs were to be called

Kit
Dodsworth,
VAD, No. 12
General
Hospital,
Rouen

'Nurse'. But the men went on calling us 'Sister', and the real Sisters didn't like it a bit.

The amateur nurses regarded the new ruling as professional jealousy. The trained nurses' point of view was based in professional pride. A nurse's training was hard and arduous, and the worst paid of all professions. A Probationer, before the war, was lucky if she earned £12 in her first back-breaking year of menial, grinding work, and in some of the big teaching hospitals, where there was keen competition for places, Probationers not only had to pay a premium for their training but received no salary at all for the first two years. There were long hours of duty and long years of study before a nurse inched her way towards the coveted professional qualification and an appointment as a Staff Nurse. Even then, it might take five, six, even ten more years of hard and dedicated service before she earned promotion to the exalted rank of Sister. It was not surprising that she was proud of her status and that she was reluctant to share the hard-earned title with mere amateurs, however obliging and hard-working. But the wounded Tommy, who regarded any girl in uniform as his personal angel of mercy, cared nothing for the finer delineations of professional etiquette. It was all one, and they were all 'Sister' to him.

With so many volunteers who had nothing to do with nursing wearing quasi-nursing or Red Cross uniform, the use of the word 'Sister' became almost universal. Red Cross workers dished out tea at railway stations, handed out comforts on hospital trains, helped in canteens. Red Cross clerks and administrative workers whose job was to try to trace the missing were often seen in hospital wards interviewing men who had been in an action in which a soldier had disappeared. Red Cross workers took charge of post offices in camp hospitals and distributed mail round the wards. Even the flag-sellers the soldier met in the streets when he was on leave in Blighty were frequently dressed in a uniform that was indistinguishable from the outdoor dress of a nurse. What was he to call them? The universal appellations of 'Matey' or 'Chum' would obviously not do. 'Madam' was much too formal. 'Miss' had a cheap teashop ring about it. The answer, which offended no one and flattered some, was to call everybody 'Sister'. But just as the exalted personages who actually *were* Nursing Sisters were irritated by VADs sharing the title, the nursing VADs were equally jealous of their own standing as nurses and were anxious not to be mistaken for anything else.

Mabel Bone, VAD, Staffordshire 2

I had been wearing a uniform similar to a nurse's outfit when I was working with the hospital supplies depot, but when I reached the age of seventeen I was able to join the VAD and work part-time in the local hospital. We had a large red cross on the bib of our aprons and they looked very bright and new. We used to bleach them to a faded pink, so that they'd look more like the well-laundered aprons of the VADs who'd been working in hospitals since the beginning. We still went on collecting for the Red Cross, and another VAD and myself used to go in uniform to a football match on a Saturday to collect from the crowd. Of course, we wore our uniforms, as everybody did, and we used to sprinkle ourselves liberally with carbolic or ether, just so that there would be a hospital smell about us. We were so proud of being *real* nurses that we wanted to everyone to know it!

In the big military hospitals where the hierarchy was unmistakable and discipline much stronger than in the happy-go-lucky atmosphere of hospitals in France, the situation was more delicate. The patients could be forgiven for their ignorance, but the orderlies were supposed to know better. Most of the orderlies were middle-aged men, well over military age, who had volunteered for this hard and taxing work as medical orderlies in the Royal Army Medical Corps. In their ranks were retired businessmen, artists, sculptors, stockbrokers, writers. Corporal Ward Muir, in private life, was a successful novelist and journalist. 'For the duration' he was serving as a orderly at the 3rd London General Hospital in Wandsworth and, like all the orderlies, spent his days at the beck and call of the nursing staff.

The old hand knows better than to address a mere nurse as Sister – if the genuine Sister is within earshot. Unfortunately a certain complication here obtrudes itself. There is a being called the Staff Nurse. She wears a Cape (one speaks the word Cape with a capital). Because of her Cape she resembles, at a slight distance, that other but more august Cape-wearer, the veritable Sister. Closer inspection reveals the trifling detail that the Staff Nurse, though Caped, is not Striped. Sister sports two stripes on her cuff; Staff Nurse has none.

Both ladies frequently roll up their sleeves. How are you to fathom whether there are stripes on a cuff when the cuff is crumpled in a tight screw around the top of a shapely forearm, the owner of which is performing deft miracles with forceps and fomentations? It is a hopeless fix for the newcomer. He will be wise to lie low and say nothing, until he has ascertained from some informative neighbour the straight tip as to which is Sister and which is Staff Nurse. He can trim his sails accordingly, addressing the Sister as Sister always and the Staff Nurse as Sister sometimes. When Sister and Staff Nurse are both present and he is addressing the latter, he must contrive to use no title. If he calls her Nurse she will not like it and, if he calls her Sister, Sister will not like it. So there you are.

When I was first put into a ward to serve as an orderly I was instructed beforehand that the only person to be entitled Sister was the Goddess with the Stripes. Eager to be correct, I addressed the Staff Nurse as Nurse. Her lips tightened. In a frigid voice she

Corporal Ward Muir, RAMC, 3rd London General Hospital, Wandsworth

informed me of the significance of the Cape; all Cape-wearers held a status equivalent to that of a commissioned officer in the Army, and must be treated as such by privates such as myself. All Cape-wearers were to be accorded the proper courtesies and addressed as Sister. Finally I was dismissed with an injunction to hurry and finish my incompleted task.

'Very good, Sister,' I replied.

Half an hour later, I was beckoned aside into the ward kitchen by Sister herself. She gently apprised me that, as I was a new recruit, she thought perhaps I was not yet aware of the accurate modes of address and the etiquette customary in a military hospital. Et cetera, et cetera. She had overheard me call the Staff Nurse, 'Sister'. . . . Enough!

Ida
Haigh, VAD,
No. 5
Northern
Hospital,
Leicester

In the military hospital where I worked, my Sister wouldn't even allow VADs to be called Nurse. We were 'Miss So-and-So' and that was that. In the early days you couldn't really blame them, because we were very ham-handed, and my Sister was extraordinarily charming and kind under the circumstances. When I had only been a few days on the ward I dropped a jar on to the glass shelf of the dressing trolley and broke it. There was an almighty crash and everything went all over the floor. Of course, I was shaking in my shoes. Sister Woods looked at me over her glasses and said quite mildly, 'Miss Haigh, you are *not* an unmixed blessing.' She let me off very lightly, although she must have been annoyed because every piece of equipment had to be accounted for, and it was tedious and time-consuming for Sister to have to indent for new things and explain how they had got lost. You had to have the exact quantity of everything, and no less and certainly no more!

We were always having breakages with all those piles of washing up, and so Sister had 'acquired' extra plates from somewhere. When inspection day came round she had to get rid of these plates that were over the quota, so she sent me off with another nurse to hide them. We couldn't think where to put them, and eventually, as the inspecting officer was going to arrive any minute, we put them in the cistern of the WC. Unfortunately, in the middle of the inspection, someone who wasn't in the secret pulled the chain – and that was the end of the plates!

Kit
Dodsworth,
VAD, No. 12
General
Hospital,
Rouen

Thermometers were my great trouble, and I broke so many that the dispensary sergeant began to disbelieve my excuses. One day I was taking temperatures and was holding a jar with six thermometers in it when there was a sudden flash of lightning, followed immediately by a loud crash of thunder. I started violently and dropped the jar on the floor – so, bang went all the thermometers. The next morning I went to the dispensary and told my sad tale to the sergeant. He roared with laughter and said that I could not possibly send in a ridiculous excuse like that. I said that it was the truth, but he persisted that I must think of a better one than that. At last he promised to think of some suitable ones himself, and a few days later I was in the dispensary and found the colonel just going through the sheets. As luck would have it, he had just arrived at the absurd list of excuses that had been invented for me by the sergeant. I couldn't understand why he grinned at me the way he did, but I found out later! The sergeant had a very vivid imagination and there were six of the most impossible excuses I ever heard. One was that a patient had bitten one in half. Another, that a patient had fallen out of bed with the thermometer in his mouth. I was ragged about it for days after, but I never dared to tell the truth because the poor man had really tried to do his best for me.

The patients were strongly conscious of what it meant to be an underdog. 'Laugh and the Nurse laughs with you,' remarked one wag. 'Sister enters, and you laugh alone.'

It was a little unfair on Sister, who was responsible for the overall smooth running of the ward and realized the dangers of what she looked on as undue familiarity with the patients.

Matron was like a battleship as she sailed down the corridors from ward to ward, and if you saw her approaching, you stood rigid until she had rolled away. Every morning we reported to her for uniform inspection and orders, including how to behave on the wards. No showing of ankles. Black shoes and stocking, white spotless aprons, collar, cuffs and cap, and on no account be familiar with the patient. Treat them well, look after them well, but eyes down and remember they have womenfolk of their own.

Maisie Bowcott, Nursing Probationer

We were allowed to talk to the Tommies, but they kept a very close eye on us. The House Sister didn't like me and I couldn't do anything right. The uniform dresses reached the ground, and apart from the fact that they were awkward to work in, the skirts got shorter as the war went on. Of course, we wanted to wear the fashionable short skirts like everybody else. So we used to hitch them up with our belts so that they were calf length. House Sister came up one morning, looked at me very disapprovingly and said as she went out, 'Nurse. Lengthen your dress by at least two inches.' The boys asked, 'What was that she told you?' I said, 'She told me to shorten my dress two inches.' And they said, 'Oh good!'

Kathleen Yarwood, VAD, Dearnley Military Hospital, Birch Hill, Rochdale

As soon as we arrived at Rouen we were formally presented to the colonel, and then Matron gave us a lecture on exactly how we were expected to behave.

Kathleen Rhodes, VAD, No. 11

Stationary
Hospital,
Rouen

'You must remember that you are on active service and these are the rules:

1. You are not allowed to have civilian clothes in your possession and you must not leave your own part of the hospital.

2. You are not allowed to go out to luncheon or dinner – or to go riding, driving or boating with anyone of the opposite sex, and *no* dancing!

3. You must always be in camp by 7 pm.

If you do not obey these regulations you will be sent home at once, and remember that there are hundreds of would-be nurses in England who would gladly take your places. You are none of you indispensable.'

There were hundreds, thousands of girls in Blighty who were only too anxious to serve abroad. Now, in the autumn of 1915 they were to have their chance. All reservations about sending VADs on active service were swept aside. Everyone was needed and the handful of VADs who had gone to help on the Western Front had proved their worth. Now, anyone who had had three months' hospital experience at home, and who was twenty-three or over, would have the chance to go abroad – either to hospitals in France or to join the harassed, overworked, trained Sisters and Nurses who were struggling to care for the awful flood of sick and wounded from Gallipoli and Mesopotamia in hospitals in the Middle East.

Chapter Nine

On the battlefields of Gallipoli the real enemy was the terrain of the peninsula itself. It was a dry land of sand and rock, of almost vertical cliffs, narrow beaches, deep ravines and gullies. Under the devastating fire from the well-placed Turkish positions that rained down on the men of the Gallipoli force as they attempted to land on 25 April, it was something of a feat to have clambered on to the peninsula at all. By the end of eight months, most of the objectives which were intended to have been secured at the end of the first day had not even been approached.

Clinging to the clifftop gullies, scrambling over precipitous heights, digging in as best they could in the arid earth, the soldiers hung on to the precarious toeholds they had consolidated in the first hours of the landing – steaming, sweating, dying of wounds, and tormented by a raging thirst which unsuitable rations only exacerbated. It became a bitter joke that the best way of beating the Turks would be to shoot over unlimited supplies of salt bully beef and dry army biscuits and wait for them to die of thirst.

Worst of all was the disease. The troops were decimated by fevers and dysentery, and the difficulty of evacuating the sick and wounded loomed as large as the problem of landing desperately needed supplies on the shallow coves of a rugged coastline where there were neither piers nor jetties, causeways nor even the slightest protection from the shells and bullets of which, unlike the British, the Turks seemed to have an inexhaustible supply. Hospital ships were anchored in the Bay of Mudros. But they were too large to be of use in the peninsula, and small ships had to be used as ferries to evacuate the casualties. Mary Fitzgibbon served on one that plied between Helles at the tip of the peninsula and the base of Mudros.

We never got off the ship at all. They brought the boys down on stretchers or on muleback, down these steep paths on the cliffs that were almost vertical. We could see them from where we were. We spent weeks ploughing up and down the Dardanelles on the *Essequibo*, a small ship, one of the Royal Mail ships. Small as it was, we couldn't go in near the shore because there were no harbours, no landing places. They brought the boys out on barges and laid them in stretchers that were really just shallow wooden boxes, two at a time, and then they were swung on to our ship by a crane. Most of the time

Sister Mary Fitzgibbon, QAIMNS (R)

we were under shell fire. The wounded were easy enough to deal with, but the sick! They were in a terrible state, all suffering from dysentery and enteric. Their insides had simply turned to water, and all they had been able to do for them on shore was to tie their trousers tight round their legs with pieces of string. We had to rip their trousers off with scissors, and then we washed the boys as best we could. We couldn't do very much for them because we only had them for a few hours – just the length of time it would take to get them back to Mudros. Of course, they were all running a high temperature and they wanted to drink, drink, drink. All we could do was to strip them off, clean them up and put them to bed. We didn't have many actual beds, they were mostly stretchers, and the boys were laid out all along the decks. We had to step over them, just lying there, as we tried to attend to them. Then we simply sailed back to Mudros, where they were put on hospital ships. From there they went to hospitals in Alexandria or in Malta and we set off again back to Gallipoli to pick up more. We had wounded as well, of course – because there were many wounded – but it's the sick I remember. I'll never forget them. Just pouring with dysentery – sick, miserable, dehydrated and in terrible pain. It was pitiful to see them, so weak, and blood and water pouring out of them. We had medicine that we gave them, but we could really do very little for them.

The original plan to attack Gallipoli had been born of the need to try somehow to break the deadlock on the Western Front. As far back as January it had seemed that instead of committing the New Armies of Great Britain and her Dominions of Australia and New Zealand to the stalemate of the trenches, there might be another area where they could stab Germany in the back and force her to divert her forces from the west, where they stood impassive against France and Britain, and from the east where they faced the Russians. The various possibilities were mulled over. Greece and Italy were still hovering on the neutral sidelines. If Greece were to throw in her lot with the Allies, it would be possible to send a force through Salonika to relieve tiny Serbia, still holding out although on the verge of collapse. On the other hand, if the Dardanelles, which was the sea route to Constantinople, could be secured by the Allies, then Constantinople itself could be taken. The Turks would then be knocked out of the war, and the Germans and Austrians would be forced to turn about to defend their back door.

But the plans were made hastily. The commanders responsible for its execution, and the soldiers who had to achieve the results, were thrust into a situation about which they were ill-informed, ill-prepared and ill-equipped. An abortive naval attack had given the Turks ample warning that a landing was likely to be attempted, and thousands of men had been moved into the peninsula to man the fortifications and trenches sited and disposed by the German staff officers who were attached to the Turkish forces. It was impossible for the Allies to advance.

Towards the end of May, with little to show for the valiant efforts of the British, Australian and New Zealand, and French troops who were fighting an impossible battle in alien terrain against formidable odds, London debated the question. Should the campaign be continued, should it be intensified, or should it be abandoned? There was a sharp division of opinion. Winston Churchill, who had been one of the prime enthusiasts for the whole Dardanelles operation, impelled by the same qualities of patriotism, obduracy and tenacity which, a quarter of a century later, would be in tune with the circumstances and the times, vigorously supported a renewal of the effort, and others including Lord Kitchener – a powerful ally – supported him.

Eventually the argument which tipped opinion in favour of a fresh assault was that 'withdrawal would have a very bad effect on British prestige in the East'.* The attack was on.

But while the arguments were being debated, precious time had been lost. There had been a political upheaval in London, and in May a coalition government had come into office. As a result there had been a certain amount of reshuffling, and decisions had been shelved. Winston Churchill, who as First Lord of the Admiralty had been involved in the Gallipoli operations from the beginning, now lost his post but was given a place on the War Council as a member of the Dardanelles Committee, and from this position he continued to press for a renewed attack.

It was 6 August, in the middle of the torrid hot season on the dusty, fly-blown peninsula, before the assault could be mounted, and it went wrong from the beginning.

The objective was to sweep across the peninsula, cut off the Turks and dominate the 'narrows' of the Dardanelles Straits. As a diversion, there was to be a heavy attack at Helles on the toe of the peninsula. The troops clinging to the fringe of land around Gaba Tebe – now known as 'Anzac' – were to be reinforced, and here the main charge would take place. Further north a new Expeditionary Force would land at Suvla Bay.

The troopship sailed. The transport sailed. The hospital ships sailed. The nightmare began. The Turks were too strong; the terrain was too difficult; the attack made hardly any progress at all.

In the operational briefings for the landing at Suvla Bay, it had been airily stated that 'water is plentiful in the Anafarta Valley', but no one had remarked that in order to avail themselves of this generous supply of water the troops would first have to capture the land. It was simply assumed that they would and, in any event, fresh water would be available to tide them over the early stages of the attack. Every soldier

* The final Report of the Dardanelles Commission (Part II Conduct of Operations, etc).

had a full water bottle containing one and half pints. Five lighter-ships loaded with 80,000 gallons of fresh water would arrive on their heels, and there would be more than enough to supply each man with the minimum ration of half a gallon a day 'for all purposes'. The arrangements seemed more than adequate, but no one could have foreseen that through a series of sinkings and collisions it would be twenty-four hours after the landings before even two of the five water-lighters reached the shores of the peninsula; and that the one lighter that eventually limped into Suvla Bay would be grounded on a sandbank, so far out that its hoses would not reach the shore.

Twelve more hours went by before it could be refloated, before the desperately needed water could be pumped from the tanks. The tragedy was that there were no water carts, no tanks, no receptacles of any kind into which they could pump it.

The soldiers who were near enough to see the water arrive made a dash for the beach, heedless of anything else but their raging thirst. There was nothing the frantic supply officers could to to control them. They watched aghast as a rabble of men crowded round the hoses, thrusting the narrow necks of their long-empty canteens into the gush of water, and were rewarded with a scant pint apiece for every gallon or so that flowed uselessly on to the beach. Some who were unable to get through the press of the crowd around the nozzles stampeded into the sea and used their jack-knives to stab holes in the body of the hoses. Most of the fresh water ended up in the sea.

There should have been water carts; there should have been mules to drag them and to carry fresh water in panner tanks to the men in the line. In fact, they had been loaded on to a supply ship in the harbour of Alexandria and carefully ticked off the meticulous indent of the transport officer, whose duties did not include the responsibility of studying the terrain on which they would be landed at the end of the voyage. Five days later, he was doubtless astonished to see the entire shipment return intact. It had been impossible to unload it. Nothing on hoofs or on wheels could have stumbled or trundled up the trackless cliffs that rose from the edge of the sea. Without water, the strength of the troops ebbed away as surely as the water from the torn hoses had ebbed into the seas of the Aegean. The advance ground to a halt.

Suvla Bay, in the words of General Sir Ian Hamilton, was 'a jungle ringed by high mountains'. At Anzac and at Helles the cliffs rose sheer from the narrow beaches, and the troops who had been there since April had burrowed into clefts and gullies beyond, much as their Stone Age ancestors had honeycombed shelters out of the rocks ten thousand years before. With its back to the sea, the army was holding the merest fringe of coastline. There was no room for reinforcements; there was no room for reserves; there was no room for hospitals, for casualty clearing stations or for anything more than the most rudimentary aid posts behind the lines. Even at the 'front', among a turmoil of rocks and boulders, there was no question of laying out a conventional system of trenches in the restricted space. It was next to impossible to fit in latrines. Authority, recognizing the difficulty, directed that such latrines as there were in the trenches should be dug extra deep, but in places where rock rang against a spade eighteen inches beneath the gritty surface of the earth there was no solution to the problem.

With an adequate supply of timber and corrugated iron, both latrines and kitchens could have been made relatively fly-proof, but the ships carrying the badly needed material, like the ships which had carried the fresh water, had been sunk on the way. Not that it made much difference, for the Turks in their trenches just a few hundred yards away paid little attention to such matters as sanitation, and there were flies everywhere. They buzzed in voracious clouds on the ordure, on the rubbish and debris in front of the Turkish parapets; they buzzed round the heads of the soldiers, in the ears, and mouths and the noses of the men who lay dead to the world in sleep; they buzzed in millions over the dead bodies that lay decomposing in the narrow strip of No Man's Land that separated the trenches. The interminable droning of insects, the heat and the stench were almost worse than the fighting, and disease claimed almost as many casualties as the guns.

Alarmed by the sharp rise in the number of men who had to be evacuated in August and September, the Surgeon General ordered the medical officers of four battalions to examine the men in the line, and the disturbing fact emerged that of these 'fit' men, 50% had 'feeble hearts', 78 per cent had diarrhoea and 64 per cent had sores of the skin. It needed no mathematician to work out that a number of unfortunate soldiers were suffering from all three. When such a man was wounded in the firing line, who could blame a hard-pressed orderly, doing his best to tend the casualties lying packed together on the tiny beaches, swept by shellfire and bullets, exposed to the elements, for failing to slot him into the right pigeonhole? The men were evacuated willy-nilly from the chaos on the beaches on to whatever ship first sailed into the bay.

Ships like the *Essequibo*, on which Mary Fitzgibbon was serving, were intended for the worst cases that needed immediate attention. For the 'walking wounded' and milder cases of sickness, there were ordinary transport ships which had only been intended to ferry the light cases to a camp hospital on the island of Mudros, little more than an hour's sailing away. But the hospitals at Mudros were already full, and even the hospital ships at anchor on the bay were often too packed with earlier casualties to be able to take any more on board. There was no alternative but to order the transports to sail on to Alexandria, two days' journey away, and if they could not unload there, to sail on for two more days to Malta. Soon even the appalled authorities were referring to the transports as The Black Ships.

The conditions on board were indescribable. It had been laid down in regulations that men who were suffering from gangrenous or suppurating wounds should be kept on deck in the open air. The fever and dysentery cases were carried below, into a hold that no one had had time to clean since it had been unloaded of horses or cargo. Packed together in the hot and fetid atmosphere, often with no pillows, occasionally with no blankets, with little in the way of medicines, with one bedpan to thirty or forty men, with little medicine and barely any nourishment and with no care other than the necessarily cursory attention of a handful of orderlies, the men were in a pitiable state. Collapsed, dehydrated, dying and dead, and after sometimes as many as five days at sea, they were carried from the ships that brought them from the peninsula.

Sister Cathy Mellor, newly arrived in the second batch of nurses rushed out from Britain, wrote home from No. 15 General Hospital, Alexandria.

Sister Cathy Mellor, No. 15 General Hospital, Alexandria

The first fortnight I was on duty in a dysentery ward, and what an experience it was and what hard work, because I had never nursed such cases before. Treatment: keep them clean, diet, rest and Emetine; hypodermic injection of the latter. They soon get into an emaciated condition, enteric is nothing compared to it. In a very short time they look exactly like the babies with summer infantile diarrhoea – those babies who are stricken and die in about forty-eight hours. And how they suffer. It is brutal. I have never seen anything like it.

They lie there in agony, night and day. Oh, the pity of it all. Great strong men, young, looking as old as men of sixty years. I am not exaggerating at all. Several died while I was there, suffering terribly and conscious up to the last moment. One man from Scotland asked me to write to his mother and say, 'Alex was too weak to write'. That was the only message. It struck me as being just about enough to heartbreak her.

Sister Adeline Palmer, QAIMNS(R), The Citadel Hospital, Cairo

Last week I was transferred upstairs to the dysentery wards, and another Sister and myself are in charge of 230 men.

There is a good bit of treatment, and none of the patients are confined to bed, as we are not allowed to keep them if they are ill enough for that. They are treated with Emetine injections, and enemas of sodium bicarb., silver nitrate and tannin; none of them go down for dressings, so we two have them all on our own.

These 'light' cases, disembarked in Egypt and distributed among busy but well-established hospitals, were the lucky ones. There was no shortage of trained nurses, for there was a pool of sisters in Egypt waiting to go to other parts of the Middle East, and they were quickly sent into the hospitals to cope with the rush. In Malta things were worse. The hospitals were newly opened, understaffed, and, at the end of a far longer voyage, the proportion of seriously ill patients was far higher. They lay beneath a tangle of grubby mosquito nets in the old stone-floored barracks of the Malta garrison, and died like the flies that buzzed around them. The nurses who had been rushed out to help in the emergency, fresh from efficient home hospitals, were appalled at the conditions, shocked to see for themselves the terrible toll the soldiers were paying for Winston Churchill's pet scheme to stab the enemy in his back through the Dardanelles.

But although many people laid the blame squarely on Winston Churchill's shoulders, it was a view that was neither entirely true nor entirely fair. Opinion on the Dardanelles Committee of the War Council had been sharply divided, and Lord Kitchener, too, was strongly in favour of continuing the campaign in the Dardanelles. When he left for the peninsula to see for himself, he was adamant in his opinion; within a few hours of his arrival he had completely reversed it. On the evidence of his own eyes, Kitchener was appalled at the realization that the Gallipoli campaign, which he had sanctioned and supported at a distance of some fifteen hundred miles, could not possibly work. He was even more shattered by his own soldierly judgement that, from the beginning, it never could have worked. Before he left the shores of the peninsula he ordered that the troops should prepare to evacuate.

Almost five weeks elapsed before the evacuation could take place, for it had to be carefully planned. Even with the most careful attention to detail it was estimated that casualties would be between 20 and 40 per cent. The ultimate success of the operation was due in large measure to the co-operation and ingenuity of the soldiers themselves. They knew that they had to leave on tiptoe, to creep from the trenches one by one in the hours of darkness to be ferried in small groups to the troop-transports moored offshore, and that it must all be done without giving the enemy an inkling of what was happening. If the Turks started shelling the troopships they would all be done for. As the ranks in the trenches thinned out, the men who were left worked frantically to keep up the same amount of desultory night firing which the Turks were accustomed to expect. The last handful of all set up mechanical devices that would keep rifles firing, and ignited long fuses that would send coloured flares shooting up and hand grenades exploding long after they had gone. Then they too crept away with muffled boots to the waiting ships. It was the only good news to come from the Middle East in the whole of that year, and was the only 'victory' of the costly Gallipoli campaign. The army had deceived not only the Turks but the German navy as well.

With all the activity around the Mediterranean, the coming and going from Gallipoli and the endless movements of shipping, German U-boats had no shortage of targets, particularly now that troopships, supply ships and ammunition ships were plying back and forth to Salonika, where they had been concentrating since the beginning of October. Some battalions of the Australian and New Zealand troops had already gone from Gallipoli to join the Salonika force, and thirty nursing Sisters from New Zealand were detailed to be sent to join them by the first available transport. It was unfortunate that the first available transport was the *Marquette,* and that all the available hospital ships were said to be fully occupied with the Gallipoli casualties. It was unfortunate because the *Marquette* was an ammunition ship and under normal circumstances no nurses should have been on board. She was sunk on 23 October within sight of Salonika. One of the twenty-six Sisters who survived actually saw the torpedo approaching.

Sister
A. Sinclair,
No. 1 (NZ)
Stationary
Hospital

It was just a straight thin green line in the water. We could hear the swish quite distinctly, and the next moment there was a crash. We donned our lifebelts and got to our stations. There was no panic and luckily the steamer took seven minutes to go down. The launching of the boats was a terrible failure. On the port side, one was launched on top of the other, crushing and injuring some, because the ship by this time had a huge list to port. I was on the starboard side and the first boat that was launched tipped over, and those who were not shot out into the sea then had to get out as soon as it touched water, because there was a huge hole in it.

Ten of the Sisters were killed or drowned, and when the news of the tragedy reached New Zealand it caused a wave of indignation, rousing violent anti-German feeling that a 'hospital ship' had been sunk with New Zealand nurses aboard. Feelings ran high everywhere, for these were the first nursing casualties of the war. But the *Marquette* was not a hospital ship. As a troopship with an ammunition column on board, she was a legitimate military target. The real scandal was that while the non-combatant medical staff was sent to Salonika on the *Marquette,* the hospital ship *Grantully Castle,* protected by the Geneva Convention, sailed empty for the same destination. It was one thing for 'Our Boys' to be exposed to the hazards of war; it was quite another thing to expose 'Our Girls' to the same risks. As the year drew towards a close, almost the only news that lifted the hearts of those at home in Great Britain, Australia and New Zealand was that at last most of the boys had been safely evacuated from the Hell of the peninsula. But before they escaped they had been overtaken by one final horror.

In November the weather turned. It became cold and stormy, with deluges of rain that flooded trenches and dugouts. It was worst of all at Suvla Bay and when the wind veered suddenly to the north and the troops, with nowhere to shelter, were swept by an icy blizzard of snow, they were literally frozen where they stood. The ships were stormbound and could neither bring relief nor evacuate the casualties. By the time they were able to reach the men marooned on Gallipoli there were more than 16,000 cases of frostbite, most of them from Suvla. By the time many of them reached hospital their fingers and toes were already dropping off and their bodies were filled with a creeping poison, for their uniforms had frozen like boards, stuck to the sores on their bodies and turned them gangrenous.

The apologists remarked lamely that at least the Gallipoli campaign had caused the enemy huge casualties and kept his attention from straying to more sensitive areas of the war. It was a moot point. The number of Turkish troops engaged was estimated to be almost 300,000. In 'containing' them it had been necessary to employ at least 400,000 British, Anzac, French and Indian troops, including those of the back-up services on Lemnos, Mudros and Imbros. The stark fact was that 117,549 soldiers had been wounded or killed on the peninsula and almost 100,000 had been evacuated sick. Nearly half of the sick had since died. Suvla Bay and Anzac were evacuated on 18 and 19 December and although the final remnants of the Gallipoli force at Cape Helles would not be evacuated until 8 January, to all intents and purposes the campaign was over.

Many heads rolled, including that of Winston Churchill, who was given no alternative place on the War Council when the Dardanelles Committee was dissolved. So he kitted himself out and took himself off to France to fight with the army.

Churchill liked to think of himself as a soldier, but although as a young man he had been commissioned into the 4th Hussars, the discipline of the peacetime regular army did not appeal to his temperament. Churchill liked war – or, at least, he liked action and by dint of using influence and friends in high places he usually managed to attach himself to whatever regiment happened to be where the action was. He joined the Malakand Field Force on the North-West Frontier while his own regiment was 'vegetating in Southern India'; he was with the 21st Lancers at the cavalry charge at Omdurman; with the Lancashire Fusiliers in a brief, inglorious episode in South Africa, which ended in his being captured by the Boers; and, after his escape, he was with the South African Light Horse at the Relief of Ladysmith. Succeeding generations of young aristocrats had been acting in precisely such a manner for a century or so. But times had changed. This was a new kind of army, a new kind of warfare. Churchill held the rank of major, but in the eyes of many his buccaneering experience of soldiering did not equip him for a command where he wanted to be – at the Front! In terms of service he was a comparatively junior officer. As an ex-First Lord of the Admiralty he could hardly be treated as such. It was suggested that he should be given command of a battalion, or even a brigade – but the scheme leaked out and aroused controversy at home. A Question was asked in the House, and the plan was temporarily shelved. Churchill, bitter at having been made a scapegoat, and anxious by some means or other to get at the Hun while he waited for a decision, spent a fortnight in the line with the 2nd Battalion, the Grenadier Guards; a little time on semi-official visits to other regiments; and a great deal of time at GHQ, lobbying acquaintances on the senior staff. Eventually he was delighted to be given command of the 6th Battalion of the Royal Scots Fusiliers, then serving on a quiet sector of the Front. Shortly after Churchill took over, Corporal Bill Morgan of the 10/11th Battalion, the Highland Light Infantry, witnessed a curious incident.

Corporal
W. Morgan,
10/11th
Battalion,
Highland Light
Infantry

We were badly cut up at the battle of Loos in September and the 9th Scottish Division was sent down the line to be reinforced. The casualties had been so heavy that remnants of the different regiments like the 10th and 11th HLI, and the 8th and 10th Gordons, were amalgamated. Then we were sent into the quietest part of the line at Armentières, between Le Bizet and Ploegsteert. There was hardly a shot being fired from either side, it was a case of live and let live, and we were to remain here and build up to full strength because it was before conscription and recruiting was very slow.

I was on my way back to Company Headquarters, because I was a runner and I had just been delivering a message. When I went into the front line from the communication trench I had to turn right, but in the first bay on the left there was an officer pumping rifle grenades over at the Jerry front line. When I got back to my own stretch of trench, everyone was up in arms about it and the Sergeant Major asked me if I saw who was doing it. I told him it was an officer in the next line, so he went along to tell him off. When he came back he said, 'You'll never believe who that was. It was Churchill!' After that the Jerries really let us have it, and there were a lot of unnecessary casualties.

The troops felt particularly aggrieved because the stretch of line was so quiet that it was regarded as a 'showplace', Churchill had not been their only illustrious visitor. The men of Bill Morgan's company had been astonished to be ordered to spruce up and rehearse a dramatic incident for the delectation of cinema audiences in Britain. It was part of the newsreel coverage of a visit to the Western Front by the Minister of Munitions, Lloyd George. It all went off according to plan. The cameraman got some splendid shots of Lloyd George talking to the men in the trenches. At a prearranged signal a soldier mounted the fire step, fired one shot from his rifle at the unsuspecting Germans across the way and fell back dramatically into the trench. On cue, two stretcher-bearers dashed round from the next traverse, picked up the casualty and under the concerned gaze of Lloyd George carried him off to the next bay of the trench, where he made a rapid recovery. The troops were much amused. They found Lloyd George a congenial gentleman and cinema audiences at home would no doubt be deeply impressed by his intrepid foray into the danger zone.

But no one was going to risk Lloyd George's life in a sector where there was likely to be trouble, for he was arguably the most important member of the War Cabinet. The newly appointed Minister of Munitions was making it his business to step up production of the armaments the Army so badly needed. The shell shortage was not yet over but the shell scandal was. The failures of 1915 had been due to lack of munitions and firepower. Everyone was agreed on that; and all other factors were obscured by this apparently self-evident truth. General Haig, who had now succeeded Sir John French as Commander-in-Chief, stated his view categorically. 'When more shells are accumulated we can walk through the German lines in several places.'

That was the goal, to turn out more shells and to build up a mighty arsenal that would demolish the Germans in one huge assault by the British and French when the winter was over and summer came to the Somme. In the meantime, for the next few months, Fritz must be kept busy with small-scale skirmishes on brigade or battalion fronts, which would have the useful side-effect of toughening the soldiers of the New Army and giving them valuable experience. Mark time. Build up. Wait for the summer.

But the Germans had plans of their own.

Part Two

1916 – 1917

Graham Carey (bearded) American Field Service, Ambulance Unit No. 3, about to set off with a friend (Powel Fenton) from the battlefields of Alsace to spend a few days' leave in Paris in 1916.

The Rev. Leonard Pearson (*right*) as an Army Chaplain in 1916, photographed with a brother officer on a pavement in Amiens in front of an inappropriate backcloth. Within weeks he would be acting as anaesthetist at No. 44 Casualty Clearing Station during the battle of the Somme.

Nurse Margaret Ellis (*kneeling, centre*) with a group of VADs, wearing Red Crosses on their uniforms, and another 'Special Military Probationer', Mildred Tanner (*right, back row*). SMPs did a year's intensive training in British hospitals and were then qualified to nurse in military hospitals in Britain and abroad.

(*Below*) Kit and Eve Dodsworth were torpedoed on the troopship *Aragon*, on their way to serve in the Middle East, on 30 December 1917. Minutes after this photograph was taken, and the sisters and VADs in the lifeboat had been picked up by a trawler, the ship on the right – which had been standing off to rescue survivors – was sunk by the same U-boat.

Daniel Sargent and Tingle Woods Culbertson were torpedoed on board the cross-Channel steamer *Sussex* on their way to serve with the American Field Ambulance in France in 1916. (*Right*) This is one of the photographs taken by Culbertson which he sold for 'no small price'. Moments earlier the Spanish composer Granados and his wife had slipped from the now empty liferaft beyond the upturned boat.

Kit Dodsworth's wedding in Alexandria, 18 November 1918. Seated are the bride, Kit, and bridegroom, Captain 'Pip' Vaughan Phillips. Behind, between Pip's brother officers, are Colonel French, who was 'so kind' to Kit and Eve aboard the *Aragon*, and Eve, the bridesmaid.

(*Inset*) Lorna Neill in the romantic uniform she wore as a helper at the canteen at Revigny. Later she exchanged it for the less glamorous uniform of an ambulance driver. The Cantine Anglaise at the station at Revigny. The grateful poilus preferred to call it the ' Cantine de Dames Anglaises '. Apart from a road bridge which replaces the old level-crossing and the removal of the temporary canopies, the station and square were quite unchanged when the author visited Revigny in 1979 . . . and found that some people still remembered the 'Dames Anglaises'.

VAD Ambulance Nurse Clare Tisdall, snapped with her younger brother while he was convalescing from wounds. 2nd Lieutenant Charles Tisdall, 9th Royal Sussex Regiment, returned to France and, four days before his nineteenth birthday, was killed by a sniper as he was digging out one of his men who had been buried by a shell explosion.

Nurses who came to France with the 1st Harvard Medical Unit in 1915 exchanged the comfortable quarters in Massachusetts General Hospital for billets in draughty bell-tents at No. 22 General Hospital, Camiers. Girls involved in the hard reality of wartime nursing may have smiled wryly at sentimental postcards like this one (*below right*) – but they were printed and sold by the million.

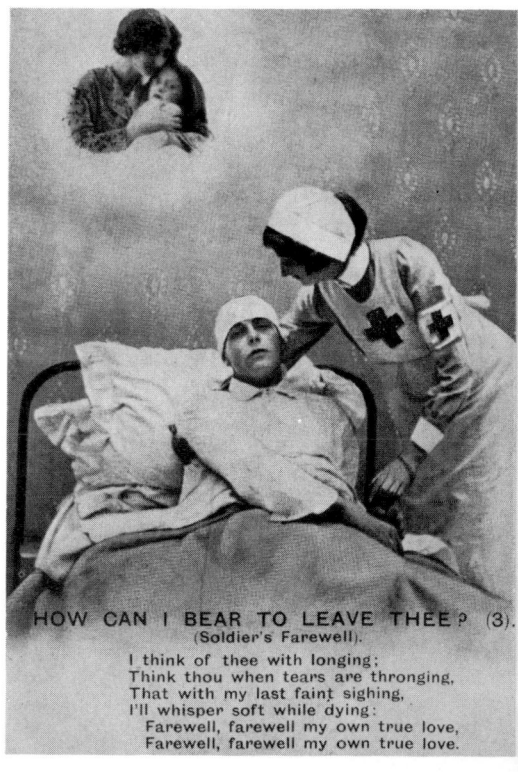

HOW CAN I BEAR TO LEAVE THEE? (3).
(Soldier's Farewell).

I think of thee with longing;
Think thou when tears are thronging,
That with my last faint sighing,
I'll whisper soft while dying:
Farewell, farewell my own true love,
Farewell, farewell my own true love.

Dr Daniel Reardon of Quincey, Massachusetts. His first patients were men of the King's Royal Rifle Corps who were wounded at Hooge on 30 July 1915. The American doctors wore the uniform of British Army Officers with RAMC insignia, but without badges of rank. Before they left for France, the non-combatant American doctors were taught how to deliver a full military salute.

No. 22 General Hospital, Camiers, photographed by Dr Daniel Reardon the day after it was taken over by the 1st Harvard Medical Unit. The bell-tents that were the nurses' quarters are on the right of the picture and the hut in front of the marquee wards was the nurses' 'ablutions'.

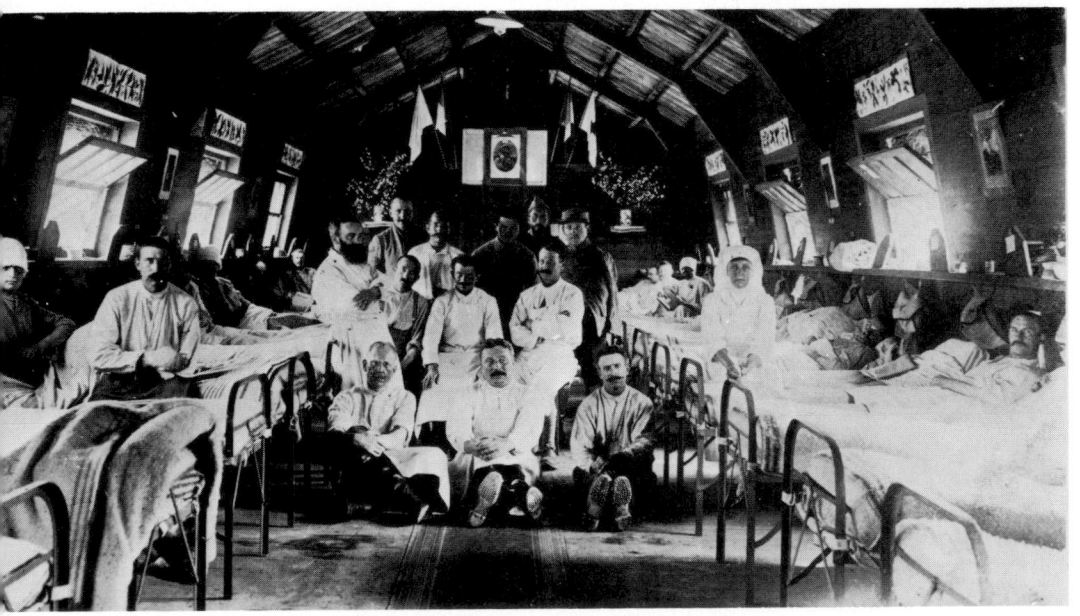

A ward hut in the French military hospital at Revigny where Kitty Kenyon's sister Winifred nursed. These convalescing soldiers had been wounded at Verdun.

The entrance and A-line tent wards of No. 26 General Hospital, Camiers, with a fine crop of rhubarb (*left*) ready for harvesting. The RAMC orderlies, often helped by 'up-patients', made gardens round the tents to improve the look of the camp and also to provide a few fresh vegetables. This picture was taken in 1917 when there was an increase in air raids at the base, and the duckboard paths were covered with camouflage nets so that they would not reflect in the moonlight. Shortly afterwards a number of the well-worn marquees were replaced by huts.

A bombed ward at No. 7 Canadian General Hospital, a casualty in the summer of 1918. Pictures like these, sent home from France, roused considerable anti-German feeling.

October 1914. Nurse Lucilla Bailey and other nurses of the London Hospital worked all night to prepare for the influx of wounded soldiers after the fall of Antwerp.

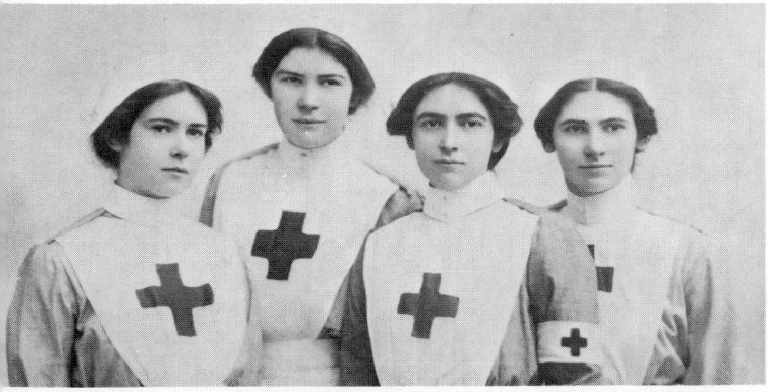

(*Inset*) The Pole sisters – (*from left to right*) Gladys, Hilda, Lily and Muriel. Kent 60 Voluntary Aid Detachment set up its first auxiliary hospital in their father's church hall. (*Above*) Some wounded Belgians, in borrowed clothing, are well enough to sit outside while the VADs of Kent 60 pose at the door of the auxiliary hospital. (*From right to left*) Trixie Batten (commandant), Muriel Pole, Winnie Alston, Hilda Pole, Marjorie Pattison, Annie O'Brien and Dolly Batten. (*Below*) From church hall to hospital at eight hours' notice. Almost as soon as the wounded Belgians had been admitted on 15 October 1914, the local photographer was called in to take a picture. It was his idea that the wounded should wave patriotic flags. The Pole girls' father, the vicar of Christ Church, provided the war map on the wall – but the British line marked on it was already outdated.

VAD Sidney Noel Brown. Crippled feet kept Noel Brown out of the army, but he 'did his bit' by working as a VAD at Queen Mary's Hospital for limbless soldiers at Roehampton. Between them the eleven men in wheelchairs (*below*), fitted with temporary artificial limbs, have only one real leg. Sidney Noel Brown snapped this group of his patients waiting for transport to take them on their weekly visit to the Saturday afternoon match at Chelsea football ground.

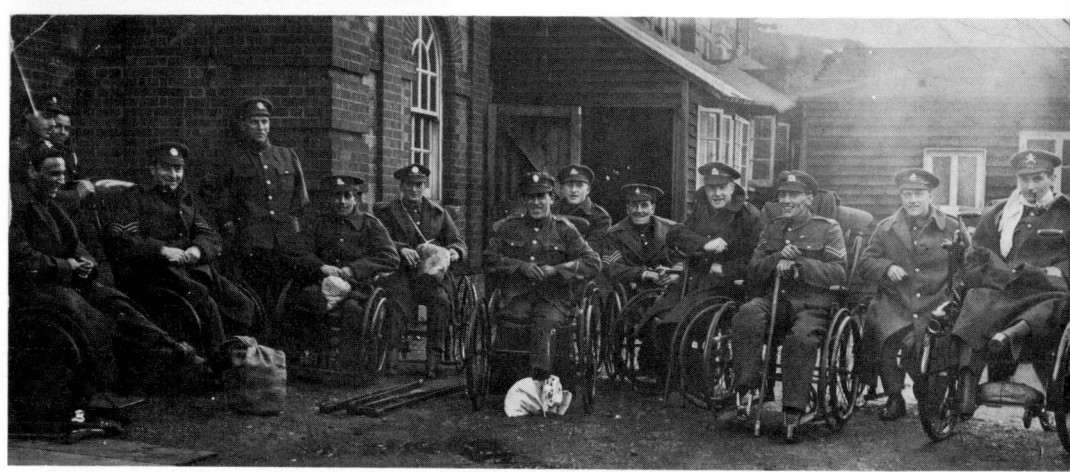

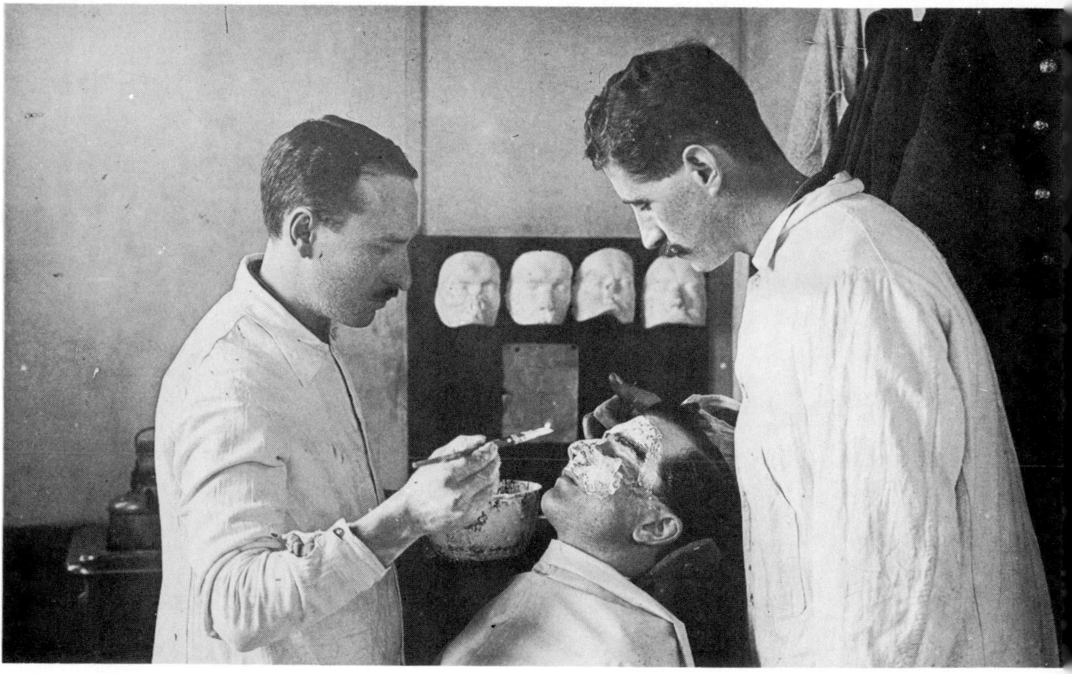

'New' faces for old. Captain Derwent Wood, RAMC, a sculptor and member of the Royal Academy, evolved a painstaking method of making delicately painted masks for soldiers whose faces had been mutilated by wounds. The first stage was to make a plaster cast of the disfigured face.

Chapter Ten

At the beginning of 1916 the Germans were at the zenith of their fortune. Serbia (which had never really mattered much) had been finally overrun. The Russians, torn by the first stirrings of internal strife, were struggling on the Eastern Front. The Allies had abandoned Gallipoli and, still bleeding from huge losses, were unable to budge in the West. It seemed a propitious time to deal a blow that would bring the French to their knees and force Britain to throw in the sponge.

Verdun. They had almost taken it in 1914 but Verdun had held out, as it held out almost until France itself had collapsed under the weight of the Prussian war machine in 1870. Verdun. Like two dogs worrying a bone, France and Germany had been snarling over it at intervals for a thousand years. Verdun. A citadel town, manned by a permanent garrison, surrounded by impregnable forts built on encircling ridges that were in themselves natural defences. Verdun. A bastion, a bulwark, the place above all others which the French army would rush to defend.

That they should rush to defend it was the cornerstone of the German strategy. It was not part of Von Falkenhayn's original plan to take Verdun itself. But the city lay deep in a salient and if the French army could be lured into it, under the guns ranged round it on three sides, it could be blown out of existence. Successive waves of reinforcements could be pulverized in their turn, and with very little expenditure of her own resources of manpower, Germany could bleed the French white. Then, as Von Falkenhayn gloated in anticipation, with 'England's best sword knocked out of her hand' the Allies would be forced to sue for peace. Verdun would be the bait. In January the Germans prepared to set the trap.

Flamethrowers, used experimentally on the unfortunate guinea-pigs of the Rifle Brigade and the KRRs at Hooge the previous July, were now available in numbers sufficient for full-scale attacks. There were 150 of the massive 'Minnenwerfers' that could toss huge bombs the size of oil-drums, and 1,200 guns ranged across the narrow front where the first attack would come – one for every 150 yards of trench. Behind were the 'heavies', the long-distance naval guns and the mammoth 'Big Berthas'* which could fire long-range shells weighing a ton apiece.

* The name 'Big Bertha' was later erroneously used for the 'Paris Gun' – the long-range gun used for the bombardment of Paris which fired comparatively light shells over an immense distance.

Thirteen ammunition trains brought two and a half million shells from the arsenal of the Ruhr, and when they were piled in well-camouflaged dumps in the hills and woods behind the German front; when camps had been set up; when every barn had become a billet and every village a garrison; and when the guns had been dragged into their final positions, there was hardly a yard of the occupied countryside that had not been taken over by the military. From the air, the roads linking farms and villages became crawling masses of field grey as the soldiers moved towards the front.

But the weather was too poor for aerial reconnaissance to be effective. When they were not grounded by mist and blizzards and actually did get into the air, the aircraft were only able to spot a handful of new gun positions, and noted the satisfactory information that no jumping-off trenches appeared to have been dug, a fact which seemed to rule out a large-scale infantry attack. They were not to know that the Germans had begun to burrow dugouts into the earth and that the bulk of the infantry concentrating for the attack was concealed from prying eyes in deep underground shelters. However, buzzed and harried by German fighter planes that clustered in a protective umbrella in the wintry February sky, it was amazing that the French had been able to penetrate the barrage to see anything at all. Skirting the dogfights, German bombers slipped round behind their backs on raid after raid.

The casualties, both civilian and military, meant hard work for the hospitals. In a château near Revigny, some forty kilometres from Verdun, where Kitty Kenyon's sister Winifred was working as a voluntary nurse, the operating theatre was working round the clock. It was two days before she was able to snatch time to write home with her latest news, and when she did the 'news' was not of the kind that was likely to reassure anxious parents who had two daughters nursing in supposedly 'quiet' zones at the Front.

Urgency Cases Hospital   Revigny
                                                    Feb. 23 1916
Dear Mother and Dad,

I daresay you will have already seen in the papers that we have been having air raids here – three in a day too – aeroplanes twice and then Zepps! We had a splendid view of all of them and were in at the death. . . .

At 9 pm on Monday 21st I walked down the path to the operating theatre, with two others. Suddenly, on our right, in the direction of Revigny, we saw lights like stars shooting up into the sky (these were shells). Next moment two searchlights flashed out far closer than those we had seen before. Then in one of the beams we saw a long thin shape – a Zeppelin! The shells burst very close. Another moment and – 'It's *hit*!' we cried,

It crumpled a little about three-quarters of the way along, and then that end turned down a little. It turned pink, and then in a second it burst into flames, lighting up the whole sky. It turned completely end-up and slowly, slowly, fell through the sky leaving a long trail of fire behind it. The queer part was that hardly anyone heard any noise after the very beginning (I suppose we must have been making so much ourselves), for apart from other things the Zep must have dropped lots of bombs after she was hit, as the field where she fell is full of huge holes, fifteen or twenty feet across.

A lot of us started at once to walk to Revigny. We got on to a cart-track, very muddy, then across a ploughed field, the other side of which lay the Zep, blazing. There were crowds, mostly soldiers, round the Zep, and a few men on duty to prevent people going too close, but in spite of that you could go right up to it and get pieces of the framework. It was a gigantic pile of blazing scrap iron, and bodies could be seen among it, but I'm thankful to say I missed seeing those. But it was most eerie, the blaze, the crowd, the noise and the mud.

We came back a different way, rather longer, but along a track all the time. This brought us past the guns, two of them only, seventy-fives and we saw the gunners and shook hands with them and congratulated them. They fired twenty-six shots altogether and I think three hit her. The altitude at which they fired was 2,500 metres (about 9,000 ft). All this information is first hand. We've just seen a long account in today's *Daily Mail* (Continental edition) and there is a lot in it which isn't a bit true. Whether the other English papers will have the same mistakes we don't know, for they won't be here for two days.

21 February was the eve of the attack. At dawn on the 22nd, the earth started to shake as the massive guns which had been lying low, deep behind the lines, roared out and sent their monster shells flying into Verdun. In the salient surrounding it, the field guns fired the first salvoes of the eight hours' intense bombardment that would soften up the French lines before the German infantry attacked.

The sound of the guns, thudding across the lands of Lorraine, could be heard a hundred miles away in the Vosges, where despite gales and blizzards the armies still battled among the frozen mountains. Ambulance Section No. 3 of the American Field Service still struggled on, bringing the wounded down the precipitous, snow-packed roads from the aid posts in the high peaks. No. 2 was already on its way from Bar-le-Duc to Verdun.

As the twenty ambulances crawled northwards in an endless stream of lorries piled high with ammunition and equipment, passing regiments of infantry marching towards the battle, the sound of the guns seemed to Frank Hoyt Gaylor 'like a giant beating a carpet, getting louder and louder as we approached'.

Frank Hoyt
Gaylor,
American Field
Service,
Ambulance
Section No. 2
We started from Bar-le-Duc about noon, and it took us six hours to make forty miles through roads covered with snow, swarming with troops, and all but blocked by convoys of foodcarts and sections of trucks. Of course, we knew that there was an attack in the neighbourhood of Verdun, but we did not know who was making it or how it was going. About four o'clock in the short winter twilight we passed two or three regiments of French colonial troops on the march with all their field equipment. They were lined up on each side of the road around their soup kitchens, which were smoking busily. We were greeted with laughter and chaff, for the most part in an unknown chatter, but now and again someone would say, 'Hee hee, Ambulance Americaine,' or 'Yes, Inglish, goodbye.'

Soon they began to meet the refugees. When the bombardment had started, the civilians were given five hours to leave the city. They struggled down the road against the tide of reinforcements and transport flowing into the maw of the Verdun salient. Whole families, pushing handcarts with wide-eyed shivering children perched on the feather-beds that surmounted a wobbling pile of household goods; an old woman plodding alone with a bundle on her back, carrying in a birdcage an enraged pet cat, which was spitting and tearing at the bars with its claws; grandfathers, leaning on sticks, bowed under the weight of lumpy sacks or small children on their shoulders. One tight-lipped shopkeeper pushed a perambulator overflowing with postcards, ornaments, pictures, statuettes, ribbons and laces – the stock in trade of a souvenir shop in Verdun.

Forcibly halted by the stream of refugees, drumming their fingers impatiently on steering-wheels, revving their engines in impotent frustration, the young American drivers watched them with mingled pity and exasperation and inched forward at the least hint of a gap. In the distance, fingers of fire and flame jabbing into the darkening sky beckoned towards Verdun. They had picked up enough information on the way to be able to guess at their destination, and inexperienced though they were in military tactics they marvelled that the Germans were attacking down from the tip of the salient, rather than trying to cut it off from east to west.

The French soldiers were badly in need of the help of the American and British volunteers, for the organization of the French army's medical services was based on the requirements of a swift war of manoeuvre and it was swamped by the demands of the actual circumstances that had now prevailed for over a year.

Lying wounded on the battlefield a French soldier was as good as dead, for there was little chance of his being brought in, and if he had the luck to be rescued and taken to a hospital there was only one chance in three that he would leave it alive.

By the end of the war, of France's 1,300,000 dead more than 400,000 had died of wounds, a proportion that was larger by far than those of any other nation and was due in considerable measure to the makeshift conditions and lack of skilled care in all but a few of the hospitals. At Le Petit Monthairon, four miles south of Verdun, where the château had been turned into a hospital at the beginning of the war, conditions had been no worse than in most others; now, in the heart of a horseshoe of fire and explosions, swamped by casualties wounded in the first hours of the bombardment, they were indescribable. This was the destination of Ambulance Section No. 2.

The château reeked with ether and iodoform. Pasty-faced, tired attendants unloaded mud, cloth, bandages and blood that turned out to be human beings; an overwrought doctor-in-chief screamed contradictory orders at everybody, and flared into cries of hysterical rage. Ambulance after ambulance came from the lines full of clients; kindly hands pulled out the stretchers, and bore them to the washroom. This was in the cellar of the dovecote, in a kind of salt-shaker turret. The uniforms were slit from mangled limbs. The wounded lay naked in their stretchers while the attendant daubed them with a hot soapy sponge – the blood ran from their wounds through the stretchers to the floor, and seeped into the cracks of the stones.

Henry Sheahan, American Field Service, Ambulance Section No. 2

As soon as the unit arrived, the drivers were ordered to carry the patients who could be moved to the nearest railhead, at Revigny. It was only ten miles away on the main road, but such was the congestion of troops rushing to the line that it was five o'clock in the morning before some of the ambulances got back. And all the time the guns never stopped firing. It was the beginning of what the German General Ludendorff would later describe as the 'hell of Verdun'. It was to last for ten long months.

In the first twenty days the American boys in their small Ford ambulances carried 2,046 wounded over 18,915 miles of the nightmare road which the soldiers had already begun to call 'la Voie Sacrée'. It was the artery of the battlefield, for it was the only way into the salient. Every gun, every bullet, every shell, every loaf of bread, every drop of ration wine, every wagon, every horse, every officer and every man of the countless regiments that were thrown pell-mell into the battle had to travel it to get there. Day and night the endless stream of traffic never abated.

Groaning under the onslaught of a million iron-rimmed wheels and the constant pounding of marching feet, the surface cracked and crumbled. A dozen times a day a top-heavy car or wagon lurched into a pothole and overturned, blocking the road and causing long delays. In Bar-le-Duc where the road began and ended, great bottlenecks of troops and vehicles waited for hours to take their place in the slow-moving caterpillar on its interminable crawl to the front. White sheets, painted in huge black letters with the word *Verdun* above a pointing arrow, were stretched on poles at street corners. At night the only light in the blacked-out streets of the town was the dim glimmer of the lanterns set behind them to illuminate the signs that pointed towards the Voie Sacrée.

Ambulances did not have priority. After one painfully slow journey to the railhead at Revigny, when two of the three wounded he was carrying in his ambulance were found to be dead on arrival, Frank Hoyt Gaylor remarked bitterly, 'Ammunition and fresh men are the all-essential things. The wounded are the *déchets*, the "has-beens", and so must take second place.'

Everything took second place to the need to save Verdun, to save France itself. There had been appalling mistakes on both sides. The guns had been stripped from the mighty forts that protected Verdun, and their garrisons had been removed on the orders of one general who believed that they had no role to play in 'modern' warfare. When, as the Germans approached, a hasty order was given to man the forts, in the confusion it was never passed on. Through a hole in an outer wall, which had been conveniently breached by a heavy shell, the astonished Germans walked into mighty Fort Douamont, tracked down a handful of soldiers sheltering from the bombardment in the deep underground passages, and went through the formality of disarming and taking them prisoner. It cost the French 10,000 lives to get Fort Douamont back again. But it was many months before that happened.

As for the Germans, their initial advantage had been thrown away by the very effectiveness of their trump-card. The terrible bombardment of their artillery, firing on one narrow front in a greater concentration of firepower than had ever been unleashed before, so shattered the land beyond that the German infantry, which should have leapt across the French positions, had to scramble and crawl, to plunge into the craters made by their own shells. The lyddite fumes tore the breath from their lungs as they struggled out again towards the ragged lines of French infantry, whose determination to defend each centimetre of native soil verged on the fanatic.

It was on this flame of patriotism, fanned to white-heat at Verdun, that the French Command depended. The French poilu's willing support of the precept that every metre of French soil captured by the Germans should be regained at once, whatever the cost, blinded the authorities to the realization that the morale of even such an army as this could conceivably crack. In their short-sighted passion for France and Glory, the marshals and generals on whose orders the infantry were thrown into the inferno took little account of the poilu as an individual.

The shilling a day of the British Tommy was a princely sum by comparison with the poilu's miserable five sous – a twentieth of a franc. There was no rota, nor even any hint of a system that would give the poilu more than the dimmest hope of occasional home-leave. And if he escaped from the dangers of battle and the misery of a spell in the trenches, there were no canteens, no rest centres, no clubs where he could relax.

It was hardly surprising that when the 'Dames Anglaises' set up a free canteen in the one-time waiting room of the station at Revigny, the French soldiers fell in love with them, to a man.

The small town of Revigny was literally the end of the line. Further north towards Verdun the railway had either been destroyed in the fighting of the Marne and Aisne, or had been severed by the German line as it looped south before swinging back to encircle Verdun. It was to Revigny that the reinforcements came, pouring out of the troop trains at the battered station, forming up among the ruins of the station square to march to the barracks or, if the situation at the front was desperate, to march straight out of the town towards the Voie Sacrée and Verdun.

The canteen was financed entirely by private subscription and run by a group of philanthropic ladies. Steel magnate John Summers had been one of the people who had given generously to its funds, and his donation paved the way for his daughter Maud and her schoolfriend Lorna Neill to go and work at Revigny as volunteers. At nineteen, both girls were too young to serve abroad with any official organization, but the *Cantine Anglaise* was only too glad of their help and the poilus were astounded and charmed to find two pretty young girls so near the front. Lorna Neill, almost straight from boarding school, and demure in the white-coiffed uniform of a French Red Cross nurse (in which, according to the commandant, Mrs Culling, she 'looked about fifteen'), was thrilled to the marrow at being part of the drama, and wrote lyrically in her journal in the style of the school essays which, a very short time earlier, she had been writing at Bentley Priory.

The Place de la Gâre at Revigny at three o'clock on a winter's morning is not an inspiring or an enlivening spot. A few miserable-looking, blue-clad figures loaded with equipment are lounging under shelter of the leave-paper 'guichet'. On one side of the square, however, stands a long wooden 'barraquement' brilliantly lighted. The lights cheered up all one corner of the square. They shone on three big notices showing in white letters the words 'Cantine Anglaise', 'Café Gratuit', 'Bouillon Gratuit'. They shone over the long open windows fitted up as a counter, on the Union Jack and the Tricouleur, rather the worse for wear but still hanging bravely over the window. At the end of the open windows is a woman in a white veil and apron, though tonight her pristine beauty is slightly spoiled by a large number of mufflers, woollies and coats intended to keep out the cold.

The train having disgorged its load at the station, the first weary

Lorna Neill, Cantine Anglaise, Revigny (her journal, February 1916)

poilu appeared, struggled wildly with a refractory knapsack, dragged a battered and wine-stained 'quart' from its mysterious depths and dashed up the fenced-off passage labelled 'Entrée'. In three minutes the Place de la Gare, which had been dead and quiet as the grave, is a sea of men in blue. They struggle behind the 'barrière', laugh and shout and swear and pass in a never-ending stream before the window. A roar of laughter rose from the crowd who have managed to edge themselves near to the centre of the canteen. From one of the windows a gramophone was playing 'Tipperary', which to the French soldier is the symbol of all that is English. The men are all warmed and comforted by the hot drinks and by the cigarettes and, above all, cheered and encouraged beyond believing by the knowledge that their sufferings and their sacrifices are not un-remembered.

This is the work that the canteen does all day and all night. Things are bad in the Verdun sector and 10,000 men pass through the entrance before the windows every twenty-four hours. It is not possible to speak to every man when they come in such numbers, yet each one feels the better for his cup of coffee, his two cigarettes. They go away content, for it is pathetic to see how little will please a soldier. The Frenchman has the knack of saying pretty things, and many a man has called the canteen 'La Maison du Bon Dieu'. Unfortunately an earthly Maison du Bon Dieu, unlike the heavenly one, has an end, and one of the hardest things a 'cantinière' has to do is to say, 'Non, il n'y a plus,' to a smiling poilu who says, 'S'il vous plâit, Mamselle, une petite cigarette Anglaise.'

But in spite of occasional shortages Lorna was able to write home to her mother in more practical terms:

The following is a list of things we gave out during February, which is a short month.
250,000 cups of coffee
 15,000 cups of tea
 15,000   ,,   ,,   chocolate
 22,000   ,,   ,,   soup
_____

302,000 total number of cups
_____

Which as you will see makes an average of over 10,000 cups every twenty-four hours. In addition to that we gave 63,000 cigarettes, 3,500 presents, 600 loaves, 310 tins of beef. That's not bad, is it? Whew!

The 'Whew' was justified. For all the excitement of the war, of the guns booming in the distance, of the regiments passing through on their way to the battle, for all the flattery of tender glances and the virtuous satisfaction of distributing bounty, it all added up to a great deal of very hard work.

The determination of the French not to give way at whatever cost had been distilled into a phrase that already had a ring of immortality. *On ne passera pas*. They shall not pass. Just as the Germans had foreseen, regiment after regiment was flung into the storm of flying steel that raged in the torn and pitted valleys and slopes around Verdun, where whole villages had disappeared from the face of the ravaged earth and whole battalions were blown to oblivion. *On ne passera pas*. But now the struggle was bleeding the German army white, just as Von Falkenhayn had planned to bleed the French, and the 'slight expenditure' of manpower with which he had hoped to achieve his object was mounting into a deficit that was draining the German resources faster than they could be made good.

Germany was fighting with one hand behind her back. Although Russia showed signs of weakening, she still had to maintain her position on the Eastern Front; and in France and Belgium a strong force must be maintained in order to repulse the attack the British would surely make to relieve the pressure on the French line at Verdun. But reserves had to be found from somewhere, and there was no alternative but to bring in the half-trained and inexperienced men from Germany and to call up new recruits to replace them in the training camps. Now they had to think about revising the original plan, to finish the battle swiftly before the British intervened, to take Verdun before the strength of their own army ebbed away.

But that overcautious advance in the opening stages of the battle had already deprived the Germans of their initial advantage, and their own mighty arsenal had acted against their interests. Even when they wrested a strip of mangled earth from the grip of the French, it was impossible to bring up supplies, impossible to bring up ammunition and impossible to move the guns forward. Both guns and reserves had to be pulled back from the line to a position that considerably weakened their capacity to support the infantry in front. Devastated by the lethal fire of the apparently unlimited supply of the seventy-fives – the quick-firing guns which the French rushed back to Verdun – debilitated by almost arctic conditions of snow and bitter winds, demoralized by the tenacity of the French defence, decimated by casualties, the German troops hung on, crawled forward, wavered, stuck.

It was not surprising that Lorna Neill, snapping a group of newly captured Germans as they boarded a train at Revigny, noticed that they looked remarkably pleased to be out of it.

I never felt sorry for the Germans at all. We identified so completely with the French soldiers, and they were so violently against the Germans and told us such dreadful stories about them and the things

Lorna Neill,
Cantine
Anglaise,
Revigny

they had done, that it never occurred to us to think that they were suffering too.

A lot of the poilus came from places which the Germans had occupied, and they got no news of their wives and families. Very occasionally a soldier would get a postcard or a photograph, possibly sent through Holland which was neutral. But there was never any writing on them. All he knew was that they were alive. I remember one man very well indeed. He was a corporal and his home was in Lille, which was occupied by the Germans, and he was desperately worried because there was a rumour that they were deporting women to Germany. He showed me two photographs. The first was of a little boy about six years old with curly hair and a fat smiling face. 'Look', he said, 'this is my "petit gars" as I knew him. And *this* is what I received a fortnight ago.' The next photo was of a woman in black with a boy standing by her side. He was tall and very thin, with an old anxious face. 'It is the same boy', the soldier said, 'and that is his mother. They seem well, maybe just a bit thinner.' There were tears in his eyes, and then very suddenly, his face changed. I've never seen such hatred on any face, and he started to rant and rave and storm at the Germans and all their works. He said that he had been an engineer, but he had transferred to an infantry regiment, really just to get his own back on the Germans. He was on his way up to the front, to Verdun, and he talked in a very blood-thirsty way about what he would do when he got there. That was all he wanted to do – kill some Germans with his own hands.

In that sort of atmosphere it was very difficult to feel much sympathy for the Germans, and we ourselves heard all sorts of horror stories. Revigny had been invaded by the Germans in the early part of the war before they were pushed back. The town was almost in ruins, and every civilian and peasant had a tale to tell about terrible things they said the Germans had done.

There was a lake not far away and it iced over that winter. They said that there was a quantity of German corpses under the ice, killed in the fighting in 1914. I don't know if it was true, but we believed it. And we used to go there to skate. It didn't bother us a bit. It left us quite unmoved. In fact, looking back, the thing that strikes me is how we managed to enjoy ourselves in those circumstances, because we did. We had a wonderful time, in spite of the terrible tragedies that were going on around us. Whether we were heartless, or just very young, or whether it was the circumstances under which we were living and the excitement of it all, we really managed to enjoy ourselves. And it *was* exciting. To be there near Verdun, when it was all anyone could talk about – Verdun, Verdun, Verdun – was immensely exciting.

Verdun had become more than a battle; now it was a symbol of struggle and freedom. And Verdun needed all the help she could get. At the beginning of March another group of young Americans crossed the Atlantic to join the American Field Service, to form new sections and also to bring some of the original units up to strength. They too had casualties. Daniel Sargent, from Wellesley, Massachusetts, was destined for Section No. 3. He was to take the place of Dick Hall, who had set off at midnight on Christmas Eve to fetch a load of wounded from the battlefield on the mountain and had been killed by a shell on the way.*

I suppose I joined the ambulance for patriotic reasons. Although America wasn't in the war, there was a lot of propaganda about the wickedness of the Germans. I wanted to do something. You might say, 'Why did any of us go?' It wasn't always for noble reasons. There were people who wanted to get away from their wives, people who were disappointed in love, and of course some people wanted to go for the adventure. I don't think I particularly went for the adventure myself, but I got it just the same!

Daniel Sargent,
American Field
Service,
Ambulance
Section No. 3

He got it sooner than he expected, because Sargent was one of seventy-five Americans who sailed for Dieppe on 24 March on the steamer *Sussex*. She left the port of Newhaven shortly before eleven in the morning. For the first half-hour of the voyage the grey bulk of a coastal patrol dirigible hovered overhead, watched by interested passengers on the deck of the steamer far below. But as it disappeared, the bitter cold sent some of the passengers below to the warmth of the first-class dining saloon in the bow of the ship and the first sitting for lunch. It was a decision that was to save their lives.

There were 500 or so passengers on board, all of them civilians, for the tiny *Sussex* was a civilian boat, plying the same cross-Channel route that she had travelled in peacetime. In wartime the journey took twice as long. Although the *Sussex* rigidly adhered to the international agreement that no military supplies or personnel should be carried, although she had no escort of destroyers, although in theory she should have been safe from attack, it was a wise precaution to zig-zag across the sea just in case the captain of some lurking German U-boat was not familiar with the small print of the Hague Convention. The passengers were a mixed bunch of French and British civilians; relatives going to visit wounded soldiers; a handful of Belgian officers in mufti; nurses returning from leave or en route to the hospitals; Granados, the Spanish composer; one journalist, Edward Marsh of the *New York Sun*; and seventy-four other American neutrals. Among them were Dan Sargent and Tingle Woods Culbertson of Philadelphia, both on their way to

* Richard Nelville Hall of Ann Arbor, Michigan, was given a soldier's funeral and buried in the French Military Cemetery at Saint-Amarin in Alsace. The cross was inscribed, 'Richard Hall, an American who died for France'.

Paris to report for duty at the Neuilly headquarters of the American Field Ambulance Service. They had become acquainted on deck and now they were laughing together at one of the long tables in the first-class saloon.

Sitting alone by a porthole was Miss Collum, a radiographer, who was returning to France after her first leave at the end of a year's service at the Scottish Women's Hospital at Royaumont. She was one of an élite group. The Scottish Women's Hospital Association had been started by the redoubtable Dr Elsie Inglis, and its hospitals were completely staffed by women doctors and specialists who had battled their way into the masculine strongholds of the medical profession. They had also had to battle their way into the war and through the prejudices of masculine authority, which no longer dared to disparage their medical skill but had grave doubts about the ability of all-women hospitals to exert the indispensable military discipline. That particular prejudice had been triumphantly refuted in the first months of the war. Now Dr Frances Ivens was running the hospital at Royaumont, and two more units, one led by Dr Inglis herself, had gone to work in neglected Serbia where, among other horrors, typhus was raging. They were still there when Serbia fell, and had been held prisoner for four months before the Germans agree to repatriate them. Just three weeks earlier, on 29 February, they had arrived back in England – thin, tired, haggard and worn by privation. The newspapers were still full of it, and Miss Collum was taking back to Royaumont a bundle of cuttings with stories of their exploits.

The passengers who had lunched at the first sitting were back on deck and those who had chosen to wait for the second had just taken their places when a torpedo struck the *Sussex* and sheared off the bow, instantly killing the diners and stewards in the first-class saloon.

V. C. C. Collum, Scottish Women's Hospital Association, Royaumont Unit

I was standing on deck just over the place where the torpedo cut the *Sussex* in two. There was a terrific bang and the next thing I knew was the sensation of hurtling through the air. I was blown on to the top deck. When I came to I saw a woman's dead body, a piece of something gruesome near me, and a solitary man standing by the davits staring down into the sea. I was temporarily speechless and deaf, but managed to reach his side. I saw him pick up a lifebelt and put it on. I pointed to it and to myself. He fetched another from somewhere and tied it round me – upside down as it transpired! Then he swarmed down one of the ropes of the falls. I looked down. Drowning in that green water suddenly seemed horrible, and I determined to make an effort to save myself. Somehow I followed that man down the rope – I had no power in my knees to cling to it, so let it slide through my gloved hands – and, half unconscious, waited till the swaying of the steamer brought me over the boat and I dropped into it.

It was a gargantuan effort, because Miss Collum had serious internal injuries. The other passengers looked at her, appalled. There was a great gash across her head, another on her chin and her long hair, sticky with blood, was plastered half across her face. As they drew away from the *Sussex* with three passengers at the oars, the sea trickled into the leaking boat. There was nothing to bale with but bowler hats, and soon the icy water crept up to their knees.

We were a bit envious of the people in the boats at first. Culbertson and I were standing chatting on the deck at the stern when the torpedo struck. It was like hitting the rock of Gibraltar, a tremendous bang, and the whole front of the ship was blown completely off. The noise was tremendous, people screaming and an ear-splitting sound as the ship let off steam. We were drenched in clouds of steam, but we were all right. Where I was, right in the stern, no one was hurt. They shouted through loud-hailers that women and children were to go to the lifeboats and that the rest of us should go get a life-preserver. So we did that and put them on, and Culbertson and I stood at the rail looking at the people in the lifeboats, thinking that we were going to go down and that they'd be OK. Then we saw that most of the lifeboats were damaged and sinking, and there was nobody to man them. One had capsized when it was being launched and all the people were killed or drowned, and we were still afloat. It was all pretty worrying. But Culbertson didn't seem to be worried at all. He had his camera and he started taking pictures. He snapped all the people crowded together with us on the deck. And he snapped photographs of the lifeboats with all the people in them. He said, 'We've got to go down, but I'm going to take some pictures of people on the boat, because if they go down and we're saved they'll be worth money'. I thought it was very strange. Money was the last thing I was thinking about at all. I was thinking about other things. But Culbertson was a real American, in the business sense. Very much an American. And in some of the pictures, the amazing thing is that people are actually smiling at the camera! I didn't feel like smiling.

I was watching Granados, the Spanish composer. I knew him because we'd crossed together from the States in the *Rotterdam*, and he was on the *Sussex* on his way back to Spain. He had his wife with him, and it was very sad. She was a big fat woman − she must have been 300 lb − and she couldn't get into a lifeboat. He wouldn't go without her, he wanted to be with her to the end. So he got her on to a raft, a very small raft and she was so very large. I'll never forget the sight of her kneeling on this raft. It was the most terrible sight I've ever seen. Granados was clinging to the raft as it drifted away, and I saw him just slip over the thing and drown. It was a terrible thing to see. Then it began to seem as if we were better off where we were, because it looked as if we'd stay afloat for a while.

Daniel Sargent, American Field Service, Ambulance Section No. 3

V. C. C.
Collum,
Scottish
Women's
Hospital
Association,
Royaumont
Unit

After about an hour the ship's officers signalled to us to go back to what was left of the ship. A stout elderly Frenchman suddenly became hysterical, and jumped up and shouted that the submarine was still nearby and we should be attacked again and killed if we went back. The rest of us felt that we should be drowned anyhow if we stayed adrift in that boat, as the sea was getting up and there was no vessel in sight. It seemed likely that the dancing maniac would upset us all, so I called up all my mental energy and by sheer will-power quelled him. My voice had come back. He collapsed, suddenly, white and shaking, and never said another word.

The few survivors of those who had taken to the boats were dragged back on to the drifting stern of the *Sussex*. She was listing badly, her bulkheads groaning under the strain. The injured were laid in the aft saloon. Miss Collum heard an American voice say, 'Where's that Red Cross worker we saw in the dining saloon? Why isn't she helping to tend the wounded?' Lying semi-conscious on a leather bench, with her Red Cross uniform concealed by her thick civilian overcoat, numbed by the pain of a badly crushed foot and bleeding from an internal haemorrhage, Miss Collum felt disinclined to announce her presence. There was a deafening commotion from next door, where some of the crew had broken into the bar and were getting uproariously drunk. A Belgian officer braved the rabble to snatch a bottle of brandy for the injured. There was no sign of rescue and it was beginning to get dark.

On deck, Culbertson had long ago finished his film. The sea began to roughen, the wreck was listing badly and the remaining bulkheads groaned under the strain. Clutching his precious camera, Culbertson turned to Sargent. 'If we go down and we have to swim for those lifeboats,' he said, 'and you're on one and I find there's no place for me, I'm going to hand the camera to you and you can keep it. It's yours. But remember, don't sell the photographs for any small price!' Dan Sargent was too astonished, too cold and too scared to make any reply.

Rescue came at eleven o'clock that night in the shape of a French trawler, which took Dan and Tingle and the rest of the able-bodied into Boulogne, for the *Sussex* had drifted far to the north. The injured had to wait for the arrival of a destroyer of the Dover patrol to take them back to England. When they reached Dover in the early hours of 25 March, Sargent and Culbertson were already on their way to Paris.

Daniel Sargent,
American Field
Service,
Ambulance
Section No. 3

When we got to Paris the story was in all the newspapers and we were all reported dead. All of our names were listed dead, drowned without a trace, because we'd drifted way off-course and I guess the story had gone to press before the trawler found us. Culbertson and I went and booked in to a good hotel, and we got a real heroes' welcome when they knew where we'd come from. We sent cables back home, then Culbertson got on the phone. In no time at all some people came around – French representatives of an American publisher called McClure Company – and Culbertson took them into his room next door to mine. When they left I said to him, 'Well, how was it, Culbertson?' He said, 'Well, I don't know. I suppose I could have got more, but I think I got a pretty good sum'. I said, 'How much did you get?' He said, 'Sixteen thousand dollars'. And that was a *lot* of money in those days*

That evening the two young men celebrated in style. The following morning they reported at Neuilly and within a week they were on their way to the front, Culbertson to join Section No. 1 and Sargent to join Graham Carey with No. 3 in Lorraine. He believed that he had just survived the most terrifying experience of his life. But he was wrong, for within a few weeks of his arrival the section was on the move again, this time to Verdun.

* Two of the pictures taken by Tingle Culbertson are reproduced elsewhere in this book. Culbertson himself did not survive to enjoy the fruits of his acumen. When the USA entered the war, he transferred to the army and was killed in 1917. Fifty people were lost in the torpedoing of the *Sussex* and thirteen, including Miss Collum, were seriously injured.

Chapter Eleven

If the first six months of 1916 constituted a breathing space for the British army, it was not particularly noticeable in the hospitals. Between the end of December and the beginning of May the 'normal wastage' of trench warfare and small-scale local attacks amounted to 83,000 killed and wounded. It was true that the British had taken over a part of the line from the French in order to relieve their badly stretched forces, but on the British front there were no major battles. All the strength, all the men, all the materials must be conserved for the one tremendous blow which would be struck in the summer.

But still the casualties flowed in. Not all of them flowed quickly out again, and there was a large backlog of men wounded in the first two years of the war – the blind, the paralysed, the limbless. With patients requiring long-term care, and fresh convoys of recently wounded arriving with depressing regularity the resources of the home hospitals were being strained to the limit and new problems were constantly challenging the ingenuity of the medical officers.

In the early months of 1916 a visitor wandered into the transport lines of a Royal Army Medical Corps Unit at Neuville St Vaast. He watched with interest as the farrier corporal threw bundles of hay to the ambulance horses, which were tethered in neat lines and protected from the mud of the field by wooden standings. Strolling back past the barn that served as a forage shed, he noticed a chaff-cutter lying outside. 'What's that?' he asked. 'That!' replied the corporal. 'That's our amputating machine!'

Agnes Howard, VAD, No. 1 Military Hospital, Dover

I was sent to Dover Military Hospital in December 1915 and there we received the worst of the wounded from the hospital ships – the boys who were suffering from gangrene or perhaps were likely to haemorrhage but couldn't be sent on to other hospitals because they were too ill. I remember one South African boy in particular who had already lost one leg, which had been amputated in France. We did the best we could for him, but eventually the surgeon decided that there was no alternative but to remove the other leg. He knew he was going to have the operation and he was terribly worried about how he would manage without any legs at all, but it was a very bad case of gangrene and there was no choice. He talked to me about it and I tried to comfort him and cheer him up. He was really very brave.

When they were ready for him and the orderlies had put him on the trolley to wheel him to the theatre, he took hold of my hand and said, 'Now for the great adventure!' They brought him back from the theatre but he never regained consciousness after the operation. He just slipped away. Even the surgeon wept.

But thousands of lives were saved by rough and ready amputation, and when the stumps were healed they needed specialist help. Most of them went on to Queen Mary's Hospital at Roehampton, where Sidney Noel Brown was a VAD. In a hospital which specialized in the care of limbless soldiers, many of them 'double amputees' who were quite helpless, the work was extremely heavy and male VADs were particularly useful, although even they found the back-breaking work of lifting and carrying the patients a strain. Inevitably most of the orderlies were either unfit or too old for the army. It was no longer an army of volunteers, as it had been in its enthusiastic heyday at the start of the war. To some extent men were still volunteering, and there were always youngsters who were only too anxious to enlist as soon as they reached military age, but the extravagant expenditure of men and lives and the likelihood of heavy losses to come had made it a matter of urgency to devise a scheme that would ensure a steady supply of recruits. In January conscription had been introduced and Sidney Noel Brown had been called up with the eighteen-year-olds.

The standard of fitness required by the army had been revised since the chaotic early days of the war when medical examinations could be either so perfunctory that obviously unfit men were passed for army service, or so punctilious in the observation of the standards which had been set for the pre-war regular army that otherwise fit men were rejected because they had bad teeth or did not reach the regulation height. Now there were dentists as well as doctors attached to army units, and a man was passed 'fit, subject to undergoing dental treatment'. Small, tough men, many of them from the poor areas of cities like Liverpool and Glasgow, were formed into bantam battalions and earned a reputation for being tough fighters. One astonished general, who was inspecting the 16th (Bantam) Battalion of the Highland Light Infantry before they went into the trenches, stopped before a particularly diminutive specimen, whose appearance suggested very little in the way of a threat to the Kaiser's Army. 'Could *you* kill a German, my man?' 'Aye, sir,' came the confident reply, 'but he wid have to be a wee one.'

But there was no place in the army for Sidney Noel Brown, for he had been born crippled. When he came before the Medical Board, the Medical Officer looked at Sidney's bare feet, congenitally clubbed and twisted. They bore the scars of many operations, which had straightened them to a point where Sidney could at least walk, as he had been unable to do for the first eight years of his life.

'Go and get dressed,' said the MO, 'and come back to see me when you've got your clothes on.' A few minutes later he raised his eyebrows at the sight of Sidney Noel Brown dressed as a member of the Red Cross. 'So, my lad, I see you're already in uniform.'

'Yes, sir,' replied Sidney. 'I've been in the Red Cross for two years now. 32nd East Putney VADs, sir. I do air raid duty mostly, and sometimes night patrol at Streatham Hospital. I work during the day, sir. I'm articled to a chartered accountant.'

The MO nodded approvingly. 'What's the position?' he asked. 'Have you any trouble with your legs or feet?'

'Well, they're not too strong, sir. I've got these special boots with whalebone in them to support them, but I don't have much movement in the ankles and that sort of thing.

'Take up dancing, my lad, take up dancing. It will strengthen your feet and do you a lot of good,' advised the MO. 'And you continue what you're doing. Keep on with your Red Cross work. You're much better there than in the Army.'

But it was hard to be out of it when all the rest of your friends were going in. The next best thing, decided Sidney, would be to give up his job and work full-time for the Red Cross.

Sidney Noel Brown, VAD, Putney 32, Queen Mary's Hospital, Roehampton

I went up to the Red Cross headquarters in Pall Mall and asked if they could give me a full-time job. They said, 'Well, they want VAD staff at Queen Mary's Hospital in Roehampton.' That suited me down to the ground because I was in the habit of going there every Saturday and Sunday to help the nurses with odd jobs. Sometimes I played the piano in the wards and the men liked that, and on Saturday afternoons we used to take a whole bunch of them to Chelsea Football Club when there was a match. There were men there with no legs at all, lots of them, and they had to be carried to wheelchairs, put on the bus, carried again into the wheelchair when we arrived at Chelsea and then looked after during the match. So I was very used to it, and the Matron knew me, and I liked it there very much. They were a wonderfully cheerful lot. As a matter of fact, we had our own football club, which I organized myself, because the chaps were very keen on football. Some of the patients who played for us had only lost an arm, so they could play perfectly well. We even had one chap in the team who had a foot off, and he was able to play with an artificial foot. They would have a go at anything, those lads.

The whole experience of Roehampton changed my life. It was one of the happiest places I've ever been in. The atmosphere was really quite extraordinary. I'd been crippled all my life and I'd spent four years in the National Orthopaedic Hospital and had twelve operations. When I came out at the age of eight I was put in irons right up to my waist, and even when I went to bed and the irons were taken off my legs were put in splints, because I wasn't allowed to bend them. Of course, as I got older they got better and I got these special boots and could walk fairly well without the irons, but I used to have a tendency to be a bit sorry for myself until I went to Roehampton. That experience completely changed me. It made me fight.

I started as an orderly in the wards, but owing to the weakness in my feet I couldn't really manage it. Matron saw that it was too much for my feet, so she had me put into the pack stores. I did that job for about six months and then the adjutant discovered that I had been articled to a chartered accountant and knew how to compute. So he had me transferred to his office to take care of the Capitation Department. It was very interesting indeed.

Every morning first thing I had to interview all the patients who had come in the day before and take down all their particulars, full names, regiments, injuries – one leg, two legs, one arm, two arms, and so on. Then having taken all these details on a card index I'd go back into the office and enter them up in a register, give each one a number and enter them in order. Every month I had to go through these registers and the card index and claim the capitation grant of three shillings a day for each patient. That's where the accounting came in, although I found it a bit tough going at first, adding up sheets and sheets of figures, but it was exceedingly interesting. The best thing about it was that they put me into proper khaki uniform, which pleased me very much. But, of course, I was still attached to the 32nd VAD. I worked at the hospital seven days a week; five and a half days in the office and then I would go home on Saturday at lunchtime, change into my VAD uniform and go back to the hospital to take the lads to the football, and back again on Sundays to do some voluntary work.

Another job I had to do was to supply the artificial leg people with boots. I used to ask their size – and in the case of men with no legs I used to get some funny replies! If there was one foot, you had to have a boot the same size as the other leg. If a chap hadn't any legs you had to have boots to fit the artificial legs. The Saxone Shoe Company in Putney used to supply these boots, and once a week the patients who were waiting for the boots used to come in to one of the huts where I had a cupboard full of them, and the Saxone man used to come along to measure them and fit them.

I used to be amazed how short a time it took these boys to get used to walking with artificial legs – it was usually about a month, or six weeks at most. I could tell by my capitation lists, because I knew just how long every man was in hospital and it was very seldom more than six weeks. A tremendous number passed through Roehampton. I started in 1916 before the Somme and the number on the list then was about 2,500. By the time I left two and a half years later, there were 25,000 numbers. So I personally had interviewed something like 22,000 or 23,000 limbless soldiers and sailors. It's incredible when you think of it!

Limbless soldiers were a common sight on the streets, hobbling on sticks, swinging on crutches, sometimes helpless in a wheelchair or with one empty pinned-up blue sleeve, where an arm had been amputated. Their all-too-visible wounds attracted a great deal of public sympathy. As their numbers grew, so the design of the artificial limbs improved; legs became lighter and more flexible, hands more resilient and ingenious, capable of gripping and lifting. No effort was spared to research and incorporate new ideas that would help to make the future tolerable for those who had not only done their bit but had left a bit of themselves on the battlefield. No ex-soldier of this war would have to stump through life on a wooden leg or with an ugly hook attached to the stump of his arm. But there were cases when stumps were too rudimentary for an artificial limb to be fitted, where a man had lost both legs and an arm, where all four limbs had been blown off or amputated. Such men would be helpless for life, and 'life' was a long time for a boy of nineteen or twenty.

But worse fates could befall a soldier than the loss of a single limb. You could get along without an arm or a leg. You could hardly get along without a face.

Plastic surgery was born of the necessity to try to repair the ravages of faces wrecked and mangled by shell splinters, and often a single case would demand the skill of half a dozen separate specialists. An ear, nose and throat man to create new nostrils so that a soldier could breathe without a nose; to rebuild a gullet so that he could eat; to insert a plate in a shattered palate, so that he could speak. An eye surgeon would be needed if his sight could be saved, or, where it could not, to trim and clean the empty sockets or create a new one to receive an artificial eye. Most delicate of all was the work entailed in rebuilding a shattered jaw and, where part of the jawbone had disappeared completely, inserting a contraption of teeth and wire. Nothing like it had ever been done before. There had never been any need.

Dr Kazanjian, who was not a doctor but a dentist, had come over with the 1st Harvard Medical Unit and rapidly became an expert in jaws. He had no official right to perform operations, but although he was completely unqualified as a surgeon his skill as a dentist, and knowledge of the structure of that particular part of the anatomy, combined with a natural talent and a passionate interest in his cases, soon convinced the qualified doctors and surgeons of the unit that he was the best man for the job. Kazanjian developed his technique to such a degree that he could not be spared when the rest of the unit returned at the end of their six months' service. He was still there in 1916 when the 3rd Unit arrived, and there was no question of his leaving.*

* On his return to America at the end of the war, Dr Kazanjian took both medical and surgical degrees and became one of the fathers of plastic surgery in the United States.

But the surgical work at the base hospitals in France, skilful though it was, was necessarily rough, and it was not until the soldier was well enough to be repatriated to a hospital in Blighty that the real work could begin. By 1916 a specialized hospital for facial injuries had been opened at 42 Brook Street, London, and a small group of surgeons were taking the first tentative steps in the development of the techniques of skin-grafting and bone-transplanting. They were also experimenting with injections of wax under newly grafted skin, which covered a flat angular plane, in order to pad it into some semblance of a cheek. It was a long, tedious business. Sometimes as many as a dozen separate operations had to be performed on a single case, with long intervals between them. The surgeons at Brook Street pooled their knowledge with colleagues working in other military hospitals, for there was a limit to the number of in-patients and even out-patients that a small specialized unit could handle.

But there were very few out-patients. Even in the intervals of healing and waiting, how could a man be sent out to meet the world when all that remained of his face was, perhaps, one eye, one ear, the brutalized remnants of a lipless mouth and two small orifices that represented nostrils but in no way represented a nose? How could relatives, wives, children, fiancées be expected not to recoil in horror from a gargoyle whose only recognizable feature was a shock of boyish hair? In the hospitals, at least, they were steeled to such sights.

> There was a man with one side of his face blown away. The skin had grown over it, but he was still bandaged and I was told to syringe his face and to put a screen round him while I did it. I chatted to him while I was taking the dressing off and I must have smiled. He said, 'How can you smile when you look at me, Nurse?' It must have meant a lot to him, because later he wrote in my autograph book:
>
> 'Remember, dear Nurse, to keep that sweet smile,
> It helps us lame dogs over many a stile.'

Grace Bignold, VAD, No. 1 London General Hospital

'*Always* look a man straight in the face,' one Sister instructed her staff. 'Remember he's watching your face to see how you're going to react.' It was easier to smile, to catch a man's eye, to look him straight in the face when you were doing a dressing before the wound had healed. Hideous though it was, in a raw, bleeding state it was not much worse than similar horrors on an arm, a leg, an abdomen, a back. A little more unpleasant to dress, perhaps, because the patient's breath, mingling with stale blood in the mouth and passages before the raw flesh healed, was peculiarly foul, and it was hard to sustain a smile during the close-quarters business of adjusting drainage or feeding tubes. Professional detachment helped. But the real difficulty arose much later when the wounds had healed, when the surgeons had done their best, when soon the man would be discharged from hospital, and he was still a gargoyle. Then, when one searching eye watched for a nurse's reaction, it was difficult for her not to drop her eyes in natural embarrassment.

The surgeons had done what they could, but they were not artists. Francis Derwent Wood, on the other hand, was a sculptor and an Associate of the Royal Academy. He was also an RAMC orderly at the 3rd London General Hospital, one of the hundreds of middle-aged men, like Corporal Ward Muir, who had joined the army as orderlies. The fact that their official title was 'Nursing Orderlies' caused some amusement in the light of the fact that nursing was the only job they were neither expected nor allowed to do. It was the orderlies who carried the stretchers, who wheeled patients to the operating theatre, who set trays, dished out meals, and took on the less pleasant chores connected with bedpans. It was the orderly who washed and shaved the helpless, carried legless men to the bath, supplies from the stores, letters to and from the postroom, and humped the daily baskets of dirty linen to the laundry. It was the orderly who washed up forty sets of crockery after every meal, boiled forty eggs for breakfast every morning, made forty mugs of cocoa every evening and answered urgent calls of 'Orderly!' forty times a day. In the hierarchy of a military hospital even the status of the humble VAD was one notch above that of the lowly orderly. 'One-third housemaid, one-third waiter and one-third valet, that's us', remarked Ward Muir without rancour.

A year ago Derwent Wood had been performing the same indispensable but undemanding chores as a private; now, in 1916, he had risen to the dizzy heights of a commission with the rank of captain in the Royal Army Medical Corps. It had all started with the splints, which had been a problem from the beginning. There was hardly any such thing as a straightforward fracture, because the bullet or shell splinter that smashed the bones of an arm or leg also ripped the flesh, so that there was no possibility of encasing the whole leg with its open wounds in a plaster cast. Sometimes it was possible to devise a series of casts with 'peep holes', through which wounds could be dressed while the limb was kept rigid. Dr Daniel Reardon had devised one for a patient at No. 11 General Hospital at Camiers but there was always the danger of creeping infection, which could fester and swell undetected beneath the cast.

Coming into close contact with such wounded men during the awkward business of helping them use bedpans, Derwent Wood's skilled eye assessed the problem and came up with a solution that could only have occurred to a sculptor. Why should the splints not be moulded and cast to fit the arm, the leg or the back of the patient, so that a fractured bone would fit comfortably into it, be held completely rigid and yet leave the wounds free and accessible? It was fortunate that the Commanding Officer of No. 3 London General was not so hidebound by professional medical etiquette as to fail to spot a good idea when it was put to him. He also recognized talent when he saw it and, in a matter of days, Private Derwent Wood had been promoted from house-maid/waiter/valet to sergeant in charge of the splint room. A second brainchild brought him a commission and the opportunity of starting an entirely new department.

The Tommies called it the Tin Noses Shop; its official title was the Masks for Facial Disfigurements Department. The hurly-burly of the ward was all very well for men with bandaged faces, but when the concealing dressings eventually had to be removed a disfigured man could hardly be exposed to the torture of the pitying or horrified scrutiny of the outsiders and visitors who were constantly coming and going. He could not be hidden behind screens for ever. It answered only part of the problem to move him to a single room when one was available, where only sympathetic doctors, nurses, orderlies or compan-ions from the main ward would have the right of entry, and which could be darkened, if the patient chose, when visitors came to see him. Often he preferred not to have visitors at all. When they did come the nurses dreaded the scenes that occasionally took place, where in spite of Sister's gentle preparation in the case of mothers and her occasionally stiffening lectures in the case of young wives and fiancées, some girls had to be brought out of the room in fits of hysterics. Restored with brandy in Sister's office they would sit wringing their hands: 'Oh Lord, help me, what am I going to do? What am I going to do?' It was a natural reaction which struck little sympathy with Sister, who was rather more concerned about what her patient was going to do.

In the quiet single rooms there was time to brood. Despite the care and vigilance of the staff, and despite their support and assumed cheer-fulness, there were occasional suicides, discreetly hushed up by the hospital authorities, and cases where the patient lost the will to live and quietly died. The standard telegram was used in either case:

REGRET INFORM YOU PRIVATE SMITH 10TH ——SHIRE REGIMENT DIED THIS EVENING AFTER A RELAPSE.

Carrying one such telegram to the postroom while he was working as an orderly, Derwent Wood reflected bitterly on the guilty thankfulness with which the telegram would no doubt be received at its destination. Over the months, in the ward and in the splint room, he did quite a bit of brooding on his own account and in October he made another appointment to see the Commanding Officer.

The Tin Noses Shop was the result. It was set up in one half of the splint room, enlarged and embellished now with rows of plaster casts of heads and faces. On the walls was Derwent Wood's 'rogues' gallery' – long rows of studio photographs of young soldiers. Many of them bore inscriptions: *To Mother, from Tom; To Florrie — all my love, Jack; To Jessie, all the best from your cousin Fred.*

Those photographs, which wives, sweethearts and relatives had urged the boys to have taken before they went off to the Front, were indispensable to Derwent Wood's work because his aim was to manufacture a mask that would as closely as possible resemble the original face.

It was pointless to manufacture a mask to fit contours which were going to shrink, so the wound had to be finally and irrevocably healed before Derwent Wood could begin. It was a job that required tact as well as skill. When a man had looked at himself in a mirror and knew that the sight of his face was unbearably repulsive, it took courage to leave his darkened room, come into the brightly lit studio and sit still and unblinking (if he still possessed eyelids to blink with) while the sculptor and his assistant stared into his face, inspected it from every angle, probed, measured, compared it with the once-familiar face in the photograph, and prepared it for moulding. Often, in his off-duty moments, Derwent Wood's friend, Ward Muir, hovered in the background, fascinated by the procedure.

Corporal Ward Muir, RAMC, No. 3 London General Hospital

The patient had lost, perhaps, one eye, a slice of the adjacent cheek and the top part of the nose. In such a case the whole of the upper half of the face, including the entire nose and the surviving eye, must be moulded. It is first painted over with oil. The eyebrows are smeared with Vaseline. The moustache, if any, receives the same treatment. This is to prevent the plaster of Paris which is about to be applied from sticking to the hairs. The patient, leaning back in his chair as though about to be shaved at the barber's, closes his one remaining eye and has a snippet of tissue paper placed on its oily lid to protect it. A similar snippet protects the hole that once contained the other eye. Quickly a film of plaster is brushed on to the face; heavier dollops of plaster are applied to the film; and soon the face looks as though its upper features have been richly lathered. The lather grows thicker and thicker, more and more solid, drier and drier. At length the correct moment has arrived and the lance-corporal assistant – who was a sculptor's moulder in civil life – detaches and lifts off from the patient's face a faintly steaming shell of plaster. The inner surface is a negative replica of the gargoyle which is to be restored to a natural appearance.

This was the first of a long series of delicate processes. First, a plaster of Paris positive was made from the negative, for the purpose of removing imperfections, tiny bubbles in the plaster, cracks and, inevitably, lumps and bumps. They were filled in or filed off and the cast rubbed down and smoothed. Then another negative had to be made of the refined version, and a new positive – this time in plasticine. The sole reason for making the plasticine positive was to open the eye which had been closed when the original plaster was applied, so that a new eye could be matched to it. When this was done, with a few strokes of the sculptor's knife, a new plaster of Paris negative was made from the plasticine and from it another positive cast of the soldier's injured face, now with an open eye. It was with this cast that the final process began.

The work was minute, elaborate and finely detailed. The eyeless socket was filled in, given an eye and an eyebrow to match the other; the concave cheek was built up to match the good cheek; the nose was remoulded; part of the forehead restored. Working in meticulous detail, the lights of his studio workshop often burning into the small hours of the morning, Derwent Wood sat at his bench for hour after hour, and with the injured man's photograph propped up in front of him he worked on the cast to produce a portrait of the soldier as he had been. Sometimes it took weeks of work before the mask itself could be contoured and moulded from the plaster likeness.

At first it was a question of trial and error. The main problem was to decide on a suitable material. Cloth could not hold a firm shape; papier mâché was too thick and was not durable; plaster was too heavy. The final choice was thin electroplate, the merest fraction of an inch thick. Its appearance in its unfinished state was not impressive; an irregular piece of metal with an oval hole to receive an eye, a jutting projection to form the upper part of the missing nose at one side of it and, on the other, a curve to replace the missing cheek. At this stage, in spite of anxious pleas, Derwent Wood never allowed a patient to see the mask. Standing behind him he slipped it over his face, measured and adjusted it and sent him off with a hearty promise that it would soon be ready. When the sculptor had convinced himself that the shape and fit were perfect the mask was sent to be silverplated. Later it was tinted to look as nearly as possible like flesh. Eyes were the problem. Francis Derwent Wood was a fanatical perfectionist and instead of using commercial glass eyes, which seldom gave more than an approximate match, he spent painstaking hours painting exact replicas of existing eyes (right down to the veins in the white) on to the oval glass discs that fitted into the oval 'eye socket' in the mask. Real hair would not adhere permanently to the metal, so eyelashes were made of hair-like slivers of silver foil painted, like the eyebrow, to match the patient's own colouring. It was all done in oil paints. Fired enamel had been tried, but the result was found to be too glossy and artificial. The mask had to blend into the patient's own skin tones as unobtrusively as possible, and so delicate was Derwent Wood's work that in many cases it was impossible to detect the join. The masks were a perfect fit, as light as a membrane and with the strength and firmness of metal, and when, as so often, there had been damage to the lachrymatory or the salivary glands, and the man with the ruined face was further afflicted by constant discharging from his mouth or his eye socket, absorbent pads which could be placed in the hollows behind the mask did a great deal to relieve his embarrassment. Spectacles hid a multitude of flaws, besides holding the mask securely to the wearer's face, and a generous false moustache could go a long way towards camouflaging a scarred and twisted mouth.

One sergeant patient of Derwent Wood's actually took to waxing the ends of his moustache and stoutly declared, to the sculptor's pleasure and admiration, that he believed he was a handsomer,man now than when he had joined the army. Underneath was still the ravaged face. There was nothing that anyone could do to alter that. No painstaking efforts could give a man back the face he had lost; no one could heal his deep psychological wounds. Even the masks were temporary affairs that would last a few years at most. But they helped. They gave back self-respect. They were a buffer against the world. From behind one of Captain Derwent Wood's masterpieces, a disfigured man could look the world in the face knowing that the world could look back at him without shuddering at the sight.

Convalescent wounded soldiers had the freedom of every town, city and village in England. By courtesy of the management, they filled whole rows of the best seats at theatres and 'picture palaces', travelled free on public transport and stylishly in the motor cars of willing volunteers, who took them for country drives when the weather was fine. There were concerts for wounded, tea parties at private houses, and bazaars to raise money for the long-term care of the permanently disabled at which a few of the wounded themselves were often decoratively present. Wounded soldiers and sailors were a surefire attraction at any social event. In the bright suits of hospital blue, white shirts and red ties, which were set off by white arm-slings or bandages on their heads and feet, supported by crutches or leaning on sticks, the wounded attracted a wealth of sympathy and attention. Heads turned to look at them, women clucked sympathetically, girls smiled invitingly from park benches, landlords, turning a blind eye to the Defence of the Realm Act, under which it was an offence to supply alcohol to patients in military hospitals, would supply free beer to wounded Tommies who ventured into pubs, and city gentlemen would press half-crowns into their not unwilling hands with a sympathetic nod. Altogether a wounded soldier could have quite a satisfactory afternoon out.

But such largesse only came the way of the wounded who presented a traditionally picturesque appearance. If a man was too badly disfigured, even if he was blind, people averted their eyes; if he had no visible wounds, no bandages to reinforce his heroic image, he got scant attention. This distinction caused a certain amount of resentment among the gassed and the many sick men who had succumbed to fever or dysentery in Gallipoli and the Middle East and had now been sent home to complete their convalescence in hospitals in Blighty. Thin and gaunt, yellowed but whole, they glared in baleful resentment as people fussed over their glamorous, bandaged comrades. They particularly resented the cash that jingled in their pockets, the proceeds of the tokens of appreciation pressed on them by individual representatives of a Grateful Nation. At St Luke's Military Hospital in Bradford a group of the gassed patients in Ward 3 (Medical), who were allowed out in the afternoons now that they were recovering, embarked on a ploy which they might have thought twice about had they realized that it was Sister's afternoon off.

It was a fine day, so I went for a walk with my friend Beatrice Bee, who also happened to be off duty, and we ended up by going into a café for a cup of tea. It was very full and there were a lot of wounded soldiers in their blues. When we were drinking our tea, I looked across and, to my horror, I saw three of my boys, and they were *swathed* in bandages. Well, of course, not one of them had so much as a scratch on him and there they were, arms in slings and legs tied up, crutches propped up by their chairs. We finished our tea and the boys hadn't spotted me, so I went across to them as we went out and stopped by their table. 'Are you enjoying your tea?' I said. They were completely dumbfounded and looked very embarrassed, and eventually one of them, an older man who came from Devon, as I did myself, said, 'Oh yes, Sister, very much.' 'Good,' I said. 'Well, when you get back, I should like you all to come and see me in my office.'

Sister Henrietta Hall, QAIMNS (R), St Luke's Military Hospital, Bradford

Of course, they turned up very sheepish, and I asked them to explain themselves. They said, 'Well, Sister, if you're walking about with bandages on, you collect a lot of money and people ask you to tea and we get very friendly with some of the girls. We didn't mean any harm.' I said, 'What a dreadful thing to do, when the people of Bradford have been so kind to you! Now, tell me, who bandaged you up? I know you couldn't have done it yourselves.' Of course, they denied that any of the nurses had helped them, but it was obvious that it was a professional job and someone must have got the crutches out of the store. They all protested that no one had helped them, but they couldn't possibly have done it alone. Obviously it wouldn't have been my Staff Nurse, but there were five VADs in my ward, so I had them all in and questioned them. They all denied it too, but they were probably in on it, because they were very sympathetic to the boys. We all were, but it was up to me to maintain discipline, so I told them that I would have to report them to the Major. After they went out the Devon man came back in. He was older than the rest, a married man, certainly over thirty. He apologized again and I told him that he, at least, ought to have known better. He said, 'Well, Sister, don't report this to Major. It won't happen again.' 'No,' I said, 'it musn't happen again!'

It seems very funny, looking back, but at the time I had to be very strict. It was a very happy ward, and yet you couldn't let them get away with too much or things would get out of hand.

I once gave some boys the shock of their lives. I'd been out for the evening and I was wearing civilian clothes and came back about 9.30 when it was almost dark. If the wounded were given a pass to go out they had to be back by 7.30, and coming along the wall of the hospital on my way to the main gate I saw a bunch of boys just about to climb over it. As I approached one of them turned round and called out, 'Come on, girlie, and give us a leg up.' But the words were hardly out of his mouth when another boy shouted, 'Good God, it's Sister!' You should have seen them scramble! 'Right', I said '9.30 tomorrow morning in my office'. So I had them on the carpet and gave them a proper dressing down and told them they had to be in at the proper time, half-past seven, in the future. I didn't report them. I should have, but I didn't.

You couldn't help but feel sorry for them. They'd been through such a dreadful time, these gas cases, and it took a very long time for them to recover. Even when they were on the mend, if there was a change in the weather or very cold it would affect the lungs. We always kept the windows open, and if we could we put them out on the veranda. The eyes were often affected very badly, so they had to be bathed and treated, and some of them had awful coughs. They simply couldn't get breath at all and it was very frightening for them. We had oxygen by the side of the bed and frequently I would have to send one of the nurses to sit there and hold the mask, perhaps for half an hour, and then have a rest and go back again. They simply couldn't breathe without oxygen when they were very bad.

In a military hospital the discipline was pretty strict. Everything was regulated: what time they got up; the fact that they must shave every day; what time they had to have baths; and when the Medical Officer came round in the morning, those who were able had to stand at attention by the foot of their beds. They were with us such a long time that we got very fond of them, and I sometimes used to think that the Medical Officers were a little bit hard on them. Sometimes when a young boy of nineteen, say, had gone out I used to think that perhaps Major could have put off his going back just a little longer.

I remember one particular Cornish boy I was very sorry for. He had been gassed at Ypres and he'd been with us a long time. He was absolutely terrified of going back to the Front – because he was almost well again – and he used to beg me to get him off going. I had to say, 'Well, there's nothing I can do about it, but I'm sure you won't be going back just yet.' One day just as I was going round the ward with Major I saw this boy unscrewing his hot-water bottle. They all had their own thermometers in a little holder above the bed, and out of the corner of my eye I saw him put the thermometer into the neck of the hot-water bottle. When we got to him he was standing at the foot of his bed with the thermometer in his mouth, as they were all supposed to do. Major said, 'This boy's got a very high temperature, Sister.' I said, 'Has he?' He said, 'Yes, a very high temperature.' And he asked the boy, 'What's the matter? Do you feel ill?' The poor boy didn't know what to say and he just mumbled something, so I had to step in. I didn't give him away, I just said to the Major, 'I think he'll be all right, but I don't really think he's ready to be discharged yet,' and of course he wasn't.

About once a month his people came up from Cornwall to see him, and his mother begged me to get him out. They were farmers and he was an only child. I remember the mother saying, 'He *would* join up, you know. He didn't have to go because we run the farm, but he *would* join up.' She was in a dreadful state, crying in my office. They wrote to me several times and thanked me for what I'd done.

I'd done very little, but the boy eventually went to a convalescent home. I don't think he ever went back.

Sister's bark was a good deal worse than her bite, and running a ward of forty seriously ill or wounded men was a heavy responsibility with only one trained nurse, who often had sketchy qualifications, and a handful of VADs with no qualifications at all. It was when the men were convalescent that the trouble began, and with their returning strength they also developed a disturbing tendency to fall in love with the VADs. Sister Hall, who was young, pretty and, at twenty-six, not above falling in love herself, understood such things better than some older martinets, but it was impossible to turn a completely blind eye. Any romantic inclinations that showed themselves in the ward had to be quickly squashed in the course of a short sharp interview in Sister's office, but she would not have dreamed of sacking a badly needed, efficient VAD so long as she remained on the right side of military discipline and propriety. 'Just don't meet him outside while he's a patient here,' Sister would advise wearily. 'And *don't* meet him in the grounds. Wait until he goes convalescent. Then you can do as you please in your own time.'

But it was difficult to heed such advice when the whole atmosphere, in the hospitals and out of them, was heightened by the excitement and poignancy of the war itself. When every wounded soldier was hailed as a romantic hero. When every gramophone in every ward in every hospital was churning out the plaintive strains of 'Smoke Clouds Set Me Yearning'. When every errand boy was whistling 'If You were the Only Girl in the World'. When every visiting pianist started off with rousing renderings of 'Tipperary' and 'Pack Up Your Troubles', and inevitably drifted into the strains of the song that caught the popular imagination in 1916. It exactly hit the prevailing mood of the million young people caught up in a weary round of work and killing, pain and suffering, toil and endurance, meetings and partings. The excitement and heroics had turned sour. It seemed as if the war was never going to end, and already they had seen horrors enough for a lifetime.

There's a long, long trail a-winding
Into the land of my dreams,
Where the nightingales are singing
And a white moon beams.
There's a long, long night of waiting
Until my dreams all come true;
Till the day when I'll be going down
That long, long trail with you.

It was hard not to cling together. It was easy for a bond of warmth
and sympathy to be mistaken for a deeper emotion. It was dangerously
easy for pity to turn to love. But in most cases Sister was right. It was
unwise. It could be dangerous. Duty must come before romance. In any
event, there would soon be no time to think of such things. It was the eve
of the biggest battle of the war. The hospitals in France were clearing
out to make way for a new batch of wounded, and the men and the guns
were already moving into position on the Somme.

Chapter Twelve

The Somme began where the harsh industrial north country of France left off. A land of rolling downs, of woods and meadows, of gentle hills, quiet streams, peaceful villages and hamlets that inclined some British soldiers to feel homesick for Sussex and Hampshire. Before the summer of 1916 there were worse places to be. It was a quiet sector of the line and 'live and let live' was the more-or-less unwritten rule, particularly in the French sector where both sides had not been above indulging in a little quiet fraternization. When water was scarce, and a solitary well was inconveniently situated in the middle of No Man's Land between the front-line trenches, French and Germans who happened to meet each other in its vicinity would discreetly look the other way. It was not unknown for French and German bathing parties to swim in full view of one another in adjoining stretches of the same river, and there were rumours that in some sections of the line French and German officers were in the habit of crossing No Man's Land by invitation to enjoy an evening socializing in the Mess of the battalion opposite. When the British army extended its line and took over part of the French sector in order to relieve the pressure on their overstretched allies, these rumours – true or false – caused a certain amount of moustache-bristling among senior officers, and in accordance with their instructions to 'keep the Hun busy' the sector livened up in the months before the battle.

The Somme offensive had been intended originally to be a combined Anglo-French operation, but the French, still struggling at Verdun, were no longer in a position to make anything like the contribution they had intended when the the plans had first been made six months earlier. Now, at best, they could provide sufficient men to attack on the southern stretch of the twisting fifteen miles of front; the main brunt of the battle would be borne by the British. But confidence was high. The planning had been meticulous down to the smallest detail, the troops were fresh, enthusiastic, even in high spirits, for it was the first time that Kitchener's Army, though tried and tested, would have had a real chance to 'have a go at the Hun' in a major battle. Officers and men alike were the pick of the volunteers. It was known, of course, that the Germans had built strong defences – observers could hardly miss the belts of barbed wire that stretched many yards deep in front of their trenches – but this time the Allies were taking the initiative. This time there were enough men, enough guns, and, for once, huge stockpiles of ammunition and massive mines which would breach the German lines at their strongest points. This time, for a full week before Zero Hour, there would be a massive bombardment which would so destroy the wire and pulverize the enemy in his trenches beyond that the Tommies would be able to stroll across No Man's Land at a steady pace with, as one particularly optimistic staff officer put it, 'rifles at the port'.

At half-past seven in the morning of 1 July, as soon as the barrage lifted, they started off towards the enemy lines.

They attacked shoulder to shoulder, line after line, wave upon wave, straight into the sights of the German machine-guns. Far from being pulverized, they were ready to chatter into action as soon as the bombardment moved on, and the German soldiers were able to rush up from underground shelters reaching deep into chalky earth, where they had escaped the bombardment virtually unscathed. No shells were powerful enough to penetrate the shelters and tunnels, even if the British had guessed that they existed. The high-shrapnel shells designed to explode above the wire and scatter the shrapnel over a wide area, slicing through the thick iron strands, had hardly touched it. The Germans were quick to recover from the huge explosions of the mines, and in their rush to defend the positions beat the British to the lips of the craters.

In the early morning, just before the battle, Geoffrey Mallen took his cinematographic camera into an assembly trench behind Hunter's Lane, the jumping-off point for the 29th Division, and filmed some soldiers of the 16th Battalion, The Middlesex Regiment (which happened to be a Public Schools Battalion), as they waited to go over the top. They were delighted to be the object of such novel attention. They nudged each other and beamed and winked at the camera. They lit cigarettes and pantomimed their excitement for its benefit. They gave the thumbs-up sign. They were full of beans and full of confidence. Within an hour almost half of them lay dead or wounded.

The medical arrangements had been made with care. Advance dressing-stations were clustered along the length of the line, with well-sandbagged collecting centres a little distance behind them. It was at one of these, known as Minden Post, that Geoffrey Mallen set up his cine-camera a little later in the day. He filmed a queue of walking wounded, waiting four deep for attention, and although there were more medical personnel concentrated in one small area than there had ever been throughout the war it was obvious that the men would have a long time to wait. The 1st and 2nd Armies, which were not taking part in the battle, had been combed for all the medical staff and transport which could be spared. Specialist surgical teams of doctors, nurses and anaesthetists stood by, ready to move quickly to where they were most needed. Operating centres were sent forward, near the line, to deal speedily with the seriously injured who would otherwise not have survived the ambulance journey to the casualty clearing stations.

It all looked very neat on paper, where the crosses denoting the medical units were drawn thick on the map as far back as Doullens. The

Director of Medical Services at advanced GHQ at Beauquesne had perhaps no reason to suppose, as he glanced with satisfaction at the blown-up version of the map on his office wall, that the provisions were not more than adequate. But they were swamped within the first hour, and at that point he should have changed his opinion and faced the fact that the three empty hospital trains waiting in the area would be far less than enough to take the wounded from the casualty clearing stations down the line to base. Twenty more were available, and by a previous arrangement a telephone call to the Assistant Director of Railway Transport at Amiens would have brought at least some of them quickly into the area. But perhaps the DMS could not bring himself to believe that the information which was coming in could possibly be true – for the casualties were ten times, twenty times, fifty times as many as anyone had anticipated. In the first twenty-four hours, 24,000 wounded had passed through the field ambulances in a steady flow, and by the middle of the afternoon the casualty clearing stations were so overcrowded that unless they could clear at least some of the wounded, there would be no room for new arrivals. It was only then, when the gravity of the situation became glaringly obvious, that the DMS made the telephone call to Amiens. It was only then that the orders were telegraphed to the ambulance trains which had been standing by all day to receive them. It was many hours before they reached the Somme. Every wheeled vehicle of the back-up service was brought from miles around, from as far away as the base, to run an emergency shuttle service to take the wounded away from the clearing stations, but in spite of Herculean efforts, many of them were still there by nightfall and it was impossible to shelter them all.

It was fortunate that the heat of the day was followed by a warm night. In the tents and marquees the wounded lay on the beds and on stretchers between the beds, and when the stretchers ran out (which was early on) they lay on the ground, in the passageways and on the naked earth outside. As the guns thudded and flashed through the night a few miles away, lighting the starlit sky with flashes of yellow glare, doctors, nurses, surgeons and orderlies worked flat out. They could only attend to a fraction of the 12,000 wounded who had reached the casualty clearing stations by evening, and fresh convoys of ambulances kept on coming all through the night. When the ambulance trains eventually came to the rescue – and eighteen reached the sector the following day – the hospitals at the bases were equally flooded and equally over-whelmed. It was only possible to keep and care for the most danger-ously wounded. The others must go straight to England, and in most cases there was not even time to clean them up or even to change the first rough field dressing which had been clapped on to their wounds in the heat of the battle many hours or even days earlier. For the push was still going on, and the casualties poured in until it seemed to the frantic doctors and nurses, drivers and stretcher-bearers working round the clock in the wards, in the ambulance columns, transports and trains, that there must hardly be a whole soldier left at the Front to fight the battle. In the first four days, in one hundred journeys, the hospital trains carried 33,392 patients from the casualty clearing stations to the bases at Boulogne, Rouen and Le Havre. Most of them loaded up at the railhead at Vequement, behind the southern part of the line where the fight was fiercest, and unloaded at Rouen. From there the patients could be put directly on the hospital ships on the river, or sent on by train to embark at Le Havre.

The hospital at Le Havre was comparatively small, perched above the quayside in pre-war waiting-rooms and offices overlooking the berth where the transatlantic liners had lain before the war. It was an ideal site, because the hospital trains could run straight on to the quay as the boat trains had done in peacetime. The wards were high and airy, with long windows opening on to the balconies where once, in another world, smartly dressed people had stood waving and cheering departing or arriving friends aboard luxury liners. The nurses found them equally convenient for waving off patients bound for Blighty. But there was no time for that. In the first days of the battle, the tiny hospital on the Quai d'Escale took in one thousand patients needing urgent treatment, and as in the casualty clearing stations there was hardly room to move between recumbent bodies.

Elizabeth Storer, VAD, Quai d'Escale Hospital, Le Havre

The hospital trains were doing a shuttle service and so were the ships. We had hardly time to look at what was going on, but we could hear because the trains ran right under the wards. Day and night there was a constant rumble as they arrived to unload and immediately start off back again, empty, to the railhead to fetch the next train-load of wounded. It was fortunate that it was fine weather, because sometimes there were so many waiting to go that the stretchers were lying all over the quay waiting for a ship to come in. The ships went back and forth all the time, and we could see them even at night passing on their way to embark the wounded from there. Later in the war, after some hospital ships had been torpedoed, they were all camouflaged and dimly lit, but then it was a brilliant spectacle because they were all painted white and in the darkness they were ablaze with lights.

I was on night duty during that period, which was not quite so bad as the chaos of the daytime, but nevertheless we were absolutely exhausted. One night I had to be in constant attendance on a patient who was one of the ones lying out on the veranda. I had a chair to rest in and I must have dropped off. Next day the RAMC colonel told me, jokingly, that he had come in to look at the patient and had entered in his report, '*Both nurse and patient were sleeping peacefully.*' It was a dreadful thing to fall asleep on duty, but the colonel didn't upbraid me because he knew what we were going through and he himself must have been as worn out as any of us.

They packed the wounded on to every inch of the hospital ships, not only into the wards and saloons below but into the Sisters' and doctors' own quarters, and when even they were full they laid the stretchers on the deck alongside the 'walking wounded'. Some of them were able to act as voluntary orderlies during the voyage. Their wounds were slight, but in the wholesale evacuation, with the base hospitals already over-crowded with serious cases, there was simply no time to sort out the men who in normal circumstances could have been returned to their units after a few days' local treatment. Leonard Chamberlen, a Second Lieutenant in The Rifle Brigade, had been sent to a base hospital with a bad ankle, which he had sprained severely by falling into a shellhole when carrying a wounded man from the line. He was amazed and delighted a few days later to find himself on a ship bound for Blighty. But the wholesale evacuation did nothing to relieve the crisis on the Somme, where the armies, in urgent need of reinforcements for the next stage of the battle, lost men for weeks or months who should only have been absent from the ranks for a matter of days; and the ranks were badly enough depleted as it was.

The reserves had already been moved up. Now huge drafts of rein-forcements were on their way from Blighty.

There was elation at home when the first news of the battle arrived, and there was rejoicing over the glowing newspaper headlines at a million breakfast tables. FORWARD IN THE WEST. START OF A GREAT ATTACK, FIERCE BATTLES ON THE SOMME. It would be many days before the casualty lists could be compiled, and more than a week of anxious waiting before telegrams could be sent to the relatives of the killed and wounded. As time passed, despite early reports that casualties had not been heavy, dread began to mount in families who guessed that their boys were in the battle. The wounded were despatched by train to hospitals all over the country, and they came in such numbers that no one could fail to see that the reports had been false and that the casualties had been appallingly heavy. Kathleen Yarwood, who worked as a VAD at the military hospital housed in what had been the old Dearnley workhouse in Rochdale, was spending her day off at home when the wounded arrived. She and her mother rushed to the garden gate.

They were coming up the road past the house, a huge, long proces-sion of walking wounded. At least, they were supposed to be walking wounded but some of them weren't really fit to walk at all, and there weren't nearly enough ambulances to bring them from the station. They'd rounded up as many private cars and motor lorries as they could get to carry the worst cases, but the rest had to make their own way to the hospital and it was a good few miles from the station. They had to go along Entwhistle Road, then right up the Halifax Road to Birch Hill. If they could walk at all they had to manage on their

Kathleen Yarwood, VAD, Dearnley Hospital, Birch Hill, Rochdale own. It was heartbreaking to see them, although they themselves were very cheery as they went past. One would be helping another, and some of the better ones were pushing some of the other chaps in the bathchairs which they'd managed to rush down to the station, and of course there were masses of Red Cross workers and people helping them along. The roads were lined with people watching and rushing into their houses and out again to give them drinks of water, barley squash, biscuits, chocolates, cigarettes – anything they had. They were walking past all day – all day long they went past our house up the road to Birch Hill. It was shocking.

When I got back on duty the state of the hospital was unbelievable. They'd even had to use the recreation rooms, and there were men on stretchers lying across the billiard table. In the ordinary wards it was so bad that they'd had to put every two beds close together, with three lightly wounded patients in the two beds and a second layer of patients on two stretchers balanced on the bed rails on top of them. There was absolutely nothing else that could possibly be done for the moment, because we received something like three times as many wounded as we had expected and we couldn't possibly accommodate them all. It was only like that for that one first night. Next day we were able to rearrange things and send some of them off to other local auxiliary hospitals.

The same thing was happening all over Scotland and the north of England where they had sent the walking wounded, who were best able to stand a longer journey. Boarding out was the only answer in the first few chaotic days, and harassed Red Cross area organizers spent hours on the telephone ringing local vicars, schoolmasters, even friends and private householders to beg a few nights' shelter for a handful of wounded soldiers.

The most critical cases had been unloaded and sent to hospitals as close as possible to the ports of arrival. Those who could not be accommodated, and those who were seriously wounded but likely to survive a longer journey, were sent on by train to Birmingham, Bristol, Exeter, Leicester, Norwich and Plymouth. But seven out of every ten hospital trains were directed to London, and during the first days of the Somme they rolled in almost every hour to Charing Cross and Paddington stations.

Claire Elise Tisdall, VAD Ambulance Nurse, The Ambulance Service, London District

Our job was to travel with the ambulances taking the wounded from the trains to the hospitals. During the Somme we practically never stopped. We had to go to the station and wait for the trains to come in – long grey trains they were, with red crosses on the outside – and we all lined up and stood there waiting. There were detachments of stretcher-bearers with their own commandants, and they went into the trains and carried the men out. Then the stretchers were carried down to the long line of ambulances drawn up inside the station.

They'd load four men into an ambulance, and when you heard your name called you jumped in too. The commandant would give you a card and say, 'You're to go to No. 3 or No. 4 General Hospital.' We went all over London. No. 3 was on Wandsworth Common and there was a big one at Tottenham, another big one at Bethnal Green, and hospitals in Lewisham, Fulham, Hammersmith and Hampstead. During that Somme push we often had to take them to the outlying hospitals, even as far as Richmond, because the big hospitals were so very quickly filled up. On the way there we had to take their names and details in a little notebook, and when we got to the hospital we had to get a receipt for their kit and then drive back to the station again to wait for the next convoy. Of course, we had to look after the men on the journey and we had some very serious cases during the Somme. I'll never forget it. I was up for seventeen nights before I had a night in a bed.

The worst case I saw – and it still haunts me – was of a man being carried past us. It was at night, and in the dim light I thought that his face was covered with a black cloth. But as he came nearer, I was horrified to realize that the whole lower half of his face had been completely blown off and what had appeared to be a black cloth was a huge gaping hole. That was the only time that I nearly fainted on the platform, but fortunately I was able to pull myself together. It was the most frightful sight, because he couldn't be covered up at all.

A lot of the boys had had legs blown off, or hastily amputated in France – just newly done, because they couldn't keep these cases. They had to keep sending them on during the Somme, because there were others coming in all the time. These boys were the ones who were in the greatest pain, and I very often used to have to hold the stump up for the whole journey, so that it wouldn't bump on the stretcher.

We were quite worn out, and the drivers were absolutely exhausted as well. My driver fell asleep one night when we had a terrible load of very badly wounded men. It was in the middle of the night, and the ambulance went right up on the pavement with a great lurch and then banged down again. The men were nearly knocked off their stretchers. They *screamed*. I thought the whole thing was going over and I jumped up and tried to hold them, but I could do very little. Then, fortunately, the ambulance righted itself and the driver stopped and pulled back the little window between his cab and the body of the ambulance. He said, 'Are the chaps all right?' I said, 'They're all right now. What happened?' He said, 'I fell asleep. I'm frightfully sorry. We just missed a lamp post.' I must confess that I nearly panicked that time.

There wasn't very much we could do for the boys; we just had to get them to hospital as quickly as possible. We had our kit with us, slung over our shoulders, and we also had to take a water bottle. In the kit we had to have a tourniquet, scissors and emergency bandages, just in case you had to rip anything off or try to stop a haemorrhage.

But most of the time you just had to talk to the boys and keep them happy. They always wanted a cigarette. We carried cigarettes with us as a matter of course, and that was the first thing they wanted. I was often quite frightened if a man had a heavily bandaged face and I put a cigarette between his lips and lit it for him. I was always afraid that he would set the dressings on fire. But that never happened. All we could do was try to comfort them, try to get them in a position that was as comfortable as possible, talk to them and tell them they were safe. Sometimes they were sent back with drainage tubes in their wounds and you had to watch that, because when the tubes got clogged up with pus it was terrible for them. If they'd been a long time on the journey they *did* get clogged up, and they were then in great pain. Of course, most of them were in pain anyway from sheer exhaustion. There was nothing to do but comfort them as best we could.

I remember talking to one boy who had his eyes and head bandaged. We were taking him to the Fulham Eye Hospital and he was very upset. He kept saying that he couldn't see, and I said to him, 'Don't worry, sonny, this is a very good hospital and they'll be able to do something for you there. They can do wonders these days.' And he said, 'It's no good, Sister. They won't be able to do anything for me. Both my eyes are out.' He was only nineteen.

These were the most dramatic cases, of course. Mostly they were fairly straightforward wounds, or multiple gunshot wounds. The ambulances were open at the back and people could see straight inside. The public weren't allowed in the station; it was always very quiet there, with just the long lines of ambulance drivers and VADs and detachments of stretcher-bearers waiting. The two platforms where the hospital trains came in were always cordoned off, but crowds used to gather outside – especially in those first two weeks after the Somme battle began.

People were very sympathetic. They weren't sightseeing in a ghoulish sense, but I did have trouble with children sometimes. That was at the New End Hospital in Hampstead. Most of the hospitals had courtyards where we could unload in privacy, but at the New End Hospital in Hampstead you had to unload in the street and the wounded had to be carried over the pavement and into the building. One awful morning during the Somme period, after the school holidays had started, there was a bunch of boys on the pavement, schoolboys of eight or ten. They were only children and perhaps meant no harm, but they gathered round the ambulance as we were unloading the men and shouted, 'Coo! He's got no hands.' And, 'Blimey! Look, he's bleeding.' It was very distressing for the men, so I called to them and told them to go away while we got the stretchers in. But when we came out after we had delivered the Tommies, this wretched bunch of children was still there and one of them actually said, 'Cor, Miss, that was lovely! When are you going to bring us some more? Bring us some more tomorrow.' I completely lost my temper and I simply rounded on them. I don't know what I said, but I can tell you that they ran for their lives, and we had no more trouble after that. It was very upsetting for our boys, being stared at like freaks and commented on like that, even if they were only children. And they were badly wounded. All of them were Red Label cases.

A label with a broad red stripe meant, 'Look out for danger'. A man with a Red Label was likely to haemorrhage. If he had a head wound, a man with a Red Label required careful lifting and handling if he were to survive at all. A man with a Red Label might go into convulsions or require any one of a dozen kinds of emergency treatment at any moment. In normal circumstances, most of the 'Red Labels' who arrived with the first thousands of wounded from the Somme battlefield would never have been sent on the long journey to Blighty, but there was no room for them in France. Many died. Those who still retained a flicker of life were taken straight off the boats to the hospitals in and around Southampton, where the work was heaviest of all.

I had applied to join the VAD. I did the examinations and I wanted to work at the hospital. I'd been at school with the daughters of the Medical Officer of Health for Southampton and he had now been made a colonel and was in charge of the University War Hospital, so he spoke to the Matron about me. But she said, 'No, I can't have you, you're not old enough.' I was only seventeen, so I went on making spaghnum moss dressings, and doing canteen work and singing at concerts. Then, when the Somme started, I got a letter from the Matron saying, 'If you still want to come, *come now*! We should be most grateful if you could give us any help. We are absolutely inundated.'

There were four flats in the hospital and the wards were called Upper South, Lower South, Upper North and Lower North. We were never free from ambulances. They brought us all the Red Label cases, the people who were haemorrhaging and not fit even to go to Netley Hospital, which was only a few miles away. But we were only a ten-minute run from the docks, and within a week or two of the beginning of the campaign we were so overrun that they put up a number of huts in the field at the back of the hospital and I worked in one of these huts on a horrible duty – three o'clock in the morning until one o'clock in the afternoon. We used to think that we really had the heaviest work, and in a sense we had, because the patients were so ill that the nurses were working all night. The day staff came

Gwynnedd Lloyd, VAD, University War Hospital, Southampton

on at eight o'clock and from then on you were busy helping them with the dressings, and a million and one other things.

Of course, at that point I wasn't allowed to do any real nursing because I was completely inexperienced. The duties were making beds and waiting on Sister, taking trolleys round while the nurses did the work, and going round twice a day collecting ashtrays and rubbish in a bucket. But I had done my first aid and before very long I had learned how to do some simple dressings. I saw some terrible sights and I suppose it must have bowled me over a bit at first, because I remember Sister saying to me one day, 'Nurse, can't you smile a bit more? The men would like to see you smile, I'm sure.'

The Southampton hospitals recruited help from miles around. Every nurse, every VAD, every orderly who could be spared from the small auxiliary hospitals in Dorset, Hampshire and Wiltshire were rushed to Southampton to help. Gladys Stanford was sent for to go from the small hospital at Stirminster Marshall to Highfield Hospital, Southampton.

Gladys
Stanford,
VAD,
Highfield
Hospital,
Southampton

I was called for during the battle of the Somme, because they were simply swamped. There were extra beds up everywhere. At Stirminster Marshall we'd only had walking cases and slightly wounded, although we did occasionally have men who died. But at Southampton they were in a terrible state, straight off the ships, and doing the dressings was terrible. We didn't give them anaesthetics for these dreadful dressings – there just wasn't time to administer them. By that time I was doing dressings myself, because having been two years at Stirminster Marshall I'd had a good deal of experience. Sister did the worst ones and she did all that she could. But she was literally doing dressings all day long, they took so long to do – it was a constant round. There was no question of VADs not helping, because everyone just *had* to.

There was one man who must have been splattered all over with shrapnel. It took five nurses to do his dressing, little bits of him at a time. His leg was fractured and we had to roll him over on his side, because his back was completely riddled with holes. It was a terrible dressing to do. It took such a long time and so many of us to do it. Later we had a special splint made for him, because his leg was all wounded as well as being fractured, and we had the splint made in pieces so that we could turn it back in different sections to dress the various wounds without disturbing the bones. He was most heroic. He stood it all absolutely wonderfully and I never heard a murmur out of him. Then, later on when he was getting better, he had a tummy upset. He moaned all day about it, and we thought it was so funny!

Most of the dressings were hot fomentations, and to do any good they should have been done several times a day. But at that time they could only be dressed once a day, as a rule, because there just wasn't time to do more. We used to soak the wounds in saline, and for some of the multiple wounds we even had to have sectional beds. There was one very badly wounded leg; you had to lift it up, take away a part of the mattress, put a bath underneath and soak the leg in this fluid. I got a very bad septic hand doing that, because the VADs didn't wear rubber gloves. Only the Sister wore gloves, and if you got the slightest prick it always went septic. If you knew that you had pricked yourself you had to soak the scratch in your off-duty time in disinfectant, but somehow I hadn't noticed that I had a tiny cut on my hand, and every day I was putting my hands into a bath of solution where this septic leg had been soaking. I certainly got the infection from that.

When every pair of hands was needed, it was a terrible time for a nurse to have to go sick. In the rush of caring for the wounded there was no time in a hospital to look after the minor ailments of a nurse, but in their run-down condition – with too much work, too little sleep and precious little time to snatch a meal before they were too exhausted to eat it – the nurses' minor ailments often turned into major ones. With early treatment it might have meant three days off duty; as it was, Gladys Stanford was ill for three months and at one point it seemed as if she might lose the hand altogether. No one could spare time to look after sick nurses and she went home to Cranbourne in Dorset where the family doctor, Dr Charles Girling, was called in to lance her swollen hand. He looked worn and anxious, for his boy, Jack, had reached his nineteenth birthday just in time to be sent to France, where men were badly needed to bring the army up to strength after its losses on the Somme.

Jack Girling himself regarded this as a tremendous stroke of luck. He had been almost seventeen when the war began, and had spent the last eighteen months worrying that it might all be over before he was old enough to get into the fight himself. At Wellington College, a public school with a long military tradition, they took the war seriously.

Jack Girling was a brilliant all-rounder. He had won an entrance scholarship to Wellington in 1910 and sailed through five happy years at the College, collecting prizes as he went – the Frew Chemistry and Mathematical Prizes, the Carr Literature Prize, the Bates-Blewett Prize – but no one could call him a swot, for he picked up most of the sporting honours as well. He was head of his House, a member of the First Eleven football team, a College prefect and, as if that were not enough, had attained the exalted rank of Lieutenant in the OTC. On the whole, it was fortunate that this paragon was also blessed with a sense of humour and a modest personality, otherwise his success might have gone to his head.

At Christmas 1915, Jack Girling's school career ended in a blaze of glory when he won an Open Mathematical Scholarship at Corpus

Christi College, Oxford. But before the holidays began, before the results of the scholarship had even been announced, Jack had already applied to join the Army. He was given a commission in the Special Reserve, attached to the 3rd Battalion of the Hampshire Regiment. It was better than nothing, but in Jack's opinion it came a poor second to fighting in France.

Then the battle of the Somme began, and more men had to be sent out quickly. Jack's name was put on a draft which was about to leave for France to reinforce the 1st Battalion – that regular battalion of warriors who had been in France since August 1914. It was almost worth the six months of impatient waiting. Boarding the *Viper* at Southampton was almost like setting off for the annual OTC training camp, but a hundred times better. It was a hot, sunny day, and the sea was calm. The crossing passed without incident until they reached Le Havre, when the ship had to anchor to make way for a hospital ship just leaving the Quai d'Escale. The troopship was bound for Rouen and as it rocked gently, waiting for the signal that would allow it to swing across the harbour to the mouth of the River Seine, Jack whiled away the time by composing some verses that seemed to fit the occasion. In a quiet corner of the deck, roped off from the troops and reserved for 'officers only', he scribbled them in his notebook.

> At last has come the time for which we always used to pine,
> We're all aboard the *Viper* and we lounge and smoke and dine,
> And watch the wheeling seagulls and the distant shores of France,
> And the sunlight on the water and the waves which gaily dance.
> And soon we'll heave the anchor up and then we move away,
> And potter up the river on this super glorious day,
> And when we get to Rouen, sure, we'll have a genial spree,
> For we do not care a buffer now, we've wandered o'er the sea.
>
> For everyone is happy now, as happy as can be,
> We've had as good a crossing as you'd ever hope to see,
> We lie about and smoke and read and wallow in the sun,
> For now at last we're off to strafe the godforsaken Hun.
>
> > For we're all off together,
> > We're making for the War,
> > We don't need to worry,
> > Or grumble any more.

Soon a light far away on the shore flashed *Viper* the signal to proceed. The anchor was hauled up and they set sail across the mouth of the harbour. As the hospital ship with its load of wounded headed towards Blighty, the *Viper* turned into the estuary of the river on the last lap of the voyage to Rouen and the first stage of the journey to the Front.

Chapter Thirteen

The 1st Battalion of the Hampshire Regiment was in urgent need of the draft of reinforcements that arrived on board the *Viper*, but it would take more than one such draft to restore its fighting spirit and its fighting strength. It did not have a single officer left. All twenty-six had become casualties on the first day of the battle of the Somme and 559 of their men had also fallen. Of the men who had marched up to the assembly point before the battle, rather less than half limped out again. The same appalling pattern was repeated in several score battalions. Except in the southern part of the line where there had been a measure of success, in spite of the valour of the troops, in spite of their spirit and perseverance, the line had advanced a few hundred yards at most and in some places at the northern end of the sector, hardly at all.

Now the survivors needed rest, time to recover to lick their wounds, absorb reinforcements and pull themselves together again into composite fighting units. The 1st Hampshires travelled to the north and there, at the beginning of August, the new boys joined them at Elverdinghe in the back area of the Ypres salient. It was far enough back for relaxation, for swimming and boating in the fine hot weather, and for the battle-scarred remnants to restore themselves. It was also peaceful enough for the new contingent of officers to get to know each other at convivial dinners in the Officers' Mess in Elverdinghe Château. Nevertheless, although there was little activity in the Ypres salient, Elverdinghe was near enough to the line for the new men to become accustomed to being under shellfire. The guns were still busy. Jack Girling found it 'blissful' to be near the action at last, although he was surprised to discover that, on the whole, he could do without the palpitations induced by explosions that came a bit too near. But it was all part of a plan to accustom the schoolboy soldiers to the sounds of war. Gradually they moved towards the line, first into dugouts in the banks of the Yser Canal, and then into the trenches in front of Ypres at the apex of the salient.

It was thrilling to move through the shattered city, to see the now-legendary ruins of the Cloth Hall tower silhouetted against the darkening sky, to feel that you were walking in the steps of countless stalwart battalions, to march as they had done up the notorious Menin Road, to cut across the fields to Sanctuary Wood and, at last, file into the trenches at the head of your platoon. They were within yards of Hooge, where this time last year The Rifle Brigade and the King's Royal Rifle

Corps had fought their terrible battle in the face of liquid fire. Now it was a 'quiet sector'. Both Allies and Germans were busy elsewhere, at Verdun where the French were gradually gaining the upper hand, and on the Somme where the battle would continue for three long months. But, quiet or not, there was no doubt that they were truly in the line at last. The Very lights blazed and sparkled in the sky; there was the intermittent crackle of machine-gun fire, the desultory boom of the guns, with an occasional shell exploding close enough to cause a half-horrified, half-thrilling *frisson*. Having posted his guards and seen that the rest of his platoon was lodged as comfortably as possible, making his way between the yellow mud walls of the trench to crawl into a dugout, Jack Girling would not have changed places with the King himself.

The previous tenants of this desirable area had already gone south to the Somme. Everywhere reinforcements were on the move, not merely into the Somme battle-line, where the troops were now hammering into the lethally fortified woods that lay on the slopes of the once-gentle valleys, but into the hospitals and, most urgently of all, the casualty clearing stations near the Front. Although nothing could approach the magnitude of the early casualties, which had rocked and swamped the medical organization in hospitals as far behind the line as Inverness in Scotland, the losses were still heavy and the casualties severe. As more and more troops went into the line, more and more stretcher-bearers were needed to carry them out. It was not a job that could be done by raw personnel, no matter how well-trained, and as the new units arrived in France they too were sent to quiet sectors to replace the experienced men who were needed in the thick of the battle.

But even in a quiet sector, it was seldom that the stretcher-bearers were able to sleep all night undisturbed. There were always panics. A trench raid with its inevitable casualties, or even a case of 'wind up' when a nervous sentry, suspecting a movement among the eerie shadows of No Man's Land, loosed a few rounds of rifle-fire and provoked a burst of answering fire from the lines opposite. When there were casualties in the front line, the battalion stretcher-bearers carried their comrades to the aid-post a hundred yards or less behind. From here the stretcher-bearers of the Field Ambulance took them down the line. Mostly it was a dangerous job.

Private
A. F. Young,
2/4th London
Field
Ambulance,
RAMC

It was agreed that each of us should be on duty for two hours, which meant remaining up fully dressed; having been allotted the hours 4 to 6 am, I kipped down with two others happy in the knowledge that I'd a good six hours in front of me.

Some time later consciousness returned, and I dimly began to realize that something was happening. My first thoughts were of being out at sea in a terrific storm with the wind and waves doing their best to batter the ship to pieces. But a few seconds later it struck me that the dugout was shaking to the accompaniment of what seemed like Hell let loose, and the atmosphere outside was alive with almost every form of projectile that we and Jerry could muster. Something 'had happened' and this 'something', according to the orderly who arrived from the regimental aid-post a little later, proved to have been a raid on Jerry's trenches. He added that there would be a good number of casualties and that several cases were waiting in the MO's dugout to be transferred to the ambulance dressing station.

Three of us adjourned to the regimental aid-post, which was a sort of half dugout and half lean-to built into the side of the trench and strongly supported by sandbags. Pausing at the entrance we saw on the floor of the dugout two shadowy forms on stretchers, well covered up with blankets, while several men less seriously wounded sat around slumped in exhaustion.

'That man's been badly wounded in several places by shrapnel,' remarked the MO, pointing to one of the stretcher cases, 'and you'd better get him to the dressing-station as quickly as possible. The others can wait until daylight.'

Two of us lift the stretcher and the third man leads the way, flashing his torch. Step by step we picked our way over the duckboards. It is useless to try and maintain the regulation broken step to avoid swaying the stretcher. Slowly we wind our way along the trenches, our only guide our feet, forcing ourselves through the black wall of night and helped occasionally by the flash of the torch in front. Soon our arms begin to grow tired and the whole weight is thrown on to the slings, which begin to bite into our shoulders; our shoulders sag forward, the sling finds its way on to the back of our necks; we feel half-suffocated. A twelve-stone man, rolled up in several blankets on a stretcher, is no mean load to carry, and on that very first trip we found that the job had little to do with the disciplined stretcher-bearing we had spent so many weary hours practising.

We are automatons wound up and propelled by one fixed idea, the necessity of struggling forward. The form on the stretcher makes not a sound; the jolts, the shakings seem to have no effect on him. An injection of morphine has drawn the veil. Lucky for him. Another hundred yards brings us to a half-way house. There is no house, merely a heap of ruins to mark what had once been the site of a brewery, but beneath the ruins are cellars that house a dozen or so stretcher-bearers. They will take over our 'case' and complete the journey to the dressing-station. In a few minutes we part from our patient, with a slight feeling of envy at the thought that in a few days he will probably be in Blighty.

No matter how primitive the conditions of working in the hard-pressed casualty clearing stations, they were luxury compared to working in the front line.

Captain Geoffrey Keynes, who had visited No. 55 Casualty Clearing Station at Heilly on his way into the Somme fighting, certainly thought so, and he had said as much to George Gask, the surgeon in charge of it. He had now been working for a full year with the 23rd Brigade of the Royal Field Artillery, and for most of the time they had been in the hottest spots of the line. Geoffrey Keynes was tired and dispirited, sickened by the deaths of so many of his fellow officers, bored with sick parades when things were quiet and, when the action was brisk and casualties were heavy, dissatisfied with doctoring that amounted to little more than first aid. His vocation was surgery, and his interest had been whetted by his first rough-and-ready experiences early in the war. Behind the line, where surgeons were badly needed at the casualty clearing stations, he felt that life would be more useful as well as more interesting. George Gask had been sympathetic and promised to do what he could to have Keynes posted to his unit. It couldn't happen too soon, reflected Geoffrey Keynes, as he trudged forward with the artillery to Montauban Alley. Behind them was the recently captured village of Montauban. In front on three sides, the horizon was bounded by the three terrible woods: Delville Wood directly in front; High Wood a mile away on the left of it; and masked by the lie of the ground to his half-left, the wood of Mametz.

It was 17 July, Glasgow Fair Monday, and by an ironic quirk of fate the Glasgow Highlanders had spent the holiday weekend in High Wood, fighting their bloodiest battle of the war. Most of it was still in German hands, and most of the boys – whose civilian friends and relatives at home in Scotland were returning from the traditional day's sail 'doon the watter' on a Clyde steamer, or from enjoying themselves at the sideshows and booths of the fair on Glasgow Green – were lying dead or wounded. Eight more weeks were to elapse before the wood would finally be secured, and although in this sector the German army was still swaying from the blows of the last seventeen days, for the moment it still had the upper hand.

Captain Geoffrey Keynes, Medical Officer, 23rd Brigade, Royal Field Artillery

At 9.30 that evening we had just finished our supper of bully beef when suddenly small shells began whistling over our heads at the rate of thirty or forty a minute, making no detonation as they hit the ground. Our gunners were at first completely mystified; but presently another one fell near us, and it became apparent that it was a new form of gas shell. We were in a shallow trench, and while the officers were putting on their gas-masks I thought it better to climb up into the open air, where the concentration of gas was much lighter, and so I escaped with only a mouthful of gas. But one man was badly gassed, and I had to carry him half a mile to a collecting post. The journey was so exhausting that when I eventually reached it I had to rest for two hours. When I returned to my unit it was getting light and raining, but the shelling continued until after 4.30 in the morning. We reckoned that at least 3,000 shells had been used, and began to look around to see what effect they had had.

My first unpleasant impression was that only by a miracle had I escaped stepping, during the night, on one of the many German dead bodies that lay about in the long grass, where they had been for several days. Their faces were pitch black and decomposing. It appeared that the bombardment had been aimed at a neighbouring crossroad, where we found the way blocked by dead mules and horses, some disembowelled by direct hits. I noticed one of our men sitting at the roadside; he was bolt upright but had no head, again the result of a direct hit. As a gas attack, however, it had been a failure, in spite of the enormous expenditure of material.

On 22 July we moved forward again. Our headquarters were situated between two six-inch howitzer batteries, with another close behind. It would be difficult to imagine a more unpleasant situation or a more likely target for the German guns. I spent the afternoon preparing some sort of dugout which would provide a pretence of safety. Then at last came the message that I was to join a casualty clearing station forthwith. With profound relief, I made my way to Carnoy and so by stages during the night to Heilly. Later, as the battle went forward, we moved to Dernancourt, behind Albert.

By the end of August, after more than two months of battering by battalion after battalion, brigade after brigade, attack after attack, High Wood finally fell. Five days later, the bastion of Thiepval, which had been an objective in the first day's fighting, also fell. The Somme campaign had fallen into a pattern which General Haig described as a 'plan of leisurely progress'. Although this phrase had a reassuringly conservative ring it meant, in practice, a series of often futile attacks, withdrawal, a pause for breath and yet another attack by fresh troops. All too often the sole result was a few hundred more names on the casualty lists and a rush of convoys to the casualty clearing stations, where the intensity of the work reflected the sequence of events in the line.

The hospital was too far from the front line to be in any danger from enemy shells, but the sound of the guns was the incessant background of our lives, and we could often anticipate the arrival of casualties by noting the increased intensity of the bombardment. It sometimes reached a level that had to be heard to be believed. There were days of comparative inactivity, but at other times the surgical teams had to work for an indefinite stretch of time. We simply kept going as long as there were patients to attend to. I remember one period vividly when I worked continuously for twenty-one hours before I was able to collapse into my bed. After I had been sleeping for only three hours, another convoy arrived and I was roused to go

Captain Geoffrey Keynes, RAMC, Medical Officer, No. 55 Casualty Clearing Station to the operating theatre. I operated continuously for another twenty-one hours. Then the same thing happened again – I was called up after only three hours' sleep. By then I was so low physically that at first I literally could not stand up. It took me a good half-hour before I could collect my faculties and begin my duties.

Strange things were happening at casualty clearing stations. In some operating theatres at the height of a push, two surgeons would be working between them at four or even six operating tables, moving from one to another, leaving less qualified, and sometimes even unqualified assistants to handle the routine tasks of stitching up, dressing and even anaesthetizing, while they concentrated on the more delicate work of repairing damaged organs and searching for shrapnel, bullets and shell splinters buried deep in the wounds. For many weeks during the Somme battles the Reverend Leonard Pearson, whose official position at No. 44 Casualty Clearing Station was that of Padre, seldom left the operating theatre.

Captain the Reverend Leonard Pearson, Chaplain at No. 44 Casualty Clearing Station

I spent most of my time giving anaesthetics. I had no right to be doing this, of course, but we were simply so rushed. We couldn't get the wounded into the hospital quickly enough, and the journey from the battlefield was terrible for these poor lads. It was a question of operating as quickly as possible. If they had had to wait their turn in the normal way, until the surgeon was able to perform an operation with another doctor giving the anaesthetic, it would have been too late for many of them. As it was, many died. We all simply had to help and do anything that was needed. I did a lot of stretcher-carrying and helped to strip the men of their filthy uniforms. We had to cut them off with scissors, and there were some nights that we cut and cut until our fingers were simply raw. We had over a thousand beds, and half the time that wasn't enough. We had to keep the worst cases and send anyone who could possibly travel down to the base.

Sometimes the operating theatre was going day and night and I had to act as anaesthetist. There was a sort of cup, a wire cup with gauze in it, and you had to hold it over the man's nose and mouth and drop the anaesthetic on to it very carefully, keeping a close eye on the patient. Of course, the surgeon was there too, working at another table – because we had these operating tables side by side – and I could call for help if anything went wrong.

I remember one case. He was a man of tremendous size, a colonel, and they brought him in and laid him on the table and the surgeon said, 'Get on with the anaesthetic.' But I couldn't get the man under. I did my best. I had two orderlies holding him down, but no, he wouldn't go under. I said to the surgeon, Wesley, 'Well, what shall I do?' Wesley was busy operating and he didn't even look up, he just said, 'You *must* get him under.' Then, to my horror, the fellow ceased breathing. I thought I'd given too much chloroform and I was very worked up. I said, 'Now, Wesley, what about it? This chap's stopped breathing. Can't you come and look at him?' Wesley simply said, 'Well, pull him around, pull him around. I can't leave *this* chap.' He was amputating a leg and it was a question of tying off the arteries so that the man wouldn't bleed to death, very delicate work which he couldn't leave.

I tried every possible means to restore the patient, jerking his arms round, pressing his chest and, finally, just when I thought I would have to give up, he took one gasp and began to breathe.

When Wesley had finished with the other chap he came over to my patient and started to take his arm off at the shoulder, but as soon as the operation began he started to sink and he died on the table. I felt very badly about it and, later on, when we had a moment to spare and we were together in the Mess, I said to Wesley, 'I'm terribly sorry about that man, dreadfully sorry.' I felt it was my fault. Wesley said, 'You musn't say that. Nobody could have done better than you did. I expected the man to die because his physique was not up to the life within it. It certainly wasn't your fault.' He never chided me at all, and I went on giving anaesthetics because no one else could be spared to do it.

One day when we were operating like that, a surgeon came into the theatre. He was an Inspecting Officer from the base, and I thought we were for it then. But he must have realized the situation. He said to me afterwards, 'You're doing very well, but don't tell anybody about it. Just keep it under your hat that you're giving anaesthetics.' So I did. Of course, I had my other duties as well – mainly burials at that period. At the very worst times I was burying over a hundred a day. I remember another surgeon in the middle of one period when the operations had been going on, one after the other – in fact two or three at a time – for almost twenty-four hours. In the middle of it all he turned away from one table and looked up as another one was being carried in, and he shook his head. He was covered in blood – we all were – and he said, 'This isn't a hospital, it's a butchery.'

By the end of two months' bitter fighting since the disastrous losses of the first day, 23,000 more men had become casualties and the total gain on the Somme front was a tiny strip of land just over a mile deep. The armies pushed on through the month of September, but now – particularly among the Australians of the Anzac Corps, which was bearing the brunt of the fierce fighting in the middle of the sector – there were mutters of 'Murder' and 'Slaughter'. Some battalions had lost so many men, had been reinforced by so many fresh drafts, that they now contained very few of the original members in their ranks. On 1 September, when the 13th Battalion of the Australian Imperial Force was relieved after forty hours' desperate fighting at the bastion of Mouquet Farm in yet another assault which had gone badly awry, they sent in a casualty list of ten officers and 231 men. In forty hours they had also won between them thirty-two Military Medals and had triumphantly reinforced the reputation implied in their nickname of 'The Fighting Thirteenth'. They were sent north to the Ypres salient to recover, to rest, to absorb reinforcements. When they left again for the Somme on 26 October they were again up to their full strength of 1,028 men. But someone took the trouble to do a calculation. The battalion had also been 'up to strength' when it landed on Gallipoli in April the previous year, but of that Gallipoli force, of the 1,028 men of the battalion, only 157 were left.

In October there was a wholesale move as battalions which had been decimated at the beginning of the Somme campaign – but now rested, re-formed and (it was hoped) refreshed – were being brought back in again while the remnants of those who had taken their places were to be withdrawn. The 1st Hampshires was one of the units that was now on its way back.

It was about this time that the troops began to sing a new verse to an old song which had started off by being rude about sergeant-majors.

> If you want the old battalion
> I know where it is,
> I know where it is,
> I know where it is.
> If you want the old battalion
> I know where it is,
> It's hanging on the old barbed wire.
>
> I saw them, I saw them,
> Hanging on the old barbed wire.
> I saw them, I saw them,
> Hanging on the old barbed wire.

Officers discouraged the soldiers from singing it on the march. A great many of them appreciated the sentiment, but regardless of their own feelings it was their job to keep up morale. However, the troops had their own methods of putting a brave face on things. For six weeks, division after division battered up the slope against the defences of Guillemont village. Time after time they were thrown back again. Time after time the ragged remnants of battalions were withdrawn, decimated and demoralized. Like High Wood, Delville Wood, Mametz Wood, Thiepval and Beaumont Hamel, the name of Guillemont was already imbued with overtones of horror which the passage of a whole generation would not erase. Yet even before it was finally secured on 3 September, the soldiers who had come out of it alive were singing, with a cynical sangfroid that bordered on bravado, a ditty which they set to the unlikely melody of 'Moonlight Bay':

I was strolling along
In Gillymong,
With the Minnywerfers singing
Their old sweet song. . .

But they had advanced a few miles – indeed, five or six miles at the southern end where the British sector met the French, who had also made considerable headway. With an optimism which was hardly based on the evidence of the three preceding months, the commanders believed that one more attack might allow the army to capture the Transloy ridges and outflank Bapaume. By the first week in October the Germans had been pushed back into their last line of defences around the town. But already the weather had turned to wintry conditions of rain and chill and the captured ground had turned to bog.

On the first day of the Michaelmas term, which should also have been Jack Girling's first day at Oxford, the 1st Hampshires moved into bivouacs round Montauban, near the spot which, almost three months before, Geoffrey Keynes had been so thankful to quit. Now the woods had at long last been subdued, Guillemont had been secured, Ginchy was taken, and around Montauban was a desolate sea of mud and ruins where tents and tarpaulins flapped in the wind. Sheets of rain swept across the blank expanse, where despite the efforts of clearing-up parties the terrible debris of the battles still lay between the gun lines. It was far from being an ideal place for a camp, but so difficult was the torn-up land to negotiate that it was impossible in a single day to cover the six miles from the jumping-off line of 1 July to the area of attack. Long before they reached the apex of the line, to the left of Les Boeufs, the men would have been exhausted.

As it was, it took the best part of a day for the 1st Hampshires to struggle up the three scant remaining miles from the camp, and when they finally arrived there were no proper trenches to take over. It was a dreadful night of pouring rain and pitch-black darkness. The relief took a long time, and when it was eventually completed there was little time left for the exhausted battalion to rest before the attack began at 3.40 am. Despite their blooding in the Ypres salient, for Jack Girling and his fellow platoon officers it was the first time 'over the top' – and it was a disastrous one. There were two days of fierce fighting in support of the 1st Battalion of the King's Royal Rifle Corps before the battle died down, the relief came up, and those who had survived struggled back to bivouac and reorganize at Guillemont. By comparison the miserable camp at Montauban had been luxury. For the 1st Hampshires spent the next three nights in shellholes with no shelter other than what they could contrive from sheets of corrugated iron and sandbags.

On the 22nd they moved forward again, to the same stretch of line, and this time the 1st Hampshires were to lead the attack. The plan and the objectives were identical to those of five days before. The troops would attack under the cover of a creeping barrage of sheltering gun-fire, the shells falling ahead of them as they advanced, so that the Germans could not leave their trenches to meet them, or even raise their heads to sight the guns on their parapets, without being blown to pieces. But it was not exactly a repetition of the fight of a few days earlier. The Germans, well aware that the attack would soon be renewed, had worked out a tactic which was the answer to the creeping barrage – a long-range barrage of fire from machine-guns massed on the ridges far beyond. The first of the British shells began to fall. The troops prepared to launch themselves towards the morass where the Germans were spread out in a series of almost undetectable outposts, and immediately the machine-guns began firing in unison from the Transloy ridges, far beyond the reach of the unwitting British field gunners. The bullets spat like hailstones on the parapet, and as the men left the trenches they advanced into a curtain of fire. Before he had led the men of his platoon more than a few yards towards their objective – Hazy Trench – Jack Girling was hit and died at once.

WAR OFFICE TELEGRAM.
TO DOCTOR C. GIRLING, WIMBORNE, DORSET.

REGRET INFORM YOU SECOND LIEUTENANT
C. J. GIRLING, FIRST HAMPSHIRE REGIMENT,
MISSING PRESUMED KILLED.

He was one of several hundred casualties, most of whom were reported as missing, for although the attack made a little progress it was several days before the objectives of Gunpits, Dewdrop, Hazy and Misty Trenches were behind them. When the 2nd Battalion of the West Yorkshire Regiment took over the new line on 12 November and spent four days holding it, they were overcome by the stench of the heaped-up dead at their backs. Dewdrop and Hazy were literally filled with bodies, and around them corpses lay scattered on the tumbled earth. Under cover of darkness two burial parties were sent out, but they were so sickened by the task that they achieved little; the bodies were already disintegrating with putrefaction. The line advanced no further, and in such an exposed and unhealthy place, constantly under shellfire that pulverized the living and the dead alike, there was no choice but to leave the dead where they lay, gradually sinking into the mud and into oblivion.*

* Second Lieutenant Charles John Girling has no known grave and is com-memorated on the Thiepval Memorial.

There was little more action on that front, apart from some feint attacks to divert the attention of the enemy from the last battle of the Somme campaign in the north. There, where the line had hardly moved at all since 1 July, in one last desperate effort in the wet, cold days of early November, the troops managed to take the village of Beaumont Hamel across a field of their own unburied dead. The cost of the Somme campaign had been enormous; the gains had been minimal. And just four months later, in the spring of 1917, the Germans cocked a last cruel snook at the men who had succeeded in throwing them back from the citadels of the fortified redoubts they had thought to be invincible.

Towards the end of February, a British aeroplane with engine trouble was forced to land in the untouched countryside to the east of the Somme battlefield. The crew jumped out, to set about the routine business of destroying maps and firing the plane before the enemy could reach it. To their amazement, a group of villagers came running towards them across the fields, shouting and laughing, 'The Boche have gone. The Boche have gone.' Somewhat in the manner of the evacuation from Gallipoli, the Germans had crept away and removed themselves some seven miles back to the newly constructed, heavily fortified shelter of the Hindenburg Line. If the British wanted the shattered, untenable strip of fought-over land, they could have it.

They left a trail of havoc in their wake, and when the British army recovered from its surprise and pushed forward on their heels, a great silence fell over the shattered and leafless valleys of the Somme. The grass began to push up among the empty and useless trenches, and although the guns still rumbled to the north and the east there was time as least to pick up the dead. Even if few of them could be identified, at least they could be given a decent burial.

So many men were reported 'missing, presumed killed' that the Red Cross set up a special bureau for tracing them. In most cases there was not much that could be added to the bald information supplied in the casualty returns, but occasionally a man of the same company or battalion who had been wounded in the same attack could say if he had seen a soldier injured or captured, or could relieve the terrible anxiety of suspense by stating positively that he had seen him killed.

Day in, day out, all through the Somme campaign and long after it ended, in the wards of hospitals at the bases in France and in hospitals the length and breadth of Britain, Red Cross workers and volunteers, armed with long lists of names, gently interrogated the wounded who might know something of the fate of their comrades.

We had a very nice man who came round trying to find the missing men. He was a lawyer in Bradford. That was his war work and he used to come every Sunday evening without fail to talk to the boys – those that could talk – trying to find out if they knew the missing men or knew what had happened to them, and very often he did find some

Sister Henrietta Hall, St Luke's Military Hospital, Bradford

of their comrades. The trouble was that it did tend to upset the boys a little bit. It took them back to those experiences just when they were beginning to forget them. All the same, I often used to think that it was a good thing for them to talk about it rather than bottle it up, because it always came out in some way and they used to have dreadful nightmares. It helped if they could talk and I always used to make a point of speaking to them. Even when we were busy I made time for it, because I thought that it was really necessary and a very important part of nursing them.

I had an armchair in my office and I often used to say to a boy if he was upset, 'Come and see me this morning, about half-past eleven, when I've finished the dressings. Come and talk to me for a little while and tell me your troubles.' Often they were very upset about having to go back, especially when they'd been talking to the searcher about the action when they'd been hit, talking about a friend who'd been killed. It reminded them. But if they could get it off their chests, privately in my office, even have a bit of a cry, which they would have been ashamed to do in the ward, I used to think it made them feel a little bit better.

Long after the battle had died down, the work of tracing the missing, burying the dead and tending the wounded went on. Another year was dragging to a close, and it was already the third Christmas of the war that everyone had said would be 'over by Christmas' more than two weary years before.

On Christmas Day every sick or wounded soldier in every hospital, casualty clearing station, hospital ship or train, in every theatre of the war, at home and abroad, received a message from King George V. It was inscribed in gold letters on a white card embossed with the Windsor Insignia. On it the King expressed *grateful thanks for hardships endured and unfailing cheeriness. The Queen and I are thinking more than ever of the sick and wounded among my sailors and soldiers. From our hearts we wish them strength to bear their sufferings and a speedy restoration to health.*

The soldiers were delighted to receive them. Sister Hall went round her ward on Christmas morning, and handed a card to each man and wished him a Merry Christmas. The sick and the gassed men in her medical ward had as happy a festive season as the efforts of the nurses and the townspeople could provide in the way of treats and entertainments. But in London where a thick black fog rolled over the city on Christmas night, seeped into every crevice and clung thick in the air for the next two days, the gassed patients coughed, choked and occasionally died for want of breath.

Chapter Fourteen

In January the temperature dropped to zero, to below zero, and stayed there. In France frost and snow covered the battlefields, lay in trenches, covered dugouts, and the bitter cold seemed to bore and gnaw into the bones. It was common knowledge that there had never been such a winter, but there had never been a winter in which so many people were living virtually in the open, or at best were protected from the elements by thin coverings of wood or flapping canvas. Even towards the coast, where the salt sea air tended to discourage snowfalls, the hills, the valleys and the sand dunes were covered with snow that lay for weeks. In the hospitals there was a scant supply of coal to warm the huts and marquees, because the British coal miners were on strike. To make things worse the Channel ports were fogbound for days at a time, and the last straw came when Boulogne harbour was blocked by a ship that had sunk at the entrance. Rations were tight; comforts were few; people fell ill and the officers' hospital at Etaples and the Sick Sisters' hospital at Hardelot were almost as busy caring for sick medical personnel as the short-staffed hospitals were in caring for the convoys of sick men who came down from the trenches.

Within a fortnight of his arrival with the 3rd Harvard Medical Unit, Dr Henry Potter was stricken with agonizing neuritis. 'Most Beautiful Lady', he wrote to his fiancée, Bessie Miller, back home in the USA.

> I got a hard cold when I first landed here – no fire, wet blanket, leaky tent and all that sort of thing, and of course it had to settle in my weak spot, my right supra-orbital nerve. I went on with my work for three weeks, aching most of the time, then after this week I got a lot worse. On the 5th I quit and went to hospital at No. 24, a few miles from here. I was able to keep warm and dry there and improved steadily, coming back on duty this morning. I'm much better, and if I can keep dry will nearly be all right in a week.
>
> Our cold weather keeps up. Sixteen days of the severest cold that France has known in the memory of anyone living. The hills are drifted deep with snow and are beautiful under the setting. The ponds are frozen ten inches thick. It is just midnight now, and most of us are up because we hate to go to bed. It is about 20°F outside, not very cold, but the wind is howling and the tents are flapping and blowing with a noise like a ship's sails when she comes up into the

Dr Henry Potter, 3rd Harvard Medical Unit, No. 22 General Hospital, Camiers wind. Louis has just come into the Mess with the news that his tent has split from the peak to the ground. Altogether it is quite a sporting life. Everybody has a cold; Sniff is down with pneumonia; Miss Grayson, one of the nurses, is very sick with typhoid; Pitts has drawn so much money from the field cashier to pay his poker debts that they won't give him any more until March; and so it goes. Are we downhearted? No!!!

Bess, dearest, I can't help wishing that I had a fairy carpet just for tonight. I'd fly away from this roaring wind and the flapping tents and the stiff fingers and the sore feet, and come and snuggle up close to you in some nice warm place, and if I got some hair in my mouth I'd like it ever so much.

You would be interested if you could look into the Mess. We sit round the little stove in a close semi-circle, a dozen or so of us; our fronts are not warm and our backs are freezing. Pitts in the middle is roasting his French chestnuts on top of the stove; the phonograph is going and everybody is working, and either reading or writing. It is quite a remarkable thing to me that there is practically no friction around the men here. All the cold and wet and red-tape is taken as part of a great adventure.

In that winter's lull in the fighting along the vast frozen length of the line, the elements were the real enemy. It was worst of all on the Somme. After the Germans retired to the Hindenburg Line they left behind a frozen tundra – pock-marked with shellholes, scarred by a network of now-useless trenches, and devoid of any shelter but the concrete chill of old dugouts, which were swiftly occupied by squeaking packs of the outsize, blood-bloated rats that preyed on the corpses of long-dead soldiers. The few dreary encampments that marked the staging posts of the long haul through the wilderness to the new front line offered little in the way of comfort to the half-frozen infantry who trudged up to man it.

Although there was little fighting in the winter wastes, and little was expected before the spring, it was not possible to withdraw large numbers of men to the comparative comfort of billets in the rear and to garrison the line with a skeleton force. Forty-eight hours were as much as a battalion could be expected to remain in the open trenches, and large numbers of troops had to be frequently rotated if the fighting force was not to succumb *en masse* to exposure, pneumonia or trench-feet. As it was, the large numbers of men sent down the line suffering from trench-feet caused the army such anxiety that special orders were issued. Every man must carry a spare pair of dry socks at all times. At least once a day every man must remove boots and stockings and rub his feet with whale-oil, and every platoon officer was to be held responsible for seeing that this was done.

But it was not easy to persuade a shivering soldier to divest his icy feet of what little protection they had. When the trenches were merely frozen hard the problem was less acute. When the sun came out or when the thermometer rose a degree or two above zero and the icy ground began to thaw, the soldiers sank up to their knees into a layer of icy slush. In such conditions it was physically impossible to carry out the whale-oil-rubbing, foot-inspection drill. Frozen and wet, stiff and numb, with no means of exercising to restore the circulation, already impeded by tightly-bound wet puttees, the feet of the unfortunate infantrymen turned into one vast and excruciating chilblain. In the worst cases, men were literally unable to walk. In the face of mounting casualties, GHQ grumbled and roared, threatened and sent demands for explanations to corps, to brigades, to battalions and to companies in the line, warning dire consequences if the situation did not improve. The exasperated CO of the 16th Battalion, the Highland Light Infantry, driven to distraction by the continuous badgering, eventually wrote to Brigade, 'I have given you every explanation that is humanly possible. If you are not satisfied, I must refer you to God Almighty.' He heard no more.

The 16th HLI had been particularly unfortunate. They had lost the admittedly high proportion of some two hundred men – one in five of the strength – with trench-feet, but in the conditions in which they were holding the Serre sector it was hardly surprising.

Men stood knee-deep in the posts. They could not lie down to sleep or, in places, even sit. When fatigue became unbearable, two men, in at least one known case, stood and slept back to back while a third kept watch to prevent a collapse in the mud. The approach to the front line by Nairn Dump was over a light railway track on which progress was made by leaping from sleeper to sleeper; to miss a sleeper was to be bogged to the waist or filthily submerged.*

The 16th HLI was a Glasgow Battalion, and its soldiers considered themselves to be very tough indeed. Regardless of the fact that it was a respite from the trenches, they felt it to be something of an indignity to be sent down the line with such unsoldierly complaints as trench-feet or frostbite. But both were exceedingly painful complaints.

They were dreadful, these Glasgow boys. They were shockers, worse than any, because they were always up to something. One of the little HLI boys came in with bad feet – they were really bad, because he had lost several toes which had to be amputated. But as soon as he was allowed to get up for a time, he was always round the ward tormenting everybody who was still in bed. By his way of it he was helping me, because the soldiers who were fit to get up used to do

Margaret Ellis, Special Military Probationer, No. 26 General Hospital, Camiers

* From the Battalion History.

light duties and give us a hand with various things and do anything they could for the other wounded. But this little one was more of a hindrance than a help, dropping things all over the place, talking to patients who didn't want to be talked to, asking questions, never at peace for a minute. He really kept going much longer than he should have done, wearing himself out and everyone else as well, because he would suddenly fling himself down on his bed and say in his broad Glasgow accent, 'Ach! My pair taes.'

Kathleen Yarwood, VAD, Dearnley Military Hospital, Birch Hill, Rochdale

Some of the trench-feet and frostbite cases were so bad that they had to be sent home. We had a tremendous number of frostbite cases at the beginning of 1917. In fact we had a whole ward of them, and another nurse and myself were in charge of that for quite a long time. We had to rub their feet every morning and every evening with warm olive oil for about a quarter of an hour or so, massage it well in and wrap their feet in cotton wool and oiled silk – all sorts of things just to keep them warm – and then we put big fisherman's socks on them. Their feet were absolutely white, swollen up and dead. Some of their toes dropped off with it, and their feet looked dreadful. We would say, 'I'll stick a pin in you. Can you feel it?' Whenever they *did* feel the pin-prick we knew that life was coming back, and then we'd see a little bit of pink come up and everybody in the ward would cheer. It was very painful for them when the feeling started to come back, and some of them had to have crutches. They couldn't walk at all, because they simply couldn't feel their feet.

Sister Grace Buffard, TFNS, No. 2 General Hospital, Rouen

We had a tremendous number of men in that winter with chest trouble, and it wasn't so very easy to treat them in those conditions because all our basic training didn't apply. In a proper hospital when you make a linseed poultice, you close all the windows and see that there are no draughts before you make it, so that it will stay really hot when you can put it on the patient, and will do the most good. I remember standing looking round the tent and thinking, 'How on earth can you close all the windows – there aren't any?' We just had to do the best we could.

Sister Mary Stollard, QAIMNS, Beckett's Park Military Hospital, Leeds

All that winter we took in bronchitis and rheumatism cases. Some of the bronchitis patients were as bad as the men who were gassed, but the rheumatism cases really were the worst. It was pathetic to see these young men absolutely crippled with rheumatism, sometimes doubled up as if they were men of eighty instead of boys in their twenties. We set up a special department to treat them with hot baths and heat treatment, massage and electrical treatment. Most of them got better, but some of them had to be discharged from the army because the rheumatism had taken such a hold. They suffered terrible pain with it. They came out of the wet trenches simply crippled with rheumatism.

There is a nice distinction made on the record cards between sick and wounded. Any man who is hurt by an act of the enemy is wounded whether it is a gunshot wound or gas pneumonia, while any man not hurt by an act of the enemy is sick. It makes no difference whether he is shot by his own rifle, burned by a premature powder blast, breaks his leg by falling in a charge, or is smashed up when troop trains crash together; he is a sick man on the records. A man may come in with a gunshot wound and die of pneumonia, but he dies of wounds. On the other hand, he may come in with feet frozen and die from amputation and secondary haemorrhage, but he dies a sick man. The point is that a wounded man draws a pension in case of disability, the sick man does not.

Dr Henry Potter, 3rd Harvard Medical Unit, No. 22 General Hospital, Camiers (his diary, January 1917)

The surgical service is light just now while the medical service is heavy, so I have offered to go on the medical side until the surgical work picks up. They jumped at the offer and I am to fill up my ward with medical cases, making a mixed ward of it. Most of the medical cases are labelled PUO,* or laryngitis, lumbago or bronchitis, but they are all essentially the same thing – debility, owing to exposure and fatigue. They come in dead tired with pains all over and a cough. The chief things they need are bed and food.

When the sick outnumbered the wounded, when there were consequently fewer serious cases, fewer operations and fewer deaths, the burden of work was lighter. There was time to walk on the snowy hills behind the camp, to go for a blow along the beach in the cold sea-winds that cleared the head of the smells of poultices and disinfectants. There was time to tramp to an inn in a country village, or to a friendly farm, for a bowl of coffee made with unchlorinated water and an omelette made from fresh eggs. It was a welcome change from the eternal stewed tea and stewed beef of hospital fare. In the once-fashionable resort of Hardelot, six miles to the north, the Pré Catalan provided a civilized tea, or a meal for the better-off; and six miles to the south, the twin resorts of Le Touquet and Paris-Plage offered sufficient delights to make the long walk worthwhile. A pair of personable nurses could usually depend on getting a lift in a lorry, an ambulance or occasionally – with discretion – a staff car, even though they had to crouch in it out of view. Lifts were against the rules – and it seemed to the nurses that most other things were too. When Margaret Ellis and her friend Dorothy Waddington contrived to spend an afternoon off together and went into a smart teashop in Paris-Plage, the waitress firmly steered them away from a

* PUO (Pyrexia of Uncertain Origin) was the ubiquitous 'trench fever' thought to have been caused by lice.

table by the window and ushered them to a discreet corner at the back. 'Sisters no like windows,' she declared in a voice resonant with experience. Sisters did *not* like windows, but most of them were prepared to take the risk of being seen in public with officers, and Le Touquet was a happy hunting-ground. Unabashed by conventions that hardly seemed to apply in the free and easy atmosphere of active service, undeterred by the rule that officers and nurses were forbidden to be seen together off duty, young officers, starved of feminine company, ogled the girls wherever they went. The girls, more than willing to risk the disciplinary consequences, smiled back encouragingly, allowed themselves to be drawn into conversation, and were easily persuaded to allow the officers to mark their appreciation of the pleasure of their company by allowing them to foot the restaurant bill.

Margaret Ellis, Special Military Probationer, No. 26 General Hospital, Camiers

Of course, in normal times or even at home we would never have dreamed of 'picking a man up', as they used to call it, because we were very well brought-up girls, but out there it seemed the natural thing to do. You were there more or less doing the same thing and certainly for the same reason. We were all part of the BEF, and that seemed to be as good as an introduction. The whole country around there was one huge military base, so there was never any shortage of officers. We knew perfectly well that every time we went to Paris-Plage we would meet someone. Of course, you'd never have dared if you'd been just on your own, but if there were two of you and two of them it seemed quite safe, even if it wasn't quite proper.

We used to walk over the bridge from Etaples and there would be two of them behind us, talking rather loudly, intending us to overhear. We would pretend to be absorbed in our own conversation and act as if we were quite oblivious of them, but we knew very well that before we had gone very much further we would let them talk to us, and if we liked them we would possibly spend the afternoon with them, and let them give us tea.

Sometimes, if we had an evening off we would meet for dinner, by arrangement. There used to be a little restaurant in Etaples, where you walked in through the kitchen to the restaurant, and they would serve you lovely chicken and delicious things to eat that we didn't normally have. Most of us had money from home, but we weren't particularly well-off and we never used to have to pay for anything with all these officers about. And it was perfectly safe because mostly they were on the move and would be off again in a few days, so there was no danger of any of them being a nuisance. They probably enjoyed it as much as we did.

Of course, we had to be very careful not to be seen with them on the road back to the hospital, because our Matron, Miss Hartigan, had absolutely gimlet eyes. One evening Dorothy and I were walking back from Etaples. It was almost dark and we were going under the railway bridge, where it was even darker, when a car went past with Matron in it. Next day I was called up to the office and she said, 'Miss Ellis, did I see you wearing a red scarf with your outdoor uniform?' Well, it wasn't a red scarf at all, but I did long for a bit of colour so I had a grey scarf with just a little red stripe in it. Matron said, 'Well, please do *not* wear it again. It is not part of the regulation uniform.'

I was working in a casualty clearing station near Corbie where we took the men straight out of the trenches. The discipline wasn't so strict as it was at the base, but nevertheless we had to toe the line. I was in charge of the officers' ward and I used to make tea in my Sister's bunk at the end of the ward, and it was rather good tea. We were absolutely fed up with chlorinated water. Everything that we ate, if it was cooked in water, seemed to taste of chlorine, so I got hold of one of the engineers and I said to him, 'For pity's sake, will you let me have some water that's not chlorinated?' He said, 'Well, Sister, if you'll be sure to boil it, I'll let you have it.' Every night he used to bring us a bucket of water that hadn't been chlorinated. I made tea with it that was absolute nectar compared to what we usually had to drink, and the officers soon got to know about it. Those of them who could get out of bed used to come along to the end of the ward after lights out and say, 'Any tea, Sister?' Some of the officers attached to the clearing station used to come in as well, and one evening I was having quite a little party when the Night Sister arrived unexpectedly. What a strafing she gave me – and them too! How dare they come in! How dare I allow them in! She was a real battle-axe. The men were so anxious to talk to us, just to be friendly, but it was strictly against the rules. It wasn't 'done' for them to come to Sister's bunk. That was sacrosanct. Some of these older Sisters, well, they weren't really human, we used to think. Of course, we were very young, but we perhaps had more regard for these men; we were sorry for them and there was no harm in it at all. It was completely innocent but it was against the rules, so that was that.

Sister Mary Hall, QAIMNS(R)

It was absolutely ridiculous how they enforced that regulation about not going out with officers. It was useless to try to be above-board about it and pointless to ask permission, because it simply wouldn't be granted. I was actually not allowed to go out with my own father, and he was a general in the Army! He had been slightly wounded by a shell splinter and came down to the base to the officers' hospital, which was No. 24 at Etaples. I was working in the ward when Matron herself came to tell me and gave me permission to go over and see him. He was only in bed for a few days and then he was allowed up while he waited to go to England. He wanted me to go for a walk with him, but father or not, general or not, I wasn't allowed to

Kitty Kenyon, VAD, No. 4 General Hospital, Camiers

go. Matron said, 'No. You may invite him to tea in my office, but you may not go out with him. You know perfectly well that VADs are not allowed to walk with officers, so I'm very sorry but you may not go out with your father.' And there was nothing I could do about it, because Matron's word was Law.

Kit
Dodsworth,
VAD, No. 12
General
Hospital,
Rouen

My brother-in-law was on the staff of General Seeley and he was once sent to Rouen for a few days' leave because he had been slightly gassed, though not sufficiently to have to go into hospital. He arrived quite unexpectedly one afternoon when I was on duty. I was sitting near the entrance to the marquee, massaging a synovitis knee, and I saw him walking past the end of the lines. I was so astonished that I said aloud, 'Good heavens! I think that's my brother-in-law.' 'Ah yes,' remarked one of the men, 'and I think it must be my brother, Douglas Haig.' However, in a few moments he came into the ward and my reputation went up in leaps and bounds, being hailed by my Christian name by a real live brass-hat. There were one or two wounded men from his brigade in the ward, so I took him round to their beds and he had a few words with them. Eve and I were nearly due to go off duty and so my brother-in-law waited for us and took us out to tea. After we had had tea we were rather at a loss to know what to do. We weren't allowed to go to any public place of amusement accompanied by any man in uniform of whatever rank, so there really seemed little that we could find to do to pass the time.

Then my brother-in-law had a brilliant inspiration and asked us if we would like to have a real bath. We hailed the idea with glee, because a camp bath is quite sufficient but not very luxurious. We'd been having tea at the Hôtel de la Poste, so he went to reception and engaged a bedroom with a bath attached and Eve and I disappeared into it and stayed there until dinnertime! The bath was heavenly, and so was the lovely thick carpet on the bedroom floor. I spent quite a long time with my shoes and stockings off, just walking up and down the floor. We had dinner in the hotel and thus finished a glorious afternoon. It solved the problem of what to do when we had an afternoon off. Especially when the weather was bad we frequently went back to the hotel and demanded a bath and bedroom, where we could rest happily in luxury for a few hours.

There was no shortage of senior officers in Rouen, which was the cavalry base depot, and in No. 2 General Hospital for officers the hierarchy and the military discipline was at its stiffest and most unbending.

Sister
Grace Buffard,
TFNS, No. 2

It was all very different from the clearing stations where I worked at other times. The ward rounds were something to behold. Of course we had them every day, but every week there was a special one with a whole procession of high-ups making a tour of all the wards – the Colonel, his ADC, Matron looking very grand, the other MOs, and several more. Tuesday was the morning for this full-scale inspection, and when I went on duty in my officers' ward on a Tuesday morning they made a great clatter with spoons, plates and anything else they could get hold of to make a noise. They used to all call together, 'Sister, it's wind-up morning, wind-up morning. Have you got the wind-up, Sister?' And I used to say, 'Don't you dare move your feet, any of you. You've spoiled the crease in the counterpane.' We had to have everything just so.

General Hospital, Rouen

Where the men were recovering or less seriously sick or wounded, the discipline hardly mattered. Everyone was used to it as a fact of life and accepted it with no more than an occasional grumble. But in the wards of badly wounded, some of the VADs felt that some of the Sisters who had come from the large teaching hospitals in London to work in France had brought with them too many rigid ideas of order which would have been better left behind. When she first arrived at No. 4 General Hospital at Camiers, Kitty Kenyon wrote indignantly in her diary,

> I don't like my ward. The only thing that really matters is that the beds are tidy, and at every odd minute the Sister sends me off to tuck the blankets in more tightly, no matter if the man is sleeping or has a hideous wound which every movement jars. A convoy came in one night and we have a gunner with both legs off. He had to have his first dressing off with gas, and that made him struggle so they haven't been able to give it again and the pain he has is horrible. He was delirious yesterday and has been in theatre today. But his pillows must be turned so that the openings are away from the door, and he has to be held up again while the stupid, newly-arrived VAD turns and sorts each pillow – wishing she could swear.

The patients were strictly segregated by rank – men and NCOs together, officers in their own wards. It was a practical arrangement made with the good of both groups in mind. An officer was trained to be a leader, and even a nineteen-year-old Second Lieutenant was expected to set an example to the men under his command. It would not do, authority felt, for an officer to be worried that his image of infallibility might slip under the stress of pain or the inevitable indignities of being a bed-bound patient. Nor would the Tommies in wards of their own feel that they had to be on their 'best behaviour' under the eye of their superiors twenty-four hours a day. Any discipline that ruled in the ward must come from the hospital, and the hospital alone. Everyone knew exactly where he was and everyone could therefore relax. For much the same reason the officers were further divided by rank whenever possible, because a humble Second Lieutenant could hardly be expected to feel comfortable or relaxed with the godlike figure of a colonel or a brigadier in the neighbouring bed.

Dorothy Bradridge, VAD, No. 2 Red Cross Hospital, Rouen

I was working on the brass-hat ward, which meant that there was no rank lower than a major and they were all in separate rooms. Bruce Bairnsfather was one of my patients – or rather he was a patient while I was there, because VADs were only allowed to do very humble tasks in that ward. He was the cartoonist who invented the famous character of Old Bill, and on the wall of his room he had drawn a lifesize cartoon of a VAD sweeping dust about and raising great clouds of it with some gusto. She had a very plain face to my mind, because we actually considered ourselves to be a very good-looking lot of VADs. I was foolish enough to ask him why he hadn't drawn a pretty VAD. 'A pretty VAD?' he exclaimed. 'Well, that's probably because I've never seen one.' It served me right for fishing for compliments! However, I always liked to feel that I got my own back on him at mealtimes because I always left his tray until last, and I left his bell unanswered as long as I dared. Needless to say, he was not a surgical or a serious case, so he was able to spend quite a time decorating the walls.*

The patients were fond of drawing on the bare walls, and nobody minded because it cheered the place up a bit. This led to an embarrassing occasion once when we had a royal visit. Queen Mary came with the Prince of Wales and a whole entourage of brass-hats. We knew she was coming and there had been tremendous 'spit and polish' for days beforehand. I think perhaps she had not been expected to go into this particular room because it had rather a *risqué* drawing on the wall. It was a stockinged female leg with a garter at the top – very shapely and seductive-looking. But just at the side of the garter a large mirror was hung, so that when anyone glanced at it they naturally assumed that the rest of the picture was hidden behind the mirror. Needless to say, everyone pushed the mirror sideways to see what was underneath. That is exactly what the Queen did, and like everyone else she saw that there was no continuation of the picture but simply the words *Honi soit qui mal y pense.* She was not amused! Her face simply froze, so none of the other people who were following her could laugh either. Walking behind the Prince of Wales as part of an unofficial 'Guard of Honour' I could see the effort he was making not to laugh aloud. His shoulders were absolutely shaking!

King George V, who was visiting hospitals rather nearer the Front, might have appreciated the joke more. There was a shortage of wounded and Dr Cook, who was in charge of the casualty clearing

* Captain Bruce Bairnsfather was suffering from mild shellshock.

station at St Omer which had been earmarked for the royal visit, was incensed to discover that a number of picturesquely wounded soldiers were to be brought from a neighbouring clearing station in order to impress the King. Men were drafted in to tidy up the grounds, and whitewash was splashed on every surface and every object which might be expected to come under the royal eye. Dr Cook did not approve of whitewash in any sense of the term.

I was told that His Majesty would come through one of my wards, so I decided to have an interesting show for him and collected cases from various parts of the hospital. When he entered the ward, he enquired what cases were there and I told him I had a representative collection of the various 'war diseases' met with in France. He was interested at once and asked me to explain them to him, so I showed him cases of war nephritis, dysentery, trench fever, 'soldiers' heart',* shellshock, epidemic jaundice and poisoning by gas. He asked me to explain the Haldane Oxygen Apparatus and was much interested in the special treatment which I had devised for gassed cases. He spoke to all the patients and spent about twenty minutes in the ward. 'However did you catch that?' he asked the man with epidemic jaundice. 'Well, Your Majesty,' replied the patient, whose face was as yellow as a daffodil, 'I was bathing in a pond and I only found out afterwards that some of the Chinese had been bathing in it before me!' The King laughed heartily. He was pleased with his visit and after his tour of inspection he had tea in the Sisters' Mess. Altogether he stayed over an hour and a half – by far the longest visit he had paid to a medical unit in France. I was happy to be able to show that it was not just the wounded who were war casualties.

Captain J. B. Cook, RAMC

At least the hospitals in France were spared the visitations of well-meaning ladies who dutifully visited wounded soldiers in their local hospitals. Many were elderly, many wore themselves out with the effort. All of them believed that they were 'doing good' but their visits were often as much of a trial to the objects of their beneficence as they were to themselves.

* 'Soldiers' heart' was defined by Arthur F Hurst in *Medical Diseases of the War* (Edward Arnold 1918): 'Soldiers not infrequently suffer from symptoms due to functional circulatory disturbances during their period of training, and still more often whilst on active service. In neither case do the symptoms differ from those which may occur among civilians, but their relative frequency has led to the adoption of the term "soldier's heart" to describe the various functional cardiac disorders specially common among soldiers. The effect of active service on the heart was first investigated during the American Civil War, and the present war has given an opportunity for a renewed study of the subject.'

Rifleman
Bill Worrell,
12th Battalion,
King's Royal
Rifle Corps

The worst visitors were the ones that came round selling religion. After I was wounded I was taken to Chelsea Military Hospital, and although visitors were only allowed on Wednesday and Sunday afternoons the Hot Gospellers could get in at any time. They were mostly middle-aged ladies who would make a dash for the first wounded Tommy in his bed and, after giving him a cigarette to establish good relations, would hand him religious tracts and try to save his soul whether he wanted it saved or not. When these people came into the ward, the troops who were allowed out of bed made a bee-line for the door and the recreation room. The bed-bound could not escape so they would pretend to be fast asleep. These ladies were not to be put off so easily. If a hand was left out of the bed-clothes they grabbed it and held on to you until you opened your eyes.

There was a Sergeant Tom in the next bed to mine, who had been wounded in the stomach, and in spite of his pretending to be asleep one of these old dears came and plopped herself down beside his bed and took his hand. He kept his eyes closed but held her hand also. Then he slowly drew her hand under the bedclothes. After a moment she gave a little shriek and went running out of the ward, straight into Sister's office. Shortly afterwards Sister Carter came out, marched up the ward and we could see that the sergeant was for it! When she reached his bed, before she could say anything he looked up at her and said, 'You must have heard me scream, Sister. I was lying here fast asleep when suddenly I found a hand being very familiar under the bedclothes!' He got away with it, but Sister made it quite clear that she didn't believe a word of it, and warned him severely not to play any such tricks again. Sister liked to think she was a martinet, but she mellowed on acquaintance.

Sister Carter mellowed considerably towards Bill Worrell when she discovered from the wounded hero's mother on the first visiting day that although his military age was twenty he was exactly seventeen years old, and she embarrassed Bill by passing this interesting information on to the rest of the ward. Bill Worrell was badly wounded in the face and stomach and was unable to get out of bed. He was also unable to understand why the other soldiers, the nurses and even the visitors laughed and made cooing noises as they passed the end of his bed, and was infuriated at not being able to see what prompted the laughter at his expense. When Sergeant Tom's wife came the next visiting day and collapsed, like the other visitors, into a fit of giggling, he demanded to know why. 'It's nothing,' she said. 'Just a notice asking visitors not to feed the infant.' Further enquiry elicited the information that the notice was embellished by a baby's feeding bottle full of milk, and a small blue potty. Bill, condemned to answer to 'Babe' for the rest of his two months' stay, was convinced that the irrepressible Sergeant Tom was the perpetrator of the jest, and he was somewhat annoyed that Sister, normally all too ready to enforce good order and discipline, had connived at the joke and allowed the undignified adornments to stay on the foot of the bed until he was able to get up and remove them himself.

In the opinion of the American Sisters serving in the voluntary hospitals in Britain and France, the discipline which prevailed in British military hospitals was ridiculous. The American Sisters could go where they liked, with whom they liked, could dance if they wished and – most infuriating of all to the British nursing staff, hemmed in as they were by petty regulations – were allowed to have parties in their Mess at No. 22 in Camiers. Here they invited the very officers and male medical staff of the British hospitals with whom the British nurses were forbidden to associate outside working hours. It caused a certain amount of bad feeling which was not alleviated by the fact that the Tommies were loud in their praises of the Americans.

It was hardly surprising that the American girls felt very slightly smug and that they tended to look down a little on the British girls – or at least so the British girls felt – and particularly on the VADs. Although a very few American 'Nurses' Aides' (which were their equivalent) would arrive at a later date, the American nurses then serving in France were all fully trained and experienced. They worked every bit as hard as the British girls, undertook the same unpleasant jobs, spent hours of their off-duty time writing to relatives of patients and to ex-patients, and lived under the same uncomfortable conditions. Who, they felt, could grudge them a little democratic fun? But the British girls next door went on muttering darkly about parties, attended by *men*, held in the American Nurses' quarters. The rumours were true, but the parties took place each afternoon between the sedate hours of four and five in the huts of nurses who were off duty, and tea was the strongest beverage served. Henry Potter, faithful to his 'Most Beautiful Lady', the dashing Bessie Miller, to whom he wrote every other day, did not go in for socializing but wrote in answer to Bessie's carefully nonchalant enquiries:

You were asking about the nurses. Oddly enough I'd just got back from a walk with two of them and Pitts. There are seventy of them here and I should think their general ability is well above the average. We practically don't see anything of them except during our ward work, and everything is very businesslike there. They live in three buildings some little distance from us and their area is taboo for all males, except from four to five when they serve tea. I've never been over there, and I don't think many of the doctors go. Their most constant guests are the officers from the Machine Gun School about a mile down the road. They live two in a room and each room has a little stove, so they are better off than we are.

The nurses have to cut their own wood. It seems to me that they have a pretty hard time. They get up at six-thirty, breakfast at seven and get into the ward at seven-thirty. They are through at 6 pm. It certainly must take a good deal of nerve to stay on duty in a cold ward all day, with the thermometer usually around forty. Many have chilblains and several have ulcers on their fingers from the cold. There are always ten or twelve off sick. They all seem to like it and several have been here since the first unit came in 1915.

Pitts announced this noon that he was going to take a walk with two nurses, and when I told him that two of each was the smallest number that were supposed to go walking together he suggested that I make the fourth. We went up over the hills to the east, through the snow, saw lots of rabbits, no end of quails and a mole or two, stopped for tea at a French inn about four miles out but couldn't get it, and got back by six o'clock. I had a good time but should have had at least a thousand times better if one of my companions' name had been B. Miller.

The officers from the machine-gun base were only too happy to visit the hospitable Messes of both doctors and nurses at the American hospital, where the atmosphere was free and easy compared to the stiff formality of any association they were able to enjoy with the British girls. All invitations had to go through Matron. It was Matron who decided whether or not they might be accepted, and Matron who laid down the rules and conditions.

Kathleen Rhodes, VAD, No. 11 Stationary Hospital, Rouen

There was an enormous convalescent camp a little distance up the road from our hospital where they had great entertainment talent among the staff, and every now and then we were invited to concerts there – a great treat for us, as we were not allowed to go to any public entertainments in the town of Rouen.

When our Matron received an invitation for her staff we had to walk up the road in twos, just like a school crocodile, escorted by a Regular Army Sister. But we had a very sporting one who, when we reached the con. camp concert hall, turned a blind eye to the row of cavalry subalterns who were all waiting for us with boxes of lovely chocolates. To their great joy – and also to ours – Sister allowed them to sit beside us.

It was inevitable that echoes of discontent should reach across the Channel, and should eventually be given an airing in the correspondence columns of *The Times*.

To The Editor of The Times
Sir,
Some few weeks ago a letter appeared in *The Times* asking for recruits for the VADs. In case the response to this appeal was not equal to expectations, it would not be difficult to indicate some of

the causes of so regrettable an occurrence. In many ways the conditions of service for British nurses in France, both trained and partly trained, are unnecessarily irksome and unpleasant, and dissatisfaction is widespread and profound among Army nurses of all degrees, though it seldom finds expression otherwise than privately.

First I take the question of privilege leave to England, which is granted normally every six months. Nursing is arduous at the best of times, but on active service during the campaigning season it is doubly or trebly exacting. That is all the more reason why leave should be given as regularly as possible. I can recall but few cases of a nurse under the rank of matron getting her leave (other than sick-leave) at the due date. Nine, ten, even twelve months are usual intervals, so much so that they are accepted as the normal expectation. During the winter months, hospital cases have been so light that every nurse in France could have been given a fortnight's leave without detriment to the patients.

My next point is that not enough is done to provide healthy relaxation for nurses. The weekly 'half day off' is abrogated by some Matrons at the slightest hint of increased military activity, often quite needlessly. Their monthly 'day off' is, even at the slackest season, almost unknown. Concert parties and entertainments are discouraged, although they are not forbidden; the latest regulation, I understand, is that nurses may not 'dress-up' for them but may perform or sing in uniform; the co-operation of medical officers or other males is tabooed. Dancing is a healthy form of exercise and relaxation from the strain of nursing which is strictly forbidden, even at Christmas. No grievance of the nursing services is so widely and bitterly resented as this Puritanical ordinance. Those who control the Colonial and the United States nursing services permit their nurses to dance, much to the advantage of their health. The invidious spectacle thus arises of a British hospital existing side by side with a Colonial or an American one, with this galling and insulting regulation in force on one side of the boundary fence but not upon the other; and it is actually the case that British nurses in their quarters can hear the dances which the British medical officers with whom they work may attend but they themselves may not.

It sounds incredible, but it is true, that on occasions when rumours to the effect that this regulation has been evaded have reached the administration, the plan has been adopted of requiring every nurse in the hospital concerned to sign a paper saying whether or not she has ever broken the rules – not merely on the occasion in question but ever since her arrival in France; and disciplinary measures have been taken against those who have incriminated themselves in response to this un-English and possibly illegal method of inquisition. I was glad to hear recently that, at one hospital where this was tried, every sister and VAD, whether or not she had actually offended, signed a confession of having done so; this defeated the authorities, who had to let the whole affair drop.

This letter has been written at the instigation of no one, and in consultation with no one, but solely to draw attention to various points actually observed in France which appear to be more or less gross abuses in the opinion of

A Mere Man

The letter from 'A Mere Man' was the opening shot in an explosive correspondence that continued for some weeks with a further salvo from 'A Mere Nurse': '. . . a very unfair statement of the feeling of the great majority of nurses and VADs . . . These excellent nurses go out to France to work, not to play . . . A few frivolous nurses and VADs may agree with "Mere Man" but the majority of them will not be grateful to him for misrepresenting them.' The aunt of a VAD 'agreed perfectly . . . One point has been omitted – viz., the really scandalously insufficient arrangements made in some hospitals for the housing of the VADs and Nursing Sisters in France . . . tents through the winter . . . no proper heating or means of washing . . . water and toothbrush frozen . . . My niece dressed in gloves and so was able to finish her toilet just before her hands got stiff with the cold.'

'Pro Patria' joined in the fray. 'Nursing staff in France are treated by the average Matron as if they were inmates of a reformatory. . . . Why is it out of the question for British nurses to have the opportunities for recreation accorded to their nurses by the Colonial and American authorities? But they know they can count on us in spite of all, so I fear that we shall continue to be treated as inmates of a penitentiary. . .'

'The Mother of an Uncomplaining VAD' also supported 'A Mere Man'. 'His facts cannot be denied . . . stated in scores of letters to parents last winter . . . damp beds insufficiently supplied with blankets . . . hot-water bottles frozen hard and she had to break the ice before she could perform her ablutions . . . do not desire a bed of roses . . . a slur on the upbringing and the education of these girls of the upper middle-class . . . Puritanical regulations . . . recognition of their noble patriotism. . .'

Eventually, Lady Ampthill, who was Chairman of the Joint Women's VAD Committee, wrote plaintively from Devonshire House:

I am going out to France tomorrow, and if I can have any places and names I should be very glad to investigate any cause of complaint. . . We are, I am glad to say, having a steady flow of recruits for VAD service, and as the new members are largely sisters of VADs who have been nursing since the beginning of the war I think this is the strongest argument that the complaints cannot be very general, and that VADs will continue to come forward as they have done in the past for the sake of the sick and wounded.

It all made very little difference, except in one important respect for which they had indirectly to thank the American Sisters who were housed more comfortably in huts. Huts were now ordered to be provided for the accommodation of all nurses in camp hospitals. The British girls still envied their Colonial and American colleagues their greater freedom, but the time was fast approaching when even that attitude would soften, for Uncle Sam was stirring his limbs and deciding that he had had rather enough of looking on at the war.

Chapter Fifteen

Both at home and abroad the neutrality of the United States had been a sore point from the beginning. Winston Churchill – half-American himself – had sent a memorandum to the Prime Minister in September 1914, with a copy to Lord Kitchener. 'Nothing', he wrote, 'will bring American sympathy along with us so much as American bloodshed on the field. What is wanted now is that there should be an announcement made that we will accept the services of Americans who come to Canada or England and volunteer.'

The trouble was that some over-enthusiastic Canadians were not content to wait for Americans to cross the border to enlist, and in blatant violation of the neutrality laws they sent recruiting officers into the United States. In the summer of 1916 the German Ambassador lodged an official complaint at the White House about recruiting advertisements that had appeared in the press. They were not precisely 'recruiting advertisements' but the intention was clear. Many American newspapers had published photographs of groups of 'Canadian' soldiers, who were actually Americans, accompanied by encouraging captions. A typical example appeared in the *Pueblo Chieftain* in February 1916:

> Officers and a few men of the American Legion, now 1,400 strong, all citizens of the United States, who are enrolled in Canada for war in Europe. The men are now in training in Toronto. It is expected that the Legion will soon be 5,000 strong, then it will go to the trenches in France. Citizens of the United States who want to fight are welcome to the Legion.

Americans serving in Europe as non-combatants were just as partisan as their fighting compatriots. Within weeks of his arrival Dan Reardon wrote home, 'If we had any neutrality when we left the United States, it has rapidly gone. We now may be neutral, but as the fellow said, "We don't care a damn who licks the Germans!"'

And there was no doubt about Graham Carey's opinion. He wrote to his mother, 'I think young fellows at home are perfectly crazy not to take such a chance as our outfit offers for seeing the war and lending a hand.' Carey had lent a hand to such effect that he was one of the first of the boys of the American Field Service to receive the *Croix de Guerre*.

Early in 1917 the son of family friends was similarly honoured. Mrs Carey telegraphed her congratulations to his mother and Mrs Chapman replied:

> Sylvania
> Barrytown-on-Hudson
>
> My dear Agnes,
>   Thank you ever so much for your telegram. Your own boy has the same record. I can't help believing that these young men – the whole class of them – are somehow giving the country that elixir which it stands in such need of.
>
> Yours affectionately,
> Irene Jay Chapman

Now the American Field Service had earned itself a new name – 'Friends of France'. In 1916 a book of that title was published about its exploits (with the thinly veiled purpose of recruiting more volunteers) and Theodore Roosevelt wrote a resounding preface.

> The little group of Americans told of in this book, who during the past two years have dedicated valiant effort and, not infrequently, risked their lives in the service of France, can best be thought of as only a symbol of millions of other Americans, men and women, who would gladly have welcomed an opportunity to do what these men have done – or more. For, notwithstanding official silence and the injunctions of Presidential prudence, the majority of Americans have come to appreciate the meaning, not only to France but to all the world, of the issues that are today so desperately at stake, and their hearts and hopes are all with France in her gigantic struggle. . . .

Roosevelt's words struck a chord of sympathy in a growing number of Americans at home in the United States, where President Wilson was growing more and more unpopular for his policy of non-involvement, and for contenting himself with sending notes of protest to Germany and trying to mediate from afar. When it was no longer possible to withstand the mounting pressure at home and from abroad, and the United States, infuriated by the sinking of many of her ships by German U-boats, finally declared war on Germany and her allies on 3 April 1917, America exploded with pent-up emotion.

Henry Potter wrote excitedly in his diary:

> An exciting day. The United States has declared war at last. Our chief feeling is one of relief that the suspense is over. We had a little jollification tonight. An orchestra, punch, and lots of toasts. Afterwards we went over to No. 11 where Cabot got up on the chair and made a speech.

Dr Henry Potter, 3rd Harvard Medical Unit (his diary, 3 April 1917)

Letters arriving from the States expressed equally jubilant sentiments. A family friend of Potter's wrote:

> Well, we're all in the fray now. Perhaps it seems a long holding-off to you fellows over there, but there was a lot had to be done before Uncle Sam said anything, and, all in all, there must have been thousands of preparations made that couldn't be done in a minute. . . . We girls have been cutting out shirts, and playing 'Sister Susie' in other ways. Today, tomorrow and Friday the class in Preparation of Surgical Dressings meets – three hours at a lesson, for eight lessons – and I really got up out of bed to go down today, for I've one of those *achey* feverish colds that I found lying loose in a snowbank Easter Monday. Yes, sir – ten inches of snow that day and some of it left yet. Sunday, Dr Arthur called for me to go out and try his new motor car and it's a beauty – then your mother invited me in for tea and, would you believe it, we had to try three churches later to get into one – finally got in at The First Baptist and, as luck would have it, the sermon had come first and so we got all the music – rather good!

The Easter snowstorm that had so unseasonably swept the north-east coast of the United States had its counterpart in north-west France. The blizzard struck as the troops went over the top to fight the battle of Arras in the first move of the long-planned spring campaign. It was ill-starred from the beginning, and there was acrimony in high places. The battle was to be part of the offensive that was the plan of the French General Nivelle, and for its duration the British army was placed under his overall command – a situation which was naturally not to the liking of the senior British commanders. It was particularly galling to Haig, who was anxious to proceed with his own plan to attack further north. He still believed that, given the right circumstances, it was possible to crack the German lines, and that a breakthrough could take place from the salient that surrounded Ypres. But Nivelle was equally optimistic, and he was only slightly put out when his plans were disrupted at the eleventh hour by the fact that the Germans had retired along part of the front and entrenched themselves in an unprobed and formidably fortified new line, some distance behind the old one.

The main attack was to take place on the French front in Champagne, with the British attacking around Arras in an effort to draw off the German reserves. They attacked in the freak snowstorm that swept the front on Easter Monday. It was 11 April before Henry Potter had a chance to write up his diary.

Dr
Henry Potter,
3rd Harvard
Medical Unit,

The big push has started. For two days the convoys have been coming in. On the 9th we took in fifteen hundred in twenty-four hours. Every ward is full and the D lines are crowded. The B line has

forty-three pretty bad cases in it. Working day and night. The
operating room starts about 8.30 am, and four table are going steadily till one o'clock next morning. I don't see how the Op. room nurses
stand it. 273 operations in four days. Cabot is a tireless worker, but
he has a disposition that could sour milk.

No. 22
General
Hospital,
Camiers
(his diary, 11
April 1917)

But again the attack had gone off at half-cock. The tanks, instead of
being concentrated on one part of the front, were spread out across nine
miles. At Monchy-le-Preux, where The Rifle Brigade and the Royal
Fusiliers had attacked the hilltop village, the cavalry that should have
supported them was late in arriving and, charging up the hill, was wiped
out by deadly fire from machine-gun posts well-sited on its crest. The
solitary tank was bogged down. And when the troops, in spite of fearful
odds, succeeded in throwing the Germans out of the village, they were
left clinging to its ruins, watching impotently as the Germans dug in on
the other side, because there were no reserves available to pursue the
advance.

But one piece of good news was received with elation at No. 11
Canadian Hospital, and by the Americans at No. 22 next door. The
Canadians, with some Scottish troops, had captured the important
objective of Vimy Ridge and were firmly entrenched on top of it. It was
the most important strategic gain of the battle – a victory sufficient to
distract the attention from the fact that otherwise the advance had been
small, and that although it had achieved its objective of drawing the
Germans' attention to the north, Nivelle's own attack in the Champagne sector was a disastrous failure. When the French attacked on the
16th their gain was precisely 600 yards, and their losses were enormous.
During the French attack there had been a lull on the British front, but
on 26 April Potter recorded gloomily:

Hustling again. The fight has been on again for three days in front of
Arras. The Germans are fighting hard and giving ground very slowly.
The convoys are mostly very badly wounded men.
    The opinion, among them, seems to be that the tanks have had
their day. The Germans have a short, easily handled anti-tank howitzer that is very effective. One man in A7 – face and hands burned,
compound fractures of both legs – told me that his tank was completely riddled. The gasoline tank exploded and all on board were
killed but him. He is going to die. He said that of ten tanks that
started out from Froiselles yesterday not one came back.

Dr
Henry Potter,
3rd Harvard
Medical Unit,
No. 22
General
Hospital,
Camiers

Already he was counting the days until his return to America, and
exulted on 1 May,

. . . the first day of my last full month here. Although if there were
really an American force coming over here soon, I think I'd consider

it my duty to stay here and join them when they arrived. But that doesn't seem at all likely. I don't believe any American troops will be over here inside of a year.

After the initial euphoria of America's declaration of war, the question of the arrival of the US troops was also exercising the minds of British and French politicians. The moral effect was splendid, but when would the Yanks arrive in sufficient numbers to be effective? General Pershing himself, although he planned to lead a token force of American soldiers to Europe as speedily as possible, was reluctant to join the war until he could put a fully-trained American army into the field under its own command. This, he estimated, would be early in 1919. Meanwhile, recruiting was well under way.

The Red Cross embarked on a brisk recruiting campaign of its own. By 10 April, 30,000 new members had enrolled in Boston alone, a record that was only beaten by Providence which netted 30,700 new members – over 12 per cent of the population. But on the whole, their role would be confined to bandage-making and sewing, for the United States was now priding itself on the professionalism of its Red Cross Nursing Service. 7,000 fully trained nurses, which the Red Cross described as 'the cream of the nursing profession in this country', had been enrolled by arrangement with the National Association of Nurses. It was a natural pride, but it led to an assumption that was as tactless as it was untrue.

> Our Red Cross Nursing Service is organized and officered by professional nurses. England has recently undergone a sad experience from pursuing opposite tactics before war came. There the Red Cross Service was largely made up of non-professional women with some training in hygiene and first aid. When war came this service attempted to supplement the work of the British army nurses, and it was not until professional nurses were called in to the rescue that a frightful muddle was straightened out.*

Such half-truths and misapprehensions stemmed directly from the widespread publicity that had naturally been given to the exploits of lady-adventurers three years earlier, during the first weeks of the war. But the resulting confusion, the misinterpretation of the role played by the British Red Cross, caused a certain amount of ill-feeling between the battle-scarred VADs and the American nurses who were about to arrive in Europe with the United States army. It was natural that Europe should have long outgrown the fervour of war fever which had spread like a bush fire in the early days and which had now ignited the

---

* *The Red Cross Magazine* (official publication of the American Red Cross), May 1917.

enthusiasm of the Americans. It was equally natural that some well-intentioned American individuals, inflamed by the cause and by the warmth of their welcome, should have behaved in a manner that was less than tactful towards the war-weary band which had been working flat out for the best part of three years. One of them was Lorna Neill, who was somewhat put out when an American mission arrived at Revigny. She wrote her parents a full account of the occasion.

It was a 'Mission Militaire', the first bit of the American army to come up to the Front to inspect transport, to read, mark, learn and inwardly digest how it is done. I told Mrs Culling, who groaned at having to get up and say pretty things at that hour; I told Antoine who groaned at the idea of getting the hot, coffee-stained, dusty canteen of six o'clock in the morning into the neat, cool, orderly, shining place it normally is at ten, by only eight o'clock. However, we worked hard all night and, at about six, Mrs Osbourne (a young widow) and I went home worn out. I woke Mrs Culling up and she said that she thought Mrs O and I ought to have a bath, dress in snowy white and come over and look at the Mission; it would be an event anyway. It was rather funny, because last night at dinner we'd been discussing America very freely. The Revigny commanders appeared to think the Mission pretty important, because the whole place was spotless at six – pebbles down in all the holes, and all the debris which is usually scattered over the square at that hour in the morning cleared away.

Lorna Neill, Cantine Anglaise, Revigny

So I awoke Maud out of a dreamy slumber and had a bath and dressed again, and we all departed over to the canteen and nearly pulverized the garrison and the few men who were waiting for the nine o'clock train, by playing the gramophone to them at that hour. Mrs Osbourne and I were nearly asleep and the others had had no breakfast, but we flung ourselves about the canteen in attitudes of easy industriousness, and waited while Mrs Culling told various commandants what she thought of American Missions who came at eight in the morning. Well, we waited and we waited, and we grew sleepier and sleepier. At last, at ten o'clock, a very shiny Pullman car, simply spattered all over with Stars and Stripes, appeared and in two seconds the canteen was full. Led by our pet colonel in his very best clothes and all his medals they came, and there appeared to be masses of them. Mostly French, however, French officers in blue and gold and medals, with beautiful manners, and amongst them about five Americans.

We were not prepared for anything very wonderful or very soldierly or very smart – *but*! They wore sort of imitation khaki made of some cotton material very badly fitting, very ordinary and, I regret to say it, dirty. There was one man in particular I noticed. He was enormous and his tunic, or 'vest jacket' as I've no doubt he'd call it, was stretched over his enormous middle, straining at the unpolished buttons and running into tight creases. It was buttoned right up to the neck and he obviously had not the French habit of tucking a serviette into his coat when he ate. He looked at us and began at once to tell us about fifty-six 'vurry fine young women who crossed in the same steamship as us, nurses mind you, who'd be out here in no time. Some dear lady in New York had given each of them a cunning silk bathing suit, with a neat pocket in each side to hold brandy in case we were torpedoed. It was surely vurry amusing to see them trying to slip them over their heads'. There was one man, the chief he appeared to be, whose face I liked and he was quiet. They didn't stay long but the fat man, as he was going, waved his hand at us with a patronizing air and said he hoped we'd have vurry good luck. He said it several times, as much to say, 'Of course, you aren't expected to come up to our fifty-six fine young women, and when we start a canteen you will no doubt retire, but still – do your best'.

Well, they will profit by all our mistakes and all our failures and all the blood we have shed as well as by all our successes, so we shall see what they can do. After all, we have always known them to be a nation of businessmen, and it certainly is a slick business proposition to wait until you have a sure thing and then plump your money right down and rake in the profits. Many of the young Americans who have been driving ambulances out here since the beginning see this and say so to us.

The ranks of the ambulance drivers were about to thin out drastically, for now that their native land was well and truly in the war, many of them (including Graham Carey and Dan Sargent) set off joyfully for Paris to join the US army.

The US army – or at least its vanguard under General Pershing – arrived in England on 9 June on the same day that Henry Potter reached London on his way back to America. The Americans, arriving on the White Star liner *Baltic*, slipped into the port of Liverpool in complete secrecy. Even the men of the Royal Welch Fusiliers who were drawn up on the quayside to welcome them had no idea why they were being paraded. The Americans were suitably gratified by their reception, but they were intrigued by the fact that the column of Fusiliers was headed by a goat. It was their mascot and it had been presented to them by King George V himself. Groomed and glistening, trotting smartly on the end of its snowy white rope at the head of the band, it attracted considerable attention. 'Say, General', one staff officer called out, having scrutinized the engraved silver plate that shone between the goat's polished horns, 'these guys got this goat as a present from the King!' 'Yeah?' replied General Pershing. 'Well, maybe we ought to get the President to give us a grizzly bear!' Amid amicable laughter General Pershing inspected the guard of honour, and the band played 'God Save the King' and 'The Star

Spangled Banner' – a melody that for the next few weeks was to follow the Americans wherever they went.

They played it that night at the Alhambra Theatre of Varieties in London's West End when a contingent of fifty American staff officers was invited to attend a performance of *The Bing Boys are Here*. Dr Henry Potter was thrilled to be in the audience, thrilled to see the uniformed Americans, thrilled at their reception. The boxes were draped with flags – a medley of Union Jacks and Stars and Stripes. The manager, Mr Foster, was so excited that his speech of welcome from the stage was almost incoherent, and the orchestra had to rescue him by striking up an encore of 'The Star Spangled Banner'. The audience rose to its feet and cheered and cheered and cheered.

The King received General Pershing and a contingent of his warriors at Buckingham Palace. London went wild. Small groups of Doughboys were mobbed in the streets, and glowing reports of their welcome were flashed back home to inspire the laggards.

Tin Pan Alley burst forth with a song that swept the United States and soon arrived in London where, billed as 'The Sammies' Marching Song', it became the show-stopper of the musical *Zig-Zag*. 'The Sammies' Marching Song' was 'Over There'.

Over There, Over There,
Send the word, send the word Over There,
That the Yanks are coming,
The Yanks are coming,
There's a drum drum drumming in the air . . .

It was an instant success and soon everyone was humming it, including the troops on the Western Front. But as time passed and, apart from a fêted few, there were few signs of an American army materializing, they developed their own ironic parody. 'They're coming over. They're coming over', sang the troops on the march, 'and they won't get there 'til it's over, Over There!'

It was hardly fair. It had taken a year for the British to recruit, to equip, to train an army and to put it into the field. Why should the Americans be expected to achieve the same object any more quickly? But time was slipping past. It was high summer now. The troops were tired and, yet again, were gathering their strength and preparing their dispositions for another battle.

Chapter Sixteen

America's entry into the war was a tremendous shot in the arm to the French. In spite of their superhuman feats at Verdun, in spite of the fact that they had thrown the Germans back and regained large tracts of the lost ground, their morale was not high, particularly in the army, where there were murmurs of rebellion and, in some divisions, insurrection which amounted to mutiny. The military authorities overreacted, clamped down on discipline, ordered summary, random executions (many sentences, in the event, were not carried out), but they were perceptive enough to realize that high sentiments of Death or Glory were no longer enough to fire the dispirited souls of exhausted men. A leave rota was introduced; more attention was paid to the comfort and morale of the poilus; and a national tribute was paid to the army on Bastille Day, 14 July, when ragged representatives of the defenders of Verdun carried their tattered standards on a triumphant march through the cheering crowds of Paris.

As a mark of honour to their French allies, and as a mark of gratitude for their own reception, General Pershing decreed that his troops should observe the date as an official holiday and join the French in their celebrations. It was a repeat performance of the celebration that had taken place ten days before on America's Independence Day, when the Doughboys had been fêted in the French capital and the population had gone wild with delight. All of a sudden, thanks to the Americans, Paris was again living up to its reputation for fun and gaiety, and the troops who managed to wangle a few days' local leave to visit it appreciated the cheerful atmosphere to the full.

At the Gâre du Nord, bands of do-gooding ladies met every leave train and waylaid the soldiers with pressing invitations to join their escorted sightseeing parties – anxious that the innocent Tommies or Canucks or Anzacs should not fall into the clutches of other 'ladies', equally pressing in their invitations, whose object was to part them from their money and their virtue alike. Being a senior officer, Colonel Nicholson of the Territorial Highland Division, who was spending a few days' well-earned leave in Paris, was immune to the blandishments of both parties and had a thoroughly enjoyable time.

Colonel W. N.

We saw four plays and one cinema in our three days' visit. The plays were suited to foreign soldiery, and, as Paris was still wildly enthusiastic at America entering the war, every possible flattering allusion turned on to the Americans. 'Yankee Doodle' received loud cheers; it seemed to be the only American tune they knew. English music-hall turns, such as 'A Broken Doll', were given in American settings. We were honoured with the announcement of 'English Grand Military Music' – which appropriately enough turned out to be 'Take Me Back to Dear Old Blighty'.

Nicholson, CMG, DSO, Territorial Highland Division

It was 'appropriate' because, in contrast to the virile exuberance of the newly arrived Americans, there was hardly a soldier on the Western Front who did not dream of 'Blighty' and of escape from the long weary war.

Take me back to dear old Blighty,
Put me on the train for London town,
Take me over there,
Drop me anywhere,
Birmingham, Leeds or Manchester,
I don't care.

How I want to see my Best Girl
Cuddling up as close as she can be,
I ti-tiddly ity,
Carry me back to Blighty,
Blighty is the place for me.

The words were set to a jolly tune that bounced cheerfully from the plush-covered walls of the theatre. The audience, festooned with streamers thrown from the stage, stamped and cheered and joined in the choruses. The soldiers had the time of their lives. They were on leave. However brief the respite, for the moment they were away from it all.

Back at the base, just one step away from the horrors of the Front, the entertainments struck a more poignant note.

The Machine Gun Corps just down the road used to have a lot of concerts and, if we possibly could, we used to go to them. The wounded had their own hospital concerts, so these were for 'Troops Only', and the Tommies came from all the base units for miles around. There were two rows in front reserved for nurses, but there wasn't a square inch of the rest of the hall that wasn't khaki. They sat on shelves, they sat on bookcases, they stood on window-ledges, they even propped ladders outside the windows and stood on the steps. When there were no chairs left, they sat on the floor and the overflow sat at the side of the platform itself. The atmosphere was unbelievably excited. Everyone went as early as they could to get a place, and gradually the noise mounted, talking and scuffling feet, cat-calls, an

Dorothy Nicol, VAD, No. 11 General Hospital, Camiers

incredible din as the audience waited, and then absolute silence when the concert itself began. I can't imagine that any artistes had ever had such an audience. They roared with laughter at every allusion; they joined in every chorus; they *encored* every item and brought the house down with thunderous applause.

There was an officer who I think must have been a professional actor. He nearly always did the same thing, but we never tired of it. First he recited in his normal voice a ridiculous 'little poem that started:

Way down in Deadwood Valley,
Where some of the boys were rough,
Parsons, he was a bit of a scamp,
That's when he drank enough,
She was a little slip of a girl,
A girl with a pure white soul,
And if one of the boys should insult that girl,
With death he should pay the toll. . . .

It was a silly little poem, but we thought it was the funniest thing we had ever heard. He did it straight the first time and then he would recite it in the character of various famous actors, and he added bits to it as well. He would say:

She was a little slip of a girl –
(Probably a VAD!)
A girl with a pure white soul –
(*Not* a VAD this time!)

We pretended to be very embarrassed, but we loved it really. The artistes didn't spare anyone – VADs, Sisters, Matrons, sergeants, sergeant-majors, officers, colonels, we were all fair game for jokes, and the men used to cheer like anything. At one particular concert, in the very front row, were four officers with very badly wounded jaws, and they had all sorts of contraptions in and about their mouths – gauze and pieces of wire. One little man came on to the stage and sang 'Old King Cole' in quite an ordinary manner, and then he went on to sing it as various ranks in the Army would – a private, an NCO, and ended up as a very posh colonel. He was terribly funny and he was *encored* over and over again. These poor officers just in front of us laughed so much, though they were obviously in terrible pain, that they were laughing and groaning at the same time, and the little man on the stage looked down as he was singing and was obviously worried. After his turn was over he came down and shook hands with the officers and apologized for having made them laugh so much, but they assured him that it had been worth it!

In between the turns there were always choruses of popular songs and everyone joined in. It was terribly moving to hear all these hundreds of men singing in unison, and sometimes it cut you to the heart. It used to make my throat constrict and I had to open my eyes very wide in case I would cry. There was such a tension, such an emotion, such a nostalgia – you could hardly define what it was, but the atmosphere was tremendously emotional.

The very worst time was at the last concert of all, before I went back to England. I didn't want to go, but my contract was about to finish and I couldn't sign on again because my mother was ill. It was a grilling hot evening towards the end of July, just before the battle of Passchendaele started. A comedian sang a frankly immoral song with a chorus that went:

> I will have a night tonight,
> The missus is out of sight,
> The woman who lives next door to me,
> Her old man has gone out to tea,
> She has invited me in, you see,
> I will have a night tonight. . . .

Everybody joined in the chorus – even the VADs and nurses, and we were supposed to be very proper. And then there came a complete change of mood. The pianist started to play, and men started to sing 'The Long, Long Trail', and it was almost unbearable. I simply couldn't take it and found myself fading out of the singing after the first two lines.

> There's a long, long trail a-winding
> Into the land of my dreams,
> Where the nightingales are singing,
> And a white moon beams. . . .

I don't know whether it was the sad tune or the words, or because I was leaving soon, but that particular evening everything got me. I looked out of the window and saw a stream of ambulances going very slowly along the dusty road. At the same time, through the other window overlooking the railway line, I could see a train full of men and horses and guns going up the line. It wasn't the first train of the evening – they'd been rumbling past all through the concert – but that one going by, just when they were singing that song, overwhelmed me. I just managed *not* to disgrace myself. It was too much seeing the ambulances coming in and the train going up at the same time – too much to think of all the pain and hurt and suffering.

There was an attitude of war-weariness that was hard for the newly arrived Americans to understand. Nell Brink landed in France with one of the first contingents of nurses which was to be attached to the American Force.

Nell Brink
Reserve Nurse,
US Army
Nurse Corps,
No. 27 Base
Hospital,
(University of
Pittsburgh),
France

We were very excited when we landed in Le Havre. We were there for some time while they decided what to do with us, and we stayed in an hotel and had French lessons every morning. We met some very interesting soldiers there. There was a whole regiment of Anzacs, wonderful men, who looked so jaunty in their uniform with the cowboy hats turned up at the side with a big sunburst badge on them.

One morning we were having breakfast in the hotel and two English officers came into the dining-room. They seemed very serious. We knew that people had been in the war for years before we got into it, and I never forgot that, because I felt at the beginning that I was an amateur, a beginner. But these English officers came over to our table, they had recognized our uniforms, and knew that we were newcomers and wanted to talk to us. They were on their way back to their outfit from leave, and we told them that we had just arrived. I said, 'Well, it will probably be some time before our men get into the trenches' – because our men were only just arriving then in August – 'but we're raring to go.' I was really stricken when one of the officers said, 'Oh yes? Well, we'll probably be killed by that time.' They just seemed to take it as a matter of course.

It made me think a bit. We were so excited about everything. It seemed such an adventure that it was difficult for us to understand.

But the Americans who had been in Europe since the beginning had no difficulty in understanding. They were war-weary themselves. Marion Daniels, who had now worked for two years with the Harvard Unit at No. 22 General Hospital, and had renewed her contract again and again, was approaching a state of exhaustion which at last made her contemplate returning to America. It had all been worthwhile. Every mail brought letters from patients, grateful for their treatment; for the small gifts which she had stowed in their 'Dorothy bags' before they left; for the letters and parcels she had sent to them in base hospitals in Blighty; or comforts she had sent them at the Front, long after their discharge.

The burden of letter writing took many ungrudged hours of every nurse's scant off-duty time . A Ward Sister had always a batch of letters to write in reply to concerned enquiries from the anxious families of soldiers under her care, and most of the staff nurses and VADs kept up a correspondence with ex-patients they had looked after, sometimes years before. Gladys Stanford was still writing to Ernest Meddemen, wounded near Ypres in 1914 and one of the first patients at the auxiliary hospital where she had nursed in the early part of the war. Now, he was a casualty again.

Dear Miss Stanford,

Just a line at last thanking you for your card, which I received a long while ago. The envelope was smothered with postmarks when I got it; it had travelled. Well, Miss I have been in hospital three months with nerve troubles and am now in a convalescent camp, having been in hospital again with tonsilitis. But I am all right now and expect to be discharged from here in a day or two.

If you write back, will you put the following address:

4314 Pte. E. Meddemen,

No. 4 Coy. DCLI,

attached 6th Entrenching Batt.,

BEF, France

I have had rather a bad time since I left Wimborne. I only wish they would let me come back there to get better; I couldn't content myself anywhere else. I know I should have recovered in half the time, but still I'm quite well now, so that's the main thing, isn't it?

Looking now, I often think of the delightful times I've had there. Do you remember the cycle into Wimborne, when on the return journey Charlesworth fell off? I have often laughed.

I remain yours sincerely,

Ernest Meddemen

A prompt reply was sent off to the new address and reached Meddemen at the Entrenching Battalion. Reclassified and regraded after 'nerve trouble', he was no longer fit to take part part in the war as a front-line fighting soldier. He wrote back gratefully:

Dear Sister,

Just a line in answer to your nice cheery letter and cigarettes and writing pad, which I received quite safely and thanks awfully. It was quite good of you to send them, but I really think you had been kind enough while I was at Wimborne, without putting yourself to all the trouble. But I am very grateful to you, it is just like you Sisters, always seeing we don't want. Well, Sister, that nerve trouble was brought on (so I believe) by trying to dodge bullets, shells, bombs, etc. The doctor says it was Neurasthenia. I had awful headaches, red mist in the eyes and could not sleep at night, and hideous dreams. I don't want it again, I would rather be hit.

'Shellshock' – a word which the authorities discouraged – was a vexed question. Both in the line and out of it, there was an all-too-ready acceptance of the fallacy that 'nerves' was an excuse for 'funkiness' or even cowardice. If it were not, why should one man break down and become a nervous casualty while a comrade who had had the same experience in the same circumstances remained apparently unaffected? It was assumed that the answer was to be found in the calibre of the man.

When special Neurasthenic Centres were set up, and when (much later than their French colleagues) the British Medical Authorities began a programme of research into the causes of 'shellshock' and into the background of individual casualties, they were struck by the exceedingly high incidence of breakdowns among the very men who, through training and a high degree of discipline, ought to have been able, in their view, to withstand the stresses of battle and bombardment – the regular soldiers of the pre-war army. Although they had, admittedly, been longest on active service, this gave the lie to the theory, held by some, that discipline would prevent 'nerves' as well as cure them.

Further probing provided further food for thought. Large numbers of the regulars had originally enlisted because of poverty, or unemployment, or because a home had been broken up through the death of one or both parents. In the case of many such men it was significant that the space in his paybook set aside for recording the details of next of kin showed the name of a brother or sister; a distant relative; or even, occasionally, an orphanage. This fact, when it emerged in statistics, was a clear indication to the authorities that 'instability of character' often stemmed from instability of background. But the question of 'shellshock' was a great deal more complex, and as time went on it became increasingly obvious that men who were likely to become nervous casualties could not be lumped together in a single category.

Its manifestations ranged from the symptoms of total paralysis and deaf-mutism to curvature of the spine; from violent hysteria to the type of debilitating nervous weakness which, years later, would be known as 'battle fatigue'. Although casualties naturally multiplied when there were major battles, a man could be sent down the line in a shocked condition at any time, simply as a result of one trivial incident which finally made him snap and drained him of what strength he had left after months and years of fatigue, strain, exposure, exhaustion and, as in Meddemen's case, an accumulation of experiences of 'trying to dodge bullets, shells and bombs, etc.'

Sister
Mary Stollard,
QAIMNS,
Beckett's Park
Military
Hospital,
Leeds

In the early days, when the men first came in, they were young and enthusiastic. 'I'd like to have a pop at the Boche. I'll teach them this, that and the other. I'd like to go across and give them a good old stabbing.' Those were the things they used to say. But little by little, that attitude changed. They didn't want to go back and they would do almost anything to stay in England.

We had one man who cried and cried, and our MO, Colonel Vining, was very sympathetic with him. He'd been out in France for eighteen months. The Colonel said, 'I'm going to discharge him, Sister. He's done his bit.'

They were very pathetic, these shellshocked boys, and a lot of them were very sensitive about the fact that they were incontinent. They'd say, 'I'm terribly sorry about it, Sister, it's shaken me all over and I can't control it. Just imagine, to wet the bed at my age!' I'd say, 'We'll see to that. Don't worry about it.' I used to give them a bedpan in the locker beside them and keep it as quiet as possible. Poor fellows, they were so embarassed – especially the better-class men.

They used to tremble a great deal and it affected their speech. They stammered very badly, and they had strange ideas which you could only describe as hallucinations. They saw things that really didn't exist, and imagined all sorts of things. And, of course, they were terrified of going back. They used to say, 'I'm not going back to the Front again. Sister, will you tell the Major? Try and get me out of it?' I had to say I couldn't do that, but not to worry about it, perhaps they wouldn't be going back. But most of them did get better eventually, because these were only the milder cases. The men who were more seriously affected went to special hospitals later on.

Sister Henrietta Hall, St Luke's Military Hospital, Bradford

We had one chap called Fidgett. He was recovering from shellshock and he wasn't in a bad way at all, but when he had the experience that put him in this nervous state his hair had stood straight up on end and it was *still* up on end months later. Nothing would make it lie down, not water or hair oil or anything. He used to wear a little black cap, because it looked so odd, and that was the only thing that would keep his hair down on his head.

Elsie Broderick, VAD, Fulham Auxiliary Hospital, Hammersmith

Before I was old enough to go as a VAD to No. 1 London General I worked as an orderly at the convalescent home on Streatham Hill, and a great many men there were getting over shell shock. One of the first things I was told was that when I was serving meals to the up-patients – and most of them got up for meals there – always to put the plate down very carefully in front of them and to let them see me do it. If you so much as put a plate down in front of them in the ordinary way, when they weren't looking, the noise made them almost jump through the roof – just the noise of a plate being put on a table with a cloth on it!

Grace Bignold, VAD, No. 1 London General Hospital

Anything made them jump, a door banging, any sudden noise. And one night I was absolutely terrified. Night Sister wanted to go to supper, and we must have been short-staffed because she asked me if I would go up and sit with her patient while she went off for half an hour. The man was seriously ill, and he must have been delirious or shocked because although he was sound asleep and I was sitting on the other side of the room by the fire his leg kept shooting up into the air. I could see this shadow leaping up the wall, and when I turned round there was his leg shot up in the air. I was very frightened.

I got quite used to carrying shellshocked patients in the ambulance. It was a horrible thing, because they sometimes used to get these

Claire Elise Tisdall,

VAD
Ambulance
Nurse, The
Ambulance
Column,
London
District

attacks, rather like epileptic fits in a way. They became quite unconscious, with violent shivering and shaking, and you had to keep them
from banging themselves about too much until they came round
again. The great thing was to keep them from falling off the stretchers, and for that reason we used to take just one at a time in the
ambulance, because you'd never have been able to cope with four
cases at once as you could with the ordinary wounded.

Of course, these were the so-called milder cases; we didn't carry
the dangerous ones. They always tried to keep that away from us and
they came in a separate part of the train. But it happened one evening
that there was one too many of us nurses, so I didn't go with an
ambulance and I was left on the platform. I noticed that some of our
men from the column were still there, and then I noticed another sort
of ambulance come into the station, not one of ours. It was completely closed up. I said to one of the men, 'What's this ambulance
coming in? Haven't we done the train?' He said, 'No, Sister, this is
from the asylum; it's for the hopeless mental cases.' I didn't look.
They'd gone right off their heads. I didn't want to see them. There
was nothing you could do and they were going to a special place.
They were terrible.

Gwynnedd
Lloyd,
VAD,
University War
Hospital,
Southampton

I nearly got carved up with a knife once. We had a patient who had
shellshock, and he went beserk one night when I was on night duty. I
was walking up the ward to see to him when one of the other men
called out to me and said, 'Don't go any further, Sister, he's got a
knife.' And two beds further on there was this chap throwing himself
about. He wasn't particularly after me, he was just going berserk. The
other men got him, picked him up, put him on the bed and sat on
him, while I sent for the Medical Officer and the Night Sister. We had
a sort of kitchen where the men used to be able to make tea or coffee,
and he'd got this knife from the kitchen. They took him away after
that, to a special hospital. He had been all right up until then, just
nervous and quiet. I was amazed when he suddenly went beserk.

Captain
Lionel
Gameson,
RAMC,
Medical
Officer, 71st
Brigade, Royal
Field Artillary

I was scratching a hole for a body one dull and depressing evening
when I heard (or felt) a couple of shells pass over my head. I saw them
burst by two of B. 71's men who were working in the open some way
behind the battery. One man fell. I found that he had a wound of the
thigh with a fractured femur and a pretty brisk haemorrhage. It was
lucky for him that I'd happened to have been mooching around just
then. His companion escaped. I sent him to Headquarters' dugout
for my stuff, while I hung on to the bleeding. Having fixed up the
casualty and got more help, we carried him to Linder's aid-post. The
little incident, after this longish carry, seemed to be closed. Later that
night, however, I had a stiff time with the boy who had not been hit.

I knew very little about this youth. He had been classed as normal by all who knew him, and had always come up to scratch. He was used to seeing people hit, to seeing his friends hit, and to having his immediate surroundings violently disturbed. Yet this stray incident broke him. He had acted quietly and well in helping me with the wounded man and in the business of getting him cleared (by far the most exacting part of the job), and had gone back quietly to his battery. It was late that same night that I was called to him. I found him gibbering.

The scene is still most vivid to me: the deep German dugout, the usual passage running from end to end, the usual tier of bunks. The place was dimly lit by a few candles. My patient was sitting up in his cramped bunk, leaning forward, gripping hard to an upright with both hands. In most of the bunks were men who stirred as they slept. Some woke but did not complain of the boy's shouting. I spent the better part of the night with him. The conditions were not ideal for such a consultation. I quite completely failed to comfort him. Finally I gave him an injection of morphia, and waited until this rather handsome, undoubtedly intelligent child had drowsed into restless sleep. Early in the morning I took him to the aid-post and he went down the line from there. I have no record of his name. I cannot remember what diagnosis I sent with him.

The question of diagnosis was a pertinent point. In the early part of the war, shellshock cases were few and were generally the result of having been blown up or injured by an explosion. Shellshock counted as a wound, giving a man the right to a wound stripe, the status of a wounded soldier, and, should he not fully recover, considerably strengthening his bargaining position in the matter of pension rights. As the fighting went on and the strains of war began to throw up new forms of mental disturbance which could not be attributed to isolated incidents or obvious causes, the Army grew disturbed at the number of cases arriving in hospital on whose labels Field Medical Officers had written 'shellshock (W)' rather than 'Neurasthenia (S)'.* Orders were issued that the use of the blanket term 'shellshock' should cease forthwith. It was a matter of simple economics – not merely (as some Medical Officers indignantly assumed) because of the wish to avoid the post-war expense of an inordinate number of disability pensions, but because of the economical use of manpower.**

* 'W' denoted 'wounded', 'S' sickness.
** At the beginning of 1921, more than two years after the war had ended, 65,000 men suffering from various forms of neurasthenia were receiving a pension. The number had dropped to 50,000 by the beginning of 1922, but even years after the Armistice there were cases of man developing some form of disabling neurasthenia as a result of their war experiences. Some 30,000 pensions were still being paid to severe cases as late as 1938.

It was easier for a harassed Medical Officer to scribble 'shellshock (W)' on the label of any man with a nervous disorder who had to be sent down the line, but it might subsequently be discovered at the base hospital that the casualty was simply suffering from strain and exhaustion, which a few days of rest and nourishing food would put right. But having been diagnosed as a shellshock case and – with no overt intention of malingering – sincerely believing that shellshock was the basis of his trouble, he might continue to complain of the symptoms, such as continuing and severe headaches; blurring of the vision; indeterminate aches and pains; a stumbling gait; even a limp. The ease with which many men reaching Neurasthenic Centres in Britain were cured by as little as one session of hypnosis and suggestion led the authorities into the uneasy belief that a high proportion of patients had not been suffering from shellshock at all, and that the evacuation and expensive specialized treatment of large numbers of such men, together with their unnecessarily lengthy absence from the ranks, was bad housekeeping and a misuse of the medical resources which were badly needed for the wounded and genuinely sick. A new system would have to be introduced, and it was to be brought into force in time for the next big push – the battle for Passchendaele or, as it was later to be called officially, the 3rd Battle of Ypres. On 7 June 1917, seven weeks before the start of the battle, an order that did not mince words was issued to all medical personnel.

General Routine Order No. 2384

CLASSIFICATION AND DISPOSAL OF OFFICERS AND OTHER RANKS WHO WITHOUT ANY VISIBLE WOUND BECOME NON-EFFECTIVE FROM PHYSICAL CONDITIONS CLAIMED OR PRESUMED TO HAVE ORIGINATED FROM THE EFFECTS OF BRITISH OR ENEMY WEAPONS IN ACTION.

(1) All officers and other ranks who become non-effective in the above category, and whose transfer from their unit or division is unavoidable, will be sent to the Special Hospital set apart for their reception under the order of the Army Commander.

(2) The Regimental Medical Officer, or officer commanding a medical unit, who in the first instance deals with a case which it is necessary to transfer to the Special Hospital, will not record any diagnosis. He will enter on the Field Medical Card or other transfer paper the letters 'NYDN' (Not Yet Diagnosed, Nervous) only, and note any definitely known facts as to the true origin or the previous history of the case. . .

(5) . . . In no circumstances whatever will the expression 'shellshock' be used verbally or be recorded in any regimental or other casualty report, or in any hospital or other medical document, except in cases classified by the order of the officer commanding

the Special Hospital. The DAG, GHQ, 3rd Echelon, will notify the commanding officer of the unit of any case so classified.

(6) These orders do not apply to cases of gas poisoning, which will be dealt with as heretofore.

(7) All previous orders and instructions on this subject are cancelled.

For the 3rd Battle of Ypres, nineteen casualty clearing stations were distributed in the back areas. No. 62 at Haringhe (facetiously known as 'Bandaghem') was designated to receive all the NYDN cases, and there, instead of being automatically evacuated to the base, they would stay for one month for treatment and close observation. This, it was felt, would be sufficient time to weed out cases of simple exhaustion and 'funk'.*

The steep rise in the rate of shellshock cases admitted on the eve of a battle caused the authorities to suspect that some men were being sent down as casualties, either because they were acutely frightened or because of what many of their own officers and comrades would have described as 'lack of grit'. It was true. Such men were a liability in the line and, in an engagement, they were a danger to themselves and to others. It was tempting to get rid of a man who was in such a state of fear and 'nerves' that his nerve was likely to crack altogether under the stress of the battle.

It had nothing to do with fear, but with the inability to overcome it because of a congenitally nervous disposition. In the trenches in the hours before a battle, as the noise of the bombardment that preceded the attack reached a deafening crescendo, the tension mounted. In the lull that fell when at last it stopped and the minutes ticked towards zero, a man would have been an automaton if the sweat did not stand out on his forehead, if his heart did not palpitate, his mouth become dry, his hands tremble, his stomach turn over with a thrill of mingled apprehension and excitement. In those moments there were few men who did not wish themselves elsewhere, but since they were not elsewhere, since they had 'a job to do' for which most of them had volunteered, since they were all in it together, all but a tiny handful were able to master their emotions.

* During the three months of the campaign, roughly 5,000 cases were admitted to No. 62 CCS. The new system was vindicated by the fact that only 16 per cent of the patients were in the long term affected sufficiently seriously to require evacuation to the base. 55 per cent were returned direct to their units and 29 per cent were sent for a month's healthy outdoor work on French farms, well away from the firing line, under a scheme which had been arranged with the Army Agricultural Officer. Of the 16 per cent evacuated to base, 4 per cent were cases of medical or organic disease admitted in error to the NYDN centre. Of the remainder, two-thirds were cases with purely psycho-neurotic symptoms and the rest were cases of psycho-neurosis with medical complications.

Rifleman F. C. White, 10th (Service) Battalion, King's Royal Rifle Corps

Everybody was afraid. If any man says he never felt fear, I don't care who he is, he's a liar. You all tried not to show it, but everybody felt the same. But when the whistle blew and you went over the top, your fears all went. You never thought about the danger once you were out there in among it, but it was that waiting, waiting, waiting in the trenches to go over that got your wind up.

Rifleman F. Scarbrow, 12th (Service) Battalion, The Rifle Brigade

Were we brave? I don't think we were brave. We'had a job to do, and we did it. Of course, I used to be frightened sometimes, like a scared rabbit. But it was the comradeship among the troops that used to keep us going. I've never experienced anything like it before or since, and not just between the men. We had this sense of comradeship with the officers too, and apart from the major battles I had some very happy times when I was in the trenches.

I remember one night I had a touch of flu, or PUO as they used to call it, and I wasn't feeling well. Some of the boys were going out on a trench raid, and before they went over, my platoon commander, Lieutenant Arthur, took off his greatcoat and gave it to me to keep me warm, and told me to crawl into a little bivouac, lie down and try to rest. It was an hour or so before they returned. They'd had a stiff time and lost one or two chaps, but the first thing Lieutenant Arthur did when he got back into the trench was to come along to look at me and ask how I was feeling. That's the sort of comradeship we had in the battalion. It kept our morale up through all the bad times.

To be 'windy' was one thing; to be 'funky' was another. Windiness was almost universal and men 'did their job' in spite of it; 'funkiness' meant shirking the job, and the majority of infantrymen held 'funk' in contempt. A funky man was an outcast, a pariah. But a nervous temperament did not necessarily exclude courage. It took considerable courage as well as a degree of desperation to shoot off your trigger-finger, to blast a hole in your foot, or even, as occasionally happened, to commit suicide rather than face the ordeal of 'going over the top'. Every soldier knew the consequences. He would be evacuated to a special hospital (at Passchendaele it was No. 61 Casualty Clearing Station at 'Mendingham') and nursed under guard, until he was sufficiently recovered to face court martial and the inevitable severe punishment of imprisonment, or even death. The alternative was to run away, and in cases of cowardice or desertion in the face of the enemy, if no mitigating circumstances were proved, the death sentence was automatic.

Captain the Reverend Leonard Pearson, Chaplain at

The casualty clearing station moved up to the Ypres salient just before the battle. We weren't expected to take in any casualties until two days after the battle began, so the evening before – which would be 29 July, the day before the troops went into the line – it was a beautiful evening and I went for a walk. I met a young officer and I recognized him. He'd been one of my drill-sergeants in the Boys' Brigade years earlier when he was only a boy, and we stopped and spoke. I said, 'What are you doing here?' because I knew where his unit was and this was some distance away. And then he broke down. He said, 'I can't face it'. I said, 'Well, there's only one alternative, isn't there? You wouldn't want that'. He said, 'Yes, I know that. Don't think I don't know that. There are fifteen men in the cage now, waiting to be shot'.

No. 44
Casualty
Clearing
Station

We spoke together for a long time, and I tried to comfort him. It seemed to help him, just to talk about it, which he couldn't have done to anyone else, and eventually he calmed down. I said, 'Well, we must get you back to your unit'. He didn't argue. He agreed. It was about a five-mile walk back to his battalion and I went with him, talking to him all the way back, and I was able to get this dear lad back again. He was killed the next day.

I was very upset about it. I think it was simply disgraceful that there should have been a death penalty. How does the average man, in the heat of battle, tell the difference between a real nervous breakdown and cowardice? I don't think it should have any place in battle at all.

An officer had a certain freedom of movement, and even five miles away from where his battalion was known to be he would be unlikely to be challenged by the Military Police, unless some confusion in his bearing caused them to suspect that he had absconded. But an unaccompanied soldier wandering in the back areas on the eve of battle had little chance of escaping, for the MPs assiduously patrolled the roads on the lookout for deserters. On that same summer evening they picked up a boy, belonging to Captain Harold Deardon's unit, and held him under close arrest until the brigade was relieved and came out of action.

Had to attend a court martial today on one of our men who had deserted before the last push and had just been captured behind the lines. He is a pitiful degenerate, has drunk a lot in his time, and is obviously of no use to anyone. I had to inspect him last night to say if he was fit for his trial, and he told me all his history. This morning, to my amazement, he asked to have me at his trial to speak for him, though I had given him no encouragement last night, when he cried and behaved like a perfect beast all the time. I went to the trial determined to give him no help of any sort, for I detest his type; and seeing so many good fellows go out during the night's shelling made me feel all the more bitter against him for trying to back down. I really hoped he would be shot, as indeed was anticipated by all of us.

Captain
Harold
Deardon,
RAMC
(his diary)

However, when I was called, he stood so drearily between his two big sentries, looking so hopelessly forlorn and lonely, with his dirty face and white cheeks, that before I knew what I was doing I found myself trying to let him down gently. All the time I was talking he kept his eyes on me, and I really never saw such a look of pitiful appeal as he managed to get into them, while he kept wetting his lips and swallowing, and wiping the sweat from his dirty-brown forehead. I said I knew he had always been a man of a highly nervous temperament whose self-control was practically nil, and that I considered he was much below the standard of the ordinary man in every way mentally. Whether I did it or not, I don't know, but he got off, and came creeping round to my aid-post afterwards to thank me.

I talked pretty straight to him then, for I felt as I had felt before I saw him cowering between the two guards, and told him he had damned well got to pull himself together and make a fresh start. He promised he would, and asked if he might come and talk to me sometimes, for the other men in his company didn't understand and would scarcely speak to him. Of course, I said he could; but it will be an infernal nuisance, and in any case he'll never make anything and will probably bolt again the first chance he gets. They tell me he'll probably get shot by his own mates the next time we go over the top, so it's a bright lookout anyway, poor devil!

Deardon's attitude of mingled sympathy and contempt, in which contempt was uppermost, was typical of the general feeling. The sufferings of the 'brave' inevitably engendered a lack of sympathy towards the weak. And in the 3rd Battle of Ypres the sufferings of the troops were prodigious.

For almost two and half years since the greater part of Belgium had fallen, the Allies had held the line around Ypres with extraordinary tenacity, and it had never been regarded as a quiet sector. In the countless artillery duels and the two weeks of bombardment that preceded the battle, more British and German shells had fallen into this tiny patch of land than into any other in any theatre of the war, churning it into an impassable turmoil of mud and slime. Through this the infantry had to struggle and fight and the guns had to be somehow dragged forward. Torrential rain streaming down for sometimes a week or ten days at a time increased the misery and the difficulties. It was a miracle that they were able to advance at all. As the army crawled forward, as the line through the morass became longer and the morass itself more dangerous, the difficulty of evacuating casualties became almost insurmountable. Now it took not two but four stretcher-bearers, then not four but eight, to carry a man on a stretcher to an aid-post half a mile away. At the worst times, it could take them two hours or more to reach it. A wounded man was lucky to get out and lucky to reach a casualty clearing station.

Although the hospitals were packed to capacity throughout the campaign, and overflowing after every renewed attack, the medical services worked superbly.

But even if a man was only slightly wounded when he reached the casualty clearing station in the back areas of the battle, he was not necessarily safe. A month before the campaign had begun, and as soon as the troops, hospitals and clearing stations began to concentrate in the area, the Germans had started to mount a campaign of bombing that was unprecedented. For they were not only shelling and bombing military targets but the hospitals themselves, and the missiles fell with such accuracy and frequency that suspicion began to grow that the attacks must be deliberate, because every hospital was prominently marked with a large red cross. There were tragic instances where slightly wounded patients, awaiting evacuation, were killed by shell splinters that ripped through the flimsy walls of marquee tents, killing or injuring patients, nurses, doctors and orderlies alike. Through all the hours of daylight, French and British flyers patrolled the skies trying to keep the observation planes and the bombers at bay, but still they got through.

One French aviator was particularly angry about it, because although he was serving in the French air force Major Charles Biddle was an American. It was by chance that he happened to be in the vicinity at all, for the French and British planes were flying in from airfields all over the north of France to fight the Germans in the air. But Charlie Biddle had been forced down by engine-trouble, and landing at an airfield near Proven he was delighted to be told that some Americans were on the surgical staff of No. 61 Casualty Clearing Station, just a mile or so away at 'Dozinghem'. While he waited for his aircraft to be repaired, he killed time by strolling over to visit them. When he got there he was even more delighted to find four friends from his native Philadelphia, because the medical and surgical staff had been augmented by a group from the recently arrived Pennsylvania Base Hospital. But some of his friends had had a narrow escape.

Dr Packard told me the Boche had bombed the hospital two out of the last three evenings. At first they thought it a mistake, but when they kept it up it became apparent that there was no mistake. This is a big field hospital in white tents and with lots of red crosses plainly visible. I have seen it myself from the air, and you can see it more distinctly than anything in the neighbourhood. A couple of days ago, a bomb had landed on a cook shack about twenty yards from Dr Packard's tent. The cook's leg came through the roof of the tent next door and the guy-ropes of Dr Packard's tent were decorated with his entrails. Another bomb landed right alongside of the tent occupied by Dillard and Vaux. Luckily, they had just answered a special call to operate that night and were not in their tent. A piece of bomb went through one of their pillows where one or the other, I have forgotten which, had just been sleeping. Their clothes were blown all over the lot and Dillard exhibited numerous holes in the seat of his pants. Fortunately he had not been in them at the time.

Major Charles J. Biddle, French Aviation Service (later US Aviation Corps)

But many had not been so lucky when, without warning, the bombs began to fall. In the guarded tent where they had put the men whose wounds were self-inflicted, and in the tents filled with soldiers wounded in the battle, four patients were killed and eighteen were wounded for a second time. It was not surprising that the staff were still full of it when Charlie Biddle arrived two nights later. Everyone was on edge.

Major Charles J. Biddle, French Aviation Service (later US Aviation Corps)

We stood around after supper at the time when Brother Boche usually came along, and waited for him to put in an appearance. We had not long to wait. Pretty soon we could hear his motors humming up in the sky, and dozens of searchlights began to look for him. They picked up one of the raiders and the show beat any Fourth of July celebration you ever saw. The machine showed clear and white in the glare of the searchlights. It was a dark night but very clear, with millions of stars. On every side were the muzzle-flashes of the anti-aircraft guns, and the sky was filled with the flashes of the bursting shells; the two were seemingly joined by streams of tracer bullets from machine-guns. Add to this the roar of the guns and bursting shells, and you can imagine what a quiet evening in a field hospital back of the front line is like.

The one Boche that we could see was driven off, but pretty soon we could hear others coming and this time so high up that the searchlights could not find them. As we stood there listening the sound of the motors seemed to have almost passed over us, when suddenly *siz-bang-bang,* and five or six bombs landed plumb in the camp. We threw ourselves flat for a moment and then went to see what had happened. You could hear cries coming from the direction where the bombs had fallen, and the air was filled with dust and smoke. One bomb that fell within about seventy-five yards of us killed three men and wounded about six. Another one lit right in a ward – imagine the effect when it was full of wounded soldiers!

The effect was even worse at No. 62 Casualty Clearing Station a mile away, where many of the shellshocked men in the Special Centre, whose labels were inscribed with the letters that stood for Not Yet Diagnosed (Nervous), ran amok in the ward.

At night there were bombs to fear, in daylight there were the long-range shells that fell with suspicious accuracy on the camp hospitals. At the base they were out of reach of the shells, but air raid after air raid like those on the casualty clearing stations put everyone in a state of nerves and caused angry anti-German reaction. For like the camp hospitals, the red crosses that distinguished hospitals at the base could clearly be seen from the sky.*

* It was never proved that the Germans had adopted a deliberate policy of bombing hospitals. It is fair to point out that, both in the packed hinterland of

It was during that summer that the long-range Gotha bombers and Zeppelins stepped up their bombing campaign on London. For the first time, civilians were at risk and could become casualties.

We had just cleared a train, and were setting off in the ambulance with four not very badly wounded patients, when the warning siren went off. One of the boys, who was a jolly young officer, said, 'Is that Jerry?' And when I said that it was, rather wondering how he was going to react, he just sighed in a resigned sort of way. 'It's *me* he's after, Sister, you know', he said. 'He's quite determined to get me. First he shells me in the trenches. Then he bombs me in the field hospital. He followed me all the way and bombed me again on the coast. Then he tried to sink the ship, and now here he is again! You've got to hand it to him really!' I had to laugh. Even in the middle of all that, I had to laugh.

Claire Elise Tisdall, VAD Ambulance Nurse, The Ambulance Column, London District

If you couldn't laugh, you were finished. At home, in the field and in the trenches, the laughter and the comradeship were the only things that made it possible to carry on at all. For morale was at a low ebb. It was three weary years since war had begun, and three weary months since they had started fighting the battle that was designed to finish the Germans once and for all, to break their line, to hammer through the encircling salient and, like a glorious sunburst, reach north to the coast and spread out to recapture the land of Belgium. Surely by now the enemy must be at his last gasp. But the British army too was feeling the strain, weakened by huge losses and by the tremendous expenditure of valiant effort. With the terrain and the weather on the side of the enemy, the troops had not succeeded in breaking the salient, but they had expanded it and crawled inexorably up the formidably defended slopes to gain the ridges and capture Passchendaele. But they were weary with the effort. So were the Germans, and it began to seem as if the side that would win the war on the Western Front would be the side that would first wear down the other.

In spite of trumpetings of victory after every small advance; despite Lloyd George's optimistic view that the war could be won on the Italian front where some divisions had been transferred in October; despite the early success of the first use of massed tanks, which had helped the infantry to batter through the German lines at the battle of Cambrai before they had ground to a stop and been pushed back through lack of reinforcements; and despite cheering indications that American troops would soon be at the Front in effective numbers, the malaise of the spirit which was beginning to spread through the weary armies on the West-

the Ypres salient and in the congested strip of territory at the base, the hospitals were adjacent to army camps, gunlines and depots, which were legitimate military targets.

ern Front had also spread to the civilian population at home. There was hardly a family in the land that had not suffered a bereavement in its inner or outer circle. In the cities the threat of bombers and Zeppelins hovered relentlessly above the heads of the population. In the coastal areas there was the ever-present danger of shelling by German ships. Convoys of badly needed food and supplies were constantly being sunk by marauding submarines. Food was scarce, rationing was strict, times were hard. The VADs and nurses who rode in the ambulances with the wounded on their way to the hospitals found that when their work was heaviest it was actually possible to go hungry.

Claire Elise Tisdall, VAD Ambulance Nurse, The Ambulance Column, London District

We got very tired and we couldn't get food half the time. They allowed us to use the canteen for the service men, so that we could get coffee and cocoa at night, and in a sense that saved our lives because there were no ordinary restaurants at the time. They had all had to close down for lack of supplies. All they were able to serve at certain hours of the day was two ounces of bread – and between two and six they couldn't sell anything at all, and that might be the only chance you'd have to eat anything. It didn't matter if you said, 'I've had no lunch. I've been working all day' or 'I'm going on duty after this, I shall have no supper and I have to work all night.' They'd say, 'We're very sorry, but we can't do it.' The regulations were very strictly enforced.

One day, when we were absolutely desperate, we went to the Charing Cross Hotel and asked to see the manager. We simply *implored* him for food. Poor man, he was so distressed. He really wanted to help, but he said, 'I can't break the law.' But he was so sorry for us that eventually he produced an omelette. He couldn't give us any bread, but we didn't care. We fell upon those omelettes as if we had never seen food before. We just had time to eat them before we had to rush back into the station to meet the next train.

It was the terrible sense of continuity that chipped into confidence and eroded the spirit in the summer and autumn of 1917. Like the Somme campaign of the year before, the battles did not finish until well into November. Just as they had done a year before, the convoys of wounded poured in after every push. Just as they had been doing then, everyone was working flat out. Nothing had changed, and it was beginning to seem as if nothing ever would. Claire Tisdall's brother had been reported killed at Ypres, and her breaking-point came on a day of sunshine that happily coincided with a few precious hours off duty.

Claire Elise Tisdall, VAD Ambulance

I had a sudden impulse to get away from it all for a while, to go out and enjoy myself and forget about the war just for a few hours, because I sometimes felt that I couldn't bear it. The whole thing was so frightful. So I thought, 'I'll walk in the park and have tea out and

I'm not going to think of it.' I put on my best dress and went out, and as I was walking along, looking at the shops, up came a woman selling flags for the Red Cross. She held one right in front of my eyes and all I could see was that blood-red cross. It was more than I could bear. I just ran from her. I ran across the road and had to stop on a traffic island in the middle, and she actually followed me and took hold of my arm and said, 'But surely you want to help the poor wounded soldiers?' I could do nothing but gasp at her, 'Go away! Go away!' She must have thought I was a brute, because I simply couldn't explain. I was so upset that it completely spoiled my outing. I didn't have the heart for it any more. I went home in tears – all because of the sight of that Red Cross

Nurse, The Ambulance Column, London District

This year, few people were tempting fate by saying, 'It'll all be over by Christmas.'

Chapter Seventeen

Christmas 1917 fell like a faint beam of light across the shadowed days of the fourth winter of the war. There were hardly enough boats to carry the huge quantities of cards, letters and parcels for the troops on active service, and the comforts that everyone wanted to send to the sick and wounded in the hospitals. Although people had been adjured to 'Post Early', there was a hold up at Southampton in early December and it took fully three weeks of gargantuan effort on all sides to ship everything across to France in the week before Christmas.

It was fortunate that the Red Cross had made sure that all their own supplies of Christmas cheer were in France by the beginning of December. In addition to the supplies sent to Italy, Salonika and the Middle East, the Red Cross warehouses in Boulogne were stacked high with 40,000 tins of sweets, four tons of Brazil nuts, four tons of filberts, ten tons of almonds, four tons of walnuts, four tons of chestnuts, twelve tons of dried fruit, 40,000 boxes of Christmas crackers, 80,000 Christmas cards and innumerable cases of coloured paper garlands to decorate hospital wards and Mess huts for the festive season. Just before Christmas, boatloads of chickens and turkeys arrived in France, plus a mammoth consignment of 25,000 Christmas puddings, which had been lovingly prepared by hundreds of voluntary groups throughout the country who had willingly sacrificed their ration of sugar and a quantity of precious dried fruit to ensure that the boys had a proper Christmas dinner. Most of the puddings were stuffed as full of lucky sixpences as they were with hoarded raisins, and were mixed with libations of stout or brandy.

It took all the considerable organizational powers of the Red Cross and a large slice of the resources of the Army Transport Corps to distribute, across the length and breadth of the Western Front, the largesse that came from every quarter of the globe. From America there was a shipment of beef; from South Africa, a boatload of grapes, peaches and nectarines; from Canada, 10,000 cases of red apples; and from Australia, a towering mountain of 'billy-cans' packed with comforts and goodies for the Aussies.

By 1917 the 'Christmas billies' had become a tradition. Back home in Australia, volunteers started packing them in August. Each community undertook to supply a certain number, filling each one with oddments of their own choice, and sent them in good time to a central depot from which they were shipped on to Australian soldiers overseas. It was a charming as well as a practical idea. The billy-cans themselves, as Australian as the strains of 'Waltzing Matilda', spoke of Home to the soldiers far away; when empty they were useful items to have on active service, and they were sturdy enough to be shipped without any further wrapping. They also held a surprising amount – chocolate, tobacco, cigarettes, sweets, a pipe, razor blades, soap, concentrated beef cubes notebooks, writing pads, candles, toffee, sardines, potted meat, socks and mittens (or at least a fair selection of these items) could all be stuffed in. All of them contained a different assortment, but the universal verdict was that they were 'Bonzo'.

The exception was the unfortunate Aussie who was particularly pleased to find in his billy-can a pair of socks knitted in the finest wool, and donned them for a long march. Within half an hour he was limping badly, and at the first rest stop removed his boots to look for the trouble. There were no protruding nails, nothing to be seen. The march continued, and by the time it ended the man was practically crippled by a mammoth blister on his foot. He found some water in which to bathe it, and when he pulled off the sock to immerse his foot in the soothing bath, to the ribald amusement of his comrades a small screw of paper fell to the floor. On it was written in a shaky hand, 'God bless you, My Dear Boy.' It was fortunate that the kindly donor was unable to hear her Dear Boy's reaction.

The language of the Australians was, at the best of times, fruity. Their undisciplined behaviour was legendary, and the more docile troops of other nationalities had a sneaking admiration for their devil-may-care demeanour and their reputation as free-booters and tough fighters. In the Christmas season of 1917, cheering news arrived from the Middle East, where General Allenby's forces were making headway against the Turks. Appropriately enough, Bethlehem had been captured and among the occupying troops was a contingent of Australians. 'Yes?' remarked one recuperating British Tommy, as an Aussie in the next bed exulted loudly over the news. 'Well, all I can say is them blinking shepherds won't *half* have to watch their bloody flocks by night now!'

The remark was made well out of hearing of the nurses; even the free-and-easy Aussies drew the line at using 'language' in front of them. Nevertheless, they did occasionally offend. The previous Christmas, at Dyke Road Hospital in Brighton, Kit Dodsworth, back from service in France but hardly more worldly-wise and sophisticated than she had been in the sheltered days before the war, had an unpleasant experience.

I was very taken aback by this episode, because most of the men were really very punctilious and never went too far, although they would always have a joke with us. We had a tremendous laugh on Christmas Eve. We had one little New Zealander who was an up-patient, and he was helping to put up the decorations. There was a stepladder

Kit Dodsworth, VAD, Dyke Road Hospital, Brighton

in the ward and he got hold of a bit of mistletoe. I was going round plumping up the pillows, and every time I went to a bed he solemnly put up his steps and very slowly climbed up them with his mistletoe in one hand and a look of blissful anticipation on his face. The steps were just above me, but he was very careful not to reach the top until I had finished and moved to the next bed, and then with a look as though all his hopes had been dashed to the ground, he sadly climbed down again, moved the steps to the next bed and started all over again. It was a real Charlie Chaplin act, and most comical. The whole ward was in fits of laughter, just as he intended.

On Christmas Morning, Eve and I went to early service in the hospital chapel. There were a number of nurses there, and as we came out we were literally set upon by dozens of men who'd been waiting outside. We were pushed from one man to another while they all tried to kiss us. I was absolutely appalled and dreadfully upset. We had an awful struggle to get through the crowd and into the dining-room for breakfast. I was in tears and felt terribly humiliated somehow, and we were terrified to come out again, but at last we had no alternative. By then the men had gone to their own breakfast, and everything was comparatively quiet. We had a very happy day in the ward, but I hardly dared to leave it. Of course, all my own boys were furious when I told them, and whenever I left the ward a bodyguard of them came with me – to protect me, they said.

Later in the day 'raiding parties' came round the wards, and I got badly caught again. There were six men, Australians, and one of them had blacked his face. They had sworn to kiss every Sister and nurse in the hospital. I was standing at the far end of the ward when I saw them come in and kiss Sister. Then they pounced on one of the other nurses and I hastily slipped out of the ward into a bathroom. I hoped that they hadn't noticed me because there was no lock on the door, but to my horror I heard them coming. I tried to hold the door shut, but there were six of them and I was forced back. They came in and, having trapped me there, started discussing in loud joking voices whether they should do it in the ward or in the bathroom. They finally decided that as there was an audience in the ward, that would be better, and they grabbed me, swept me off my feet and literally carried me in. They set me down and the black-faced man kissed me vigorously, leaving a filthy black mark on my face. My own men felt it was beyond a joke and protested like anything, but that didn't stop the Australians. I felt too awful for words and I cried for hours about it. Eve was as disgusted as I was. We heard afterwards that some English boys had told the Colonials that English girls expected to be kissed on Christmas Day. They meant no harm. We didn't so much mind being kissed – although we didn't like it a lot – it was the way they did it. Matron was on leave, and the

Assistant Matron was rather a weak character, or it would never have happened.

The unpleasant incident with the nurses at Dyke Road was not entirely unconnected with the fact that the Red Cross had received as gifts huge quantities of champagne, wine, port, sherry and brandy, and had distributed them to the home hospitals at Christmas. It was decided not to repeat the experiment, partly in deference to the Defence of the Realm Act. Apart from one innocuous glass of beer with the Christmas dinner this Christmas would be a sober one, and Kit and Eve were safe from the exuberant attentions of merry 'Colonials'. They were en route to Egypt on board the troopship *Aragon* and they had been a long time on the way.

In the transit camp near Marseilles they had been given half an hour's notice to join the ship, and there was a wild panic to get ready. Kit packed while Eve dashed to the village laundry to retrieve the washing they had left there the day before. It took a lot of argument before she was able to get it back – wringing wet – and then they had had to repack all their belongings so that the sodden garments (which comprised almost all the underwear they owned) could have sole possession of one suitcase. They could have done without carrying the extra weight of water.

We had a hair-raising journey travelling in packed lorries the ten miles to No. 13 dock. There was no one there to meet us and at last two sailor men came down over the side of the boat and we discovered we were not expected till the next day. They couldn't send us back – a *horrid* climb, up the companion stairs, hanging over the water, only a wobbly rope to hold on to and *such* a lot to carry.

Diary of
Kit and Eve
Dodsworth
(Eve)

It was 8 December, and in spite of the rush to get the party of nursing Sisters and VADs on board the *Aragon*, the ship sailed out of the harbour, anchored in the bay, and stopped there for almost two weeks. It was tantalizing to be within sight of the shore and the legendary port of Marseilles without being able to go ashore. But the days passed pleasantly enough on the packed troopship. The NCOs and other ranks were on the decks below, and the upper decks were reserved for nurses and officers who were only too ready to indulge in a little friendly dalliance. Matron foresaw trouble, and ordered her party to report to her in the first-class saloon before 'nurses' dinner' at six o'clock. The Sisters and VADs stood with downcast eyes and demure expressions as Matron warned them to 'behave, and remember that you are officers and ladies'. Eve remarked, 'Quite a sensible lecture and I'm sure necessary from the looks of some of our companions. We wore Mess dresses and white caps for dinner, which we had an hour before the men. There isn't room to have it together even if we wanted to.' The men, however, were not disinclined to associate with the nurses and the lively Dodsworth girls were soon the centre of a circle of charming acquaintances. 'The gang', as Eve was soon familiarly referring to them, strolled together on the decks, joined in the sports, sat together in an exclusive, merry *coterie* in the audience at concerts and entertainments, laughed, flirted and enjoyed themselves. The weather was fine, and in the sunshine of the Mediterranean, cold foggy England seemed a long way away. The sunniest place was the boatdeck, and as the deckchairs and benches which had catered for the relaxation of pre-war travellers had long since been removed, the girls took to reading, writing or sewing in one of the lifeboats. One by one, inevitably, 'the gang' drifted in the same direction and climbed into the boat for a pleasant session of chat and badinage. But occasionally Matron prowled the decks.

Diary of
Kit and Eve
Dodsworth
(Kit)

Eve and I were talking on deck to Captain Newman, Captain Wheatley, Captain Campbell and Major Chapman, when Matron seized Eve and dragged her away and strafed her like anything for our 'conspicuous behaviour'. 'You are positively collecting men,' blazed Matron to poor Eve. We were furious. We left the men at once and went down to our cabins. When Matron came downstairs, we went to her room and asked her what she meant by it and she was perfectly charming to us and said we were doing no wrong at all, only she was afraid other people might be jealous. So we left feeling quite bucked with life.

In spite of the long, frustrating delay, Kit and Eve continued to be 'bucked with life' and surrounded by amusing company. Even when the *Aragon* finally sailed on 21 December and Kit was stricken by seasickness, there was always a group of admirers to comfort, soothe and fuss over her when she managed to struggle up on deck. On Christmas Eve the ship anchored in a bay off the island of Malta. It was a strange Christmas. No one was allowed to go ashore, except for the commanding officer, Colonel French, whose exalted rank had not prevented him from joining the ranks of the Dodsworth sisters' admirers. But the girls had plenty to occupy them on board because on Christmas night there was to be a 'mixed dinner', with officers and nurses celebrating together, and Eve was to hostess a table. All afternoon, they sat in the lifeboat consulting 'the gang' on the design of the menu cards they were busily preparing, kindly allowing them to admire Eve's talented sketches of plum puddings and jolly sailors, and to help with the more boring jobs of filling in the background and cutting the cards to size. In the evening, after their segregated dinners, they all met again on deck and leaned over the rail to listen to the Tommies singing carols on the well-deck below. It was a warm, idyllic evening. The sky was ablaze with stars. And although the ship was blacked out, they could clearly see the shadowy forms of the men crammed together on the lower deck by the light of a few flickering candles. For once 'the gang' was very quiet. The familiar melodies in the strange setting made them feel unaccustomedly emotional. As the *Aragon* lay at anchor they stood listening, occasionally joining in, and thinking like every other soul on board of Home.

Although there was no Matron prowling the decks tonight – she had gone ashore to dine in the illustrious company of the senior officers as the guests of a shore establishment – no dragonlike figure to pounce, no eagle-eye to censure, no one felt much like horseplay or badinage that night. The officers and nurses separated with quiet goodnights and went sedately to bed.

Like her counterpart on board the *Aragon*, the Matron of Dearnley Hospital, Rochdale, was a chastening influence on the Christmas festivities. Kathleen Yarwood was working in a convalescent ward, and it had been the Tommies' own idea to manufacture a miniature cannon and set it on the table at the entrance, where it would catch the eye of every visitor. They helped the nurses to decorate the ward with garlands, draped red crêpe tastefully over the spartan white china lampshades and painstakingly printed out a bold holly-bordered card:

HELP THE TOMMIES' CHRISTMAS FUN.
POP A SIXPENCE IN THE GUN.

When Matron spotted it on her ward-round, she was horrified and delivered her opinion with some force. The very idea of soliciting money from visitors was disgraceful! The notice was promptly removed, but the gun was allowed to remain as the centrepiece of the Christmas decorations.

There was really no need for the Tommies in Dearnley or anywhere else to beg for contributions towards the Christmas festivities, because the volunteers as well as the hospital staff were determined to see to it that hospital patients should have a good time. Every ward sparkled and shone with greenery and baubles and on Christmas Eve in every hospital and convalescent home in Blighty and abroad, a stocking was hung at the foot of every bed.

When we were decorating the ward I popped some holly into one of these socks, just for a joke, so there was an interesting bulge in it and people kept putting their hands into the sock to see what it was and getting prickled by the holly. Lady Crichton and her husband came round on Christmas Eve to see the boys and give them a few sweets and cigarettes, and unfortunately Lady Crichton said, 'What have you got in your sock?' And she put her hand in to see. But she was very funny and took it in good part. Then later on Christmas Eve, Sister and I filled all the socks up. We had hunted around for things and I think Sister produced most of them, just handkerchiefs and

Gladys Stanford, VAD, Highfield Hospital, Southampton

pencils and oddments like that, sweets, cigarettes, an apple. They were all very pleased when they had them on Christmas morning.

In the field hospitals in France and even at the base, it was not quite so easy to find the 'oddments' with which to play Father Christmas to the Tommies. As far back as September, provident Sisters had written home to friends and relatives for parcels of tiny toys, pens and novelties to supplement the nuts, sweets and cigarettes that were supplied by the Red Cross Comforts Fund. Off duty, the nurses and orderlies scoured the countryside for holly and the Christmas tree that every Sister was determined to have in her ward, hut or tent. Convalescent patients who had been carpenters in civilian life were persuaded to build cribs; electricians who could rig up lights for the trees were much in demand; and when men were due to be discharged to convalescent camp, where the comforts were fewer, Sisters and doctors between them conspired to keep them in hospital just a little longer, over the festive season.

For although the comforts fund of every company (often generously augmented by contributions from the battalion's officers) provided a noble Christmas dinner of poultry, beef or mutton, Christmas pudding, beer, wine and often cigars for the men in billets – or provided a postponed celebration when battalions came out of the line – hospital was definitely the best place to be, even as a wounded prisoner. Attitudes had hardened into mutual bitterness since Christmas 1914 when British and German soldiers had declared a holiday from the war and met as friends in No Man's Land. But wounded Germans – who were normally treated with punctilious medical etiquette – received special consideration in the season of goodwill.

Sister Ruth Bruerton, who had come from the United States with one of the first contingents of army nurses in September 1917, to serve with the BEF at No. 4 Stationary Hospital on the racecourse at Rouen, was disconcerted to be put in charge of a ward of wounded Germans. By the time Christmas came, she was equally disconcerted to find that although the Germans were to be given a special Christmas dinner, they were not to be included in the handout of sweets and nuts. The nurses themselves had been given an extra ration of sugar as a Christmas treat and, by universal agreement, they spent the evening of Christmas Eve making toffee in the ward kitchen to hand out to the German boys on Christmas Day. As they worked, the men were singing carols in the ward:

> Stille Nacht, heilige Nacht
> Alles schläft, einsam wacht . . .

The same melody was being sung elsewhere in the camp and in hospitals all over France as groups of nurses went up and down the long line of huts, singing carols outside each ward. In the camps at the foot of the hills behind Dannes-Camiers it was a blustery, wet night. The bitterly cold wind from the sea had changed in the evening to a north wind that promised more snow before morning, and it brought blasts of icy air into the wards as the doors opened to admit groups of carol singers, muffled in scarves and greatcoats, candle lanterns in their damp-gloved hands, their faces rosy and glowing with the sting of the wind. Later, back in their billets, as the night nurses settled the men and turned down the lamps in the wards, the carol singers brewed cocoa and drank it as they thawed out round their tiny stoves, and went to bed looking forward, for once, to tomorrow.

The Christmas festivities were at their most uproarious in wards where the men were approaching convalescence, and at their most subdued in wards where Sisters tried to keep things quiet for the benefit of men who were very ill. But even those who were badly wounded tried to enter into the spirit of the occasion, to take a sip of champagne, to show interest in the contents of their stockings, and, even if they were too weak to join in, to listen to the merrymaking and singing without complaint.

In Margaret Ellis's ward at No. 26 General Hospital, Etaples, she was in her element – joking and laughing under the benign eye of a Sister, relaxed with Yuletide goodwill, and keeping the men entertained with a flow of North Country repartee and wit. Pretty Nurse Ellis was a universal favourite. Just before she went off duty, with aching feet and a voice hoarsened by the bustle and laughter of the day, she had a visitor. He arrived soaked and breathless from the long walk from the convalescent camp three miles away, and thrust a crumpled package into her hands.

I was terribly touched, because he was one of my men who had been discharged to convalescent camp just the week before. He couldn't have been properly fit, and it was a long way for him to come and he was absolutely breathless, with perspiration running down his face. He stood looking at me with great big eyes as I opened the parcel, and it was one of those terrible handkerchief sachets in quilted silk, in a very lurid bright pink – a horrible-looking thing. But what a thought! He must have gone to such trouble to get it – perhaps even had it sent from home – and then to go to all that trouble to bring it to me on Christmas Day. Of course I thanked him warmly, but he was one of the men who was a little bit of an embarrassment to me. He imagined things. In fact a little later I received a letter from his sister in England, as though I were engaged to the man, saying how pleased she was and so on. Poor chap. But when they were in bed and sick in hospital, they didn't react quite normally. Sometimes they had fancies . . .

Margaret Ellis, Special Military Probationer, No. 26 General Hospital, Camiers

But the best present of all came from the patients in the ward. They had obviously planned it and even rehearsed it. As Margaret buttoned her greatcoat, waved a last goodnight and 'Happy Christmas' as she went off duty, a sergeant of the up-patients called out, 'Wait a minute, Nurse!' He leapt on a chair and started to sing:

> Two young fellows were talking about their
> Girls, girls, girls,
> Sweethearts they'd left behind,
> Sweethearts for whom they pined.
> One said, 'My little shy little lass
> Has a waist so trim and small,
> Grey are her eyes so bright,
> But best, best of all . . .'

Every Tommy was listening and watching, waiting for the cue. 'Come on boys, all together . . .'

> My girl's a Yorkshire girl,
> Yorkshire through and through.
> My girl's a Yorkshire girl,
> Eh! By gum, she's a champion!
> Though she's a factory lass,
> And wears no fancy clothes,
> I've a sort of Yorkshire relish
> For my little Yorkshire rose.

Even the boys who were too weak to sit up joined faintly in the cheers, as the chorus ended. Only the 'Yorkshire rose' was speechless. The ward with its long rows of beds, the bandaged Tommies under the red blankets, their beaming faces, the lights, the Christmas tree, swam in front of her eyes. Back in her billet it took quite a bit of discreet dabbing with a forbidden powder-puff to repair her complexion.

On board the *Aragon*, still riding at anchor off the shores of Malta, the Christmas festivities were in full swing. It had been a merry day. At the foot of the stairs leading to the social hall, someone had hung a huge bunch of mistletoe, obtained from some mysterious source ashore. The obvious culprit was the dashing Colonel French. It was hardly likely to have been Matron! Kit and Eve, who had been so offended the previous Christmas by the behaviour of the Wild Colonial Boys at Dyke Road Hospital, had no objection whatever to being saluted under the mistletoe by their charming shipboard acquaintances. 'It was doing good work even before breakfast,' recorded Kit in the diary she wrote jointly with Eve. 'I was caught by Captain Newman and Captain Campbell – the impertinent children! Captain Part got me too.'

Even Matron was 'caught' when the time came for toasts and speeches at the end of the Christmas dinner.

We went to second dinner at eight and were a very cheery and happy party. Eve did hostess and Evans, Gilham, Allenby and myself were the girls, and Major Strange, Major Buxton, Captain Campbell, Captain Newman, Captain Wheatley, Captain Part and Captain Stewart were the men. We started on cocktails (martinis) and then had much champagne after that, all provided by the men. We ate turkey and plum pudding, all on fire with brandy, and after dinner there were many toasts and speeches. Both the colonels, and Matron and the skipper, except that *he* wouldn't make a speech but kissed Matron under the mistletoe tied over their table. Then, he persuaded the adjutant to follow his example. After all were drunk and fed that could be, we went up.

Diary of Kit and Eve Dodsworth, 25 December 1917 (Kit)

In spite of the toasts, the flattering attention, the general *bonhomie*, Matron had not mellowed. Matron, in fact, made a scene when she arrived in the social hall to discover that the nurses were dancing with the officers. It was strictly against Army regulations for nurses to dance in uniform. 'Stop this at once,' she yelled. The dancers left the floor, embarrassed. The pianist broke off. Colonel French pleaded with Matron, tried to jolly her along, and when she remained adamant, became exceedingly angry.
'It is dark on the deck outside,' he announced generally, 'and the music can plainly be heard out there when the doors are open.' The hall began to empty as the nurses and officers took the hint and drifted, couple by couple, out of the saloon.

The colonel went for her with the skipper and finally she dissolved into tears and said, 'Well, I see that I can't object, but I shall have to report it and I *shall* report it, and you will be sent straight home as soon as we arrive.' And she burst into tears and went down to her cabin. After a bit the colonel came out to us on the deck and told us that it was all right, and that we might go on dancing until midnight. After that, he said, he relied on us to go straight to bed. He told me afterwards that he and the captain had had an awful tussle with Matron. They had sat one on each side of her and argued with her until she gave in and fled, weeping, to her cabin. Poor woman, she made herself miserable out of sheer obstinacy.

Diary of Kit and Eve Dodsworth (Kit)

Christmas was the highlight of the long voyage. Gales raged in the Mediterranean and it was days before the *Aragon* was able to leave her sheltered anchorage for the last short lap of the voyage to Alexandria. On the third day they sighted the coast of Egypt. The ship's engines had stopped and she lay rocking gently ten miles offshore, waiting for the ship that would escort her to Alexandria harbour, while the rest of the convoy raced on towards Port Said.

Diary of
Kit and Eve
Dodsworth,
30 December
1917
(Kit)

Eve was standing by the rails talking to Colonel Bateson, Major Chamier, Captain Campbell and Captain Newman, and I was propped against the wall of the social hall talking to Colonel French and Major McLeod, when suddenly there was a terrific crash and a lot of dust and bits of wood were blown up into the air over the aft well-deck. The fall-in sounded and our companions flew at once to their posts, and we quite mechanically put our lifebelts on (they were on the ground nearby) and walked to our places in the social hall. There was no panic, although we could feel the ship beginning to list a bit. Captain Duncan who was in charge of our group told us we had plenty of time and there was nothing to be frightened of. Major McLeod was standing near and ragged us like anything as we got into the boat and went down leaving the men all there on deck. They stood there at attention and actually saluted us. Not one even looked like wanting to get into the boat. They were wonderful!

There were two crew on the boat and fourteen of us Sisters, although the boat could have held thirty, but they were supposed to get rid of the first load and then go back for the men. Then they started to lower the boat. First, we seemed to catch on the side of the ship, which was listing badly by then and made it very difficult. Then when we got clear of that, one of the davits stuck and we tipped right up on end. We had to cling on to the seats for dear life and I own to feeling a bit funny then, but I looked up and saw Major McLeod still laughing and smiling at us, so I felt all was well and I kept on laughing too. It had been a joke at the lifeboat drill among 'the gang' that if we went down, we would go down laughing, and here we were. It was really happening.

We landed in the water with a tremendous bump and a huge splash, and bounced ever so high again and then down again. However, we got clear away and came round under the poop, which was going down rapidly. It was terrible to see it because nearly all our friends were standing there, and they shouted to us and we shouted back.

The crew had got hold of the oars by now and they called to someone to take the tiller. I grabbed hold of it but I had no idea where to steer for. A destroyer was standing by, but I noticed that by then some trawlers were coming up and one was as near to us as the destroyer, so I decided to go for that, for the simple reason that it looked as if it would be much easier to get on board. When we got there the sailors hauled us on board and our boat went straight back to the ship to pick up some more. When we had got ourselves sorted out on the deck of the trawler, we managed to get to the side where we could see the poor *Aragon*. The destroyer HMS *Attack* had pulled up right alongside the ship and she was taking men off as fast as she could. But the *Aragon* was sinking fast and as she finally started to go down, the front of the ship was right up out of the water and there were men pouring down the side into the sea; it was simply a swarm of khaki all down the side and it seemed as if it would never clear before she went altogether. We felt that all our friends were drowning before our eyes.

Just before she went down she was hit by another torpedo and then immediately afterwards the destroyer was hit. It was bad enough seeing the *Aragon* go, but when that happened it filled us with an even greater horror, because all the survivors from *Aragon* were aboard. The torpedo hit her in the oil bunkers, so all the men who were thrown into the sea were swimming in a pool of oil. The tragic thing was that those who were wet, had had time to strip off their clothes on board the destroyer, and so they were naked when they were thrown into the sea. When they got into the oil, it sickened them with the fumes and made them unconscious, and it covered their bodies so that it was impossible to pull them out of the water. It was terrible to see where the ships had been, and where now there was nothing but a little floating wreckage and hundreds of swimming figures. The submarine was obviously still around and the captain of our trawler decided that it was too dangerous to risk staying there any longer. So we started back for the shore.

Our own boat was full of men who had been picked up out of the water. Most of them were wet and everything they had on them was wet too. They were pulling little sopping packets of cigarettes out of their pockets. Fortunately, before I had left my cabin I had slipped a full box of a hundred Royal Beauty cigarettes into my pocket, so I handed them round and a sailor followed me with matches. One poor Jock had had to take off his kilt while he was in the water, because he couldn't swim with that heavy weight of material about him. He was sitting shivering in his wet shirt, looking somewhat ill-at-ease, and one of the other VADs noticed his plight. I saw her disappear for a moment behind the back of one of the Sisters and then pop out and hand something to the Jock. When we eventually reached the harbour at Alexandria he went ashore more-or-less decently clad in a pair of ladies' silk stockinette knickers.

The battleship HMS *Cornflower* was in the harbour and her men lined the decks and cheered us as we passed to our berth. It was agonizing waiting to see who failed to turn up. We kept remembering that the CO, dear Colonel French, had told us that if we were hit his place was on the bridge with the captain, and that they could only leave the ship when everyone else had gone. After seeing so many men jumping off at the last moment, we felt sure that he could never have got away and we were dreadfully upset, because he had been so good to us all the time. To our great joy he came in on the third trawler. The nurses were packed into ambulances and sent off to the Khedivial Hotel, which had been taken over as a billet for nursing staff.* There was a hastily mustered reception committee of Sisters and VADs, who, Kit remarked, 'were all most kind to us, though they seemed a little disappointed that we were not all half drowned as they had seemed to expect.'

But with the kindest of intentions, someone then blundered. It was four o'clock in the afternoon and food was produced. But tea, bread and butter, and a small portion of scrambled eggs was meagre fare for 150 overexcited, ravenous girls whose only sustenance for the past eight hours had been half a tumbler of whisky. As soon as the meal was finished each was given ten grains of aspirin, a pair of pyjamas, a toothbrush and sent to bed.

Diary of
Kit and Eve
Dodsworth
(Kit)

All our nerves had gone, and we were whacked too – very tired and very sorry for ourselves. All the awfulness came over us then when we were shut up in that bedroom, and we were starving hungry because a little scrambled egg isn't really very much. By then it was evening and our bedroom windows looked out on to the main street and they had already started celebrating the New Year – there were lots of troops dancing and singing in the streets and everybody was being gay and happy, and we weren't allowed to go out of our bedrooms. We got very upset. Eve and I were standing there at the open bedroom window looking down on the street and we both started to cry, and when we leaned out and looked along the row of bedroom windows where all the other VADs and nurses were standing, looking out, they were all crying too.

It was a terrible feeling knowing that you owned absolutely nothing – nothing but what you stood up in, not even a handkerchief to blow your nose on. Next day they gave us ten pounds and a day off to go and buy some kit. The shop was absolutely swarming with girls trying to buy everything they needed, and in due course a lot of officers turned up as well on the same errand. We were anxiously looking for someone we knew and eventually we found our CO, and he asked us to tea with him at his hotel and gave us all the information we were dying to know, mainly that all our friends were safe.

That evening we moved into new billets and next day we reported for duty at our hospital.

It was New Year's Day, 1 January 1918, and the first day of the fifth calendar year since the war had begun.

* Later the Savoy Hotel.

Part Three

1918

Chapter Eighteen

The New Year toasts of 'Victory this year' were beginning to ring a little hollow in the ears of those who had drunk to the same fervent hope on four previous occasions. There was undoubtedly a feeling that something was in the air, that something was going to change, but it did not have the smell of potential victory about it. It was plain that, with crack battalions of highly trained fighting troops released from the Russian front, the Germans would very soon mount a large-scale attack in the west. It was equally plain – at least to the British military commanders – that if the attack were launched against the British front they were in a poor position to repulse it, because the Army was dangerously under strength. It was true that the reserves of men of high calibre were smaller than they had ever been before. But there were nevertheless several divisions, and a large number of newly trained but inexperienced soldiers and men of lower physical categories to supplement them.

However, they were not in France. They were still based in the British Isles and there it seemed they would stay. Too many men, in Lloyd George's opinion, had been sent into too many fruitless battles. Too many lives had been squandered to gain empty victories that advanced the line a mile or two at most and advanced the march towards peace and victory apparently not at all. With one eye on the revolution in Russia, and one ear still quivering with the reverberations of the mutinous rumblings that had so recently shaken the French army, Lloyd George inclined towards the belief that Public Opinion would not remain unprotesting for ever as the lifeblood of the nation's youth trickled through the profligate fingers of the military commanders. But the Commander-in-Chief, Field-Marshal Haig, was thinking less of attack than of defence. He needed – he demanded – 600,000 more men to bring his outnumbered army up to strength – and not merely to hold the old British sector, which ran from the Somme to the Yser, but to garrison an even longer stretch, for the British were being pressed to take over part of the French line, extending the front by forty miles.

The attitudes and the demands of both soldiers and the politicians were so widely divergent in their aims that there was no possibility of compromise. The pleas, the arguments, the rows dominated the first weeks of the New Year, and the politicians won their point. Haig was forced to give away and, with the deepest misgivings, to obey instructions to regroup his army on a scale smaller than it had been since the spring of 1915. Some battalions would be amalgamated, some divisions reduced to nine battalions instead of twelve, and with these depleted forces Haig must extend his line and arrange his defence as best he could to withstand the attack the Germans would inevitably make in the spring. There would of course be reinforcements – but instead of the 600,000 demanded by Haig, only 100,000 had arrived by the beginning of March.

A similar number of American troops had arrived as early as October 1917 and more were only too ready to cross the Atlantic, but there were complications. The Americans were depending on the British to supply a large number of the ships they would need to transport their troops. But badly though they were needed at the front, Britain could not spare a flotilla of vessels to bring them across *en masse*. The shipping resources were already overstretched keeping open the lines of communication, supplies and reinforcements to the war zones of Macedonia, Palestine, Egypt, Mesopotamia and East Africa – in addition to the immense amount of tonnage needed to carry raw materials and food to Britain and vast supplies to the Western Front. The Navy, too, was heavily engaged in anti-submarine warfare, in blockading German ports, and few naval vessels could be spared to escort troop convoys. Even when all the resources were pooled, it left a great many eager American divisions kicking their heels on the other side of the Atlantic, when they might have been in Europe and getting the first-hand experience they required before they could join the fray and tip the balance in favour of the Allies. The troops that were already there were doing useful work supporting and acting as reserves to some British and French units, others were still in the course of training; in either case it would amount to folly to throw them wholesale into a battle without further, badly needed experience.

Everyone knew that the attack was coming. There was nothing for it but to prepare deep defences, to dig new trenches and fortified strong-points well behind the line; to hope for the best and conserve what manpower was already there. Artillery duels must be played down. Trench raiding must be strictly curtailed. Wounded soldiers must not be sent needlessly to Blighty. This was hard luck on Quartermaster-Sergeant Gordon Fisher, whose wound just a few short weeks or months before would have been an automatic 'Blighty one'.

Quartermaster-Sergeant Gordon Fisher, 1st Battalion, The Hertfordshire Regiment

I was in a little 'baby elephant' hut – that's a little dugout of corrugated iron about four feet high. You could just sit in there with your knees up. One shell dropped right at the side of it. I dived out, and another shell came over and a splinter caught me across the temple, and then another in the leg. I struggled into the officers' dugout and one of the officers cut my puttees off and said, 'Oh, you've got a lovely Blighty one.'

The stretcher-bearers took me down through a lot of heavy shelling and we made it to the advanced dressing-station, which was a dugout called Essex Farm on the canal bank. They gave me a cup of cocoa and had a look at my wounds, and within half an hour a little Ford ambulance came up and I was whisked off down to Hazebrouck. They had another look at me in the casualty clearing station, and within another half-hour I was on a Red Cross Hospital train that took me down to No. 4 General Hospital just outside Calais. It was wonderful! I'll never forget slipping down between cool white sheets in a hospital bed. I seemed to have been sleeping in my clothes for years, and to get between cool white sheets straight from the mud of the Front up in Passchendaele was like being in heaven.

Soon afterwards the Matron came round the ward. At the foot of your bed you had a board that stated your regiment and when you'd landed in France, the nature of your wounds, and so on, and she looked at the paper on my board and said, 'I see you've been out since 1914. Is this the first time you've been down the line?' I said, 'Yes, Matron, it's the first time I've been down the line!' She didn't say anything for a minute, just looked at me, weighing things up a bit, and then she said, 'Are you a teetotaller?' 'Oh no,' I said, 'just a moderate drinker.' 'All right', she said, and she gave me a bit of a wink, 'I'll put you on a bottle of Bass'. I had a bottle of Bass with my lunch every day while I was in that hospital, every single day. Nobody else in the ward got it – so I've always got a soft spot in my heart for Army Matrons ever since then.

I was there for six weeks, and I certainly didn't expect to be there that long. As my officer had said, any other time it would have been a Blighty without question. But they knew beforehand that the March breakthrough was coming. They didn't know where and they didn't know when – but they knew there was going to be a heavy attack, so they started clearing out all the hospitals to make room for a lot of new wounded. It was an American doctor in charge of this ward, and he was going round marking up all the chaps that he possibly could for England. When he came to my bed he had a look at my board and he said, 'I'm sorry, old chap, I can't mark you for England'. I was definitely taken aback, so I said, 'What's the catch?' 'Well', he said, 'we've had instructions that we must *not* send any senior warrant officers or NCOs back to England if it can be avoided, so I can't mark you for England.'

What had happened was this. So long as you were still in France – even in hospital away from your battalion – no one could be promoted to your rank in your place. But once you went over the water they had to fill the vacancy in your battalion, and the result was that you couldn't go back to your own unit. Because of this they found that they had a surplus of warrant officers and senior NCOs in England – and that's exactly where they didn't want them, especially at that particular time. They wanted them at the Front. That's why I didn't get to England.

As an old soldier, after almost four years in the battle line, Gordon Fisher took things as they came. Frank Ahlquist, younger in years as well as in experience, found it more difficult to reconcile himself to disappointment. He could hardly be blamed, because he had actually been 'marked for Blighty'.

Private
Frank
Ahlquist,
2/1st Battalion,
The
Cambridgeshire
Regiment

I was in hospital in Rouen, not critically wounded but bad enough for a Blighty – at least that's what we all hoped for. We were a bunch of youngsters in my ward, and although we felt poorly sometimes we were well enough to do a bit of ragging. The Night Sister seemed a bit of a martinet to us, though I suppose she had trouble keeping us all in order. One night when she came into our ward, she left her cardigan jacket with its red piping on the bed nearest the door while she rolled up her sleeves and went to do some job. We passed it along the beds and sewed up the cuffs and the collar. She was absolutely furious – didn't see the joke at all. She reported us and we were all fined five shillings (a lot of money for us) and it was stamped in our paybooks that it had to be deducted until it was paid off.

I had just got well enough to be able to stand the journey to Blighty for convalescence. I was able to get up a bit, though not very easily. I was over the moon when I was 'marked for Blighty'. But an hour or two later, before we were cleared out, they must have got some sort of warning. They had to clear the hospital because more casualties were expected, but they also had orders to keep in France anyone who'd be likely to recover fairly soon and to send only those who needed long convalescence and treatment to England. It was a terrible moment when they told me that my Blighty ticket was cancelled. I just couldn't believe it. I could hardly control myself. I managed to hang on until the doctor and Sister had gone down a few beds further on. I couldn't put my head under the bedclothes in front of all the lads I'd been ragging with for days past, so I struggled out of bed and got up to the end of the ward and hid myself in the toilet and cried my eyes out. I stayed in there a long time before I could recover myself sufficiently to go back in and pretend that it didn't matter.

I didn't go back to the line immediately. They sent me to Trouville. But all I had wanted was to get home. I didn't even mind being wounded, if only I could have got home.

In early March intelligence reports made it clear beyond doubt that the expected attack would take place on the French and British sectors in the north-west of the line, and almost the only question which remained unanswered was, 'When?' Since the Germans had retired to the Hindenburg Line more than a year earlier, the casualty clearing stations, and even some stationary hospitals, had moved forward. Now they would have to be prepared to move back, and to move at short notice. Those in the forefront of the German attack (at whatever point it might come) would have to retire to safety, while the others – as the situation became clear – would have to be prepared for a rapid move to the battle zone to help with the care of the casualties. Moving was no simple task. Depending on the size of the unit, it required anything from fifty to a hundred motor-lorries to transport a casualty clearing station with all its personnel, tents and equipment, and vehicles could not be whistled up at a moment's notice. Careful plans had to be made well in advance.

It was unfortunate that when the German attack was launched, its main spearhead thrust against the front held by the 5th Army, where the emergency medical arrangements were at their weakest. The Director of Medical Services, Major-General B. M. Skinner, prompted by motives which can have been clear only to himself, had deliberately made his plans so fluid and indeterminate that they would serve equally well if the Army should unexpectedly advance. From the Commander-in-Chief to the rawest of newly arrived reinforcements, he was probably the only man on the Western Front to envisage such a contingency. Other armies had already selected suitable sites to which their casualty clearing stations could easily remove, and even continue their work in conjunction with the three lines of defence in the rear. This was not the case in the 5th Army. General Skinner had no intention of abandoning any of his hospitals until the very last minute. He made it known to the Quartermaster-General that, in an emergency, he would be likely to require a hundred lorries at once, and he calculated that he could move one of his stations in a single day, with virtually no prior preparation. In his view, such an emergency would be unlikely to arise. Exactly three weeks before the attack took place, when everyone else was already on the *qui vive*, he ordered No. 55 Casualty Clearing Station at Tincourt to increase its accommodation, and to indent for extra marquees and equipment in order to do so. It was the furthest forward casualty clearing station of all, in a dangerously advanced position only ten miles behind the front line. The heightened tension of the next twenty-one days did nothing to disturb his composure or his optimism. Almost on the eve of the battle, No. 38 Casualty Clearing Station arrived back from Italy and instead of acting on the advice of the Director General's staff to order it to Bray, General Skinner instructed that it should be set up further forward on the Maricourt plateau. And in contrast to the minutely detailed emergency plans for moving back which were ready to swing into action on other fronts, as late as the last week in March the DMS of the 5th Army and his staff 'were engaged in searching for suitable sites, instead of having had them already marked down for successive retirements'.*

* From the *Official Medical History of the War, Volume III.*

It was rather late in the day. The long-anticipated attack had already been launched, and in the early morning of 21 March the blow fell. Between Arras in the north to south of the River Somme, along the weakened front held by the 3rd and 5th Armies, the Germans had mustered every gun, every shell, of every variety yet devised – shrapnel shells, high explosive, gas shells, and the lethal 'blue cross' containing two-thirds of high explosive and one-third gas. The artillery had been brought up to a formidable strength, and on 18 March German soldiers billeted in villages near the front saw an interesting sight. Long processions of self-propelled guns were moving forward on 100-horsepower motorized chassis, to take up camouflaged positions. As soon as the infantry had made headway the guns would be able to move forward under their own power to support them. It was obvious that, this time, headway was precisely what the German Command intended. The crack troops from the Russian front were fresh from weeks of intensive training, which had honed their already considerable fighting skills to knife-edged perfection. Now they were poised in the forefront of the battle awaiting the order *Protzen heran* – Prepare to move.

Leutnant Herbert Sulzbach, No. 2 Battery, Field Artillery Regiment No. 5, 18th German Army

We couldn't wait to go! For weeks, ever since the beginning of 1918, we had watched the *aufmarsch* of troops and supplies building up in the area – new battalions and reserves; guns, guns, guns; mortars; crack divisions. We were really confident, because we were a crack division ourselves – experienced front-line soldiers with the same spirit as in 1914.

There were thousands of batteries besides our own firing. The noise was so deafening that I could only order the fire by using a whistle, but the spirit and enthusiasm of the gunners was so tremendous that I hardly needed to give them orders, they just kept on slamming shell after shell into the breech.

Private Jim Brady, 43rd Field Ambulance, RAMC

We were deployed at advance posts facing St Quentin and awoke to the thunder of a thousand guns and the shattering blast of shells. We were in a dugout, thirty feet deep, but even so we were absolutely scared stiff. Cracks were appearing in the rafters and sand was running down on us from sandbags that had burst. The gas-curtain half-way down the stairway had been torn to shreds, and we could feel the blast sweeping in with every shell burst.

Leutnant Herbert Sulzbach, No. 2 Battery, Field Artillery Regiment No. 5, 18th German Army

When we stopped firing, the forward guns switched to a creeping barrage and the infantry stormed across. We were part of the second line, so we got quite a surprise when we were ordered to move off very soon. We knew then that the attack must have been a big success. We were in the middle of the town of St Quentin and all ready to go, of course. It all went very smoothly. It was two days before we had to get the guns into action – they were moving ahead so fast that we just kept moving forward all the time. We were all elated. After such a long time – almost four years – of being static, it was wonderful to be moving at last and we really felt that, now we had beaten Russia, we were going to beat the French and the British and everyone else as well.

There were roughly a dozen of us in the stretcher-post at Essigny, in sight of St Quentin – two stretcher-squads of four men each, two ASC ambulance drivers, a couple of 'battle stragglers' and the MO, Captain Duncan, in a tiny 'bed-sit' along the timbered passage. We were trapped in a ring of flying steel, with no hope of escape until the barrage lifted, and by ten o'clock it had reached a deafening crescendo. We really wondered how much more we could stand, but we had to stay put in case any stretcher-cases came down from the post a kilometre up the road ahead of us.

Private Jim Brady, 43rd Field Ambulance, RAMC

Suddenly, almost as if it had been switched off, the bombardment stopped. The silence was almost as deafening as the noise had been! One of the ambulance drivers, Bob Stevens, ventured up the stairs for a look and said that everything was 'deathly quiet', the village of Essigny was completely flattened. Some of the chaps went up after him to clear the entrance to the dugout of the debris, and we reckoned that the Jerries would take about half an hour to get to us.

It was true that the German assault troops had broken through the lightly-held forward zone of the British and French defences. That had been anticipated. What had not been foreseen was that they would so quickly quell and pass over the fortified defence zone four miles behind. The intention had been that the front-line troops should retire to these strongpoints when the Germans attacked, but they were completely pinned down by the German bombardment. With little shelter from the explosions, blinded and dazed by the fumes and the gas that thickened the morning mist into a suffocating fog, and unable to escape, not many units were left with enough strength to stand fast and put up more than a token resistance when the enemy infantry followed on the heels of the inferno. The positions were quickly overrun, and as the Germans moved across the shattered trenches, deep with dead, the demoralized survivors were rounded up and sent stumbling eastward to captivity.

On the 3rd Army front, in the Arras sector to the north, resistance stiffened early on, but in the southern part where the attack had fallen on the 5th Army, the fog continued until the middle of the afternoon, adding to the confusion. The rush to evacuate the medical units in the path of the German advance made matters worse. When General Skinner had blandly assumed that fleets of vehicles could be summoned up at a moment's notice to move the clearing stations wholesale, he had not envisaged that they would have to struggle forward over roads on which a whole army was retreating. To the credit of many commanding officers who were obliged to 'think on their feet', only a few clearing stations had to abandon their tents and equipment, and only one patient, who was dying and could not be moved, had to be left behind. But in the rush of the German advance, it was inevitable that some forward dressing-stations and countless wounded awaiting evacuation were captured.

Leutnant Herbert Sulzbach, No. 2 Battery, Field Artillery Regiment No. 5, 18th German Army

Very soon after we started to move forward we saw the first prisoners coming back. They were well-built chaps, with good uniforms and equipment. I asked them where they came from and one of them was a chap from Eastbourne. It was the only English town other than London that I knew, so I was able to tell him that I'd spent a holiday there in 1907 with my parents and my sister. He was really pleased. He liked to talk to a German about his hometown. There was no bad feeling. As soon as they became prisoners, we became friends. We could only talk for a moment, because we had to move quickly on.

Private Jim Brady, 43rd Field Ambulance, RAMC

When we got into the open we were nudged into a dejected-looking semi-circle by a group of young Germans armed to the teeth, and a German officer started yelling at MacBarron asking him where the gunline was. Then an incredible thing happened. A baby-faced German standing near nudged me, and gave me a smile and a wink. 'Hello, chum', he said – just like that – in perfect Cockney. I was astounded, but I said 'Hello' back to him. 'How old are you, then?' the young Jerry asked. I managed to gulp out that I was twenty and said, 'How old are you?' 'Nineteen,' he said, 'I lived in Balham till I was fifteen.' He took out his wallet and produced some snapshots and handed me one of a group of three people. 'That's me in the middle,' he said. 'Have it, chum. A souvenir.'

Then they started rounding us up. 'March, march.' We formed up on the roadway, our hands held high. The landscape was thick with advancing German troops – waves and waves of them – infantry, flame- and gas-throwers, light artillery, stretcher-bearers, and even observation balloons floating a hundred feet up. It had never occurred to me that I'd end up as a prisoner of war.

Leutnant Herbert Sulzbach, No. 2 Battery, Field Artillery Regiment No. 5, 18th German Army

We spent the night outside Essigny-le-Grand and next day we moved still further, past the British gunlines and past their second-line positions. We were hardly called upon to stop and fire at all, and we had very few casualties. Mostly we just rolled on through the beautiful spring weather, enjoying the sunshine and trying to keep up with the 5th Guards Division, which was moving ahead even faster in front of us. We didn't come into action at all until the third day. Then we began to meet some resistance.

But the bulk of the fighting army was still falling back, and as the fighting approached Albert, the casualty clearing stations at Dernancourt, where Geoffrey Keynes was now stationed, had to fall back too. The roads were in a turmoil as reinforcements tried to hurry forward to stem the German advance against the tide of men and equipment pouring back. Such transport as there was, honking and thrusting a snail-like path through disordered packs of stragglers, had long ago been commandeered.

Fortunately we had been able to get all the nurses away, but there was nothing for it but to make our own way on foot. We had to leave most of our equipment behind, and I was put in charge of the hospital orderlies. I was terribly sorry for them, because they weren't soldiers at all – they were mostly C3 men, unfit and over-age, and that's why they were orderlies. Some of them could hardly walk. They wanted to sit down in their tracks and just stay there; they absolutely didn't care. I was exhausted myself but I had to keep moving them on, move them on all the time, *make* them go on. In the middle of the night, when we'd been marching for hours and hours on these congested roads, up came a staff officer on a horse and gave me a proper dressing-down. 'You must keep the men in proper ranks,' he said. I said nothing at all. Under any other circumstances I might have laughed, but I simply didn't answer him I was so irritated. We just plodded on.

    It happened to be the night of my thirtieth birthday. When we reached Doullens the following morning we reported to the hospital in the Citadel, where people were congregating. There were no beds to spare, and I lay down on a stretcher. I was so exhausted that I slept for eighteen hours. But even then, when things were at their absolute lowest point, it never crossed my mind that we should lose the war. I was quite certain we shouldn't. At that point I thought it might go on for as long as five years, but I never thought that we should lose it.

Captain Geoffrey Keynes, RAMC, No. 56 Casualty Clearing Station, Edgehill, Dernancourt

The weary troops, the hospitals, the personnel and the wounded were now converging far behind the front line of a week earlier – on St Pol, Fréevent, Doullens and on the important town of Amiens, frighteningly close to the base camps and the English Channel beyond. It was Holy Week and the strangest Holy Week that the Rector of St Giles, Dorset, now doing service as Chaplain at No. 42 Stationary Hospital, had ever experienced. On Good Friday he made time to write an account of it to his good friend and parishioner Mrs Lockyer, who happened to be Gladys Stanford's grandmother.*

I have been trying to find a few minutes when I can be quiet to tell you

---

* More than sixty years later, Miss Stanford still keeps this unusual first-hand account as a prized family memento.

a few of the wonderful experiences I have been through during this historic Holy Week. Our hospital at Amiens, after being suddenly transformed from a stationary hospital into a casualty clearing station and then practically into an advanced dressing-station, had eventually to be evacuated. Our stretcher casualties began to come in last Saturday morning (23 March) and in four or five days we had anything between 4,000–5,000 casualties through our hands. We had, I suppose, about 600 cases in the first convoy, the majority of them sitting and walking cases. These men were the survivors of troops who had been through six hours of continuous shelling of the most stupendous kind, then five hours of gas – and no food for forty-eight hours – and a journey of many hours in open trucks to wind up with. As fast as we could, we got them hot tea. And everyone in the hospital worked like niggers. Eventually the garden, the lovely salon and other rooms were full of these poor boys. It was a sight with these poor boys, covered with mud and blood, on the sofas and armchairs, lying on the carpets and all over the grass in the garden. Some of them were washing and shaving in the outside artificial pond with goldfish in it.

Suddenly, a good lady, a Miss Evans (unknown to me) turned up. She is a French hospital nurse. She had six bottles of wine and asked me to accept them and said she was off to get more. In the middle of it all, Madame de Bûctot, the owner of the house, herself arrived from Paris and was delighted to think we were so using her house. I thanked her properly and made the men give her three cheers. She then produced four dozen bottles of wine from the cellar and then Miss Evans returned with six bottles of champagne and a *salmon*. I know that I poured two *cases* of wine into mugs and bowls, and what others poured out I don't know; all that Madame could say was, '*Il est naturelle*'. Her niece worked away and helped to light a big stove in the drawing-room.

We took in for four days continuously. The worst time I ever had in my life was on Palm Sunday, and nothing but the most merciful Providence saved us. We had, I think, five hours of the most vicious and persistent bombing. We are not thirty yards from the big station, which was, of course, one of the chief points of interest to the Boche. We had almost finished taking in a most appalling convoy, and the stretchers were in the corridors, under the tables and all over the place. The staff were beginning to get them to bed and examine them when the bombing began. You can imagine what it is like at the top of a big hospital, lights out and at least a hundred or so wounded on every floor. But the pluck of the sisters and VADs is simply marvellous. It is something to remember to see quite young girls not only washing the most gruesome wounds but doing so hastily from bed to bed, practically in the dark except for a very much shaded candle, and bomb after bomb falling round.

It has been a strange Holy Week, but I have never realized the Passion so vividly before and the meaning of the blood shedding. O'Neile, the dear little padre, gave me a most beautiful meditation on the sorrowful mysteries as we sat on two heaps of coal in the cellar on Tuesday night.

The Passion is reproduced in the life of nearly every soldier. 'He went forth bearing the Cross for *Himself*', my text last Sunday morning. There is the Cross, the soldier's pack (O'Neile says the pack weighs the same as the Cross), and the Crown of Thorns – the tin hat – and of course the Agony, the loneliness of the soldier wounded, helpless until he is picked up. This morning (Good Friday) one saw it all again in the Via Dolorosa. The seven words – the first thing the boys ask for is a drink, so the cry 'I thirst' – and the 'bloody sweat' and the falling beneath the weight of the Cross, and then the picture of home and mother flashing before him at the 4th Station; the splendid women of Jerusalem – the good nurses; the Simon of Cyrene, compelled to bear the Cross – so like the good but unbelieving doctors, who seem often so unresponsive spiritually but so splendid in relieving the actual Cross-bearing. And then St Veronica – the Madame Bûctots and the Miss Evans and hundreds of others like them. And the stripping of the garments – the undressing of the wounded; and the hanging on the Cross – the sick-bed and the theatre and the stretcher.

It is all so vivid and full of meaning and makes one feel more and more how true the old Gospel is, and the Resurrection and Victory beyond it all.

I suppose it is the biggest battle the world has ever seen and if one comes through all right – as I hope we may – it will indeed be worth all the hardship. The magnificent courage of the men is simply unsurpassable, and no words can ever tell the heroic things that are done which will never be known.

It took everyone's courage to stand firm in the face of the losses, the tragedies, the collapse, the chaos, the sense of defeat that hung like a pall across the Western Front in the bright spring days of Easter week, made all the worse because no one knew quite what was happening. In the base hospitals along the coastline, they were too busy to brood. As the troops and the clearing stations fell back they were swamped with convoy after convoy of casualties. The distinction between day duty and night duty was soon academic, as doctors, orderlies and nurses worked almost round the clock. Meanwhile, for want of any other accommodation, the worn and weary Sisters and orderlies who had escaped from the casualty clearing stations in the line of the German advance snatched a few hours of recuperative sleep on the beds of those who were on duty in the wards.

Sister Helen Dora Boylston, US Nurse at No. 22 General Hospital (Harvard Unit)

Our first warning that the convoys were coming was the steady hum of ambulances winding down the road as far as the eye could see, with scarcely a yard between them. Nearly every case should have been a stretcher case. Ragged and dirty; tin hats still on; wounds patched together any way; some not even covered.

They were direct from the line and their faces were white and drawn and their eyes glassy from lack of sleep. There were great husky men, crying with the pain of gaping wounds and dreadfully discoloured trench feet. There were strings of from eight to twenty blind boys filing up the road, their hands on each other's shoulders and their leader some bedraggled, bandaged, limping youngster.

Matron sent us to the D Lines. She said that there were 500 in this convoy, and that there were stretcher cases on the way, and she asked if my friend Ruth, myself and Topsy Stone could clean up the 500 walkers. We thought that we could, though heaven knows how we thought we were going to do it. We made a frantic effort to systematize our work. We made a small table for the medical officer, and then a large table piled with bandages, splints, boric ointment, sponges and a basinful of Dakins for wet dressings. Then there were two smoky lanterns and an enfeebled primus stove.

Ruth, armed with a pair of scissors, stood in the doorway and beckoned the boys in, two or three at a time. Because there was so much to do it was impossible to try to take the stiff, dried bandages off carefully. The only thing to do was to snatch them off with one deperate tug. Poor Ruth! She could hardly stand it. She'd cut the dressing down the middle, the poor lad looking on with set jaw and imploring eyes. Ruth's own eyes were full. There'd be a quick jerk; a sharp scream from the lad; a sob from Ruth; and he was passed on to the Medical Officer, and Ruth began on the next.

The Medical Officer looked at the wound, said 'Wet – dry – boric ointment' or 'Splint' to the orderly sitting at the table. The orderly scribbled the order on a bit of paper and gave it to the lad, who moved on to Topsy and me. They came much too fast for us, and within fifteen minutes were standing twenty deep around the dressing-table. As the hours went by we ceased to think. We worked through the night until dawn.

When there was no space left in the hospitals, whole convoys of wounded soldiers straight from the front had to be shipped directly to England. It was a grim repetition of the wholesale evacuations of twenty months before when the British had attacked on the Somme. But it was one thing to be wounded in the cause of possible victory. It was quite another to be wounded in the course of defeat.

Kathleen Rhodes, VAD

It was the very worst time of all, because everything seemed so hopeless. Every man who had two uninjured feet had had to run for

his life, but some of them came in with very severe injuries – shattered limbs which had become gangrenous because they couldn't be
got back as quickly as they would normally have been.

By now I was the senior VAD nurse, because all the others who
were with me in 1915 had either been posted away or had resigned,
or been sent home because their health gave way and they couldn't
stand the rough camp life. I was put in charge of two huge emergency
huts with stretcher beds on the floor, and not even a proper nursing
orderly. My only help was an 'attached man'. He couldn't go up the
line because he had flat feet, but at least he was able to cope with
meals for the patients. His name was Clumpas, and he claimed to be
descended from Christoper Columbus! I was thankful for his help,
because there was no one to spare for night duty and I stayed on duty
every day until all the dressings were done. I started at 7.15 in the
morning and sometimes it was midnight or one o'clock the following
morning before I finished. When I went off to snatch a few hours'
sleep, the men had to be made as comfortable as possible and then
left alone. The Night Super would look in from time to time, of
course, and some of the less severe cases would be able to go for help
if there was an emergency. But there was nothing else that could be
done.

*No. 24
General
Hospital,
Etaples*

It was a terrible time – a very depressing time. We knew that the
Germans had broken through, but we got so little real news that we
didn't know *where* they were or how fast they were advancing. We
were warned to evacuate, and yet there was no time to do anything
but carry on and hope for the best – hope that the Germans wouldn't
suddenly arrive on our doorstep, though we thought it was quite
possible that they would. I was in the eye ward and two of the
sergeants in my ward had pistols and ammunition, because they were
machine-gunners and hadn't been issued with rifles. At any other
time they would have been taken away from them when they were
admitted into hospital, but in all the disturbance of those days the
normal routine of admission went overboard, so they had kept the
pistols and they showed them to me. They made me promise that if
the Germans really got near the hospital, I would come to them and
they would shoot me there and then, rather than let me fall into the
hands of the Germans! That really frightened me.

*Nona Mitchell,
VAD, No. 73
General
Hospital,
Trouville*

I never heard men so depressed as the wounded who came in at that
time. Usually they were so cheerful, the wounded, glad to have a
Blighty and ready to make the best of things, but the men who came
in from the retreat were hopelessly depressed. I remember one man
saying, 'You know, Sister, they'll be over here next month – and we
can't do anything about it'. Quite a number of them were saying
things like that.

*Gwynnedd
Lloyd,
VAD,
University War
Hospital,
Southampton*

I had been working in the theatre and I was coming to the end of my stint there and due to go back on the wards, but Sister Owens, who was the Theatre Sister, said she just couldn't carry on in the middle of the rush with a new person who didn't know the ropes, so I stayed on. I never left the hospital from the end of March until about the beginning of May, when things quietened down a bit. We used to have time off, but I never went into town because you never knew when you would be needed and you had to keep on loading up your drums and sterilizing things. Sometimes you'd even be in bed, and the orderly would knock on the door and say, 'Theatre' – and you'd be there until four o'clock in the morning sometimes. There were emergency operations all the time, because there was a continual stream of ambulances.

Claire Elise
Tisdall, VAD
Ambulance
Nurse, The
Ambulance
Column,
London
District

I had spent a few months in Stuttgart before the war and had had a very happy time and made some friends, but I really hated the Germans then and I was still suffering the agony of losing my brother, whom I dearly loved, at Ypres. My feelings towards them were less than Christian, but I spoke German pretty fluently at the time, so ironically I was one of the ones who used to be allocated to the German prisoners. I didn't travel with them, but we looked to see that they were comfortable and just checked them up before they left. There were four or five ambulances full of Germans, and the last one was just due to go off. I jumped in to have a quick glance around and a very pale-faced boy looked up at me and he said, 'Pain, pain'. So I spoke to him in German. I said, 'Where is the pain?' He said, also in German, 'In the leg, the knee'. I pulled back the blanket and there, to my horror – a spouting artery! I knew what to do, though I had never had to do it before: *'Search for the femoral pressure point, a hand's span from the hip to the groin, and press strongly down with both thumbs'*. I used to practise it in my bath every night, I dragged his clothes aside, hoped that I'd found it, got my thumbs down and pressed for all I was worth, and at the top of my voice I shouted, 'Haemorrhage, Haemorrhage', which was what we had to do. I kept holding on until I heard the voice of one of the one trained nurse. She said, 'Good, dear. Good, dear, that's right. Now you can let go and I'll take over'. The orderly was standing behind her with a tourniquet, which they always had at the ready, so I jumped down and she went into the ambulance and they put me into another one with British soldiers.

On the next convoy I looked out for the driver of the ambulance and asked him what had happened to the boy. He said, 'You were lucky. You stopped that in time. He would have been dead before we were out of the station. He was just spared'. And I was glad. I really was glad. It melted a little bit of my hatred and I felt quite differently towards Germans after that. Of course, I was hopelessly teased by

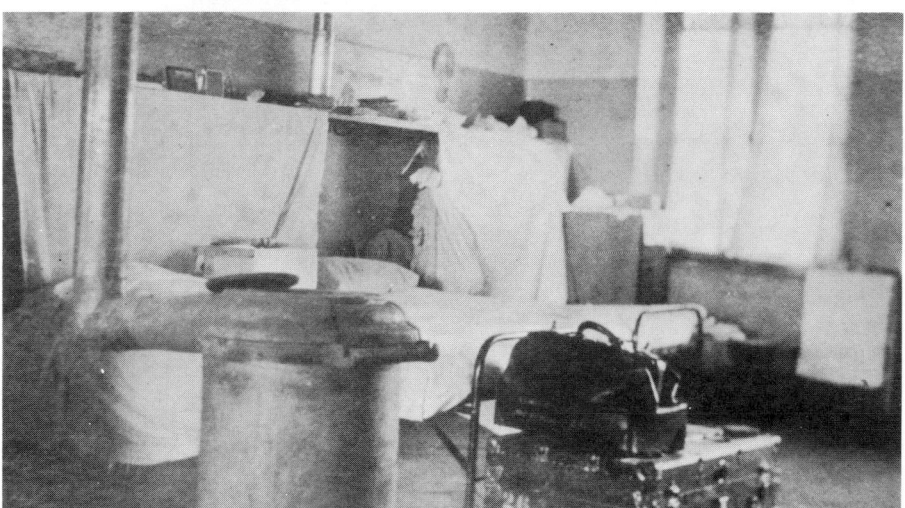

(*Top left*) US Nurse Nell Brink with a group of her patients at No. 27 US Base Hospital, Angers. Lieutenant Robarts is standing on her left. (*Top centre*) The day before she sailed from New York, she was photographed in her brand-new uniform of a US Army Nurse. (*Top right*) Just off the cross-Channel ferry, US Nurse Jane Baudin on the quayside at Le Havre en route to No. 26 US Base Hospital at Allerey. (*Centre*) American nurses in the Independence Day Parade on 4 July 1918. Paris went wild and renamed this street (Avenue du Trocadéro) Avenue President-Wilson. (*Above*) By 1918 the nurses' quarters were an improvement on the bell-tent accommodation of the early days, but they were far from luxurious. Two nurses shared this corner of a hut at No. 26 US Base Hospital.

The Kitchen. Beaufort War Hospital, Fishponds Bristol. 1526

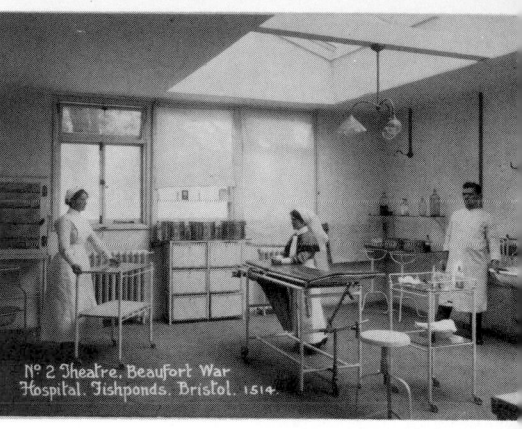

Nº 2 Theatre. Beaufort War Hospital. Fishponds. Bristol. 1514

The Laundry, Beaufort War Hospital, Fishponds. Bristol. 1533.

The Laundry, Beaufort War Hospital, Fishponds, Bristol. 1534.

Concert Hall. Beaufort War Hospital. Fishponds. Bristol 1479

M.C.Ward. Beaufort War Hospital, Fishponds, Bristol 1521

Beaufort War Hospital, Fishponds, Bristol, in 1916.

(*Above*) Happy Christmas 1917. The RAMC staff at Queen Mary's Military Hospital, Whalley, sent holly-bordered postcards of the hospital to their friends . . .

. . . but the Almeric Paget Massage Corps ordered special cards of their own (*right*). Electric treatment and massage on limbs paralysed by wounds was a feature of the hospital's work.

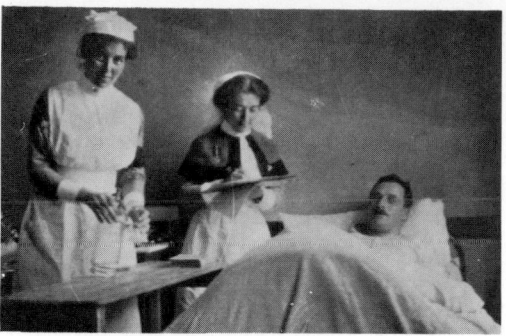

(*Left*) Sister Mary Stollard and her auxiliary nurse, Miss Dormer, photographed at a patient's bedside at the Northern Military Hospital, Becketts Park, Leeds.

(*Below left*) A patient Dr Reardon described as a ' lucky man '. If the shrapnel had entered two inches higher, he would have been dead; two inches to the left and he would have been blind.

(*Right*) Private T. Mair of the Royal Scots Fusiliers was wounded near Hooge on Sunday, 15 August 1915. Dr Reardon scribbled the diagnosis 'bullet wound left hand with compound fracture of second metacarpal'.

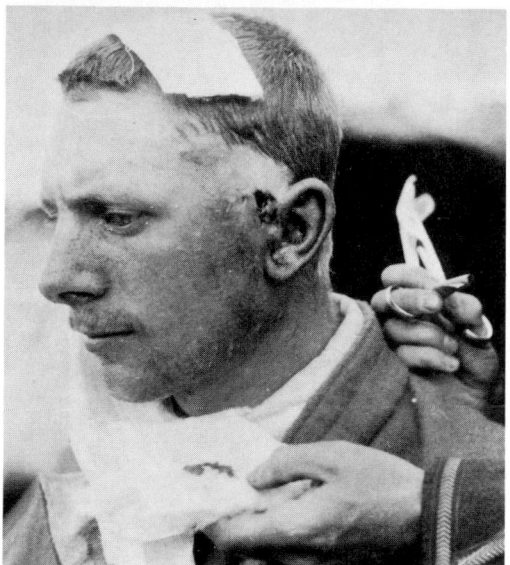

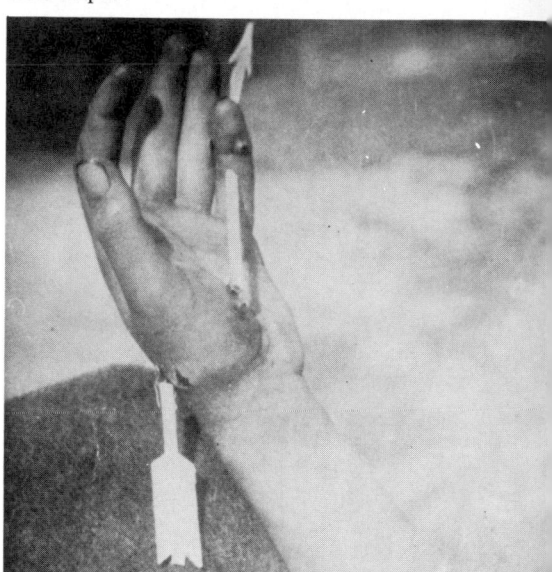

(*Below*) The model gun (*right foreground*) made by wounded soldiers at Dearnley Military Hospital, Rochdale, was the centrepiece of Christmas decorations in Kathleen Yarwood's ward. The notice on the table behind reads, 'Help the Tommies' Christmas fun, pop a sixpence in the gun.' But Matron made them take it away. VAD Kathleen Yarwood is standing on the left.

(*Above*) Fancy-dress parties were popular with these convalescent wounded soldiers at Rusthall Grange Auxiliary Hospital, Tunbridge Wells, where Hester Cotton was a VAD. Even the 'nurse' and the 'commandant' are soldiers in fancy dress.

(*Above left*) 'In the early days, when the men first came in, they were young and enthusiastic. 'I'd like to have a pop at the Boche. I'll teach them this, that and the other.' But little by little, that attitude changed.' Sister Mary Stollard, Northern Military Hospital, Becketts Park, Leeds.

(*Above*) Sister Mary Fitzgibbon with other army nursing sisters on board the hospital ship *Essequibo*, which received some of the sick and wounded from Gallipoli.

(*Right*) At Gallipoli the hospital ships could not go inshore and the wounded had to be transferred from barges by box stretchers. Sister Mary Fitzgibbon, on board the hospital ship *Essequibo*, took this photograph in 1915.

A typical 'sweetheart' pose, but Nurse Maisie
Bowcott was posing with her brother 'Nip' on
his last leave. He was killed a month later.

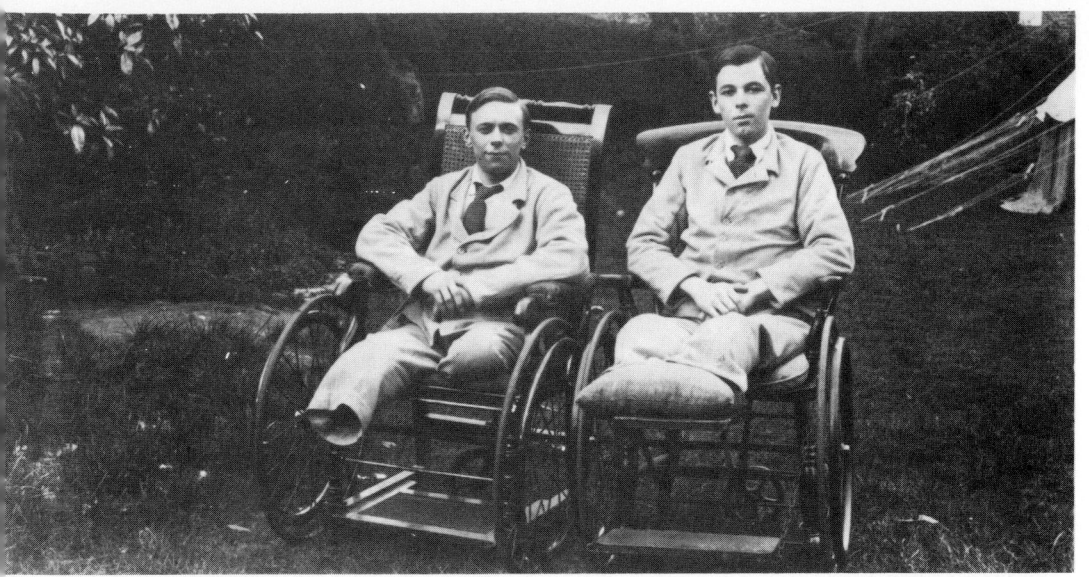

(*Above*) Private George Hobbs (*left*) and Private Arthur Hancock, both eighteen, and both with two legs amputated, were the nurses' 'pets' at Struan House Auxiliary Hospital, Reading.

(*Above left*) This photograph appeared in *The War Budget* on 10 October 1914 with the caption, 'The Duchess of Westminster has joined the Red Cross and is at the front. She has taken with her her favourite wolfhound.'

(*Above right*) Millicent, Duchess of Sutherland, with the staff of her ambulance, photographed at The Hague after their escape from German-occupied Belgium.

(*Right*) 'Dare you to come in?' The English duckling quacks its challenge to the American eagle. Cartoon published in the *New York World*, August 1914.

PEACE! This photograph was snapped at exactly 11.00 am on 11 November 1918 in the hospital ward where Frank Ahlquist was a patient. He is seated on the right on the end of a bed, with his wounded foot in a sling.

PEACE! At Nimy, near Mons, on the morning of 11 November 1918, Germaine Lauryssen saw Lieutenant Deeks of the 116th Battalion, Canadian Expeditionary Force, come up the street, and knew that the war was over. Later they were photographed together (he is on her right) with Lieutenant James Tiffin, to commemorate the occasion.

the other girls. They used to say to me, 'You've saved the Kaiser another soldier'. And they kept it up for days, asking me, 'Have you got your telegram from the Kaiser yet? You know, thanking you for saving some of his army. . .'

But the Kaiser's Army was not quite so cock-a-hoop as it had been a week earlier. After the elation of the breakthrough and the rapid advance in the southern part of the line, they had ground to a halt. The German Commander-in-Chief, General Ludendorff, had made the tactical error that was to lose him the war. The strategy of the assault had been brilliant and he had rightly calculated that if the Allied line were breached between the British and the French, the breach would widen of its own volition as the British were forced to fall back towards the sea, and the French to wheel south-east to defend Paris. Ludendorff could then thrust his army through the widening gap, encircle the French on the one hand and, on the other, force the British back across the narrow coastal strip, out of France, and out of the war. America would then have no jumping-off point from which to join battle, and with both her major allies reduced to impotence France would have no choice but to sue for peace and the war would be over.

It was a masterly plan, put into effect at exactly the right moment when the German forces were at their strongest and the Allies at their weakest. And it could have succeeded had Ludendorff removed the first reserves from the northern sector, where the 3rd Army had succeeded in halting his troops within a few kilometres, and rushed them south to support the troops who had punched a huge hole in the Allied lines. There, his troops not only lacked the high-calibre reserves they desperately needed, but were finding difficulty in advancing those that they had over the old shattered battlefields of earlier fighting. Strong reinforcement of troops and of manpower were needed to supply, support and relieve the crack regiments that had forged so gloriously ahead across the valley of the Somme. Ludendorff hesitated and lost. He would launch another attack, but in another place. On 9 April he attacked further north in the valley of the River Lys, with a secondary assault towards Ypres.

By 11 April the thin ranks of the British Expeditionary Force had been further depleted by the loss of 150,000 men killed, wounded and captured in vast numbers by the Germans – and all the reserves were used up. The following morning an Order of the Day was sent out from General Headquarters to every unit of the BEF with instructions that it was to be read by every man and woman in France and published in the newspapers so that it could be read by everyone at home. It was signed by Field-Marshal Haig and it concluded, in stirring tones:

. . . There is no other course open to us but to fight it out. Every position must be held to last man. There must be no retirement. With our backs to the wall and believing in the justice of our cause, each one must fight on to the end. The safety of our homes and the freedom of mankind alike depend on the conduct of each one of us at this critical moment.

Haig's last-ditch call to arms had an unexpected effect. It put a stop to the despair of the last three disastrous weeks and even went some way towards stemming the tide of hopelessness that, for months past, had threatened to engulf the morale of a people weary of pyrrhic victories.

If the near-defeat did not precisely restore the national morale to its former spirited level, it reunited the nation in a sense of purpose and a grim determination to soldier on – and to win.

Chapter Nineteen

Now it was the Yanks, with all the confidence of new arrivals, who were echoing the belief – long outworn among the Allies – that it would, 'all be over by Christmas' – or, in their own colourful phraseology, 'Heaven, Hell or Hoboken by Christmas'.

Hoboken, just across the Hudson River from New York, was the main port of embarkation, and as more and more men mustered to the ranks of the US army and completed their preliminary training at home, its streets rang with the sound of tramping feet and the mournful dirge of ships' sirens, as the camouflaged transports pulled away from the piers and slipped up-river past the Statue of Liberty, impassive in the grey dawn, to rendezvous with the smaller ships that would convoy them across the Atlantic into the unknown 'Over There'. For all the enthusiasm of the Doughboys it was an eerie leave-taking. 'If the Statue of Liberty wants to see me more than once', remarked one soldier, 'she'll have to turn around!'

Even if it did not match the wild enthusiasm that greeted the earliest arrivals, there was no doubt of their welcome. Every soldier, every officer, every nurse, every doctor, every civilian Red Cross worker was handed a personal message of welcome from the King.

WINDSOR CASTLE

Soldiers of the United States, the people of the British Isles welcome you on your way to take your stand beside the Armies of many Nations now fighting in the Old World the great battles for human freedom.

The Allies will gain new heart and spirit in your company. I wish that I could shake the hand of each one of you and bid you God speed on your mission.

George RI

April 1918

It was printed on the finest notepaper embossed with the royal coat-of-arms, in such an excellent facsimile of the King's handwriting that large numbers of Americans were convinced that King George had written each one personally.

It would have been a tall order. By March there were 325,000 American troops already in France; by 1 May there were more than 429,000;

by the end of May more than 650,000 – with still more training or awaiting shipment in Britain, where people were still reeling from the shock of the German breakthrough in France. Dr John Finney, who had arrived the previous July as senior medical officer of the John Hopkins Unit to set up US Base Hospital No. 18, wrote home enthusiastically to his wife:

> The stimulus of the presence over here in increasing numbers of the fresh and, in many respects, raw and untrained American soldiers is having a most wholesome effect upon the French and English psychology. Don't misunderstand me when I speak of the American soldier as 'raw and untrained'. In many respects they certainly are, as compared with the seasoned and veteran poilu and Tommy, but at the same time there is about them a certain something that is lacking in the others, or at least is not present to the same extent; namely, a suggestion of vigour and 'pep' that is present in a fresh athlete as compared with one who has played the game until it has begun to tell on his vitality – a punch that carries with it a latent power that, unless I am mistaken, will put it over on the Boche ultimately in a way that no one can deny.

But although Dr Harvey Cushing, who had seen rather more of the war, was just as pleased to see the Yanks arriving in force, he sometimes found their new-boy enthusiasm and confidence the slightest bit irritating. Travelling back to France in a troop train after a few days spent in London, he found himself in a packed 'Officers Only' compartment, in which the 'chief interest centred on two spick-and-span West Pointers – a colonel and a major – just out of a bandbox – tight-fitting, neatly-pressed thin uniforms, paper-soled pointed riding-boots – very alert and erect – also very complaining'. He was embarrassed by their conversation, and recorded the gist of it in his journal.

Dr Harvey
Cushing,
US Army
Surgeon

'Rotten town, London – had to wait fifteen minutes for our hotel bill – almost missed breakfast and the train – never want to see the d----d place again. And they wouldn't give us a check for our luggage! Now in America you can check your trunk right from your room to your destination, etc., etc.'

'Yes, just landed Tuesday; saw two "subs", think we got one of 'em; fine trip, brass bedsteads, bath, all to ourselves, twenty aeroplane squadrons on board. Going to send machines over in droves, engines not very fast, but so many of them we won't miss the few crashed by faster Hun planes. Training our men to shoot; British have been all-fired stupid; when we break through there'll be open warfare and the men'll know what to do; lots of niggers, great fighters, fine shots. Now if you had only done this at Cambrai, etc., etc.'

The patient young captain to whom this was chiefly addressed showed wonderful restraint. 'You see, we're very fed up with the war. That's the way *we* used to feel; but then we've made so many mistakes, and your country understands administration so much better and has no red-tape and will show us the way, I'm sure.'*

The fact was that it was difficult to know exactly what to do with the Americans, because they had little besides their boundless enthusiasm to contribute. The US army had so few weapons – and what they had was of antiquated design – that they would have to be supplied by the British and the French. True, there were some 170,000 old Springfield rifles and a handful of Hotchkiss machine-guns, but they had been well-nigh worn out by the training programme, and the rifles were no more than a token adornment of the husky shoulders of Doughboys streaming into Europe. As for guns, the 430 field pieces – all that the US army had – were hardly worth bringing across the Atlantic. Until the American munitions industry could sweep into production to supply the deficit, the Allies would have to make it good. The US Government had already placed huge orders with British and French arms manufacturers, but it would take time to fulfill them.**

The American Red Cross had also ordered vast quantities of goods. Although a certain amount of necessary supplies could be shipped from the United States, it had sensibly been decided that valuable time (and shipping space) could be saved by making use of the existing resources of the now-huge purchasing organization of the British Red Cross, buying from manufacturers with whom they dealt and from whom they were able to get speedy delivery on advantageous terms. The British Red Cross rocked under the weight of the orders, but finally delivered the goods.

The hospitals for the American troops had begun to arrive long before the troops arrived themselves – before even General Pershing himself had reached France with his token force in June 1917. By May 1918, Base Hospital No. 5 (calling itself The Harvard Unit, until briskly ticked off by the original Harvard Unit, which had been encamped at Camiers since 1915) was celebrating the first anniversary of its arrival. And even No. 5 had not been the first to arrive. The Lakeside Unit from Cleveland, Ohio, had beaten the Harvard men to the post by landing in France five days before them to set up Base Hospital No. 4. Other units followed fast on their heels as medical schools and hospitals the length and breadth of the United States recruited teams of doctors, surgeons, nurses and the enlisted men – many of them medical students – who would act as orderlies, stretcher-bearers and general dogsbodies.

* *From a Surgeon's Journal,* Harvey Cushing.
** By the end of the war, not a single shot from a new weapon of US manufacture had been fired in France.

As yet, there were no American wounded soldiers to nurse, but the hospital units had come at the urgent request of the British and French governments, who were quick to appreciate, as Washington had done, that such a contribution to the war effort was the most immediately helpful gesture the USA could make. While the American hospital units waited for their own troops to enter the field, they would be 'loaned' for the next year to the hard-pressed British and French, caring for their wounded. They would take in the Doughboys as the occasion arose – and it arose sooner than anyone had anticipated.

It was a repeat of the British experience of 1914. As soon as the Yanks began to arrive, there were epidemics of mumps, measles, chicken-pox, even outbreaks of diphtheria, amongst country boys now exposed to infection for the first time. Worse were the chronic sick who, just as the British boys had done three years earlier, had slipped through the net of perfunctory medical examinations. Base Hospital No. 5 had taken over the old No. 13 General Hospital, and soon Harvey Cushing was writing indignantly:

> No. 13 General is fast filling up with Americans who bear no relation to the present or any other battle – a mixed bag of 'sick', some 250 in number – hammer toes, *hallux valgus,* haemorrhoids, hernias, varicoceles, backaches – and, worse, tuberculous pleurisies, chronic heart disease, and the like. Very inefficient medical examinations at home, this would seem to indicate. It's difficult to know where to send them until American bases in England are opened – if there ever are to be any. . . . I saw a young chap this morning whose weight on enlistment was 108 pounds; he now weighs about 90 pounds, and his pack with rifle, ammunition and all else weighs more than he does. . . . Another in Arlie Bock's ward – a tailor – had a mitral stenosis, with the apex in his axilla. He had not been able to run or climb stairs for many years. A young Medical Officer thought something was wrong and called his major's attention to it, but they sent him along nevertheless. He'll have to be boarded Class C. All these people were in the 77th Division.

Young Arlie Bock, a rosy-cheeked youngster not long qualified, had boyish good looks which endeared him to the nurses, but having been put in charge of the medical wards he had little time for dalliance. On the last day of April 1917 he had been going about his business as House Officer at the Massachusetts General Hospital, and if he thought at all of the star-studded team of medicos recruited by Harvey Cushing and about to set off for France to man US Base Hospital No. 5, it was with the merest trace of envy and no expectation that a young intern of eighteen months' standing would ever be invited to join their illustrious ranks. But next day the impossible happened. George Minot fell ill. Young Dr Bock was invited to take his place on the team, and before

May was out he had exchanged the gleaming sterile setting of the Massachusetts General for the leaky tents of No. 11 General Hospital at Dannes-Camiers, with two hundred beds under his inexperienced care. He was also given the responsibility of organizing a laboratory, for the seniors had been quick to realize that, inexperienced though he was, as the most recently qualified doctor in the group his knowledge was the most up-to-date. He would therefore be familiar with the advances that had been made in the two years since the Americans had introduced the technique that prevented transfused blood from coagulating. Now it was possible to type the various blood groups, and Arlie Bock knew how.

You can't imagine the big demand that was placed on us, and that was the need for blood. We had been accustomed to matching blood for transfusion purposes to make it safe. You had Type 2 and Type 3 sera and you could find out which was suitable for any transfusion, because transfusion wasn't safe unless these bloods were typed, and they didn't know how to do this until we got there. I happened to have the material to organize the laboratory, being the youngest member of the outfit, and had the Type 2 and Type 3 sera in order to type this blood. It was supplied to me by a very great man, James Homer Wright, who was a famous Professor of Pathology at the MGH, and who invented etiology, the origin of blood platelets and so on.

Dr Arlie Bock, Medical Officer, US Base Hospital No. 5

We were in this hospital, all under canvas with tents lit by candle-lanterns, so that at night you could hardly see what a patient looked like. That was from the end of May to the first of November. Then we were transferred to the big casino in Boulogne, to the big outfit there. In that hospital it happened that Sir Almroth Wright had a laboratory. He was one of the most famous people in the world at this time, author of the so-called Ultrasonic Index and so on, and among his helpers was Alexander Fleming, who was later responsible for the discovery of penicillin. I was fascinated with what they were doing and exceedingly interested in the work that went on there. Whenever I possibly could, I used to steal away from my ward duty when things were quiet in the afternoon and go up and have tea with Wright and Fleming. They tolerated me for some reason, and we used to have many an interesting discussion about what was going on.

I used to think I got much more out of my work in France than the patients did, because I was very lucky to be associated with that kind of crew — Harvey Cushing and Elliott Cutler, one of Cushing's right-hand men, and Reginald Fitz and O. H. Roberston, and so on. A remarkably top-notch group of people, and I got in with them by sheer accident, due to the illness of George Minot.*

* George Richards Minot MD was a future Nobel prizewinner (1934) who was to become Professor of Medicine at Harvard in 1928 and win fame for his researches into the pathology of the blood, and for his discovery of the curative properties of liver in pernicious anaemia.

It made an unimaginable impression on me to see what was happening to these young men from all over the world, in the prime of life, going through what they were going through. I used to think, what's all this about? Who's looking after us anyway? What about Divine Providence and where is there any justice? It made me think about those sort of big problems and I've never seen them answered. It certainly changed my attitude – and I've never been to a church service since.

Lorna Neill, British Red Cross ambulance driver, Etaples

I never said to myself, 'There can be no God, or He would never allow such things'. I saw it the other way. I felt that there couldn't be heroism and suffering to no purpose. It was at that point that I really became Christian – in the midst of all the suffering that was all around us.

As soon as we became old enough to talk our way into the British Red Cross, Maud and I went home and managed to get accepted as ambulance drivers – which was a miracle in my case because I could hardly drive. We were sent back to France when things were at their very worst early in 1918, when the Germans had broken through and the casualties simply poured in all the time. It was very different from Revigny, where we ranked as officers in these glamorous uniforms and the French soldiers almost revered us and called us angels! In the ambulance convoy the discipline was very strict; half the time we wore boots and greasy overalls, though we had blue uniforms with tailored jackets and skirts that came well below the knees.

We were put on night duty straight away, and being the last arrivals we were given the most ancient and rackety ambulances. Mine was No. 896 and I was warned that it had a slipping clutch. We went on duty at eight o'clock and sat round a sort of common-room hut where there was a big stove, waiting for the first call. It came about nine – someone flung the door open and shouted, 'Train in. Train in'. We had to rush out and find our cars in the dark, and race down these narrow roads without any lights to see who could get to the railway-siding quickest, because the people who arrived first got the least badly wounded. They kept the very worst ones, the dying ones, until the end and took them out more carefully. There were old orderlies, C3 men, who lifted the stretchers out of the train and into the ambulance, and then the section Leader, Doris Chambers, would call the number of the hospital you were to go to and you would have to make your way there in the dark, with no lights. At first it was very difficult, agonizing, knowing the way to where you were going, because it was a huge hospital camp and there were all sorts of exits and entrances. If you went up to an exit when you were supposed to be going in an entrance, you were really in trouble.

There was an awful atmosphere of depression. We had no news, but we could tell what was happening by the very bad condition of the wounded who came down and the tremendous numbers of them, and you could feel this atmosphere of anxiety and worry around you. The men who came down would often say, 'It's been very bad up there. The Jerries are coming through'. One night I was very very tired. We'd been busy all night and about three or four o'clock in the morning I felt completely done in. I didn't really know how I was going to carry on, yet I knew there was another train to meet. So when I drew up at a hospital and dropped my wounded, I went in to one of the ward huts. There was Sister sitting quietly, as night nurses always do, behind a table, with a red light beside her, and alongside her, all down both sides of the ward, lay these boys. She looked round and came to ask what I wanted, but I couldn't even speak. She saw at once that I was exhausted and she said, 'Sit down and I'll give you something to drink'. She brought me a hot cup of tea and then she sat down and talked to me. She asked how old I was (she was a much older woman than I was, well over thirty) and she didn't say, 'You must give up, or stop, or go home – she just chatted and smiled, and was nice to me and very understanding. She pulled me together, and after a few minutes I went out feeling better, and did one more journey. Then I went home to my billet.

On the way home, dawn came. I had seen many dawns, but I always remember this particular dawn on a spring morning about six o'clock, after this terrible night. I saw it coming up gradually over the east where the battle-line was, and I knew that with things as they were, the battle-line wasn't very far away. 'Well', I thought, 'here comes the dawn, and I feel terrible. My face is filthy and I've got ashes in my mouth – how I don't know, but I have. I feel awful and I'm filthy, but the dawn is coming'. It seemed symbolic, somehow, although everything was so terrible, as if the dawn was coming for everyone. And of course it did come soon after.

Not many people, in that late spring of 1918, had the same instinctive feeling that the dawn was just over the horizon. But it was. The German breakthrough had broken the deadlock which, for more than three years, had held both sides in its vice-like grip in hopelessly static positions along the length of the Western Front. But now the troops were out of the trenches. Now there could be a war of manoeuvre and movement. Now tactics would have a chance. It was as if the brick wall against which both sides had been banging their heads in fruitless endeavour had suddenly crumbled. The Allies were being pushed back, but they were being pushed into a position from which they would be able to strike out. But as the Germans continued to thrust against the British and French, as the losses mounted, as the enemy advanced, only the most sanguine of temperaments looked on the situation as the beginning of a victorious end.

On 28 May, Dan Sargent, now an artillery lieutenant in the 1st US Division, found himself lying on a hillock overlooking the village of Cantigny a 'golf ball's drive away', the furthest point of the salient the Germans had pushed into the Somme front. It was a red-letter day for the Doughboys, because the Americans were about to go into their first wholly independent action. In order to straighten the line and improve their position the 28th Infantry was to attack the village, and Sargent's job was to observe the action and report back by field telephone to the French gun batteries in support of the attack. It was a terrifying, an exhilarating but, as things turned out, a pointless exercise. Although Sargent lay there all day fascinated by his bird's-eye view of the battle – watching the Yanks advance, wincing under the bombardment of the German counter-attack, sweating with relief as the Doughboys held on – the field telephone remained puzzlingly silent. As the afternoon drew on he wondered if the French artillery had forgotten his existence. The fact was that although the French guns had stayed long enough to support the first wave of troops as they advanced into the village, they had long ago pulled out and even now were travelling towards the east where, two hundred miles away, the Germans had attacked on the Chemin des Dames – and had broken through.

It looked like another disaster. The Front was held by a mixed bag of troops, for it had been a quiet sector. There were fresh but inexperienced American troops intermingled with exhausted French battalions and no-less-weary British divisions, which ironically had been sent to that front for a 'rest' after the hard fighting to the north. For Bill Lockey it was third time unlucky. In March he had survived the first five days as the army fell back on the Somme; in April he had come through unscathed at Villers Bretonneux, when the Germans made their last-gasp attempt to reach Amiens. Now, fighting from shellholes well behind the line they had been holding just a few days before, he was wounded in the right thigh by machine-gun fire. And the Germans were advancing so quickly that, speedily as Lockey was carried back to the rear, the sound of close-quarter firing followed him all the way.

Private
W. Lockey,
1st Battalion
(Sherwood
Foresters),
Notts &
Derbyshire
Regiment

The enemy must have advanced around the right flanks of the wood where I was wounded, because I could hear the rattle of the machine-guns and the *zip zip zip* of the bullets as they passed over me lying there, on top of the limber. The drivers, crouching low on the backs of the horses, whipped them into a gallop until they reached the outskirts of a village. Here the wounded were handed over to some men of the RAMC, who bore us off to the advanced dressing-station, No. 25 Field Hospital.

The doctors and staff were having a busy time of it, and we lay there waiting our turn to be attended to. The doctor took the bullet from my thigh and handed it to me. Then I was given a drink of hot tea, and another chap and I were placed on stretchers and carried into an empty ward. Here we were left for what seemed like hours, and all the while the din of the battle crept nearer and nearer and we got it into our heads that they must have forgotten all about us. At last some RAMC men came rushing into the ward and bore us off into a waiting ambulance. Shells seemed to be falling all around and we expected to be blown into eternity at any moment, but our luck held good and eventually we reached No. 37 Casualty Clearing Station. Here we were attended to once more. The place seemed to be filled to overflowing with wounded. After a while we were put into a marquee and were informed that the hospital was expecting to be evacuated the same night. In a short time I was fast asleep.

When I woke up it was next morning. I opened my eyes and the fellow on the next bed was propped up on his elbow, looking at me. 'Hi, mate', he said. 'Jerry's here'.

Although three train-loads of wounded had been evacuated from No. 37 earlier in the day, the late arrivals were unlucky. So many casualty clearing stations and hospitals were overrun that 45,000 beds were lost and the wounded who could not be got away in time, like the doctors and nurses who had volunteered to stay with them, were now prisoners of war. Moreover, vast dumps of supplies and large quantities of medical equipment had fallen into enemy hands. After its first exhilarating rush deep through the Allied line, the Germans' advance was halted and a new line was formed, but there was now hardly a hospital, hardly a doctor, hardly a nurse, hardly a dressing or a bandage to supply the needs of the casualties among the troops struggling to hold the Germans at bay.

Had this not been the case, Mary Ludlum would never have got anywhere near the Front. It was only by a lucky chance that she was in France at all. She was not a nurse, nor was her friend Carolyn Clarke, and the American Red Cross did not look kindly on untrained helpers. But by judicious string-pulling both girls had managed to get to France to work with the Children's Branch of the Red Cross, and for the past months they had been working in Evian-les-Bains and Marseilles looking after French refugee children. But now that the Germans were at Château Thierry, American troops were being sent into the line. Emergency hospitals were needed, and needed quickly, and until they got there the wounded would have to be carried fifty jolting miles to Paris.

It was four years and all but two months since Spink and Mary Ludlum had been tramping the streets of Paris, trying to track down the permits, visas and tickets they required for their journey back to neutral America. Now Mary was only too happy to be back again and to feel that like Robert and Spink, who were already in khaki and in France, she would soon be playing a real part in the war. At ten o'clock on 4

June the hastily-mustered party of eleven girls reported at Red Cross headquarters, and outside in the Place de la Concorde, lorries loaded with medical equipment waited to take them to the Front. The girls were warned in no uncertain terms that they would be going into danger, and the point was punched home when they were issued with gas-masks and shown how to use them. Eight of the party were trained nurses, and three were Red Cross Aides who had come to France under the wing of Miss Ashe of the Children's Branch. She was responsible for their welfare and as the gas-mask drill proceeded she paled visibly, and obviously began to have second thoughts. At the first opportunity she drew her three charges aside and in a voice tremulous with apprehension, 'asked us if our parents would blame her if we should get killed'. 'Nothing of the sort', they reassured her and, terrified that permission to go to the Front would be revoked, Mary Ludlum looked Miss Ashe straight in the eye and unblushingly assured her that, for her part, her mother would be 'pleasantly surprised if she ever saw her daughter again'. The unfortunate Miss Ashe hesitated and succumbed. The baggage was taken downstairs, and the girls climbed aboard the ambulance drawn up in front of the lorries. As the convoy moved off, as if to confirm the worst fears of their uneasy guardian tearfully waving from a window, a shell from a long-range German gun exploded with a loud report in the Tuileries Gardens across the way.

Carolyn Clarke, American Red Cross Aide, American Red Cross Hospital No. 107

We rolled along over the road, followed by the dusty *camions*, and were soon all dusty ourselves. By and by we came to a town where there were soldiers, American soldiers, and then we saw more and more. It was a great sight for us, as most of us had been working for months among the French refugees, and while we loved our work we had a desire way down in our hearts to be with and work for our very own soldiers. The soldiers certainly were glad to see us. They would turn to look at the ambulance and when they saw American women going up between their rest-camps and the Front, such smiles as lighted their faces and such cheers as they gave we never forgot.

The final destination was an old château at Jouy-sur-Morin. Until a few days ago it had been far enough behind the line for use as a convalescent home, where French soldiers could recover far away from the sound of the guns. Now, it was just over twenty kilometres from Château Thierry at the tip of the German advance, where in a few hours' time the 2nd US Division would be pushed into the line alongside the French to try to push them back. There was little enough time to get the hospital into order, to scrub and clean, to unpack supplies, to set up an operating room, to beat and air mattresses and make up beds. Nurses and aides tackled the job together and worked like demons, while corps men cleaned out a water tank, got the pump going in the yard and uncomplainingly mended the main telephone line to the Front, which had been inadvertently severed by two nurses heaving a heavy mattress over a windowsill. Within thirty-six hours of the start of the attack, Temporary Hospital No. 23 was ready to receive its first convoy, and the staff was only slightly disconcerted to find that it consisted of one solitary patient.

Sergeant Rogers of the 2nd US Division had never before attracted so much attention. The entire personnel of the hospital, including the scrubbed-up surgeon and Theatre Sister, came out on the terrace to welcome him. He was anaesthetized almost before he had time to register amazement and whipped into the operating theatre. Then he had the shrapnel removed from his hand, was tenderly tucked up in the hospital's most comfortable bed, and awoke to find himself surrounded by a bevy of excited nurses, all anxious to supply his slightest need. Sergeant Rogers thoroughly enjoyed the fuss. It was a luxury to be the only patient, but fresh from the struggle at the Front he stated with gloomy certainty that there were 'plenty more coming'. He was quite right.

Soon the wards in the house itself were so full of wounded that first one, then another and ultimately twenty French Bessoneau tents had to be put up in the grounds to take the overflow. In the elegant old salon, where the tapestried walls had been hung with sheets of white oilcloth to make a sterile operating room, the lights burned day and night as surgeons and theatre nurses worked in shifts. The aides and ward nurses were rushed off their feet receiving new patients, washing and settling them, wheeling them to the X-ray room and sparing time to reassure the nervous as they awaited their turn in the theatre.

> The boys came in ambulances and had a hard ride. When they were lifted out they would smile at us, with their eyes only if they were very weak. Occasionally one would say: 'Gee, what a ride,' but usually it was 'Hello' or 'What part of the States are you from?' or 'It's six months since I've seen an honest-to-God American girl.'
>
> When we had a rush of patients they would often have to wait a long time, and we would give them cigarettes and chewing gum and try to fix them up comfortably on their stretchers. There was no grumbling over the long waits. Often when it came to a man's turn he would say: 'Take the other feller first, he's hurt worse than me.' In the operating room they would take ether almost as if they liked it, and some really were 'glad of a chance to go to sleep'.

Carolyn Clarke, American Red Cross Aide, American Red Cross Hospital No. 107

It was small wonder that the Doughboys were exhausted. Fresh, vigorous, enthusiastic, as anxious to 'get at the Hun' as the volunteers of Kitchener's Army had been in the days that now seemed a lifetime ago, they were fighting with a reckless fervour that astonished the Germans. It also irritated the Germans to have to use up their reserves and resources in fierce defence of the land at the apex of their advance when they would rather have employed them to push out to the west, where Ludendorff was anxious to secure his recent capture of the railway line from the Aisne valley to the Vesle, which was still perilously within reach of the Allies' guns. The professional soldier in Ludendorff respected the bravery of his new adversaries and their refusal to accept defeat; but the marines and soldiers of the 2nd US Division did not see their achievement as defeat. They fought the Germans through and out of Château Thierry, into the bloody wood of Belleau, and in two weeks of stubborn, costly battering against the experienced infantry of the 7th German Army they pushed them out of it and triumphantly established a line on the other side. The Americans were elated by their gain; Ludendorff, though recognizing that they had released wearier but more wily and experienced French and British troops to man the quieter sectors, was not much disturbed by the loss of a comparatively small patch of ground. The Americans, he noted, had 'bravely attacked our thinly-held fronts; but they were unskilfully led, attacked in dense masses. . . . Our losses compared with those of the enemy . . . were very slight.'*

It was true that the casualty rate had been staggering among the inexperienced troops, intent on reaching 'Heaven, Hell or Hoboken by Christmas'. In the heat of the battle, in the fever of determination to drive the Germans back, they didn't much care which.

No. 99414 Sergeant Roger Knowles was, as his serial number implied, one of General Pershing's 'First Hundred Thousand' and a member of the 42nd US Division. They called it the Rainbow Division, because its members came from State Militia Corps all over the United States and the various units when they were plotted on a map sketched an arch across America. The Rainbow Boys had arrived in October, and by the time the Germans began the attacks of their spring campaign they had been long enough in action with the French army to consider themselves veterans.

Sergeant Roger Knowles, Stokes Mortar Section, 168th Infantry, 42nd US Division

We made plenty of mistakes at the beginning. Our artillery brigade went straight away for training as soon as we landed, and when they joined up with the outfit in February they were fresh out of artillery school and full of the dandy ideas they'd picked up. We had to take over the French gun batteries just where they stood, and it was all desolate there with miles of mud and no cover. When these artillery fellows saw the batteries they said, 'This is terrible. There's no camouflage on these guns, no nothing. We've got to get camouflage so the Boche won't spot them.' There were no trees anywhere around, so they got these trucks and they went back miles until they came to undevastated country. They started chopping branches off the trees, loaded up the truck and went back and camouflaged these

* My War Memories, Volume II, 1914–1918.

batteries all nice, just the way they'd been told to do it on the artillery course. Well, a tree grows in Brooklyn – but not *that* fast! The Boche had spotter planes over all the time, and within twelve hours they had their guns registered on these batteries and every single one was knocked out.

We learned after that. You learn to keep your head down, keep out of trouble. You don't want any casualties. Nobody ever won a war with a bunch of dead heroes.

With casualties, for whatever the reason, out of proportion to the value of their heroic gains and their valiant defence of positions held literally to the last man, it was fortunate that more troops were on the way, that acres of hutted barracks were springing up in a dozen different places to serve as American hospitals, and that contingents of nurses were crossing the Atlantic to staff them.

Private Stewart Emmery, two days out to sea on the SS *Baltic* was moved by the excitement of it all to compose an appropriate ditty:

Goodbye, goodbye, goodbye,
The decks are deep with men.
We're going out to God knows what,
We'll be back God knows when.
Old friends are at our sides,
Old songs drift out to sea,
Oh, it is good to go to war
In such a company.
The sun is on the waves
That race to meet the sky,
Where strange, new shores reach out to us –
Goodbye, goodbye, goodbye.

The decks were 'deep with men' and with girls as well. Jane Baudin was one of a group of a hundred nurses on board and didn't find it quite so 'good to go to war' in an overcrowded troopship, even though the nurses had quarters of their own.

I started out as a Red Cross nurse, and then when we got to New York we were transferred to the Army Corps because of the submarines. They put us under the army for protection so that we would be able to go across in a convoy. Our unit consisted of doctors and nurses from the Mayo Clinic in Rochester, from the University of Minnesota and from the Swedish Hospital in Minneapolis. Dr Mayo was to be head of the unit, but he was stopped in New York and sent back because of the reconstruction work and surgery that would be needed on soldiers as they came back. So Colonel Law took his place. He had been the head surgical man in my hospital, so I knew him pretty well.

Jane Baudin, US Army Nurse, Base Hospital No. 26, Allerey

We were nineteen days crossing the Atlantic, zig-zagging all the way in rough weather, all crowded together with very little in the way of comfort. All we had was a cot to sleep on and our trunk in the corner – no closets and not nearly enough washing facilities for such a number of us to be comfortable. We landed at Le Havre and then we were sent to a transit hospital while we waited to be sent to our own Base Hospital No. 26, which was just about to open. There we were, all grubby and travel-worn, and here was running water. Well, the first thing we wanted to do was wash our hair – we all had long hair and we hadn't been able to wash it on the ship. The whole bunch of us washed our hair and we were sitting out on the edge of a porch, letting the wind blow through it to dry it when this head nurse came out and yelled at us, 'Get in out of this yard. What do you think you're trying to do to the poor men in this army? Drive them crazy?' Well, we were astonished. In the first place we hadn't realized we were in sight of the wards, and in the second place we hadn't thought that hair was physical, not to the extent to rouse wounded men anyway! She was an old bat! We were glad to get out of there and on to our own hospital.

We got there just before 4 July, which was a French National holiday. As we were just opening up, no patients yet, they decided that the unit would give a party for the local French people, just for goodwill. There was a big banquet and we nurses waited on the tables.

And just as they had done a year before, thankful then for America's entry into the war and grateful now for the spirit the Doughboys were showing in the fighting, the French pulled out all the stops to honour the Americans.

Dr Harvey
Cushing,
US Army
Surgeon

4 July 1918 Paris . . . La Fête de l' indépendence, and they were actually celebrating it in England! Here it has absorbed everything. Even Bastille Day has been fused with this our own national festival. The city began to be decked out yesterday with intertwined American and French flags, and Old Glory floats on the very tip of the Eiffel Tower. A beautiful day – everyone much cheered by the fighting qualities shown by our 2nd Division terminating in their recent attack at Vaux.

Trim in new khaki, the new style 'battle caps' perched jauntily on their heads, eyes right as they passed the flag-decked saluting base and the equestrian statue of George Washington, they marched down the Avenue du Trocadéro – which, as the ultimate compliment, was from that day on to be renamed the Avenue du Président-Wilson. A contingent of US nurses followed behind, and beyond them came the French, 'waves of poilus – glorious in their *horizon bleu*'.

The crowd cheered with delight. '*Vive la France! Vive l'Amérique!! Vive Prezydonc Veelsong!!!*' The widely publicized renaming of a street in honour of 'Prezydonc Veelsong' was a happy thought, and it caused the *Maire* of Neuf-Château a certain degree of annoyance that he had not thought of paying a similar compliment to the Americans who had set up their Army Medical HQ in his town. The matter was rectified ten days later on Bastille Day, 14 July, although as Harvey Cushing noted the following morning, 'Yesterday's atmosphere of festivities was abruptly checked this morning by the news that another great German attack had been launched – from Château Thierry to the Argonne – an 80km front.' It had not been expected that the Germans would hold off forever, but Foch had hoped to get in first with a counter-offensive of his own.

After the rush of the weeks before, most of the wounded had been transferred to base hospitals. Hospitals at the Front had been cleared out ready to receive the casualties of the battle, and at Jouy-sur-Morin, Temporary Hospital No. 23 had earned promotion to the status of US Red Cross Hospital No. 107. In contrast to 4 July when they had organized a special dinner for the wounded (chicken, vegetables and doughnuts, each tray decorated with French and American flags) Bastille Day was quiet. In a triple Bessonneau-tent ward (which normally held seventy-five) Red Cross Aide Mary Ludlum was left in charge of one solitary patient, and she was giving him as much attention as had been lavished on the fortunate Sergeant Rogers five weeks earlier. An American officer ducked through the entrance of the tent and said, 'Hi, there!' Mary had no idea that Spink was in the area, no idea that he would be taking part in the coming battle. They were able to spend two hours together, walking in the rose garden, sitting on the old stone benches, talking until they were hoarse.

Later that evening, Mary and 'Caddy' Clarke went early to the room they shared together. Tomorrow would be a busy day. They didn't speak much as they prepared for bed by the light of the star shells in the distance. Mary worried about Spink. Caddy's brother had been killed with the 1st US Division at Cantigny two months before.

The Germans attacked in the small hours of the morning

We were wakened early by the sound of the guns and by the convoys arriving not long after. When we went on duty, every ward in the house and every tent was crammed full of wounded. We were stepping over stretchers on the lawn. We didn't have time to think any more, and worked all day without stopping. We were still working late at night when a German plane came over and the bombs began to fall. They just narrowly missed the tent we were in, but two others were destroyed. Three of the boys were killed. Eight were wounded and so was Miss Jeffries, who was on duty in one of the bombed tents. It was dawn before the mess was sorted out and all

Mary Ludlum, American Red Cross Aide, American Red Cross Hospital No. 107

the new patients taken care of. We went to bed to snatch a couple of hours' sleep and then went straight back on duty.

Carolyn Clarke, American Red Cross Aide, American Red Cross Hospital No. 107

German planes came over again the next night, but they dropped no bombs. Again we worked all day and into the night, and that second night after the bombing we had a thunderstorm, a regular New England one. We had no lights, only candles in the wards, and the doctors who had been operating steadily for twenty-four, thirty-six or forty-eight hours did dressings until midnight by the flashes of the storm. You might think that overwrought nerves and painful wounds would cause cross words and complaining, but not a bit of it; there were only cheering words, smiles and jokes. We had two large French windows without a pane of glass in either and blankets over them to keep in the little candlelight. All of a sudden the wind blew the blankets straight into the room, blew out the candles, and the rain poured in on our defenceless patients. The orderly managed to fasten down one blanket but the other would not stay. He and I just stood and held it, keeping out wind and rain, the room and its rows of wounded lit up by vivid lightning flashes. There was a sort of glory in it, as if we were stronger than the elements.

After the heat of the summer's day the thunderstorm that broke above Jouy-sur-Morin swept across the whole of northern France, putting a temporary stop to the battle. On either side of the line, lorries sank deep into ruts on the flooded roads that led to the Front. In Paris, where nerves were strained by the unremitting, haphazard bombardment of the giant German guns and the uneasy knowledge that the Germans were too close for comfort to the gates of the city, people started and trembled as the first thunderclaps boomed above the eastern *arrondissements*. Less than fifty miles away, sheets of torrential rain were turning fields into lakes, lashing gun-crews into the shelter of tarpaulin dugouts that were already awash. But there was no shelter of any kind at the Front, where the Germans and Allied armies faced each other in shallow, hastily-dug trenches where the water rose so relentlessly that some were soon knee-deep. In English, French and German, in the accents of Stuttgart and Sydney, of Munich and Marseilles, of Cologne, Kirriemuir, Berlin and the Bronx, the soldiers cursed, shivered and took chill. Throughout the night from Argonne to the east, the storm rolled across the face of France until it reached the Channel shoreline in the west.

Kitty Kenyon, VAD, No. 4 General Hospital, Camiers (her diary)

The lightning lit up the sky at intervals all night, and then at 4 am, as dawn was breaking (wonderful tawny golden sky with lighted clouds behind the hills), the storm broke. A flash of lightning and a growl of thunder and then it began in earnest. Flaring blue and blazing white – lighting up the cement factory chimneys as if by an acetylene flare. It was wonderful and rather terrifying. I watched from the door for a bit with Toovey, the VAD in the next ward, and saw one blaze of forked lightning rip the sky down to the ground straight ahead – we expected the chimney to go any minute. Then I went round shutting the ward windows. One minute the hut was in semi-darkness, the next in blazing light as if there were a fire raging somewhere. The rain came down in cascades (and we were thankful), and the whole thing lasted nearly an hour. As I was closing the last window the man in the bed beneath it said, 'It's better than an air raid, Sister.'

There had been all too many air raids in the last few weeks as the Germans moved their airfields forward to keep pace with their advance, and at the base they were almost a nightly occurrence. Some of the bombs fell on the hospitals, and anger predictably simmered among the Allies. There was a brisk trade in photographs of the tragic debris of bombed hospital wards – tangles of splintered planks, torn mattresses, twisted iron bedsteads. GERMAN SAVAGERY AT ITS WORST shrieked the popular newspapers in indignant outsize print. It was the last straw. The air raids on the British bases in France fanned the flames of righteous wrath which were burning up the last reserves of fair-mindedness in a country renowned for its sense of 'fair play' and objective judgement.

If it was a case of 'backs to the wall' at the Front, it was 'backs to the wall' at home too. 1918 had seen belts being tightened all round; coal was scarce and expensive, and food was rationed. Under a new Act of Parliament, men could now be conscripted up to the age of fifty-one. The cost of living soared and wage disputes erupted in a rash of discontented strikes and industrial unrest among the war-weary workers, who were having to work harder and longer hours now that their ranks had been combed through in a last effort to sweep into the Army every man who could possibly be spared from a workbench, a coal mine or a shipyard. It was all the fault of the war – and the war was the fault of the Germans.

In the summer of 1918, 'Hun baiting' became a national sport. Posters appeared on windows and walls – INTERN THE GERMANS – SIGN HERE NOW – THE MONSTER PETITION TO THE GOVERNMENT. It was organized from centres in London, Manchester, Leeds, Birmingham and Bristol, and a million people signed it in a frenzy of vindictiveness – whipped up by rallies, mass meetings and demonstrations. The targets were long-naturalized German residents, or *any* foreign resident at all who had a suspicious-sounding accent or a German-sounding name. There was a renewed witch-hunt on conscientious objectors and pacifists, and even the Government came in for open or implied criticism on the grounds of being too soft. People were tired, people were anxious, people were physically run-down and they were in no mood to be trifled with.

Public opinion was further enraged by the sinking of the hospital ship *Llandovery Castle*, and then less than six weeks later, at one-thirty in the morning of 3 August, the hospital ship *Warilda* was torpedoed en route from Le Havre to Southampton.

Sister
Jean Calder,
QAIMNS (R),
No. 2 General
Hospital, Quai
d'Escale, Le
Havre

She sailed the evening before, because now we were taking precautions and sending the ships across at night if we could. It had been a lovely, hot day and it was a warm evening, so some òf the boys were on the deck on their stretchers, well wrapped up in blankets. They'd gone off, all happy and excited, with their labels on their pyjamas, clutching these cotton drawstring bags we used to give them in hospital to keep their treasures and personal things in, and we just had time to strip the empty beds, for the night nurses to make up, before we went off duty. It was just coming up for dusk, but we could see them plainly lying there on the deck as we waved from the balcony, and they waved back and shouted – so happy to be going home.

The next morning I had breakfast in my billet and was walking along the quayside to the hospital when the station-master came rushing up and stopped me. He told me that the *Warilda* had been sunk and everyone had been lost. We all felt shocking about it, because we'd got to know the boys. To think that a thing like that should happen to them when they were so helpless – because they were mostly cot-cases. And knowing the men who were on the ship, waving them off just a few hours before, made it all a dreadful tragedy.

The situation was not quite so bad as the first rumours led the nurses to believe, but it was bad enough. 115 patients, a nursing Sister and an RAMC orderly went down with the *Warilda*. The rescued were taken to Southampton, where the badly wounded survivors were admitted to local hospitals. Later in the day, when they had been fed and cared for and kitted out with dry clothes from the Red Cross Depot, the walking wounded, the 'Boat Sitting' patients, were sent by hospital train to London. Claire Tisdall was on duty with the Ambulance Column when the train pulled into Paddington Station.

Claire Elise
Tisdall, VAD
Ambulance
Nurse, The
Ambulance
Column,
London
District

They were all thoroughly shocked and horrified. Not all of them had been in the water, but those that had were wearing all sorts of clothes which the Red Cross had given them from their comforts stores. Some had greatcoats, and some just had blankets around them over their pyjamas, with a khaki muffler and a balaclava helmet on top – because although it was summer, they were cold and terrified after having been in the water. But what made me really angry was that there were some Germans among them who'd been picked out of the water, and there *they* were, wearing these things too – things we'd knitted for our Tommies. I thought that I'd got over hating the Germans by then, but that made me furious. I remember them standing there, all huddled, and because I spoke German I understood what they were saying. 'It wasn't our U-boats,' talking in German, 'we would never do such a thing to the Red Cross.' They really believed it! And then they had the nerve to say, 'It must have been the Royal Navy.' Imagine! I couldn't bring myself to speak to them, but I told the other girls what they had said. 'Just imagine the nerve of them, to say that it wasn't them!' And to see them, huddled together with those khaki coats and things on! I was shocked. We were all shocked and angry.

But there was less anti-German feeling in France than there was in England. Nurses closer to the Front seldom saw newspapers, were less exposed to propaganda, and were too busy getting on with the job in hand to brood on the subject of 'Hun frightfulness', especially as the 'Huns' they saw in their hospitals were wounded in the same way, and victims of the same circumstances as their own wounded soldiers.

We had a wonderful ward of German prisoners and the girls loved to work there. This was towards the end of the war, and they were taking kids into the German army. Some of them said they were only fifteen years old. We had German prisoners as orderlies, and they took care of their own men and did every bit of the work. They scrubbed the floors so that you could hardly walk on them, and they were lovely to the nurses. When you passed them in the camp they'd stand right stiff and salute you. We were supposed to salute back, but we'd just smile. There was no feeling of enmity. Those young boys weren't our enemy. What did *they* know? They didn't know anything! They were just rosy-cheeked schoolboys.

Jane Baudin, US Army Nurse, US Base Hospital No. 26, Allerey

I had a German orderly on my ward at the Quai d'Escale. His name was Fritz Koch, but I never called him by his name. We always addressed the German orderlies as *Sanitäter*. He was a very good orderly and he did his work very well indeed, and was always there when you wanted him. I never got friendly with him, always treated him correctly, but it was very much the sort of relationship where the officer gives orders to the lower ranks. My ward was in what had been the old buffet of the station and there was a bar in it, all mahogany with brass rails and cupboards at the back, where we used to keep the surgical dressings. I went back years after the war, when it was a restaurant again, and I noticed that the bar wasn't half so clean and shining as it used to be when my German orderly cleaned it.

We never had anything but a formal relationship, but when our own army started advancing and I was ordered up north to a casualty

Sister Jean Calder, QAIMNS (R), No. 2 General Hospital, Quai d'Escale, Le Havre

clearing station, I was leaving the ward, going off duty on my very last day, when he came up to me and clicked his heels and handed me a letter. It was addressed to '*Schwester Calder. Hier.*' I couldn't read it because it was written in German script, but I kept it with my things and when a patient came into the CCS later who could read German I gave it to him and asked him to translate it for me. It was a very formal letter, there was nothing cheeky about it, but it was very admiring in its tone. You might almost have said that it was a love letter.

Like Bill Lockey, Harry Turner had been captured on 27 May when the Germans had struck out on the Chemin des Dames. Unlike Lockey, he had not been sent directly to Germany but into a prisoner-of-war camp behind the line and sent out on daily working parties to repair roads and re-lay railway tracks. The Germans were running short of manpower and they were running short of food. With poor rations (just slightly inferior to those of the German soldiers), heavy work and living in filthy lice-ridden conditions, many of the exhausted prisoners fell sick and had to be evacuated to Germany.

Private
H. Turner,
D Company,
50th Division,
Machine Gun
Corps

We travelled all day in a cattle train, and very late at night we stopped at Trier. There a German Medical Officer came alongside the truck and asked in English, 'Are there any prisoners who feel they cannot travel any further?' I got out with two Americans and two British soldiers and we were taken to a large nearby building. It looked like a factory from the outside but actually it was a former barracks, now being used as a hospital for prisoners of war. Here we were stripped of our clothing and put into bed, the first real bed I'd seen for many long weeks. Next morning we were taken on stretchers to a bath-room, but the water was only lukewarm. Our hair and bodies were alive with lice and more than a warm bath would be needed to get rid of that lot!

Later that morning a German Hospital Sister came to see us. She spoke no English but just looked down at each one of us, shook her head and said something about '*Krieg*'. It was the one German word we were familiar with. Sister was a lady of maybe sixty years of age, a dedicated nurse, and in the weeks that followed I got to know her well. We knew her as 'Schwester Kristina'. Nationality and war had no place in her thoughts and all she wanted to do was to get the men well, although she was greatly hampered by the shortage of food and of the facilities that you normally expect to find in a hospital.

In our ward there were many nationalities – French, Italian, Russian, Polish, American, as well as British – and all of us were in an emaciated condition and suffering from diarrhoea and dysentery. Each evening, before going off duty, Schwester would call at the ward with a big jug of water and ask, '*Wasser trinken?*' She was no linguist, but she had taken the trouble to learn the goodnight greeting of the different nationalities in her ward. As she left the room she would say, '*Bonsoir, Franzose – Buona sera, Italiano – Pokoynoy nochee, Russki – Goodnight, Englander.*' And to return the compliment, we would chorus back in German, '*Gute nacht, Schwester.*' When I left the hospital in Trier, I promised myself that when I got back home I would write to Schwester Kristina and thank her for all her kindness in getting me well again. With much regret, and some sadness, I confess that I never did.

Towards the end of the war I had charge of a ward of Germans, but they were nearly all kids. We had boys of fourteen crying for their mothers! The British army was very severe. They wouldn't allow the boys to write home and tell their mothers that they were sick; they wouldn't allow anything like that. So I got a list of their addresses and I wrote to all their mothers and let them know how they were going along, and if they were doing well or if they weren't. The letters went through Switzerland and when I came home from the war lots of the mothers wrote to me to say how grateful they were. After all, those mothers were just as upset about their kids as we were about ours. Some of the other British nurses said I was pro-German – I wasn't. I was pro-kids. I never hated the Germans. I just loved people – and especially poor sick kids.

Sister Elizabeth Nordsvan, Australian Army Nursing Service

4 August 1918 was the fourth anniversary of the war. It was about this time that Kathleen Rhodes was struck by the change of mood implied in a new version of a song which had long been familiar to the troops. A convalescent soldier on 'light duties' was singing it absently to himself as he polished a bedside locker.

The Bells of Hell go ting-a-ling-a-ling
For Jerry and for me . . .

It was the instinctive expression of a feeling that few of the infantry's rank-and-file could have put into words. A feeling that the war had taken on a monstrous character and volition of its own. That they were all being consumed by it. That everyone was in the same boat. And that nobody was winning.
But the tide had already turned.

Chapter Twenty

The Germans had withdrawn to the Vesle River, and American Red Cross Hospital No. 107 was preparing to move up from Jouy to Château-Thierry, to work with the evacuation hospitals receiving the wounded direct from the line. Even now they were sending up 'flying squads' of surgeon, nurse and anaesthetist to help with emergency operations in the field hospital, and on 6 August the Chief Nurse, Linda Meirs, drew Mary Ludlum aside. 'Now don't panic, Luddy,' she said, 'but I've just had word from our people at the field hospital that your brother's been through wounded.' It was hard not to panic when that was the extent of the news, but Miss Meirs was sympathetic. 'Look,' she said, 'I'm going to invent an errand. I'll say they want more supplies – they always do anyway – and I'll ask an officer to take them up in a *camion*, and you can go with him to assist him. When you get to the hospital, ask for his admission tag and get the straight facts.' There was no difficulty. The field hospital staff, thankful to see extra cases of dressings arriving, were too busy tending the men who lay bleeding and shocked on their stretchers to care about the irregularity of a Red Cross aide going through their paperwork. Mary scrambled through the duplicate tags of the morning's casualties and slumped with relief as she came to Spink's. *Gunshot Wound left shoulder – no foreign body – evacuated to Base Hospital No. 15, Chaumont.*

Back at Jouy a sympathetic Medical Officer put through a priority telephone call to Chaumont. The news was good and Mary scribbled a hasty cablegram to her parents in America: *Spink doing fine. Don't worry. Love, Mary.*

The cable reached the puzzled Ludlum family next day – before the official notification that Spink had been wounded. They inferred that Mary and Spink had met up with each other and assumed that '*doing fine*' meant that Spink was proving to be a successful warrior! It was kind of Mary, they thought, though perhaps unnecessarily extravagant, to take the trouble to inform them of this gratifying fact by expensive cablegram. It was not until the following day when a telephone call from the War Department in Washington regretted to inform them that Lieutenant Ludlum was seriously wounded on 6 August that they checked dates and gratefully reinterpreted Mary's cable.

That day, 8 August 1918, was the day that General Ludendorff would later refer to as 'the Black Day of the German army'.

The French and the British attacked together on a fifty-mile front from the River Oise in the south to the River Ancre on the old Somme front in the north. The Germans staggered and, taken completely by surprise, began to give way. They had not expected that the Allies could have recovered so quickly from their losses in the spring, and for once they had no idea that an offensive was in the offing. And for once too, the Allies had made their dispositions, filtered troops into the line, slid guns into position, poised reserves on strategic springboards, all in utter secrecy. Dawn broke. The battle started. The Allies pressed on, moving forward, gaining ground and – at last – fighting in the open.

Took in a convoy at 8.30. Eleven cases, six of whom are to go to theatre between now and morning. I was thrilled when I saw two khaki, mud-stained Aussies in shorts and without hats come in. It was like old times! They say we have made an advance on a huge length and that we've taken the enemy's big guns already, and goodness only knows how many prisoners.

Kitty Kenyon, VAD, No. 4 General Hospital, Camiers (her diary, 9 August, 3.30 am)

From the night of the 9th to yesterday evening the theatre has been going night and day, nearly continuously – all delayed primary sutures – the MOs *have* worked. We had convoy after convoy, mostly Australians. On the night of the 10th there was a raid, and through it the theatre was working and patients being brought back to the wards by steel-hatted stretcher-bearers. But there's no anxiety these days – how different from last year! Things are going splendidly. The men are all so pleased – but I suppose it must last through the winter.

12 August

In the light of the snail-pace battles of the last four years it was a reasonable supposition. But the weight of numbers had now shifted in favour of the Allies. Ludendorff's spring offensive had used up the last strength of the old German army, and the Germans were sick of the war. Morale was crumbling at its very core – in the homeland, where the Allied blockade, the breakdown of the distribution system of such food as there was in the national larder, had reduced the population to a level of subsistence beside which the British wartime rations looked like a Roman feast. In Britain people grumbled about the scarcity of food: in Germany they went hungry. The Germans had no tobacco, no paper, no leather, few textiles, few trains or other transport for civilian use – and there was raging inflation. Like the discontented British workers, the Germans came out on strike. But in Germany the strikes could not be explained away by war-weariness. They were far more widespread, far more crippling, far more serious in their political implications. What had begun as a murmur of revolution in January grew to a roar of grievance and, by the summer, even the throne of the Kaiser was shaking with its vibration. Too many young men had been swallowed up by the military machine; too many had died in the sodden wastes of Flanders, on the shattered downlands of the Somme, on the slopes in front of Verdun. The Germans no longer wanted victories. They wanted peace and food, and they wanted their boys home. The German people no longer stood behind the army, and home on leave from the Front, Herbert Sulzbach was shocked to realize it.

Leutnant Herbert Sulzbach, No. 2 Battery, Field Artillery Regiment No. 5, 18th German Army

Arrived at Frankfurt in the evening; this time, the reunion was more tender than ever, because my people can hardly believe being able to see me alive after these last few weeks. Lovely days of leave after that. One day I visit Frau Reinhardt, Professor Reinhardt's widow and Kurt's mother, and she gave me the last photo taken of Kurt; the next day I went to see his grave, where he lies next to his father, who was also killed in action. I visit old acquaintances, and they are all beset by this heavy care, this dreadful worry – 'Are we going to be all right?' Food is scarce, and the whole economy is slanted towards the war.

I had the depressing experience of meeting a soldier in the street who was very obvious about not saluting me. It really isn't my style to blow people up, but in this case I really lost my temper. If these stupid youths back at home make a show of letting discipline go to pieces, you have to do something about it! Whyever, if things work so well up at the Front, does a thing like this happen to you at home?

Going back in the train to Brussels, I have some conversation with a chief surgeon, who has a lot to say about the mess things are in at home ... morale is frightful. ... We must have made a lot of mistakes on the Home Front.

Low in spirits, Sulzbach returned to his battery, to face the French and Americans beyond the Vesle, and to receive

... grave and disagreeable news; the Front is being withdrawn in this sector. It will be the same here as in the case of the Siegfried withdrawal; it's the Marne down there, yes, the Marne, that's done this to us once again! It began down there with the loss of Château-Thierry, then it moved up to Fère-en-Tardenois, and now here. We feel terribly depressed and filled with pain at having to give up all that ground which was so dearly paid for.

Just as the arrival of the American troops in the field had boosted the morale of the British and French, it broke the morale of the Germans. Their newspapers played down the importance of the 'planned with-drawals' in the face of the Allied offensives, but it was plain to most people who took the trouble to read between the lines that an Allied victory was now a mathematical certainty.

At US Base Hospital No. 27 at Angers, the 'heroes of the Vesle' arrived long before the men who had been wounded at Château-Thierry and Belleau Wood were well enough to be moved on, and those of them who arrived in Nell Brink's ward considered themselves to be lucky. When she stood on her dignity and drew herself up to her full height, which was often, Miss Brink measured a full five feet from her diminutive shoes to the top of her auburn head, and she was not prepared to stand any nonsense from doctors, from patients, or even from Uncle Sam himself.

We got Over There, and, as Uncle Sam do, Uncle Sam sends us awful, horrible-looking uniforms made of grey crêpe, like in Florence Nightingale's day. And he sent us those aprons, like the butchers used to wear, with a string around their back and this white bib thing in front. Well, when I saw that I said, 'I am *not* wearing that kind of uniform for my patients. If I'm over here, if Uncle Sam thought enough of me to *send* me over here, I want to look the best I can every day, for my own patients. I want to look clean. I want to smell good. I want to look right and I want to *be* good'. I had six brand-new white uniforms made by my mother. And she also made me the nicest-looking white aprons! They were smart – in fact they were so smart-looking that the nurses going out on detached service would say, 'Nell, can I borrow a couple of your good-looking aprons?' They were cute. They had straps over the shoulders, a cute little small bib and a pretty skirt line, and when I'd first go on duty in the morning I'd wear one over my white dress, and then I'd take it off when dressings were done. So I never did wear the grey uniform.

Nell Brink, US Base Hospital No. 27 (University of Pittsburgh), Angers

There was always a good atmosphere in my ward and a lot of kidding. They always had jokes and they hadn't much sympathy for each other except when dressings were being done, big wounds and big dressings. Even then, sometimes, they were almost callous with each other. I remember one young boy with a bad gas burn. He was burned from his waist right up to his neck, and as I was doing his dressing he was saying, 'Ouch, ouch, ouch!' And some fellow across the room there said, 'What's the matter, Red? Is your silk underwear itching you?' And the boy bucked up then, you know, and never made another sound.

They didn't often cry out when they were getting the bad dressings done, but there was always a kind of atmosphere in the ward when they were finished. I used to take off my apron and say to them, 'This is the deadest ward I've ever been in! Let's sing, let's sing'. There was one little chap who had a wounded arm. He was in a baseball team and was really worried that he wouldn't be able to play baseball again, so I used to sit and bake his arm under a warm lamp and massage it for him, to get it in condition. And while I was doing that I would make them sing. 'One, two, three, four . . .' and they'd all join in singing the different parts. One day, out of the corner of my eye I saw the big door at the end of the ward open and our Chief Nurse came in with a party. Of course, if the Chief Nurse comes in, or an officer, you usually stand up – that's the routine. But we were all singing, and I never let on I saw them. They walked right through the ward and out the other door, and nobody ever said anything! And when the boys saw that I wasn't looking up and kept on singing, they just kept their eyes on me and went on singing too.

Lieutenant Ralph Robart, A Company, 104th US Infantry

Life seemed kind regardless of our wounds. We were happy with the let down, with clean beds and three meals a day. It was like going from Hell to Heaven. It was a swell hospital and wonderful facilities and all the nurses were angels, so far as we were concerned. You'd hardly know they were all tough wounds. Every day a few would be taken out on stretchers to the operating room. As they were being moved out, the rest would always whistle a funeral march.

The surgeon came round for dressings every morning and I never heard any squawking. I remember a fellow named Red Patten who'd been a football player at Aubern in Alabama. He was in the next bed to mine with a shrapnel wound and he was there before me. When I first got into hospital and had to sit up in bed to have my back dressed – there was a gash across my spine a foot wide – I remember his Southern drawl. He said, 'Lord, I haven't any right to be in this hospital at all, compared to you, boy'.

It seems funny to think back on it how bashful everybody was coming out of a man's war into a ward with girl nurses. They were from No. 27 Base Hospital, Pittsburgh. They were wonderful and they had to work terribly hard. Nell Brink was the head nurse of the ward, and she was always laughing and singing.

It was difficult to pass the time. Most of the fellows played Solitaire a lot, because we couldn't get our beds close enough to play poker together. But our principal amusement was a phonograph. It had two records, both of them Hawaiian songs, and we played them over and over.

It was Nell Brink's sister (who worked in the music business back home in the States) who had sent not one but two phonographs to entertain the wounded, and she sent parcels of new records as soon as they were released. To the relief of nurses and patients alike, a new batch arrived in mid August, long after the Hawaiian songs had begun to pall. It contained records of several of the latest hit songs from Tin Pan Alley, and among them was one which the soldiers felt was particularly appropriate to their present situation. The imagination of America had been caught by the stories of the Doughboy's heroic struggles in France, by the horror of the high casualty figures, by the pathos of the thousands of men lying wounded in their hospitals, and by the romantic image of the American girls who had travelled across the Atlantic to nurse them. The song seemed to sum it all up and, overnight, it became a hit.

There's a Rose that grows in No Man's Land,
And it's wonderful to see.
Tho' it's sprayed with tears,
It will live for years
In my garden of memory.
It's the one red rose
The soldier knows,
It's the work of the Master's Hand;
In the War's great curse, stands the Red Cross Nurse,
She's the Rose of No Man's Land.

Soon everyone was singing it. The tune verged on the lugubrious, the words carried sentimentality to a point that stopped just short of being maudlin, but it struck a note of truth. No concert programme was complete without a feeling rendering of 'The Rose of No Man's Land', sung by a plaintive tenor with one eye fixed meaningfully on a row of embarrassed nurses. And the 'Roses of No Man's Land', forgetful of their aching feet, their broken fingernails, their weary muscles and their red, chapped hands, exchanged deprecating giggles and were secretly flattered and delighted.

But as August drew on towards September, fewer and fewer nurses had the time or the energy to attend many concerts. The news was splendid. The wounded, though disturbingly numerous, were cheerful and talked happily of 'having Jerry on the run'. English newspapers were at a premium and, these days, the word 'battle' in their headlines provoked excitement rather than dread. But the hospitals were fighting a battle of their own – a new and tragic battle that began with shattering irony, just when it began to seem as if peace might at last be in sight.

The epidemic of influenza that had broken out in June and had seemed to be abating, now broke out in a new, virulent form in Britain, Germany and the United States, and in the ranks of all the armies on all the rapidly shifting fronts of the war.

As soon as it was realized that we were in for an epidemic, our own CCS, which had remained packed up for about six weeks, was opened as an influenza hospital and we rejoined it. We took over the buildings and huts which had been vacated by No. 7 General Hospital when the enemy was advancing a few months previously. The building was known as Mallasis, formerly a Christian Brothers' School about half a mile from St Omer. In addition to the main building and the Nissen huts, we erected sufficient marquees to bring our accommodation up to about 2,000. We had between thirty and forty nurses, and forty medical officers. Soon we were taking in between five and six hundred patients a day. The very bad and the very slight cases we kept, the remainder were evacuated to the base. During this rush of work we were interested to read in the English

Captain J. Cook, RAMC, Medical Officer, No. 18 Casualty Clearing Station papers an official statement to the effect that, '*Up to the present the epidemic of influenza has not affected the British troops in France.*'

The newspapers were too busy composing glowing, victorious headlines to concern themselves much with lesser stories.

ATTACK ON THE ANCRE

———

THREE MILE ADVANCE

———

MANGIN OUTFLANKS NOYON

The Times,
22 August 1918

Kitty Kenyon,
VAD, No. 4
General
Hospital,
Camiers
(her diary)

The night orderly has just been in to say that 230 stretchers are coming in and I'll have all the surgicals; the others are this new flu which is knocking everyone everywhere over like ninepins. Sergeant Franklin died last night, with horrible bronchial pneumonia after the Spanish flu that so many are dying of. They thought he would die the night before. Last night I went to the front door of the ward to look at the night and saw the stretcher-bearers come round the corner by the theatre, and I knew it must have been Franklin being carried down the road. He has been one of our orderlies for so long that it must have been hateful knowing all the last details and knowing that he would be carried out on a stretcher under a Union Jack, like so many men that he had accompanied himself. He was one of the nicest of our NCOs. The day before he was taken ill he was talking to Sister Griffiths and me about it and laughing because the men were all asking, would it send them to Blighty?

Margaret Ellis,
Special
Military
Probationer,
No. 26
General
Hospital,
Etaples

It was a terrible epidemic. There was so little that we could do for them. The only treatment apparently was to keep an even temperature in the ward, that was the main thing we were told. We just had to give them fluids and keep walking up and down seeing if anybody wanted anything. They were all incontinent so you were continually changing beds and washing. I remember doing one boy from head to foot, and ten minutes later I had to start doing it all over again.

BIG AMERICAN OFFENSIVE

———

ST MIHIEL WEDGE ATTACKED

———

ADVANCE OF FIVE MILES   *The Times,*
13 September 1918

Peggy Marten,
VAD, No. 55

The men came in enormous convoys, some of them semi-conscious. We couldn't do much for them. We gave some of them steam inhalations, but mostly it was a case of keeping them warm, keeping them nourished, hoping that they wouldn't get pneumonia. But many of them did.

General Hospital, Wimereux

I remember one man. I just happened to peep over the screen and an orderly was starting to wash him. The man's face was dark blue, so I told the orderly to stop, and I went and reported it to Sister. He died in the early evening, and then in the morning, when we came on duty, one of the medical staff came to Sister and said that he wanted her to go down and see this body. It had already started to decompose. They called it influenza but it seemed to us to be some frightful plague. It was very, very serious and it was as hard as any push that we'd had from the fighting, and the proportion of deaths was higher – much higher – than we'd had from wounds at any time. It was very heavy work and very depressing. It was so near the end. They'd gone through all that frightful thing, and then they couldn't go home.

Special Order Of The Day
By Field-Marshal Sir Douglas Haig

. . . Already we have pressed beyond our old battle-lines of 1917 and have made a wide breach in the enemy's strongest defences. In this glorious accomplishment all ranks of all arms and services of the British armies in France have borne their part in the most worthy and honourable manner. The capture of 75,000 prisoners and 750 guns in the course of four weeks' fighting speaks for the magnitude of your effort and the magnificence of your achievement. . . . We have passed through many dark days together. Please God these will never return. The enemy has now spent his effort, and I rely confidently upon each one of you to turn to full advantage the opportunity which your skill, courage, and resolution have created.

I was working in the casualty clearing station, doing the usual work. There wasn't much surgery to do. I shall never forget the sight of the mortuary tents. There were rows of corpses, absolutely *rows* of them, hundreds of them, dying from something quite different. It was a ghastly sight, to see them lying there dead of something I didn't have the treatment for.

Captain Geoffrey Keynes, RAMC, No. 55 Casualty Clearing Station, Bohain

More people died in the world epidemic than died in the entire war. It was a special form of virus. We've never had the same kind of infection again, which is fortunate, because ordinary antibiotics don't work for the influenza virus. It's very difficult to treat these cases and, even today, I doubt whether we could.

More and more of the wounded were going down with it all the time, and a lot of them were dying. I had no deaths in my ward, but the

Sister Henrietta Beanland,

St Luke's War
Hospital,
Bradford

men were very ill with severe headaches and high temperatures and
very often they were delirious. There was not much you could do. It
was all a matter of nursing, giving them good food, although a lot of
them couldn't take food. I remember I used to make Bovril with milk
– anything just to get some nourishment into them. Building them up
all the time and sponging them down, because they used to perspire
terribly with those high temperatures.

Sister
Grace Buffard,
TFNS, No. 19
Casualty
Clearing
Station,
Caudry

Even after four years of nursing men with awful wounds, the
influenza epidemic seemed to be the worst thing of all. They were
dying like flies. I was the senior Sister, and the surgeon and I spent
our whole time going round the casualty clearing station giving the
men blood transfusions. We did it for days at a time and it was the
only thing we could do to help them, to keep them alive if possible
until they got over the main symptoms.

A TURKISH DEBACLE

—

OUR CAVALRY IN NAZARETH

—

The Times,
23 September 1918

Alison Strathy,
American Red
Cross Aide,
French Field
Hospital
(her diary)

I have had to learn how to do cupping with so many French soldiers
ill during the flu epidemic, and it's certainly very effective for bad
congestion. A heavy special glass cup is used, then cotton on a rod
is dipped in alcohol and set on fire – this is popped into the cup
and out, and then the cup is immediately pressed on the back of
the thorax and remains there by suction. If the congestion is very
severe, the doctor first makes a cross-cut on the surface of the skin
and the suction draws a little blood. White skin is less difficult,
as the black skins of the Senegalese soldiers apparently contain
more oil.

Patients have been pouring in with *grippe*. I can't keep up with this
– recently we lost seven or eight with it, and fifty more patients have
arrived – French and Senegalese and some Americans. I have
twenty-six *grands malades* in one ward and fourteen in another. The
doctor says there should be one nurse to every five men! Work is
desperate. A twelve-hour day with twenty minutes for lunch. . . . I
think twenty-two patients have died now.

BATTLE FOR CAMBRAI

—

HINDENBURG LINE BREACHED

—

SERBIAN GAINS

—

BULGARIA BEGS AN ARMISTICE   *The Times,*
28 September 1918

We sailed for Europe on 29 September 1918. In the morning I was
really sick and had a very bad sore throat. But I got on the boat and
next morning they sent me to the infirmary. I was there ten days with
very little care because there was only one nurse for about twenty
girls, all with influenza. You had terrific pain all over your body,
especially in your back and your head, and you just felt as if your
head was going to fall off. The odour was terrible in that ship's
infirmary – I never smelt anything like it before or since. It was awful,
because there was poison in this virus.

    There was no one to spare to look after us, because it was a
troopship and hundreds of the troops went down with it as well.
Eighty died. They didn't bury them at sea. They wanted to take them
to Brest and bury them in military graves, but we were on the
southern route and it was very hot. They had to take all the food out
of the refrigerator and put bodies in.

Mary Dobson, US Army Nurse, US Base Hospital No. 63, Savenay

GERMAN PLEA FOR AN ARMISTICE
—
NOTE TO PRESIDENT WILSON
—
The Times,
7 October 1918

The tragic thing was the Americans. Our hospital overlooked the
common, and the Americans came down there from their depot at
Winchester to camp overnight on it before they embarked for
France. It was terrible, because they went down with influenza in the
course of that one night, and they died like flies. There were some in
tents, but they were mostly in the open. They came to us wanting
brandy and things like that, but we couldn't give them any because
the little we had we needed for our own men. But I always felt that
that was rather dreadful. In the end women volunteered from Southampton – not trained people, just anybody at all who could go along
and help to cope. They just died there in hundreds.

Gladys Stanford, VAD, Highfield Hospital, Southampton

We were asked if anyone who had a few hours off duty could go and
help out with the Americans – just to give them coffee, tea, food,
anything like that. We had to take one man into the hospital because
he had the most fantastic temperature. He was put in a special ward
and they took tests and everything. He couldn't eat. We used to give
him drink in small quantities and another VAD and I used to wring
out sheets in cold water from a big bath at the side of the bed and
wrap him in them – and they were dry in no time. That went on for
about a week, and then he died.

Gwynnedd Lloyd, VAD, University War Hospital, Southampton

GERMANY'S PEACE OFFER SCORNED

———

FRANCE REMEMBERING HER BURNING TOWNS

———

The Times,
8 October 1918

SHARP STRUGGLE FOR ARGONNE HEIGHTS

———

AMERICANS SEIZE THREE HILLS

———

The Times,
9 October 1918

Dr Harvey
Cushing,
US Army
Surgeon
(his journal,
Tuesday, 15
October)

Neufchâteau:

A cold depressing day today. Bagley turns up, after some three weeks' working his way by 'channels' to these HQ from Southampton, where they landed. The usual story. This time Transport 56 – i.e., the *Olympic*. He was Ship's Medical Officer. There had been no *grippe* in the States, but nine cases developed on the boat, with one death from pneumonia. They were held in Southampton harbour twenty-four hours before disembarking, and 384 cases developed during this brief time – very severe – temperatures of 105° frequent in men at the very outset. People standing guard would fall in their tracks. They were sent to a rest-camp near Southampton and in a week 1,900 cases developed, with several hundred pneumonias and 119 deaths before he left. Of the 342 nurses who were left on shipboard after the troops disembarked, 134 developed influenza.

SURRENDER OF TURKEY

———

FRESH ADVANCE IN BELGIUM

———

AUSTRIAN ROUT

———

OVER 50,000 PRISONERS

The Times,
1 November 1918

WAAC Elsie
Broderick,
Women's
Auxiliary
Army Corps

I had joined the WAACs as soon as I was old enough. I was stationed in Calais working with the Army Service Corps, and we used to have dances with the troops. I was dancing one night with a very nice Australian boy called Eric Birchmore. Next morning I went down with flu and I heard that he'd got it too. I remember being carried out of the ambulance on the stretcher with my hat on my tummy and I felt it was just as if I was going to my own funeral. I must have had a very high temperature, because I don't really remember much about the first few days in hospital. What I do remember was hearing that Eric Birchmore had died. And then when I was sitting up and feeling better, I was very depressed, and so I asked if they could give me anything to do to pass the time. And they said, 'Well, all we can give you to do is sewing shrouds'. So I sewed shrouds.

The Times, 1 November 1918
Yesterday there were 1,445 members of the Metropolitan Police Force and 130 members of the London Fire Brigade on the sick-list with influenza. During the twenty-four hours ending at seven o'clock yesterday morning, forty-four persons were stricken with sudden illness in the London streets and were removed to hospitals in the LCC ambulances. In Battersea undertakers have been compelled to refuse to take orders for funerals. One undertaker has declined twenty orders.

You couldn't keep pace with the deaths. You'd just walk down the ward and see that another one had died. I've hated the sight of a Union Jack ever since, because they always used one to cover them as they carried them out on a stretcher. Before they took them away we had to lay them out. I had to do it on my own one night. There was no one else there so I just had to get on with it. I put the screens round and started to lay the body out, and on the other side of the screen I heard the man in the next bed remark, 'It's hard lines, isn't it, when she's so young'. Although I was in charge of that special ward, I never had so much as a cold. I remember Colonel Barling coming into the ward one day when the patients were beginning to get better and he came up and took me by the hands. He said, 'Miss Ellis, you've done well. You've had a hard time in here and you look better and better every day.'

Margaret Ellis, Special Military Probationer, No. 26 General Hospital, Camiers

AUSTRIA GOES OUT

ARMISTICE AT THREE TODAY

ANOTHER STEP TOWARDS VICTORY *The Times,* 4 November 1918

One particularly tragic case I remember was a little girl, a very young bride, who'd been brought out to see her wounded husband. She had probably caught the infection before she left, because not long after she arrived in the ward she collapsed and was taken to the Sick Sisters' quarters with influenza. She died a day or two later and it was terribly tragic for the poor husband. Then later he caught it and died too.*

Sister Mary McCall, QAIMNS (R), No. 4 General Hospital, Camiers

* Mrs Florence Grover, aged twenty-one, is buried in a war grave in Etaples Military Cemetery, Plot I, Row C, Grave I. Private Albert Grover, aged twenty-three, who died three weeks later, is buried in Plot XLVII, Row E. Grave 5.

Copenhagen, 6 November. A Berlin official telegram states that the German Armistice Delegations left Berlin for the Western Front this afternoon.   *The Times,*
                        Reuter   7 November 1918

Mary Dobson, US Army Nurse, US Base Hospital No. 63, Savenay

When we got to Savenay I was put in charge of the flu cases, because I'd had it and they thought I'd be immune to the infection. It was raging there, because all the people that had come in were bringing it right with them. They'd said that there wasn't any in the USA, but we knew better because Camp Grant was full of it when we'd left there three weeks before. Half of these men that we were nursing had been brought in straight off the boat. We had a great big ward full of boys dying, a lot of them. They just died within twenty-four hours after they got there. The cemetery was just up the hill, and every morning you could hear the bugle blowing as they buried the bodies. It was gruesome. It really was.

Captain J. Cook, RAMC, No. 18 Casualty Clearing Station, Ypres.

During the whole month of October we had admitted and treated over 12,000 patients, so we had rather a strenuous time. After a time we got rid of them all and remained packed up and ready to move at twenty-four hours' notice. The rest was very welcome. Many of us took the opportunity of visiting the recent battlefields and places of interest in the reconquered territory. I frequently wandered over the Hindenburg Line and wondered how any troops in the world could possibly have penetrated its apparently impregnable defences. All of them did *not* penetrate – and that was only too plainly indicated by the mounds and little wooden crosses scattered by the thousand over the devasted countryside. To walk over a recent battlefield and see the graves, and the indescribable collection of broken and discarded equipment of all kinds – damaged tanks, guns, rifles, 'dud' shells, hand grenades, ammunition, food, clothing, etc. – scattered amongst the maze of trenches and barbed wire entanglements, which appear to extend aimlessly in every direction, is to me an extremely but inexpressibly sad experience, coupled with the suffering and mangled humanity brought to the casualty clearing stations.

THE ARMISTICE MEETING

—

A DECISION BY MONDAY

—

INSURRECTION SPREADS

—

RESIGNATION OF THE CHANCELLOR

—

COURSE OF GERMAN RETREAT   *The Times,*
9 November 1918

Poor Lepladdec died of pneumonia in the isolation ward upstairs – I am dreadfully distressed about it. Harman in Ward 246 has also slipped away.

The war news is wonderful and puts great heart into us all. Went by Métro to the Champs-Elysées to see the booty taken from the Huns! The Avenue Alexandre II is lined with field artillery right up to the Pont Alexandre and on either side of the Champs-Elysées, about fifteen feet apart or less, right down to the Place de la Concorde. On reaching the Concorde a wonderful sight meets one's gaze. Huge flagstaffs decorated with laurels and flying the Tricouleur and all the Allied flags. Serried masses of field guns, trench mortars, machine-guns and everything one can name in the horrible art of war arranged on every available space all around the Place. Big groups around Cleopatra's Needle and on all the islands. A huge tank and a huge Krupps cannon. The monuments, which are encased in sandbags against bombardment, are literally covered with German steel helmets – thick as peas! Just like the French to think of such a thing! On the long terrace at the entrance to the Tuileries Gardens and facing the Place de la Concorde is a whole line of various Boche aeroplanes. The stone balustrade of the terrace is edged with machine-guns – simply bursting with them! Quite an unforgettable sight!

People are walking in the boulevards with flags rolled under their arms, so as to be ready for the supreme moment.

Norah Broadley, French Red Cross Worker, The American Hospital, Neuilly, Paris (her diary)

THE ARMISTICE SIGNED

CEASE FIRE ON ALL FRONTS

The Times,
12 November 1918

On the day the Armistice was declared, there wasn't one man in the ward who knew. They were all delirious, not conscious enough to know, too ill. There wasn't one man who understood. Not *one* man.

Margaret Ellis, No. 26 General Hospital, Camiers

It was all over at last. But people were still dying – in Germany, in France, in Britain, in America. In the Middle East, in Africa, in every country in Europe. And in France in the week before the Armistice, in the British Army sector alone, almost 12,000 influenza patients had been admitted to army hospitals – and one in every twelve of them had died.

Chapter Twenty-One

The war had lasted exactly four years and a hundred days. The land fighting had ranged from trenches in the sand dunes on the coast of Belgium to the peaks of Alsace, the barren rocks of Gallipoli, the mountain passes of the Tyrol, the sands of Egypt, the hills of Macedonia, the plains of Africa. But for the British Army, the war ended, as it had begun, at Mons. There the first shots had been fired on a hot August morning in 1914, and there, just before the eleventh hour of the eleventh day of the eleventh month of 1918, the last shot rang out through the grey November drizzle.

Germaine Lauryssen might have heard them both. It had been a hard war for civilians in Occupied France and Belgium. In Mons and Nimy the stiff German officials responsible for the administration of the district had been correct but harsh in their behaviour – very different from the fighting soldiers on local leave who were occasionally billeted on the Lauryssen family. When the German army began to fall back, the Lauryssen house was requisitioned as a Divisional HQ, and there was a constant coming and going of messengers, a never-ending ringing of telephones, a darkening of expressions on the faces of the officers who grew gloomier and more anxious as the weeks passed. The boom of the distant guns came nearer and nearer. Even the Germans spoke openly of the terrible battle for Mons that lay ahead.

In the early evening of 10 November the gunfire became strangely desultory, and the long silences were almost more disturbing than the familiar thud of the guns. Germaine Lauryssen stood on the doorstep outside the house, listening and wondering. The colonel in command of the headquarters came hurrying along the street, stopped, bowed politely, and wished her good evening. Then he froze. They both heard the noise at the same time. It was the sound of a trumpet, blowing the Retreat.

Germaine Lauryssen

It was obviously a prearranged signal. I said, 'What was that?' He recovered himself and answered that it was nothing. But he left me very quickly and went into the house and soon, from our quarters, we could hear the sounds of frantic activity. They were pulling out telephone switchboards, dismantling wires and equipment. Lorries drew up outside and they started carrying the stuff out and loading them up. One little officer's batman beckoned me aside, thrust several bottles of white wine into my arms and winked at me to hide them away somewhere.

Within an hour all the troops in the village were lined up and ready to move off. As they were about to start, the colonel looked back at me and said, 'We are the last Germans you will see'. They moved off quietly and the villagers who had come out of their houses stood just as quietly watching. We were too stunned at his words to take them in properly. We had seen so many units come and go that we couldn't believe that this was the last of them. When they left there was an awful silence – a vacuum almost. We didn't know what was going to happen. It felt exactly as it had done in 1914.

We went to bed. About five o'clock in the morning we were wakened by a huge shell exploding on the level crossing. Then everything was silent again; we went back to sleep and when we woke up it was still quiet. My father went off to Mons to find out what he could and my mother walked down to the village to see if she could get any news there. My sister and I decided that if we were going to have a celebration we had better prepare the house. While we were working we thought we would celebrate by sampling the white wine which the German soldier had given me, and not being used to wine and being half starved we were tipsy in no time. I had to retire to bed and the next thing I remember is my mother prodding me and saying, 'Wake up! The English are here!'

But when I went to the front door and looked along the road it was still quiet. As I was standing there, I saw a figure appear and start to walk very slowly towards the house. He looked exhausted, he was quite untidy and covered in mud, and he wore a uniform that I did not recognize. He was a Canadian officer. I called to him to come in and within a few minutes he was sitting with us in our parlour having a drink, and he told us that the war was over.

The Canadian troops had captured Mons. The 5th Royal Irish Lancers followed on their heels. From the roadway in front of a house just across the canal, stretcher-bearers picked up the body of possibly the last man to be killed in the Great War and carried it off for burial.*

The town erupted in a frenzy of celebration. Angèle and Germaine Lauryssen put on their best clothes and hurried to Mons to join in the excitement. In the Grand Place the troops were being mobbed by the Belgians and were enjoying every minute of it. The cafés broached long-hidden caches of beer and wine. Everyone was talking at the same time. It was difficult to get precise information. No one knew exactly

* He was 256265 Private George Lawrence Price, of the 28th Northwest Battalion, 6th Canadian Infantry Brigade, killed at two minutes to eleven on 11 November 1918.

what had happened, but no one really cared. The only things that mattered were that the Germans had gone and the war was over.

Thirty miles away at Beaumont, Hauptmann Herbert Sulzbach recorded unhappily in his journal:

> The war is over.... How we looked forward to *this* moment; how we used to picture it as the most splendid event of our lives: and here we are now, humbled, our souls torn and bleeding, and know that we surrendered. Germany has surrendered to the Entente!
>
> We move to Sart Eustache: we did not find anything very pleasant there. The fanatical Belgians ran up the Belgian flag over our heads. The bells are ringing for the French marching in behind us. We have to keep calm and swallow this provocation.

Carolyn Clarke, American Red Cross Aide, American Red Cross Evacuation Hospital 114

Miss Ellis woke me in the morning of 11 November, when I had just got to sleep for the day, to say that the war was over. I said, 'I don't believe it'. Then I noticed that the guns had stopped and in their stead was the sound of bells. A Frenchman somewhere was eagerly explaining in a loud voice: '*La guerre – fini!*' It was true. The boys were not being killed any more. That night we had sixty-four patients who had been wounded before eleven in the morning and one other. He was a handsome man from the 13th Engineers and was found unconscious on the railroad track with a bruise on his forehead. He was taken to the receiving ward where the doctor in charge tagged him 'Fractured Skull' with a question-mark. We hurried him through the X-ray, which showed a depression in his skull, and sent him to the operating room before the others, as none seemed as badly off as he did. He was the first case of the evening. The doctors all gathered around and everyone was looking at him, when he began to come to. He had been over to the French Commissariat and indulged in several drinks to celebrate the day, and had tripped on the railway tracks on the way home, too far gone to get up again. The dent in his skull was a natural one. He was put to bed in one of the wards. We saw very little intoxication among the American soldiers and when we did see an unfortunate, he was usually being led along by an MP. The Engineers had a torchlight procession through our main street that night and all who could watched it. It was all right except that it waked up some of our sickest flu patients.

Evacuation 114 had moved up yet again, this time to Fleury on the Argonne front – and this time without Mary Ludlum, who had been too ill with influenza herself to go along. Even as the fighting ended, convoys continued to come in and the casualty clearing stations which had advanced with the army were full of flu patients who could not be moved. Their nurses were as busy as they had ever been in all but the worst of the fighting.

We moved up to St André after the army went into Lille, and almost immediately we started taking in wounded and many people who had Spanish influenza as well. We couldn't send them down the line because they were too ill too move, and we had ever so many deaths. We were kept very busy and it was a most depressing time – worse, in a way, when all the good news was coming through. The boys were coming in with colds and a headache and they were dead within two or three days. Great big handsome fellows, healthy men, just came in and died. There was no rejoicing in Lille the night of the Armistice. There was no rejoicing.

Sister Catherine Macfie, TFNS, No. 11 Casualty Clearing Station, St André

But there was wild rejoicing at No. 5 Base Hospital in the casino in Boulogne. During the epidemic, several surgical wards had had to be turned into medical wards and Arlie Bock and his colleague, Captain Denny, had for weeks past been working themselves to a standstill in the laboratory studying the virus, carrying out tests and experiments, trying by every possible means to save lives and control the epidemic. They had enjoyed some measure of success. The number of deaths among the soldiers was not excessive. They had even managed to produce an emergency vaccine and were proud of the fact that, thanks to its efficiency, not a single doctor, nurse or enlisted man had succumbed to the infection. That was a good reason for rejoicing and, ever since the capture of Lille by the British, the casino had been decked out in gala attire. Strings of bunting and a comprehensive display of Allied flags fluttered from the flagstaff and from every doorway, window or balcony where it was possible to fix one. In the last fortnight of the war, the flags fluttered bravely in the damp sea winds – an encouraging sight for the troops huddled on the decks of returning leave-boats as they sailed past the casino towards the rainswept harbour of Boulogne; a cheerful send-off to the wounded and the leave-men travelling in the opposite direction, bound cheerfully for Blighty.

On the morning of Armistice Day, in a matter of minutes, the flags unaccountably disappeared. It was not that Base Hospital No. 5 had nothing to celebrate, but rather that it was celebrating all too well. Everyone who could be spared, and a great many who couldn't, tore the flags from the building and paraded, waving them, around the streets of Boulogne. There were frequent stops for refreshment, and they only returned, much the worse for wear, late in the evening. But although the war was over, the convoys were not. In the afternoon, 300 stretcher-cases (mostly Americans from the 37th and 91st Divisions) arrived at the hospital. There were only six enlisted men and six officers available to take the convoy in. Not everyone had felt like celebrating.

Armistice Day was the most appalling day I've ever lived through. We had a big convoy of flu cases and Sister was very busy, so she asked me to go along to represent the ward at a little ceremony they

Peggy Marten, VAD, No. 55

General
Hospital,
Wimereux

were going to have, a little thanksgiving service in the open air by the flagstaff with the Last Post and a silence after it. And as I was walking to the flagstaff I saw two parents being escorted to the mortuary. They must have been sent for to come and see their wounded boy and got there too late, and now they were being taken to see his body. I thought, 'Here we are at the end of the war – but we're not at the end of the grief'.

In the evening my three chums and I had a little session in our hut after supper. One of the girls had been down in the town and brought back a bottle of wine and some biscuits and we were having a little party, just the four of us, drinking each other's health. Then we tossed up for the cork of the bottle because whoever got the cork would be the first to be married. And Mia Venables got it – and she was!

Lorna Neill,
Motor
Ambulance
Convoy,
Etaples Base

It was a terrible day. Sometimes we had to do fatigues, and it was my turn that day to drive the lorry to take the men to the dump to shovel coal. It was a one-ton lorry, which seemed rather big to me in those days because there weren't any self-starters and you had to swing the handle of the beastly thing. We got there and the men were shovelling the coal on to the lorry and they weren't men I knew, so I was quite alone. I was sitting in the driver's seat and at eleven o'clock these sirens went off and they went on and on. Then the men up at the Bull Ring started to blow the reveille, and we heard the bugles and we knew that it was over.

I didn't feel a bit elated. The men who were shovelling coal were quite depressed and one of them said, 'So that's it, then. The bloody war's over.' It wasn't an exciting time at all. We wanted to go out and celebrate in the evening, but they were probably afraid that Etaples and Le Touquet would be very rowdy, so everything was put out of bounds to us and we were kept in our billets and not allowed to go out. In any case, it wasn't very easy to feel jubilant when we seemed to be surrounded by rows and rows of white crosses and acres and acres of hospitals with beds full of wounded men. We just thought, 'Thank God it's over. Let's go home.'

In Alexandria, in Egypt, Kit Dodsworth, still seedy from the after-effects of influenza and overwork, had a day off and spent it quietly.

Kit
Dodsworth,
VAD, No. 19
General
Hospital,
Alexandria,
Egypt

I had an early dinner and was in bed by eight o'clock and asleep soon after that. At eleven o'clock I was rudely awakened by Eve shaking me vigorously. I hadn't seen her all day. She'd been on duty and then went off celebrating in the evening and now she was yelling in my ear, 'You must wake up! The Armistice is signed and I have got engaged!'

I sat up and leapt out of bed and hugged her. I put on my

dressing-gown and we went out on to a flat roof overlooking the main street. There was the most extraordinary cosmopolitan procession that one could imagine. Every little crowd that passed was singing its own national songs. There were French, Greek, Italian, Belgian and, intermingled with them all, the Britishers. We all sang and shouted ourselves hoarse. What a night it was! I don't know what time we eventually got to bed and to sleep. We were very happy and elated and altogether it was a happy time, because I was engaged too. Exactly a week later I married my officer at the consulate in Cairo and a few months later Eve married her doctor.

Hilda Pole spent part of Armistice Day gardening, for she had taken on the task of growing vegetables and breeding rabbits to supplement the family diet, and there was no help to be had. One of the pre-war servants remained, but a great deal of the work fell on Hilda's shoulders. Gladys had long ago left home to join the Land Army. Muriel, inspired by the pill-rolling she had seen in the early days when the auxiliary hospital first opened, was training as a dispenser. Lily had gone to Scotland as quartermaster of a military hospital. Hilda's father had retired. The Poles had moved to a smaller house, and only Hilda was left at home with her elderly parents, dividing her time between house, garden and part-time work at the hospital in Bromley. Later on she would be free to think of a career for herself, but in the meantime she was tired.

I kept rabbits to help the food shortage and did gardening, and with having such a lot to do and only being able to work part-time at the hospital, they put me in the kitchen. That was the hardest in a way, because we were getting tired of the war and it all began to get a bit tedious. You began to feel as if it would never end. We were glad when it did, but there was no celebration. I spent the afternoon of Armistice Day in the hospital kitchen, washing up and scraping carrots and peeling potatoes. And then I went home. In London and places like that people just went wild with hysteria, but in our town nothing particularly exciting happened.

Hilda Pole, VAD, Kent Detachment 60

Everybody is in the streets and boulevards and *no work* is the order of the day. The streets are absolute *vistas* of Allied flags, and everywhere people are singing, marching in processions and waving flags. Everyone fraternizes! And everywhere you hear over and over again the national anthems of the Allies and the war songs. The sound of 'Tipperary' sung by a little group brought a great lump into my throat. I couldn't help remembering the gallant men who sailed from England to the sound of it, and never returned.

Great scenes of animation going on in the Place de l'Opéra, and a British Colonial demonstration which made us feel very happy. A

Norah Broadley, French Red Cross Worker, The American Hospital, Neuilly, Paris

French aviator did stunts close over our heads – he flew quite low along the *Rue de la Paix* and then rose over our heads and the Opéra, amid great cheering. Men were standing up on the roofs and one man was dancing up there and playing around with a chimney pot. The band played the 'Marseillaise', 'God Save the King', and other national anthems.

The crowds surged down the Champs Elysées, danced in the boulevards and swarmed in the Place de la Concorde. The monuments representing Lille, now liberated from the German occupation, and Strasbourg, which after forty-eight years of German rule was standing once again on the soil of France, almost disappeared in a sea of flowers and wreaths. Children waved flags, and climbed on the muzzles of captured guns. Mistinguett high-kicked at the *Casino de Paris* in front of a packed house and an audience so delirious that the show turned into a mass demonstration of mutual congratulation and delight. In the boulevards, celebrating crowds hauled the German guns from the Place de la Concorde, collapsed exhausted and abandoned them inconveniently in the middle of the streets. Cafés, flouting wartime regulations which had not yet been rescinded, stayed open into the small hours. Nobody wanted to go to bed. The cheering, the singing, the dancing, the whistling, the flag-waving, went on until dawn. It was the start of a glorious fête which continued for more than two weeks.

By eleven-thirty in the morning, half an hour after the Armistice had been signed, it seemed as if London too had gone mad. Some policemen and Boy Scouts were seen pedalling bicycles furiously through the streets blowing the bugle-call *'All Clear'* a hundred times more enthusiastically than they had ever done at the end of an air raid. 'City gents' joined in a spontaneous parade led by a tin kettle 'band'. Office workers left their desks and rushed to the windows and when the signal for a general holiday was given they poured into the streets. Soon traffic in Whitehall was at a standstill and a long line of buses stood, unable to move, in a line that stretched from Downing Street to Trafalgar Square. The passengers didn't care. The open top-decks were 'filled with happy soldiers, cheering, singing, waving flags and exchanging compliments with the girl clerks at office windows.'* Within an hour, bus drivers were forced to abandon any idea of following an official route and keeping to a timetable, or even of eventually reaching their prescribed destination, and the happy 'conducterettes', basking in the pleasure of being hailed as war heroines themselves, gave up any thought of collecting fares. Soon most of the buses were chalked with the cordial invitation – *'Free to Berlin'*.

White-coated medical students marched down the Charing Cross Road carrying a skull on a pole shouting, *'Hoch der Kaiser!'* Flag-sellers

* *The Times*, 12 November 1918.

appeared from nowhere and did a roaring trade in the milling crowd around Trafalgar Square, along the Strand, in Piccadilly. The noise was indescribable and it seemed as if the city could not have held another person. But by the afternoon there were twice as many in the streets. People from the suburbs and from towns as far as forty miles from London made for the capital to join in the fun. They arrived by the train-load, by bicycle, packed into cars and into recklessly hired taxis. They arrived from the docks and munition factories by flag-bedecked lorry-loads. They screamed and they yelled. They cheered and they sang. They kissed and they danced. When there was no room inside they climbed on the roofs of overloaded taxis; they climbed up the plinth of Nelson's Column, and one intrepid sailor was seen making a brave attempt to scale the column itself. They streamed down the Mall to Buckingham Palace to swell the cheering crowd outside and, struck simultaneously by the same happy thought, some hundreds of exuber- ants roared off around the corner to Victoria Station to meet the leave-train from France. They mobbed the gratified soldiers and carried them shoulder-high round the station – rifles, packs and all. The sound of their cheering, the blowing of trumpets, the rattling of tin trays snatched from the buffet, almost cracked the glass in the high arched roof.

Having rightly deduced that it might take her some time to get there, Claire Tisdall had donned her Red Cross uniform and set off early to report for duty with the Ambulance Column at Charing Cross Station. But it was more difficult than she had ever imagined. The Underground train came in packed with people from the stations further up the line and was stormed by the waiting crowd as soon as the doors opened. Three trains came in and went out again, leaving Claire still on the platform. She struggled through the crowd towards a helpful porter. 'I'm an ambulance nurse and I've *got* to get to Charing Cross'.

He promised to get me into the next train and held me at the edge of the platform until it arrived. The he literally lifted me up and squeezed me in, and banged the door closed behind me. I thought my ribs were broken, but I was in.

When I got to Charing Cross Station it was absolutely calm. It was just exactly as it had been all these years. The waiting, the ambul- ances and the cars, the nurses and the stretcher-bearers. Nobody said much. It was unreal somehow, uncanny.

The train came in and was unloaded, just as usual; my number was called and I got into the ambulance with four men, all badly wounded, and was told to take them to New End Hospital, Hamp- stead. It was almost impossible to get through the streets. We got out of the station all right, but we simply couldn't get through the crowds and the traffic. We were held up a dozen times. The ambulance had to keep stopping because the way was blocked by other traffic – cars

Claire Elise
Tisdall, VAD
Ambulance
Nurse, The
Ambulance
Column,
London
District

and taxis and buses honking their horns and full of people cheering. Nobody paid any attention. Nobody noticed us at all.

The journey took almost two hours of stopping and starting, of finding a way out of the congested streets and travelling by roundabout side-roads to Hampstead. Claire tried, as she always did, to make her patients comfortable. She chatted to them cheerfully, but they had little to say in reply. As usual, in handwriting that shook as the ambulance jerked along, she scribbled the routine particulars in her notebook.

No. 20308 Private R. S. Darvell, WIR, 2nd Battalion, Quarters No. 3. Gunshot wounds of the right thigh.

No. 631205 Private W. Adams, 2/20th London Regiment. Severe wound of left foot.

No. 6542 Private G. Saysun, 1st Battalion, Gloucestershire Regiment. Gunshot wound. Skull and compound fracture.

No. 201398 Private W. MacKnight, 5th KOYLI. Gunshot wound right leg.

By the time they arrived at the hospital the men were pale with pain and fatigue. The driver jumped down and went in to report their arrival. The stretcher-bearers came out and lifted the men from the ambulance. Claire Tisdall stood on the pavement, with a nod and a smile and the usual 'Good luck, Tommy', as one by one they were carried inside. She had always hated the lack of privacy at New End Hospital. It was here that in the bloody summer of the Somme two years before she had screamed enraged at the gloating schoolboys crowding round the hospital entrance. But today there were no schoolboys, no ghouls, no sightseers. The war was over. The celebrations had begun – and they were rejoicing elsewhere.

The Aftermath

Just as it has never been possible to calculate the precise number of men who died in the Great War (the German estimates alone range between two million and four million), it is difficult to assess the number of men who were wounded. The official British figure is 2,289,860. That total includes 2,261,502 who were brought to England in hospital ships from France, leaving a balance of only 29,000 to account for patients arriving by hospital ship from Malta, the Middle East and Africa, for patients who were treated locally in those areas as well as in France and returned to the line, and for those who were wounded, taken prisoner and repatriated by normal channels after the war. It seems an astonishingly low estimate. But in the turmoil of the war, in the frantic conditions under which medical staffs abroad had to work during the big 'pushes' and battles, given the number of quasi-official, voluntary and auxiliary hospitals, it is hardly surprising that it was difficult to keep complete and accurate records.

But there are some unchallengeable statistics. In 1938, twenty years after the war had ended and on the eve of another, despite the number of men who had died as a result of war wounds in the twenty years that had elapsed since the Armistice, the British government was still paying out almost half a million disability pensions to men who were wholly or party disabled as a result of their war service.

8,000 pensions were being paid to men with one or both legs amputated; 3,600 to men with one or both arms amputated; 90,000 to men with withered or useless limbs. 2,000 pensions were being paid to men who were totally blind; 8,000 to men who were partially blind; and 11,000 to men permanently deafened by explosions. 15,000 men had head injuries so severe that through constant pain or reduced mental capacity they were unable to resume normal employment; 25,000 were still suffering from nervous disorders or neurasthenia, the after-effects of shellshock; 2,800 were epileptics. And in 1938, more than twenty years after their minds had been broken by their experiences, 3,200 were still confined in mental asylums. The list goes on:

Incapacitated by inoperable hernias — 7,000
Incapacitated as a result of frostbite — 2,200
Bronchitis, tuberculosis as a result of gassing — 41,000
Heart disease, attributable to physical strain on war service — 38,000

Crippled by rheumatism due to conditions in the trenches — 28,000
Incapacitated by severe wounds (unclassified) — 32,000

These were the wounded men whose conditions were so serious that the Ministry of Pensions (not renowned in the thirties for soft-heartedness) recognized the need to assist them financially. Probably as many again suffered to a lesser degree from the after-effects of wounds, and over a period of years many more developed conditions which were directly related to their experiences during the war. Some were able to get pensions. Others just had to put up with it.

The figures are for British soldiers only. They take no account of the permanently disabled among the American Forces and the troops of the British Empire – Canada, Australia, New Zealand, South Africa, New-foundland, India and other Dominions and Colonies – whose pensions were paid by their own governments. And, of course, they do not reflect the huge number of maimed and crippled men in Belgium, in France, in Germany, in Italy, in Russia. In order to arrive at even a conservative estimate it would be necessary to multiply the British figures many times. For most of them, time has put an end to their suffering. But some have had to carry the burden of pain and ill health through a long lifetime.

At the time of writing (February 1980) the Exchequer of their Queen and Country is still paying pensions to 27,000 disabled men who went off to fight for King and Country more than sixty years ago.

Bibliography

1914 – Field Marshal Viscount French of Ypres, KP, OM, etc. (Constable & Co. Ltd, 1919)

Military Operations in France and Belgium 1916 – Brigadier-General Sir James E. Edmonds, CB, CMG, RE (retired) (Macmillan & Co. Ltd, 1932)

Military Operations in France and Belgium 1918 – Brigadier-General Sir James E. Edmonds, CB, CMG, RE (retired) (Macmillan & Co. Ltd, 1932)

History of the First World War – Liddell Hart (Cassell & Co. Ltd, 1930)

History of the American Field Service in France, Vol. I, II & III – Told by its members (Houghton Mifflin Co., 1920)

Friends of France – The Field Service of the American Ambulance – Told by its members (Houghton Mifflin Co., 1916)

British Red Cross and Order of St John Reports for 1914–1919 – Joint War and Joint War Finance Committees (His Majesty's Stationery Office, 1921)

Final Report of Dardanelles Commission Part II – Presented to Parliament by Command of His Majesty (His Majesty's Stationery Office)

Medical Diseases of the War – Arthur F. Hurst, MA, MD (Oxon), FRCP (Edward Arnold Ltd, 1918)

Official History of the War – Medical Services General History, Vol. I, II, III & IV – Major-General Sir W. G. MacPherson, KCMG, CB, LLD (His Majesty's Stationery Office, 1921)

Hospital Ships and Ambulance Trains – Lieutenant-Colonel John H. Plumridge, OBE, RAMC (retired) (Seeley, Service & Co. Ltd, 1975)

Shock at the Front – William Townsend Porter (Atlantic Monthly Press, 1918)

Physical Remedies for Disabled Soldiers – R. Fortescue Fox, MD (Baillière, Tindall and Cox, 1917)

The Psychoneuroses of War – Dr G. Roussy and J. Lhermitte (University of London Press Ltd, 1918)

Kent's Care of the Wounded – Paul Creswick, G. Stanley Pond and P. H. Ashton (Hodder & Stoughton Ltd, 1919)

The British Red Cross in Action – Dame Beryl Oliver, GBE, RRC (Faber & Faber Ltd, 1966)

The Royal Naval Division – Douglas Jerrold (Hutchinson & Co. (Publishers) Ltd, 1927)

The Fighting Thirteenth – Captain T. A. White (Tyrrells Ltd, 1924)

British Regiments 1914–1918 – Brigadier E. A. James, OBE, TD (Samson Books Ltd, 1978)

History of the 16th HLI – Thomas Chalmers (John McCallum & Co., 1930)

A Medico's Luck in the War – David Rorie, DSO, TD, MD, DPH (Milne & Hutchinson, 1929)

Happy Days in France and Flanders – Benedict Williamson (Harding & More Ltd)

Notes of a Camp Follower on the Western Front – E. W. Hornung (Constable & Co. Ltd, 1919)

Fifty Thousand Miles on a Hospital Ship – 'The Padre' (The Religious Tract Society, 1917)

Twelve Days – Sidney Rogerson (Arthur Barker Ltd)

The Phantom Brigade – A. P. G. Vivian (Ernest Benn Ltd, 1930)

The Price of Glory – Verdun 1916 – Alistair Horne (Macmillan & Co. Ltd, 1962)

The World Crisis 1911–1914 – Rt. Hon. Winston S. Churchill, CH (Thornton Butterworth Ltd, 1923)

Behind the Lines – Colonel W. N. Nicholson, CMG, DSO (Jonathan Cape Ltd, 1939)

By Ways of Service – Hector Dinning (Constable & Co. Ltd, 1918)

The Doughboys – Laurence Stallings (Harper & Row Inc., 1963)

America's Part – Brigadier-General Henry J. Reilly, ORC (Cosmopolitan Book Corporation, 1928)

The War History of the United States Army Base Hospital No. 61 AEF – Major Royale H. Fowler, MC

Queen Alexandra's Royal Army Nursing Corps – Juliet Piggot (Clarke, Doble & Brendon Ltd, 1975)

Tales of a Field Ambulance 1914–1918 – The Personnel (Borough Printing & Publishing Co., 1935)

Medicine and Duty – Harold Dearden (late Capt. RAMC) (William Heinemann Ltd, 1928)

Six Weeks at The War – Millicent, Duchess of Sutherland (*The Times*, 1914)

The Way of the Red Cross – E. Charles Vivian and J. E. Hodder Williams (Hodder & Stoughton Ltd, 1915)

A Surgeon's Life – The Autobiography of J. M. T. Finney (G. P. Putnam's Sons, 1940)

From a Surgeon's Journal 1915–1918 – Harvey Cushing (Constable & Co. Ltd, 1936)

Four Years Out of Life – Lesley Smith (Philip Allan, 1931)

The Story of British VAD Work in the Great War – Thekla Bowser, FJI (Andrew Melrose Ltd)

With a Field Ambulance at Ypres – William Boyd (The Musson Book Company Ltd, 1916)

With the BEF in France – Adjutant Mary Booth (The Salvation Army, 1916)

A VAD in France – Olive Dent (Grant Richards Ltd, 1917)

The Grey Battalion – May Tilton (Angus & Robertson Ltd, 1933)

The Happy Hospital – Corporal Ward Muir, RAMC(T) (Simpkin, Marshall, Hamilton, Kent & Co. Ltd, 1918)

Nursing Adventures of a FANY in France – Grace Ashley Smith (William Heinemann Ltd, 1917)

Diary of a Nursing Sister on the Western Front 1914–1915 – (William Blackwood & Sons Ltd, 1915)

Unknown Warriors – K. E. Luard, RRC (Chatto & Windus Ltd, 1930)

My War Experiences in Two Continents – S. MacNaughton (John Murray Ltd, 1919)

The King's Royal Rifle Corps Chronicle 1915

Duke of Cornwall's Light Infantry – R. F. K. Goldsmith (Leo Cooper Ltd, 1970)

Before Endeavours Fade – Rose E. B. Coombs (Battle of Britain Prints International Ltd, 1977)

With the German Guns – Herbert Sulzbach (Leo Cooper Ltd, 1973)

The Home Fronts – Britain, France and Germany 1914–1918 – John Williams (Constable & Co. Ltd, 1972)

The Royal Regiment of Artillery at Le Cateau, 26 August 1914 – Major A. F. Becke (Royal Artillery Institution Printing House, 1919)

The British Campaign in France and Flanders – A. Conan Doyle

Author's Note

I wish to acknowledge my debt to all of the
following, without whose valuable assistance this book
could never have been written.

Miss R. Adcock

Mrs E. J. Anderson (VAD Elizabeth Storer)

Mrs K. Anderson (VAD Kathleen Yarwood)

682160 Pte. Louis Astorino, US Army

Dr Laurence Abel, USA

Dr Cora Allen, USA

328278 Pte. Frank Ahlquist, 2/1st Battalion, The Cambridge-shire Regiment

Mr Robert Applewhite, USA

Mrs H. H. Beanland (Sister Henrietta Hall)

6458 Sgt. 1st Class Laurence H. Blackburn, US Army Medical Corps

Miss E. B. Brazell (US Army Nurse)

Mrs C. A. Buchanon (US Army Nurse Cecil Bixler)

Mrs E. M. Bushell (VAD)

Mrs K. F. M. Burkinshaw

Mrs G. A. Bamford, USA

Dr Arlie V. Bock, USA

Mrs J. M. Bull

Sub-Lieutenant Jeremy Bentham, Benbow Battalion, 1st Royal Naval Brigade

Mrs F. M. L. Bone (VAD Mabel Bone)

Miss G. Buffard (Sister Grace Buffard)

Pte. G. Bundy, 211th Infantry Battalion, Canadian Expeditionary Force

101264 Pte. Jim Brady, 43rd Field Ambulance, RAMC

Miss N. Broadley (Nurse Norah Broadley)

Mrs Eileen Brandon (daughter of Nurse Lucilla Bailey)

Mr A. Graham Carey, American Field Service – later US Army

Miss H. Cotton (VAD Hester Cotton)

Captain J. B. Cook RAMC

Mrs A. M. C. Coney (Staff Nurse Alice Sullivan)

Mrs E. J. Cook (Sister Elsie Cook)

Miss G. N. Cooper (VAD G. Cooper)

Miss M. F. Cozens-Walker (VAD Mabel Cozens-Walker)

Mrs P. R. Costich (US Army Nurse)

Mrs N Curry (VAD Nina Robson)

Mrs A. E. Cowley

Mrs L. C. Cowper (Lorna Neill)

Mr Rudolph A. Clemen, Red Cross Headquarters, Washington, USA

Mr Carl E. Clifford, Orderly, US Base Hospital No. 5

Mrs G. Chaplin (Germaine Lauryssen)

Captain Leonard Chamberlen, 13th (Service) Battalion, The Rifle Brigade

Miss I. M. Donegan (Nurse Ida Donegan)

Richard Dunning Esq., for Miss Norah Broadley's diary

Mrs E. B. Driscoll, USA

Mrs M. David, MBE, RRG (Commandant Millicent Norton)

Mrs M. M. Davies (US Nurses Aide Mary Ludlum)

Mrs I. M. Dove (VAD Ivy Dove)

Mrs M. C. Dowling (VAD Peggy Marten)

Miss K. Duelle (US Army Nurse Reserve Katherine Duelle)

Mrs Norma T. Douglas (VAD Norma Wilson)

Mrs J. Dosseter (Sister Jean Calder)

Mrs I. F. Edgar

Mr and Mrs E. Ellis, USA

Mrs M. Evans (Nurse Mary Walker)

Mrs G. V. Francke (VAD Grace Bignold)

Mrs M. S. Faulkner (Nurse Marjorie Royall)

Mrs J. Finney, USA

Quartermaster-Sergeant Gordon Fisher, 1st Hertfordshire Regiment

Dr Merill Foote, USA

Miss F. Gordon-Waterman (Nurse Florence Gordon-Waterman)

Mrs I. E. Gould (VAD Ida Haigh)

Mrs M. L. Garnett-Clarke (VAD Margaret Rea)

Mrs Lionel Gameson

Mrs A. M. Howard (VAD Agnes Dixon)

Miss E. Hills-Young, MBE (VAD Elaine Hills-Young)

Miss B. B. Hutchinson, MBE (Driver Beryl Hutchinson)

Mrs M. Hudson (SMP Margaret Ellis)

Mrs D. M. Howe (VAD Dorothy Bradridge)

Mrs R. C. Hansen (US Red Cross Nurse Ruth Bruerton)

Mrs R. K. Hulle, daughter of Nurse Marion Daniels, Harvard Medical Unit

Mrs E. M. Hargreaves (VAD Evelyn Carroll)

Mrs H. M. Harvey

Mrs D. E. Hawes (VAD Daisy Varney)

Mrs S. A. Hay

Mrs H. E. Higgins (US Nurse Harriet English)

Mr Roy Holmes, US Army Medical Corps

2nd Lieutenant J. Phelps Harding, 165th Regiment, 42nd (Rainbow) Division

Mrs C. Hayden Phillips, USA (wife of Dr C. Hayden Phillips)

Jennifer Hassell, for Nurse Garrard's letters

Miss C. Hastings (Sister Christina Hastings)

Miss E. Hodgson (Sister Emily Hodgson, New Zealand Nursing Service)

Mrs D. Irving-Bell

Dr Benjamin A. Jackson, USA

Miss K. Kenyon (VAD Katherine Kenyon)

Sir Geoffrey Keynes, MA, MD, D.Litt., FRCP, FRCS

99414 Sergeant Roger Knowles, 168th Infantry, 42nd (Rainbow) Division

Mrs Francis Knowles, USA

27691 Sgt. W. J. Kemp, Royal Garrison Artillery

247 Pte. Clarence C. Langenheim, 166th Field Hospital, 42nd (Rainbow) Division

Mrs M. I. Lightbound (VAD Muriel Bond)

554847 Corporal Leslie Longhurst, 16th London Queens Westminster Rifles, 56th London Division

Mrs Rose A. Lynch, USA

Dr Pearce Leavitt, USA

Mrs Helena Lambert

71938 Pte. W. Lockey, 1st Battalion, Notts and Derbyshire (Sherwood Foresters) Regiment.

Mrs E. May

Mrs C. L. Mackay-Brown (VAD Charlotte Fitzgerald-Dalton)

Mrs J. McKernan (US Nurse Jane Baudin)

Mrs M. Martin (US Nurse Maud Smith)

Mrs E. M. May (VAD E. Cormack)

Mrs S. Mitchell (VAD Sheila Macbeth)

Mrs M. M. McWilliams (US Nurse Mabel Booth)

Miss E. MacKenzie (VAD Elspeth MacKenzie)

Miss J. N. Mitchell (VAD Nona Mitchell)

Mrs Pauline Margarson

Sir John Compton Miller

Miss Bertha Miller, USA (US Army Nurse in WW2)

Mrs Mary B. McCall (Sister Mary McCall)

Raymond E. Maddison Esq.

Peter Mason Esq.

Colonel Roderick Macleod, DSO, MC, Royal Artillery

Miss E. Macleod

Miss C. Macfie (Sister Catherine Macfie)

24819 Corporal Bill Morgan, 10/11th Battalion, Highland Light Infantry

Miss E. Napier (VAD Ellis Napier)

Mrs T. D. Nairn (US Nurse Mary Dobson)

Miss D. M. Nicol (VAD Dorothy Nicol)

Mr S. J. Noel-Brown (VAD Sidney Noel-Brown)

Mr Henry E. Nesbitt, USA

Mr Carl H. Nelson, USA

Miss E. Nordsvan (Sister Elizabeth Nordsvan, Australian Army Nursing Service)

Mrs Elizabeth Ogilvie, New Zealand

Mrs A. M. Ord (VAD Alice Rodd)

Mrs M. F. Oakley (Sister Miriam Pepper)

Mr Charles H. Pimlott, USA

Mr Jerome Preston, American Field Service

Mrs Pottridge, USA

Mrs Richard D. Parant, USA (daughter of Dr G. A. Moore, Harvard Medical Unit)

Miss Caroline S. Parmenter, USA

Mrs E. M. Parker (VAD Edith Crosse)

Mrs M. R. Parker (Nurse Minnie Bees)

Miss H. G. Pole (VAD Hilda Pole)

Miss M. Pole (VAD Muriel Pole)

Miss W. G. Pole (VAD Gladys Pole)

Mrs Press

Mrs A. M. Probert

Captain the Reverend Leonard Pearson, Army Chaplain's Dept.

Miss Elizabeth Potter, for letters and papers of Dr Henry Potter, 3rd Harvard Medical Unit

Mrs Elizabeth Pearce-Sharman

Miss L. Powell (Sister Lynette Powell)

Mrs D. Pilcher

Mrs E. E. Quinlan (VAD Elsie Broderick)

Mrs F. Quirk (VAD Florence Chamberlain)

Mrs C. Remington (VAD Chris Procter)

Mrs D. M. Richards, MBE (Nurse Maisie Bowcott)

Mrs Margaret Robb

Miss K. T. Rhodes (VAD Kathleen Rhodes)

Mrs D. Ricketts (Nurse Dorothy Eden)

Judge Paul Reardon, son of Dr Daniel Reardon, 1st Harvard Medical Unit

Mrs V. G. Strange (VAD Gwynedd Lloyd)

Miss L. Simmons (Nurse Lilian Simmons)

Mrs S. E. Spencer

Mrs M. Stead (VAD Madge Eaton)

Miss M. L. Stollard (Sister Mary Stollard)

Miss G. M. Stanford (VAD Gladys Stanford)

Mrs N. Shea (US Reserve Nurse Nell Brink)

Reverend Dr Richard Lyon Stinson, USA

Mrs William F. Small, USA

Miss Susan C. Saunders (Matron, The Nurses Memorial to King Edward VII [retired])

John R. Smucker Jnr., National Adjutant, US Army, Ambulance Service Association

Leutnant Herbert Sulzbach, No. 2 Battery, Field Artillery Regiment No. 5, German 18th Army

37778 Rifleman Charlie Shepherd, 13th (Service) Battalion, The Rifle Brigade

Henry Sheahan, American Field Service, SSU No. 3

Daniel Sargent, American Field Service, SSU No. 3

Rifleman Fred Scarbrow, 12th (Service) Battalion, The Rifle Brigade

Miss A. Sinclair (Sister A. Sinclair, New Zealand Nursing Service)

Miss M. Tansley (VAD May Tansley)

Mrs Edna A. Taylor (VAD Edie Rodd)

Miss C. E. Tisdall (VAD Claire Elise Tisdall)

Mrs M. Thompson (VAD Muriel Cressy)

Mrs E. Turner (VAD E. Godwin)

Z 2756 Corporal R. E. Thompson, 13th (Service) Battalion, The Rifle Brigade

267634 Rifleman Charles Tomlinson, 1/6th (Liverpool Rifles), The King's Liverpool Regiment

128025 Pte. H. Turner, D. Company, 50th Division, Machine Gun Corps

Mrs C. Vaughan Phillips (VAD Kit Dodsworth)

Mrs M. C. Veale (Sister Mary Hall)

George Walker Esq., for Miss A. Walker's scrapbook

Miss R. Whitaker (VAD Ruth Whitaker)

Mrs Washer

Mrs. G. A. Weaver

Mrs M. Wells (Sister Mary Fitzgibbon)

Mrs. S. T. Wilsdon

Mrs Herbert F. White (US Nurse)

Mrs L. Willson

Mrs M. Wade, USA (daughter of Nurse Ruth Bruerton)

Mrs R. Wolf (VAD Rosalie Cosgrave)

48529 Rifleman Fred White, 10th (Service) Battalion, King's Royal Rifle Corps

Rifleman Bill Worrell, 12th (Service) Battalion, The Rifle Brigade

Miss M. O. Wedd, Women's Land Army

Mrs A. E. F. Yates (VAD Amy Newbold)

Index

Lyn Macdonald is a former BBC radio producer who, in 1973, resigned her position in order to devote herself to full-time research and writing about the World War I era. Her other books are *1914*, a chronicle of the first months of World War I, *They Called It Passchendaele*, an account of the notorious Passchendaele campaign, and *Somme*, a history of that legendary and horrifying campaign of 1916. Like *The Roses of No Man's Land*, all three are based on the accounts of eyewitnesses and survivors, and told in their own words.

Lyn Macdonald lives in London with her husband, a journalist.